Handbook of Long-Term Care Administration and Policy

PUBLIC ADMINISTRATION AND PUBLIC POLICY

A Comprehensive Publication Program

EDITOR-IN-CHIEF

EVAN M. BERMAN

Huey McElveen Distinguished Professor
Louisiana State University
Public Administration Institute
Baton Rouge, Louisiana

Founding Editor

JACK RABIN

Professor of Public Administration and Public Policy
The Pennsylvania State University—Harrisburg
School of Public Affairs
Middletown, Pennsylvania

Available Electronically

Principles and Practices of Public Administration, edited by
Jack Rabin, Robert F. Munzenrider, and Sherrie M. Bartell

PublicADMINISTRATION*netBASE*

Handbook of Long-Term Care Administration and Policy

Edited by

Cynthia Massie Mara
Pennsylvania State University
Middletown, Pennsylvania, U.S.A.

Laura Katz Olson
Lehigh University
Bethlehem, Pennsylvania, U.S.A.

CRC Press
Taylor & Francis Group
Boca Raton   London   New York

CRC Press is an imprint of the
Taylor & Francis Group, an **Informa** business

CRC Press
Taylor & Francis Group
6000 Broken Sound Parkway NW, Suite 300
Boca Raton, FL 33487-2742

© 2008 by Taylor & Francis Group, LLC
CRC Press is an imprint of Taylor & Francis Group, an Informa business

No claim to original U.S. Government works
Printed in the United States of America on acid-free paper
10 9 8 7 6 5 4 3 2 1

International Standard Book Number-13: 978-0-8493-5327-7 (Hardcover)

Visit the Taylor & Francis Web site at
http://www.taylorandfrancis.com

and the CRC Press Web site at
http://www.crcpress.com

Dedication

To our children, Shannon, Heather, and Alix, that the long-term care system may be transformed by the time you may need it.

Contents

Foreword

Long-term care has been and remains the distant cousin of health policy. Newspapers are full of commentary on what 2008 presidential candidates have to say about "universal health coverage," the new expression for what used to be called national health insurance. However, one would be hard-pressed to describe what any of them think about long-term care. The discussion of how America is aging touches on familiar themes: the pressure on the Medicare budget, the implications for Social Security pensions, and whether the savings or the sports behavior of baby boomers is adequate for their future. It is hard to avoid endless comments on which diet should be followed for healthy living, whether lead or benzene poisoning is to become the asbestos story of the twenty-first century, or whether the impact of a growing proportion of those above 65 years should prompt smaller apartments or more handrails in modern bathrooms. But one would look in vain for straightforward discussion of long-term care—its likely scale, its financing, its connection to Medicaid spending, or its impact on family caregivers, let alone what other countries have done in this area of social policy.

This handbook brought together by Mara and Olson is precisely directed toward that relative neglect. As writing has increased about the administration and policy struggles in medical care, comparable attention has not been given to long-term care. This handbook presumes that the sharp increases forecasted in older Americans for the next three or four decades warrant extended discussion. What training will administrators in this sphere of social and medical life require? What can we learn from the experience of other industrial democracies about the financing of care for the frail? If all of us have a modest probability of needing such care, does social insurance make sense? What are the prospects for private financing, or for the continued role of Medicaid as a funder of last resort? The realities of both providing and receiving care are too readily masked. How many Americans, for example, know anything about the scale of nonelderly recipients of long-term care? The list of neglected topics, as the table of contents reveals, is long.

That is the justification of gathering such a wide range of policy and administrative writers to contribute to this handbook. The editors have for years been writing, teaching, and conducting research in long-term care. They have made presentations on the state, national, and international levels. They have also organized panels and lectures related to long-term care. This is the product of their scholarly search for the complete range of commentaries about the world of American long-term care, now and in the future. It is a welcome addition to the literature.

Ted R. Marmor
School of Management
Yale University
New Haven, Connecticut

Preface

The fastest growing part of the population is the 85-years-and-older cohort. The baby boomers have already begun to enter their 60s and the need for long-term care will escalate as they age. The growing requirement for services, with its associated opportunities and challenges, necessitates the presence of additional skilled long-term care administrators and policy makers. Moreover, long-term care administration is undergoing a process of professionalism similar to the one that took place decades ago in hospital administration. This evolution heightens the need for effective preparation for administrators and policy makers.

This text grew out of my long-standing interest in long-term care. During varied work experiences, I have seen that:

- A person, even one with diminishing abilities, could remain safely at home if there is adequate support from family and the community.
- Mistreatment of nursing home residents existed as well as conditions that put their lives in jeopardy.
- Apathy was apparent on the part of some officials whose job it was to ensure the delivery of safe, adequate long-term care.
- Isolation was often experienced during extended hospital stays by people who were dying;* their call lights tended to be answered only after considerable delay, and their requests to talk about the seriousness of their illness were frequently ignored.
- Public policy, and its many modifications, had the potential to improve the long-term care system and the lives of the people it served.
- Positive changes in institutional and home and community-based care could be made through both the public and private sectors.
- Individuals needing long-term care comprised a diverse population.

---

* Extended hospital stays took place before the implementation of a prospective payment system for hospitals. More about this change in hospital reimbursement can be found in the chapters on the financing of long-term care.

■ Advocates for younger and older people with chronic illnesses or disabilities often saw themselves in competition for the same resources and resisted cooperating to improve the lives of people of all ages who need assistance with daily activities.

My experiences have also shown me the relationship between the quality of an organization's administration and that of the services provided. The need for educated, prepared administrators and policy makers is abundantly clear. This handbook is designed as an instructive tool for the education of individuals planning to work in long-term care. It contains a wide range of information they will need as they provide leadership in the long-term care arena. This handbook is also intended as a reference for individuals already employed in this field.

Laura Katz Olson's deep interest in aging and long-term care prompted me to ask her to serve as the coeditor of this text. I was pleased that she accepted the invitation.

Cynthia Massie Mara

Acknowledgments

The preparation of this handbook has involved our collaboration with many talented individuals in the field of long-term care. First, we express great appreciation to the authors for writing about and sharing their particular areas of expertise. Through their work, each of them participates in the preparation of leaders for the long-term care system.

The editors would like to thank the following individuals for their review of and comments on various materials: Mary Brundage DeLashmutt, Susan Donckers, and Elizabeth Revell. The continual support and encouragement provided by Kay Morhard is also very much appreciated.

Three former and one current graduate student in the Penn State's Master of Health Administration program are to be particularly thanked. Nidhi Daga and Supraja Vija conducted literature reviews and provided much assistance at the beginning of the project. Deb Kephart, who is now participating in a long-term care research project, also provided helpful input. Graduate student Patsy Taylor-Moore, who has years of experience in the long-term care endeavors of state government, is especially thanked for applying her many skills as work on the handbook was brought to completion.

We acknowledge with gratitude the many clients whom we have met during our various work experiences in long-term care. They have been our teachers.

Cynthia Massie Mara

Laura Katz Olson

Editors

Cynthia Massie Mara is Associate Professor of Health Care Administration and Policy at The Pennsylvania State University, where she has worked since 1994. She is the coordinator of the Master of Health Administration program and the developer and coordinator of the Graduate Certificate Program in Long-Term Care Administration and Policy. She serves as adjunct Associate Professor of Management and Health Systems at The Pennsylvania State University College of Medicine.

Dr. Mara's research interests include health and long-term care administration and policy, the long-term care system, aging and disability, and organizational theory. Her current research focuses on assisting state government in planning for Medicaid-funded long-term care services and expenditures as the demands on these public programs continue to expand. Other studies on the state level have addressed programs financed through the Older Americans Act. Dr. Mara has conducted research for the U.S. Department of Justice on developing strategies to address long-term care needs in prison systems. She has been an invited grant reviewer for the U.S. Department of Health and Human Services Administration on Aging and the National Institutes of Health.

Dr. Mara has authored a number of professional articles; has made presentations at meetings of state, national, and international organizations; and serves as the long-term care editor of an academic journal and an editorial board member for two additional journals. She organized the Aging Politics and Policy Group at the American Political Science Association meetings and serves as president of the organization. Dr. Mara was the founder and executive director of a Medicare- and Medicaid-funded not-for-profit hospice organization. She has worked on the U.S. Senate Subcommittee on Aging and for the New York City Department for the Aging. Earlier, as an Assistant Professor of Nursing, she worked with two colleagues to establish a baccalaureate nursing program.

Laura Katz Olson has been Professor of Political Science at Lehigh University since 1974 and chair of the department since 2003. She has published six books: *The Political Economy of Aging: The State, Private Power and Social Welfare; Aging and Public Policy: The Politics of Growing Old in America; The Graying of the World: Who*

Will Take Care of the Frail Elderly; Age through Ethnic Lenses: Caring for the Elderly in a Multicultural Society; The Not So Golden Years: Caregiving, the Frail Elderly and the Long-Term Care Establishment; and *Heart Sounds* (her first novel). Currently, she is working on a book project titled *The Politics of Medicaid: Stakeholders and Welfare Medicine.*

Dr. Olson has published widely in the field of aging and women's studies. Her articles address topics such as pensions, Social Security, problems of older women, and long-term care. She has been a scholar at the Social Security Administration, a gerontological fellow, and a Fulbright scholar. She has also lectured throughout Pennsylvania on Social Security, Medicare, and long-term care policies funded by the Pennsylvania Humanities Council. Dr. Olson is on the editorial board of the *Journal of Aging Studies* and *New Political Science.*

Contributors

Arthur W. Blaser, Ph.D.
Department of Political Science
Chapman University
Orange, California

William P. Brandon, Ph.D., M.P.H.
Department of Political Science
University of North Carolina
  at Charlotte
Charlotte, North Carolina

Jan L. Brown, J.D.
Jan L. Brown & Associates
Harrisburg, Pennsylvania

Shannon M. Chance, AIA
Department of Architecture
Hampton University
Hampton, Virginia

Michael Duffy, Ph.D., ABPP
Department of Educational
  Psychology
Texas A&M University
College Station, Texas

Colleen M. Grogan, Ph.D.
School of Social Service
  Administration
University of Chicago
Chicago, Illinois

Bradley E. Karlin, Ph.D.
Office of Mental Health
  Services
Veterans Administration Central
  Office
Washington, DC

Sharon M. Keigher, Ph.D., ACSW
Helen Bader School of Social Welfare
University of Wisconsin—
  Milwaukee
Milwaukee, Wisconsin

Cynthia Massie Mara, Ph.D.
School of Public Affairs
The Pennsylvania State University
Middletown, Pennsylvania
and
College of Medicine
The Pennsylvania State University
Hershey, Pennsylvania

William J. McAuley, Ph.D.
Department of Communication
George Mason University
Fairfax, Virginia

Megan E. McCutcheon, M.A.
Department of Communication
George Mason University
Fairfax, Virginia

Edward Alan Miller, Ph.D.
Departments of Political
  Science and Community
  Health Center, and
  Centers for Public Policy
  and Gerontology and
  Health Care Research
Brown University
Providence, Rhode Island

Vincent Mor, Ph.D.
Department of Community
  Health Center, and Center
  for Gerontology and
  Health Care Research
Brown University
Providence, Rhode Island

Laura Katz Olson, Ph.D.
Department of Political
  Science and Public
  Policy
Lehigh University
Allentown, Pennsylvania

Stephen E. Proctor
President and CEO
Presbyterian Homes, Inc.
Camp Hill, Pennsylvania

**Galen H. Smith III, M.H.A. and
  Doctoral Candidate**
Public Policy Program
University of North Carolina
  at Charlotte
Charlotte, North Carolina

**Stephen A. Stemkowski, M.H.A.
  and Doctoral Candidate**
Public Policy Program
University of North Carolina
  at Charlotte
Charlotte, North Carolina

Deborah Stone, Ph.D.
Department of Government
Dartmouth College
Hanover, New Hampshire

Daniel Swagerty, M.D., M.P.H.
Landon Center on Aging
Department of Family Medicine
University of Kansas
Kansas City, Kansas
and
American Medical Directors
  Association
Columbia, Maryland

William Weissert, Ph.D.
Department of Political Science
Florida State University
Tallahassee, Florida

SETTING THE STAGE 1

Chapter 1

History, Concepts, and Overview

Cynthia Massie Mara

Contents

Early History

Local Government Contracting for Provision of Care: Outdoor Relief

A complete understanding of long-term care (LTC) in the United States must begin with knowledge of its past so as to foster awareness of the roots of current challenges and facilitate the development of innovative responses. In the early years, elder care was not of great concern. With the exception of the Native American population, inhabitants were generally young immigrants who came either on their own accord or involuntarily as slaves. Older people, especially those who were ill, seldom made the arduous oceanic voyage. Those who did were likely to die on the trip (Stevenson, 2007). After arrival, in the colonies, people often experienced cycles of poverty and disease resulting in relatively short life spans.

For those who did reach old age, illness, accompanied by medical and LTC needs, often precipitated a descent into poverty. Aging individuals who lacked relatives to provide care relied on either neighbors or, less often, on the charity of their communities. The Elizabethan Poor Law, adopted in England in 1601 and later adapted to the needs of the colonies, designated communities as responsible for disadvantaged residents. Local autonomy was fostered by distance between settlements and by unsophisticated methods of transportation (Deutsch, 1941).

The Elizabethan goal of adopting three different responses to social need did not materialize. In that scenario, the objectives were to assign people who were sick and not able to work to infirmaries, people able to work but who could not find employment to a workhouse, and individuals able to work but refusing to do so to a House of Correction. Instead, in the colonies, all were generally grouped together in the almshouse which was also called a poorhouse or a county home or infirmary (Stevenson, 2006; Starr, 1982).

One exception was New York City, which purchased Blackwell's Island in 1829. Isolated from the city, the facilities included "the Charity Hospital, Penitentiary, Alms House, Hospital for Incurables, Workhouse, Asylum for the Insane, among others." Although the functions were separated, all were under the authority of the Almshouse Commissioners. In the 1930s, with increasing specialization of care, Welfare Island as it came to be known became dedicated solely to the care of older, sick individuals (NYC DOC, 2007).

Destitution was the central criterion for receipt of public assistance, which in the early years began as "outdoor support." Using the current terminology, the local government contracted out the provision of housing, food, and care for people who were unable to provide for themselves. Some of these individuals were boarded at a physician's residence, others were "boarded round the town." At times, family members would be paid to provide care. Alternatively, the care of poor people might be auctioned and assigned to the lowest bidder. The range in quality of care was vast, although for the most part it was inadequate and of poor quality. Communities were also known to ward off people with disabilities whom they thought would become dependent on public assistance.

Development of Almshouses: Indoor Relief

Although almshouses appeared as early as the 1600s, a general shift to this more structured, institutional approach to social need, called indoor relief, was not made until the eighteenth century. Outdoor support had become increasingly expensive, inexpedient. Almshouses, the prime examples of indoor relief, were generally regarded with dread. People with an amalgam of problems, including poverty and challenges related to aging and physical and mental illness, were housed together. Moreover, widows and orphans who lacked a source of income also lived there. In an 1881 edition of *The Atlantic Monthly*, almshouses were described as "wretched places [where] cleanliness is an unknown luxury; all is filth and misery . . . inmates, sane and insane, were found, in many instances, huddled together without discrimination of age, sex, or condition" (Thanet, 1881).

Residents, who were called inmates, offered almost all of the available care. Although services were sparse, the almshouse approach was not inexpensive. For instance, in 1880, Pennsylvania spent over $1.5 million for the support of 20,310 people. Such expenses in Massachusetts totaled approximately $1.7 million. New York's 1879 costs for 57,925 people in these "poor houses" were more than $1.6 million; an additional 79,852 people received temporary assistance at an expense of more than $690,000 (Thanet, 1881).

In his classic volume, The Transformation of American Medicine, Starr (1982) notes that by the 1830s, outdoor relief was ending and almshouses had become the sole provider of publicly funded care for the poor. It was hoped that the repellent nature of almshouses would motivate people to avoid poverty and subsequent reliance on public assistance.

The Development of Specialized Care

From almshouses, where people with a wide range of conditions and situations were housed, emerged more specialized institutions. Separate organizations were developed for the care of people with long-term mental illness; curable, acute diseases; and chronic or terminal illnesses.

In almshouses, mentally ill individuals tended to receive the harshest treatment described as "simply shocking" (Thanet, 1881). In response, in the 1830s, state-run institutions for these individuals expanded. Although the function of these hospitals initially was therapeutic, over time, custodial duties took priority (Starr, 1982). The facilities, located at a distance from populated areas, had a secondary purpose. As the cities grew, so did the number of residents with mental illness, contributing to public concerns regarding security. The state-run institutions were seen as one way to address societal fears by providing housing for these individuals in a remote location. As a result, LTC for people with mental illness was separated from the rest of healthcare.

Younger disabled people did not fare better. In the second half of the nineteenth century, a physician, Samuel Howe, led a commission exploring "feeblemindedness" and ways to address the related challenges. The Industrial Revolution helped shape the term's definition. During the transformation of the country from a rural to an urban society, educational requirements increased to the current equivalent of a third grade education. Anyone not reaching that level was deemed to be feebleminded. The term included people with a sensory impairment, for instance, blindness or deafness, that interfered with communication and, therefore, with learning. Difficulty with mobility, rendering a person unable to attend school, also resulted in such labeling.

Howe recommended the development of a special school for children with disabilities.* The Massachusetts legislature approved funds for this project. Howe intended to teach the children life skills and return them to their families. However, families resisted taking their children home. Some did not want to assume the child's care; many believed that institutional care was better for their children. Thus, although Howe opposed separation of people with disabilities from the rest of society, his work served as a basis for permanent institutionalization of these individuals (Pfeiffer, 1993). As a result, the younger LTC population was isolated from society and the mainstream of healthcare.

Similarly, acute care was separated from the LTC of older people with chronic physical or mental disabilities. By the late nineteenth century, there was a rapid growth in hospitals for individuals with short-term, curable illnesses. Before the use of antisepsis and aseptic technique, the discovery of antibiotics, and the safe use of anesthetics, hospitals had been avoided. They were called Death Houses. Better care could be received at home. Only people lacking home and family would seek services there.

Anesthesia allowed surgery to be completed without pain. Antisepsis and asepsis helped prevent the infections that had often resulted in death. If infection did occur, antibiotics helped control it. These advances and others that followed greatly improved the image of the hospital. As medical capability continued to expand, the treatment of curable, acute illnesses became the focus of the hospital. In fact, admission was denied to people with chronic or terminal illnesses. Care of these individuals continued to be the responsibility of almshouses (Starr, 1982). Technological advances similar to those in the hospitals did not occur in these "poor houses" and public attitude toward them remained negative.

Chronically or terminally ill people without wealth or family remained in the almshouses. Changing public policy, however, expanded the housing opportunities

---

* Children who lacked family and who did not have disabilities were sent to orphanages.

for this group. Holstein and Cole (1996) marked six factors, occurring from 1930 to 1970, as critical to the formation of modern LTC.

■ The Social Security Act of 1935 provided pensions to older people with the stipulation that anyone housed in a public facility could not receive them. The aim of this provision was to bring about the end of the almshouses. An unintended consequence of the policy was to stimulate the growth of voluntary and proprietary nursing homes. Most were more similar to board-and-care homes than to today's nursing homes. Some older people remained in almshouses; others went to state-run mental institutions. Commercial homes, however, accepted persons with both physical and mental infirmities.

■ Beginning in 1950, the federal government began making direct payments to LTC facilities for the care of older residents and others with disabling, chronic conditions. This type of disbursement made nursing homes more appealing to entrepreneurs.

■ Congress enacted legislation to support the construction of health-related facilities, including nursing homes. The Hill–Burton Act of 1946, which funded the construction of hospitals in rural and low-income areas, was amended in 1954 to extend coverage to the construction of public and not-for-profit nursing homes (Perlstadt, 1995). Medicalization of these facilities was fostered by the amendment's requirement that they be associated with a hospital (Holstein and Cole, 1996).

■ The Kerr–Mills Act encouraged home care by providing federal funding for a variety of services, but only if the state covered community-based as well as institutional care. However, states were not required to participate in the program and many chose to ignore it.

■ The formation of the American Association of Nursing Homes, resulted in more effective lobbying on behalf of the interests of the new nursing home industry. For instance, in 1956, the organization successfully induced Congress to authorize loan programs for proprietary nursing homes, some of which were freestanding facilities; they had not been included in Hill–Burton funding. These loan programs resulted in the rapid expansion of for-profit institutions (Vladeck, 1980).

Although the intent of the federal government was to regulate nursing homes, an unexpected impact on the development of these facilities ensued. Regulations were implemented, but enforcement was rare and had the unintended result of driving smaller facilities out of the market. Subsequently, the larger, more medically focused homes thrived.

Between 1940 and 1970, the percentage of institutionalized older people living in nonmedical locations such as boarding homes declined from 41 to 12 percent. During the same time period, a dramatic increase in nursing home occupancy occurred. Certainly, the passage of Medicaid and Medicare in 1965 sparked an even greater growth in the nursing home industry (Holstein and Cole, 1996).

Themes from the past can be seen in the present. Negative attitudes toward LTC, especially institutional facilities, remain. Poor quality of care persists. Costs continue to be high and the funding of LTC presents numerous challenges both to individuals and to their government. The shift in public funding from outdoor to indoor support today plays itself out in the tension between institutional and community-based care. Such issues in LTC will most likely continue into the foreseeable future.

Basic Concepts

LTC can be thought of as a variety of services and equipment provided over an extended period of time* to people of any age who need assistance with daily activities. It can also be viewed as a difficult-to-navigate journey because passage into and through the LTC system in the U.S. can be daunting. When people realize that they need such assistance, more times than not, they do not know the route to take or even where to start. There are no signs saying "Enter Here" or "Detour Ahead." Moreover, their families and friends often find themselves on the journey as well, unaware of the ways in which LTC needs are assessed and addressed.

Answers to critical questions have often been hard to find: What services do I need? Where can I get them? Who will provide them? What will they cost? How will they be funded? When individuals develops one or more limitations in function necessitating assistance with daily activities, where do they turn? Sometimes, when care can be provided at home, they turn to their family or friends. If no one is available, especially for full-time help, they search the want ads in the local newspaper. Attention may be drawn to a notice that says, "Will care for an elderly person. Experienced." But how can people needing assistance know if the individual is really prepared to provide quality care? What happens when the helper becomes ill, needs days off, or quits? How can informal, unpaid care be coordinated with formal, paid care?

Functional Limitations

An injury or chronic condition† can result in functional limitations. For instance, arthritis may restrict a person's movement to the extent that he or she requires help with daily activities. Tasks such as bathing, dressing, eating, using the toilet, and

---

* Generally, the time span is three months or longer.
† Chronic conditions can be associated with long-term physical, developmental, mental, intellectual, or cognitive challenges.

transferring from a bed to a chair are called activities of daily living (ADLs). Other chores needed to remain independent, including grocery shopping, cooking, taking medications, and handling finances, are termed instrumental activities of daily living (IADLs). A primary focus of LTC is the maintenance or enhancement of these functional abilities for people of any age.

Denial

Many people and their families who lack financial and emotional preparation are surprised when they need assistance with daily activities; they are also distressed by the price tag, especially for institutional care. With the average annual cost of nursing home care being approximately $70,000 (Kaiser Family Foundation [KFF], 2004), only the wealthy can afford an extended stay. Others "spend down" or exhaust their resources on medical and LTC outlays and then qualify for Medicaid. Indeed, Medicaid is the primary public payer for LTC. Funded both by the states and the federal government, this social welfare program requires impoverishment as a prerequisite to receive funding.

Often, people think that private health insurance or Medicare, neither of which requires poverty to qualify for assistance, will pay the bill. But both of them provide reimbursement primarily for acute and primary care services, not LTC. In addition, they only cover relatively short-term care that occurs after acute episodes. Such services can be provided by a home health agency (HHA), a rehabilitation facility, or a postacute care unit that can be located in a nursing home.

The financial stakes in LTC are high. Although not everyone will need this type of assistance, for those who do, the costs can be catastrophic. Regardless, it is common for people to deny even to themselves that they will ever need LTC. A majority of people report not having planned for potential occurrence. A recent survey conducted by Greenwald & Associates (2006) indicates that the percentage of nonplanners has been increasing. Minimal or no LTC planning had been undertaken by 69 percent of the 21- to 75-year-old respondents as compared to 49 percent in a similar study conducted in 1997.

When asked, most people say they would not want to go to a nursing home, and many equate nursing homes to LTC. This strong preference to avoid institutionalization can be another factor in the resistance to considering any future LTC needs. For many it is easier to think, "I'll never need long-term care," and neglect to plan for this possibility, especially if the person is convinced that a nursing facility is the only option. Considering that 69 percent of people aged 65 and above will require some LTC, and 35 percent are projected to become nursing home residents for at least a short period of time (Kemper et al., 2005/2006), denial and lack of knowledge are critical issues that need to be addressed. At the same time, given the uncertainties and exorbitant costs, a significant percentage of the population is incapable of saving for these needs on its own.

Administrators and Policymakers

The LTC path is not always clear even for administrators as they seek to provide information and services to people needing assistance and to their families. Nor is the journey uncomplicated for policymakers as they search for solutions to the problems in LTC. Changing socioeconomic factors such as demography and the economy create the need for policy modification. In turn, the changing policies impact the management of LTC organizations. Clearly, providing leadership in LTC is challenging. Such work, however, is crucial in addressing current and future LTC needs.

Long-Term Care Recipients, Services, and Providers

More and more people will require assistance with their daily activities in the coming years. The U.S. Department of Health and Human Services (DHHS, 2007) estimates that between 2006 and 2020 the number of individuals above the age of 65 will increase from nine to twelve million (Barrett, 2006). Although about 19 percent of people aged 65 years or older have functional impairments, the percentage among people aged 85 or above—the fastest growing segment of the elderly population—is approximately 55 percent (Hagen, 2004). Moreover, older people have an estimated 40 percent chance of entering a nursing home and one-tenth of them will remain there for five years or longer (DHHS, 2007). Although the proportion of younger individuals needing assistance is much lower, because of their greater numbers, they represent between 30 and 50 percent of the LTC population (Feder, 2000, 2001; KFF, 2004a, b).

LTC providers, whether paid or unpaid, assist individuals in carrying out both ADL and IADL tasks. Family members, especially adult daughters and wives, offer the bulk of LTC. Despite this dependence on informal services, various societal forces are impinging on the ability of loved ones to make the associated sacrifices. Decreasing family size, increasing divorce rates, and greater employment of women have been bringing about a growing need for formal care. Yet a workforce shortage already exists and, in the face of an aging population, is expected to worsen considerably (Holahan et al., 2003; Johnson et al., 2007).

Factors Affecting Demand for and Supply of Services

Certain factors such as declines in the disability rate among older people and emergent technology can help in addressing the shortage. Disability rates declined between 1982 and 2004. However, Lakdawalla et al. (2004) argue that increasing rates of obesity in younger people may lessen this trend by 2015–2020. Alternatively, Manton et al. (2007) are unconvinced that the current obesity epidemic will necessarily have a significant impact on the future disability rates of older

Americans. Regardless, Johnson et al. (2007) found that even with an optimistic annual decline of one percent in the disability rate, the number of older people with impairments will increase by 50 percent between 2000 and 2040.

Advances in technology can also contribute to a reduction in the need for hands-on care. Although long-term services are generally considered low-tech, scientific advances that reduce the need for human assistance are expanding. For instance, telehealth can provide for the monitoring of a person's vital signs from a distance. Also, the range of conditions for which home care is possible is widening. Individuals whose medical needs, in the past, would have necessitated hospital care are increasingly receiving the required services at home (Berkman et al., 2005). As such, as Stone (2000) states, we are witnessing a blurring of acute services and LTC.

Location of Care

There exists a variety of places for the provision of LTC exists. A person's home or apartment is the location of preference. Assisted living and personal care facilities generally supply housing, meals, housekeeping, laundry, social activities, transportation, and help with medications. Assistance with ADLs may be offered by the facility or by community service providers. Continuing care retirement communities (CCRCs) offer a variety of housing options on their campuses. They include houses or apartments for independent living and assisted living and skilled nursing facilities. Adult day service centers may also be included.

Because LTC entails concern for the place within which it is provided, consideration of housing is essential. The space within which a person with disabilities lives can range from supportive to risky. Efforts to create or modify the setting to facilitate its use by persons with disabilities can help them age in place. In other words, a person with increasing functional limitations can remain in the location with which he or she is familiar and receive services at home. The person's current environment, of course, must be adapted regularly to meet his or her changing needs.

Overview of the Book

Part I of this handbook provides the context for the rest of the volume. As suggested earlier in this chapter, past attitudes toward LTC have left a strong residue in today's society. Current problems in the LTC system have served to augment such perceptions. In Chapter 2, Laura Katz Olson examines opinion polls that reflect current public attitudes toward and understanding of issues surrounding LTC, including the role of Medicaid. Consideration is given to attitudes of caregivers whose older relatives have been placed in nursing homes as well as to the preferences of older people themselves. She also examines opinions about the quality of care in, and regulation of, nursing homes. She notes that there are many misconceptions about LTC, particularly those related to its funding.

Chapter 3 by Deborah Stone forms the "heart" of the text. In it, she details her mother's experiences with LTC and her own responses to that care. Stone points out that efficiency-oriented care, although meeting regulations, lacks the human contact so craved by care recipients. The need for caregivers to provide a high-touch approach in the delivery of assistance shines through the pages.

Tension exists in LTC between the social model and the medical model of care. The former provides the recipient with more independence; the latter, it is presumed, offers more safety. In Chapter 4, Colleen Grogan examines the history of LTC to find an explanation for the deep societal conflict between these two ideals. She reviews policy changes, including those developed in response to the squalid conditions in the almshouses, to show how U.S. policy moved toward a medical model. She emphasizes the enduring conflict between the social and medical models. Do we view aging as an illness to be treated or as a natural part of life to be experienced with all its risks? Our answer seems to teeter between the two but falls more heavily on the former.

Part II focuses on the recipients of care and their caregivers. Megan McCutcheon and William McAuley in Chapter 5 present a picture of older people who receive LTC. Among other issues, they detail the characteristics of these individuals with functional impairments and their use of LTC services.

In Chapter 6, Arthur Blaser describes the characteristics of younger people who require LTC. Noting that, too often, LTC is seen only as an aging issue, Blaser focuses on the similarities and differences between the needs of younger and older consumers of care. He emphasizes that both groups would benefit from greater control over LTC decisions affecting their lives.

The high levels of informal LTC provided by family members and friends is addressed in Chapter 7 by Sharon Keigher. Keigher answers the questions: Who are the 44.2 million people who provide more than $270 billion of volunteer assistance each year to family members and friends? What benefits and sacrifices are involved? What differences are there in providing care to a spouse, parent, or a child? What policies most effectively provide support to informal providers of care? Keigher concludes by recommending the formation of more effective partnerships between formal and informal caregivers, improved integration among service providers overall, and, similar to Blaser, more participation on the part of the consumer.

The relationship between the competency of the paid workforce and the quality of care is addressed in Chapter 8 by Edward Miller and Vincent Mor. Not only do the authors explore barriers to recruiting and retaining skilled caregivers, but they also propose strategies to improve these processes, such as redesigning the workplace; improving benefits and training; and providing career ladders, loan forgiveness programs, and scholarships.

Until 1974, skilled nursing facilities were not required to employ a medical director. Daniel Swagerty in Chapter 9 notes that involvement of physicians, however, is essential for the provision of quality care. He discusses guidelines for performing the tasks of the medical director as well as the working relationship between the attending physician and the medical director.

The services themselves are emphasized in *Part III*. The idea of a continuum of LTC that is more ideal than real is discussed by William McAuley and Megan McCutcheon in Chapter 10. They argue that, in this country, there is no system in which a person can pass seamlessly from one type of service to another. They present a number of models that attempt to confront the barriers for achieving coordination of care, including the Program of All-Inclusive Care for the Elderly (PACE), Web-based care coordination, social health maintenance organizations (SHMOs), and Coordination and Advocacy for Rural Elders (CARE). They also discuss LTC services, ranging from home and community-based approaches to care offered in nursing homes, assisted living facilities, personal care settings, and continuing care retirement communities (CCRCs).

In Chapter 11, Jan Brown provides information about the changing legal environment surrounding LTC. She describes the various legal documents used in preparing end-of-life decisions, forms that can be confusing for the layperson. Cautioning that her writing is meant to convey information of general scope and not legal advice, Brown also describes four types of legal documents with which all adults should be familiar. Although an understanding of these materials is helpful to anyone above 18 years of age, it is especially useful for LTC care administrators and policymakers. Finally, Brown discusses asset protection, a topic about which there has been much controversy in recent years. She provides information about changes in asset transfer policy contained in the Deficit Reduction Act of 2005.

Supportive housing is an essential issue in LTC. In Chapter 12, Shannon Chance reviews the history of LTC from an architect's point of view. She first discusses the relationship between the physical environment and the need for and receipt of hands-on care. She then presents the evolution of construction technologies and their impact on LTC facilities. Chance interweaves national policymaking with the changing locations for the provision of care. She takes the reader from the nonresident focus of the almshouses to the emergence of housing options that are designed with consumers' needs and wants in mind. She includes the preferences of baby boomers and their likely effects on LTC architecture.

Part IV addresses issues related to the administration of care. In Chapter 13, Steven Proctor discusses not-for-profit LTC entities, including almshouses with names such as The Home for the Friendless. Although other authors describe the negative aspects of almshouses, Proctor points to the charitable intent of many persons who provided time-intense, detail-oriented leadership for these organizations. Proctor also describes the context within which governing bodies have evolved. Over time, different skill sets have been required of board members. He then discusses the changing relationships among staff, the governing body, and the chief executive officer (CEO). He reviews the responsibilities of the board, with the financial integrity of the organization as a key concern. In addition, Proctor addresses ethical concerns as well as the importance and benefits of transparency of information. He offers strategies for providing board members with clear data without overwhelming them, and includes an example of a "dashboard" that contains key indicators of the health of the organization. Proctor reminds the reader of the administrator's importance in the culture of an organization, saying, "in long-term care, leadership is the soil in which a culture of care can grow."

In Chapter 14, Vincent Mor addresses quality from an information standpoint. He presents the development of uniform quality measures for nursing homes and HHAs over time. The reader gains an understanding of the development of various measurement tools such as the Minimum Data Set (MDS) and the outcome and Assessment Information Set (OASIS) now used in nursing facilities and HHAs, respectively. Mor presents not only the original goals of quality measures, but also subsequent uses to which they have been put. He includes the measures' strengths and limitations and explores the potential of these indicators to influence consumer decision making.

In Chapter 15, Shannon Chance defines the administrator's role in the planning and design of LTC facilities. An understanding of the design process, and the series of steps it entails, is needed by administrators as they work with development teams. Chance presents a description of the roles of other team members as well. She begins by describing the types of LTC housing and related services, detailing the medical and residential models of care and addressing the emergence of hybrid forms of care. She targets often-overlooked features that can greatly affect quality associated with living and working in each of the places.

Part V concentrates on policymaking and funding for LTC. Many policy issues regarding LTC, including its financing, face the nation. However, LTC is not an issue that is often on the public agenda. William Weissert, in Chapter 14, contends that the elements essential for reform are largely absent in the formulation of LTC policy. He presents his thesis using Kingdon's (1995) model of the policy process as a framework. According to Weissert, even getting on the public agenda has proven to be a largely insurmountable task for LTC, particularly because the issue often lacks a public official who is willing to bear the LTC banner. He points to the struggles of those members of Congress and heads of public agencies who have carried that banner for a time. As a policy area with little current promise of success, LTC continues to have difficulty garnering sustained political support. As Weissert takes the reader through a story of the many barriers to LTC reform, he makes the gargantuan nature of the task ahead increasingly evident. Weissert concludes, "There is nothing easy about long-term care."

The care of persons with long-term mental illness has advanced since the days of the almshouses and custodial state institutions. Yet, as Bradley Karlin and Michael Duffy state in Chapter 17, there is a continuing, significant neglect of older people's mental health needs, especially those of nursing home residents. The authors discuss such problems, including the obstacles to services created by administrative practices and regulatory policies. Karlin and Duffy then formulate recommendations for change and point to the value of advocacy as a means of changing the public agenda and modifying policy.

If the financing of LTC could be satisfactorily resolved, the system's other challenges would seem less daunting. From the times of the almshouses up to today, public funding, private payments, or a combination of the two have not been sufficient to support this type of care adequately or meet people's LTC needs completely. Given the government's increasing reluctance to assume more of the financing of LTC, Galen Smith and William Brandon examine private financing for LTC in Chapter 18. The authors' assessment of private LTC insurance includes information on related economic principles and an exploration of the reasons for the slow growth of the private market. They discuss financing strategies such as various forms of risk pooling and ways for individuals to accumulate assets. Attention is given to government initiatives that stimulate private market mechanisms for funding LTC expenses and policy proposals to augment these efforts.

In Chapter 19, Stephen Stemkowski and William Brandon point out the complex funding mechanisms that have fostered fragmentation in LTC programs. In presenting an overview of public financing, they discuss the various government programs related to LTC and include the reasons for the current lack of success of private LTC insurance. They also address policy initiatives that would shift some of the financial responsibility for LTC from the government to the individual. In addition, the authors discuss the failure of the federal government to adopt LTC reform, the role of the states in providing strategies for change, and principles and examples of social insurance. They conclude with reasons for the reluctance to implement LTC social insurance in this country.

Finally, in *Part VI* we look toward the future. In Chapter 20, Cynthia Mara calls for a national debate about LTC. She examines the areas of change in LTC, topics that would surely be part of the debate. Denial about chronic illness and disability is very strong in this country and serves as a barrier to meaningful interchange about LTC. When fear about the related costs exceeds the emotion surrounding denial, discussion may well be possible. It will likely, however, be a time of crisis, fiscal and otherwise, in LTC.

Conclusion

This time in history is pivotal for LTC. Clearly, increasing demand, coupled with resource restraints, will force change. Administrators and policymakers face a myriad of challenges as they attempt to contain costs while maintaining quality of and access to care. Too often the seeming intractability of the problems has fostered public denial and inaction. Increased knowledge and understanding of LTC, however, can aid in the formulation of effective policies and the administration of thriving programs. The ultimate aim of these efforts is to help people with functional limitations and their families to travel more smoothly and effectively through the LTC system.

References

Barrett, L. (2006). *The Costs of Long-Term Care: Public Perceptions Versus Reality in 2006.* Washington: AARP Knowledge Management. http://www.aarp.org/research/long-termcare/costs/ltc_costs_fs_2006.html (accessed May 26, 2007).

Berkman, B., Gardner, D. S., Zodikoff, B. D., and Harootyan, L. K. (2005). Social work in health care with older adults: Future challenges. *Families in Society*, 86(3), 329–337.

Department of Health and Human Services (DHHS). (2007). *What Is Long-Term Care?* Washington: Centers for Medicare and Medicaid Services. http://www.medicare.gov/LongTermCare/Static/Home.asp (accessed May 27, 2007).

Deutsch, A. (1941). The sick poor in colonial times. *The American Historical Review*, 46(3), 560–579. http://links.jstor.org/sici?sici=0002-8762%28194104%2946%3A3%3C5 60%3ATSPICT%3E2.0.CO%3B2-Y&size=LARGE&origin=JSTOR-enlargePage (accessed April 30, 2007).

Feder, J. (2000). Long-term care: A public responsibility. *Health Affairs*, 20(6), 112–113.

Feder, J. (2001). Long-term care in the United States: An overview. *Health Affairs*, 19(3), 40–56.

Greenwald & Associates. (2006). Survey of consumer attitudes toward long-term care. In *Senior Journal*. Money Management & Insurance for Senior Citizens: Americans Less Concerned about Long-Term Care Than 10 Years Ago. http://www.seniorjournal.com/NEWS/Money/6-07-05-AmericansLess.htm (accessed June 25, 2007).

Hagen, S. (2004). *Financing Long-Term Care for the Elderly.* Washington: United States Congressional Budget Office.

Holahan, J., Wiener, J., and Lutzky, A. W. (2003). Health policy for low-income people: States' responses to new challenges. *Health Affairs*, W187.

Holstein, M. and Cole, T. (1996). The evolution of long-term care in America. In Binstock, R., Leighton, C., and von Mering, O. (Eds.). *The Future of Long-Term Care: Social and Policy Issues*, pp. 19–47. Baltimore, MD: The Johns Hopkins University Press.

Johnson, R. W., Toohey, D., and Wiener, J. M. (2007). *Meeting the Long-Term Care Needs of Baby Boomers: How Changing Families Will Affect Paid Helpers and Institutions.* Washington: The Urban Institute.

Kaiser Family Foundation (KFF). (2004a). *Health Care and the 2004 Elections: Long Term Care.* http://www.kff.org/medicaid/7208.cfm (accessed July 4, 2007).

Kaiser Family Foundation (KFF). (2004b). *Health Care and the 2004 Election: The Uninsured.* http://www.kff.org/uninsured/7155/cfm (accessed July 4, 2007).

Kemper, P., Komisar, H. L., and Alecxih, L. (2005/2006). Long-term care under an uncertain future: What can retirees expect? *Inquiry*, 42(4), 335–350.

Kingdon, J. (1995). *Agendas, Alternatives and Public Policies*, 2nd edition. London: HarperCollins.

Lakdawalla, D. N., Bhattacharya, J., and Tolley, H. D. (2004). Are the young becoming more disabled? Rates of disability appear to be on the rise among people ages eighteen to fifty-nine, fueled by a growing obesity epidemic. *Health Affairs*, 23(1), 168–176.

Manton, K. G., Lamb, V. L., and XiLiang, G. (2007). Medicare cost effects of recent U.S. disability trends in the elderly: Future implications. *Journal of Aging and Health*, 19(3), 359–381.

New York City Department of Corrections (NYC DOC). (2007). *New York City Department of Corrections History*. http://www.correctionhistory.org/html/chronicl/nycdoc/html/blakwell1.html (accessed May 24, 2007).

Perlstadt, H. (1995). The development of the Hill–Burton legislation: Interests, issues and compromises. *Journal of Health & Social Policy*, 6(3), 77–96.

Pfeiffer, D. (1993). Overview of the disability movement: History, legislative record, and political implications. *Policy Studies Journal*, 21(4), 724–734.

Starr, P. (1982). *The Social Transformation of American Medicine*. New York: Basic Books.

Stevenson, K. (2006). *The History of Long-Term Care*. http://www.elderweb.com/home/node/2832 (accessed May 19, 2007).

Stevenson, K. (2007). *The History of Long-Term Care 1776–1799: Poorhouses Become Homes for the Indigent Elderly*. http://www.elderweb.com/home/node/9641 (accessed May 12, 2007).

Stone, R. (2000). *Long-Term Care for the Elderly with Disabilities: Current Policy, Emerging Trends, and Implications for the Twenty-First Century*. New York: Milbank Memorial Fund.

Thanet, O. (1881). The indoor pauper: A study. *The Atlantic Monthly*, 47(284). Text from: Library of Congress American Memory Collection. http://www.elderweb.com/home/book/export/html/2832 (accessed April 22, 2007).

Vladeck, B. (1980). *Unloving Care*. New York: Basic Books.

Chapter 2

Public Perceptions of Long-Term Care

Laura Katz Olson

Contents

Introduction

Using a variety of opinion polls over the last several years, this chapter seeks to address issues related to perceptions of long-term care in the United States. It begins with an assessment of views of caregivers about placing their elders in nursing homes, followed by the preferences of frail older people themselves. Then opinions about long-term care public policies, especially the regulation of institutional facilities and quality of care issues, are discussed. Payment for long-term care is the focus of the next section: it looks at whether Americans understand how long-term care is funded, their ability to afford such services, and their interest in the subject generally. Subsequent sections concentrate on attitudes about Medicaid, including points of view about middle-class participation in the program, reducing government funding, and the relationship between support for Medicaid and its long-term care coverage. Finally, the chapter looks at how concerned people are about their own long-term care needs and the perceptions and misconceptions they have about Medicare and their private insurance policies.

Views on Institutional Care

Caregivers

One of the more difficult challenges faced by the United States and nations worldwide is the care of the frail elderly. Currently in the United States, about 10 million people of all ages are estimated to need long-term care; 60 percent are aged 65 and above. Certainly, adult children and spouses, especially women, do the majority of the caring work, although this is becoming increasingly burdensome for many households. This kind of labor has intensified over the decades, as increasing longevity at older ages has fostered greater physical and mental disabilities and for longer periods.

At the same time, more women must rely on their paid labor to support themselves and their families; they are often caught between nurturing their young children and tending to the needs of aging parents or parents-in-law; and the number of dependent elderly per caregiver is growing due to declining family size and more living generations. Consequently, growing numbers of middle-aged and older adults must face long-term care questions regarding one or more of their increasingly disabled aging kin. In a recent poll, sponsored by Genworth Financial National (GFN; 2006), for example, half of the respondents above 40 years replied that they have a parent or other relative who needs or has needed home care or long-term care in a nursing home or assisted living facility.

Despite the difficulties, American adult children, spouses, and others generally provide hands-on care for their chronically disabled family members for as long as they can. Only after they are exhausted, too ill, or frail themselves, and only as a last resort, do they seek institutional care for their kin. One reason many families are extremely reluctant to place their loved ones in a nursing home is because of the dearth of quality—or even acceptable—facilities. In her study, Abel (1991) found that many caretakers refuse to place even their severely debilitated elders in institutions, mostly because of the notoriously abusive conditions or their own firsthand observations of the facilities during their search for a home. Others have personal experience through visiting relatives, neighbors, and friends or even their own stays, such as after a hospitalization.

Current data suggests that many people do have direct experience with nursing homes and understand the negative implications of institutional placement. When asked if they had ever been in a nursing home, either as a patient or as a visitor, 84 percent of the respondents in a Kaiser Family Foundation Survey (Kaiser Health Poll, 2005) said "yes." Moreover, 46 percent of the total had a member of their immediate family, or someone they knew well, in a nursing home within the past three years. When asked where they get their views on nursing homes, 31 percent replied from their own experience and another 43 percent from the experiences of friends and family; only 21 percent said that they received such information from television, radio, newspapers, and other media.

Clearly, such firsthand experience does not engender a positive impression, especially in comparison with other healthcare sectors. Only 35 percent of respondents in the Kaiser Health Poll (2005) thought that nursing homes were doing a "good job" serving healthcare consumers, as compared to 84 percent for nurses, 69 percent for doctors, 64 percent for hospitals, and 43 percent for pharmaceutical companies. Interestingly, the public's generally low opinion of nursing homes appears commensurate with their estimation of health insurance companies and managed care plans: only 34 and 30 percent of respondents, respectively, gave these entities such approval.* Moreover, 41 percent of the respondents regarded residency in a nursing home as making frail elders worse off than they were prior to entering the facility; another 23 percent stated that it did not make much of a difference, not exactly an endorsement of institutional care. Only 19 percent assumed that the facility would improve their situation.

Older People

In addressing the issue of long-term care, we must include not only the needs but also the preferences of the frail elderly themselves. The evidence suggests that older people, similar to their caregivers, do not have a positive view of nursing facilities. Accordingly, an overwhelming majority do not want to be institutionalized and dread the prospect of entering a nursing home. Ultimately, frail elders want to live

---

* Managed care, viewed by public officials and employers alike as a means of reducing medical costs, has been proliferating throughout the United States. Yet, similar to nursing homes, the quality of care has been an issue.

as independently as possible, preferably in a community setting and without over-whelming their family members, whether a spouse or an adult child.

In a survey of 3000 seriously ill hospitalized patients, 26 percent said they were unwilling to, and 30 percent said they would rather die than live in a nursing home—only 2 percent said they would do so voluntarily (Kane et al., 1998). In a *USA Today* (2005) poll, one-third of the respondents indicated that they "worried a great deal," and another 20 percent were "somewhat worried" about eventually winding up in a nursing home; 16 percent and 32 percent, respectively, were "not so worried" or "not worried at all." Perhaps the lack of concern by some of these latter respondents could be attributed to the fact that they incorrectly assumed, for a variety of reasons, that they were bulletproof from such an eventuality.

Regardless, such facilities do become "home" to a significant percentage of vulnerable older people. Currently, about 1.5 million, or 14 percent of the age 85 or older population lives in nursing homes (Houser, 2007). Moreover, studies show that over 50 percent of women and nearly one-third of men age 65 and above will reside in a nursing home at some time during their life span; about 10 percent—primarily females—will stay for five years or more (U.S. Senate, Committee on Finance [SFC], 2005b).

Critically, a significant minority of disabled elders have no family to provide help. Given the dearth of publicly supported home and community care, older people who cannot pay for themselves are forced to enter an institution. Such individuals are most likely to be single women: despite a lifetime of expectations that they provide care to others, they are more at risk than men of lacking any care for themselves (Hooyman, 1999). Because older men are more likely than women to be married and even to remarry in their later years, when they become chronically ill they generally receive hands-on assistance from their wives; over 50 percent of women aged 75 years and above are single. Moreover, about one-fifth of all older people have no children on whom they can rely on for everyday assistance, and about 10 percent are without any living kin (Abel, 1991; Brody, 1995).

Public Policy

Notwithstanding the generally negative views on nursing homes by caregivers and older people alike, our public policies continue to promote institutionalization. Recently, there has been some expansion of home and community services under Medicaid; nevertheless, the national government and states continue to fund nursing facilities at ever-increasing costs.* Ostensibly a private sector industry, nursing homes appropriate billions from the public coffers annually. Currently, Medicaid

---

* In the past decade, Medicaid home care spending increased from 14 to 29 percent of Medicaid's long-term care spending (SFC, 2005a, p. 112); about 1.2 million people now receive in-home services through the program.

is paying for nearly 50 percent of the more than $100 billion total nursing home bill,* with Medicare subsidizing another 6 percent. A significant reason that states struggle with escalating Medicaid budgets is because of such long-term care costs. Indeed, institutional care represents about 35 percent of all state spending on the program.

Despite such large public sums, the private, mostly proprietary nursing home industry, which is answerable mainly to its stockholders, has relatively little public accountability or serious government oversight. As I discuss elsewhere (Olson, 2003), its workers continue to be underpaid and overworked; most facilities are understaffed, particularly with regard to nurses and nurse's aides; and financial fraud is unchecked, as is patient neglect and abuse (Olson, 2003). For instance, Turiel (2005) provides evidence that over 90 percent of nursing homes do not have sufficient staff, a situation associated with festering bedsores and other serious infections, malnutrition, weight loss, dehydration, pneumonia, and other seriously negative patient outcomes. Clearly, a significant number of Americans are acutely aware of these failings. As opposed to political leaders, studies show that the public understands some of the serious, ongoing problems related to U.S. nursing homes.

In the Kaiser Health Poll (2005), 63 percent of the respondents agreed that there is not enough government regulation of the quality of nursing homes, and 59 percent that government is not enforcing quality standards for these facilities. Similarly, 74 percent strongly or somewhat agreed that nursing homes do not have enough staff; 60 percent that its staff is often poorly trained; and 58 percent that there is too much waste, fraud, and abuse by facility managers: relatively few people strongly disagreed with such statements.

However, some aspects of the nursing home industry's public relations efforts may be paying off: nearly half of the respondents (48 percent) concurred that nursing homes are not paid enough money by Medicare, Medicaid, and other insurers. About one-fourth (26 percent) did not know, probably indicating that a significant minority of people are unaware of public expenditures for long-term care, actual daily costs of serving residents, and nursing home profits (Kaiser Health Poll, 2005).

Paying for Long-Term Care

More and more people require at least some paid assistance, yet the costs of long-term care have grown dramatically. By 2003, outlays from both public and private sources reached $183 billion annually, or 13 percent of total healthcare expenses in the nation.† Nearly half (48 percent or $87 billion) is paid through Medicaid

---

* Medicaid is the principal payer for nearly 60 percent of all nursing home residents in the nation.
† Nursing homes account for about 47 percent of total long-term care spending (HEC, Subcommittee on Health, 2005).

alone, mostly for nursing homes.* The government subsidizes another 18 percent ($33 billion) through Medicare; other publicly supported programs pay an additional 3 percent ($5.5 billion) (U.S. House, Committee on Energy and Commerce [HEC], Subcommittee on Health, 2005).

Only a relatively limited amount of long-term care is funded privately. In 2003, families paid for 20 percent ($37 billion) of the national total out-of-pocket, the vast majority for nursing home care. Even less, only 9 percent ($16 billion) came from private long-term care insurance and 3 percent ($5.5 billion) from other types of private sources (HEC, Subcommittee on Health, 2005).

Studies show that people may have an erroneous understanding of how long-term care is funded. They also tend to have an unrealistic view of whether they can afford to pay for such costs on their own, or an indifferent attitude toward the subject. One poll, sponsored by the Employee Benefit Research Institute (EBRI, 1996), indicated that at least half of respondents were confident that they would have enough money to finance nursing home or home healthcare, if they required it. Although only 19 percent of respondents in the Kaiser Health Poll (2005) expected to support their long-term care needs themselves or through family money, 30 percent did not know how they would fund paid help. The reality is that few people can afford the high costs of such assistance, and even a smaller number can pick up the tab for as long as may be necessary.

In 2000, the median net worth of elderly households—excluding their homes—was only $23,885 (SFC, 2005a). Older widowed, divorced, or never-married women tend to have even fewer resources. Moreover, such females often do not have adequate income to meet their daily needs: nearly one-third of all single women aged 65 and above had incomes at or below 125 percent of the official poverty threshold. In 2001, a Survey of Income and Program Participation (SIPP) measured the total assets of single people, aged 85 and above, who required ongoing assistance because of functional or cognitive impairments. Seventy-four percent of these elders had assets of less than $5000 (SFC, 2005c).

On average, people residing in a nursing home—which currently can cost $60,000 or more—wipe out their entire life savings after 18 months (GFN, 2006). The SIPP study showed that 84 percent of the people evaluated could not pay for even one year of nursing home expenses; another 9 percent could afford slightly less than three years of institutional care; and only 7 percent could cover three or more years (SFC, 2005c).

About 44 percent of nursing home users do finance their own care but most of them have relatively short stays and often deplete much, if not all, of their savings. Another 16 percent of residents initially pay on their own, exhaust their assets, and

---

* Nationally, on average approximately 57 percent of Medicaid long-term care is for the elderly, which amounts to about 35 percent of this group's total long-term care expenses (HEC, Subcommittee on Health, 2005).

turn to the public health program. Over one-third is forced to depend on Medicaid from the start (SFC, 2005a, d).

Medicaid, Long-Term Care, and Public Support

Medicaid and "Spend Down"

One of the more contentious issues today regarding Medicaid's long-term care provision is its use by the middle class. In the initial 1965 legislation, the federal government mandated only five basic services, one of which included skilled nursing home care for individuals aged 21 and above. Frail elders with higher income or assets than a state's welfare levels could qualify under its medically needy program; however, such individuals would first have to impoverish themselves by spending their own assets and income on medical costs until they reached the state-established standards. As early as 1975, Medicaid was paying, at least partially, for more than half of all nursing home residents, many of whom had previously considered themselves as part of the middle class.

Over the years, Medicaid has remained a key support for older people, at all income levels, who require long-term care. Indeed, by the 1990s, President Clinton and many other Democrats were defending Medicaid as "a key support for senior citizens residing in nursing homes" (Grogan and Patashnik, 2003, p. 844). Framing Medicaid as an entitlement for middle-class elderly, many Democrats in 1996 defended the program against efforts to reduce its federal outlays (Grogan and Patashnik, 2003).

Recently, however, there have been concerted attacks on the use of Medicaid by the nonpoor for long-term care. A particular focus has been on asset transfers: through various forms of estate planning, enterprising middle-class elders potentially can divest themselves of their money through gifts to their children or by establishing trusts to become eligible for Medicaid. In an attempt to control this alleged problem, in 1993 Congress increased the waiting time to five years for sheltering assets through certain trusts and to three years for transferring money to relatives before an elder could apply for Medicaid. The Deficit Reduction Act (DRA) of 2005 has tightened the rules even further: it increases the look back period to five years for asset transfers; changes the penalty period from the time of transfer to the date of Medicaid eligibility, and excludes coverage for individuals with home equity valued at over $750,000 (see Chapter 11 for additional information on changes in the look back period).

Nonetheless, unlike the current administration, Americans tend to support middle-class participation in Medicaid, particularly as it pertains to long-term care. For example, in a Kaiser Family Foundation Poll on Medicaid (2005), 55 percent of the respondents were opposed to eliminating the ability of middle-class elderly to transfer their assets to their children for the purpose of qualifying for Medicaid.

Moreover, a recent American Association of Retired Persons (AARP, 2005) survey found that fully 75 percent of the respondents opposed an extension of the look back period to five years for such money transfers.

Notably, as Judith Feder suggests, "Claims that Medicaid serves as an asset shelter for the wealthy rather than as a safety net are simply not supported by the evidence" (SFC, 2005a). Taylor et al. (1999) found that the vast majority of people who could potentially benefit from forming trusts to qualify for Medicaid did not have any; in fact, it was rare for anyone to do so. The data suggests that trusts "are far more commonly established by wealthy people seeking to reduce tax burdens and avoid probate than by modest income people seeking to avoid spend down for nursing home care" (Taylor et al., 1999, p. 7). Moreover, other research shows that older people in poor or declining health are not transferring assets but rather are keeping whatever money they have to pay for their own care (Feinstein and Ho, 2001).

The reality, as shown earlier, is that most middle-class elders either pay for their nursing home care with their own money or become impoverished before applying for Medicaid. Ironically, the new Republicans have passed legislation to lower inheritance taxes for high-income people, while seeking to prevent the middle class from preserving their small bequests.

Public Views on Medicaid

Medicaid is the quintessential entitlement program so detested today by the new conservative forces. Yet, unlike Aid to Families with Dependent Children (AFDC), it has proven difficult to abolish or even reduce considerably. After years of attack by conservative and even moderate political officials, AFDC was successfully dismantled as a national program in 1996, resulting in a drastic retrenchment in cash assistance to poor families. Despite all of the fanfare about its devastating costs, AFDC outlays were relatively modest, both at the national and state levels. Although the majority of recipients were Caucasian, the program had been labeled as a program serving indolent, dependent minority households (Quadagno, 1994; Teles, 1998).

Medicaid, on the other hand, is now the fifth largest item on the federal budget (after Social Security, defense, interest payments on the national debt, and Medicare) and the second most costly item—and in a few places the highest—in state budgets. Despite these large and escalating costs, Medicaid was left relatively intact in the mid-1990s. Since that time, there have been annual efforts to cut billions at the national and state levels, but they continue to prove relatively unsuccessful. One main reason for the sustainability of Medicaid is public support: Rushefsky and Patel (1998) argue that the failure of Republicans to reduce increases in Medicare and Medicaid in 1995 and 1996, as opposed to AFDC, "can be attributed to public opinion" (p. 239). Although many political leaders of both parties have

those households that would have purchased the policies anyway (SFC, 2005a). Certainly, they will not benefit a significant percentage of the population, materially improve the situation of current or future frail older people or the disabled younger population, or even begin to solve the U.S. crisis in long-term care.

Conclusion

On many questions, the response is mixed as to whether the public completely understands long-term care in this nation. Certainly, the way people comprehend an issue can be essential to its political outcome (Leech et al., 2002). Similarly, as Grogan (1999) asserts, if constituents are not interested and aware, politicians have more leeway and interest groups have more power.

Obviously, there is a growing need for long-term care in the United States, whether institutional or at-home assistance, given that there are increasing numbers of frail and disabled people and fewer caregivers per person requiring aid. Although we continue to publicly subsidize nursing homes, chronically ill older people and their families perceive that these are not effective, quality, or humane places. However, despite the reluctance of carer and recipient alike, frail elders—a significant percentage of single women aged 85 and above—will end up in these facilities. The evidence suggests that they are not completely aware of such an eventuality.

Nor are most people cognizant of long-term care costs and how they are funded. Large numbers of people erroneously assume that services will be covered through Medicare or their private health insurance policies. Yet the reality is that most chronically ill older people cannot afford to pay for long-term care on their own; the majority of physically or mentally disabled elderly women will be forced to spend their meager life savings to qualify for help from Medicaid. As Judith Feder sums it up: "People who need extensive assistance with basic tasks of living (like bathing, dressing and eating) face the risk of catastrophic costs and inadequate care" (SFC, 2005a, p. 2).

Polls and other survey data reveals that the public tends to support Medicaid, particularly because it serves the long-term needs of the elderly. They also generally approve its use by middle-class older people. In fact, nearly 70 percent of respondents in a Kaiser Family Foundation LTC Poll (1996) indicated that the federal government should spend more money to provide long-term care for the elderly even if it meant an increase in their taxes. Overall, the data suggests that the vast majority of the population endorses publicly supported long-term care for frail older people.

Much needs to be done to improve the U.S. approach to long-term care, including better government oversight of institutional facilities, something most adults keenly understand but have not actively demanded. As a result, proprietary nursing homes, and their influential lobby organizations, have dictated much of public policy over the past several decades, undermining a more sound and caring approach to long-term care. Our elderly—and their caregivers—deserve not only quality facilities but also greater opportunities for publicly supported home and community assistance.

References

Abel, E. K. 1991. *Who Cares for the Elderly?: Public Policy and the Experiences of Adult Daughters*. Philadelphia, PA: Temple University Press.

American Association of Retired Persons (AARP). 2005. Telephone survey of 1,011 adults, nationally. Poll conducted by ICR International Communications, April 20–24. Washington: DC.

American Association of Retired Persons (AARP). 2006. Telephone survey of 1,026 adults, nationally. Poll conducted by ICR International Communications, January 4–9. Washington: DC.

Brody, E. M. 1995. Prospects for family caregiving: response to change, continuity and diversity. In R. Kane and J. D. Penrod (eds.), *Family Caregiving in an Aging Society*. Thousand Oaks, CA: Sage.

Cook, F. L. and E. J. Barrett. 1992. *Support for the American Welfare State: The Views of Congress and the Public*. New York: Columbia University Press.

Employee Benefit Research Institute (EBRI)/The American Savings and Education Council. 1996. Telephone survey of 1,252 adults nationally. Poll conducted by Mathew Greenwald and Associates, January 3–29. Washington: DC.

Feinstein, J. and C.-C. Ho. 2001. Elderly asset management and health. In W. G. Gale, J. R. Hines, and J. Slemrod (eds.), *Rethinking Estate and Gift Taxation*. Washington: Brookings.

Fossett, J. W. and C. E. Burke. 2003. *Managing Medicaid Take-Up, Is Medicaid Retrenching?: State Budgets and Medicaid Enrollment in 2002*. Albany, NY: Rockefeller Institute.

Genworth Financial National (GFN). 2006. Telephone survey of 600 adults nationally, over age 40. Poll conducted by Public Opinion Strategies, February 27–March 1. Richmond: VA.

Grogan, C. 1999. The influence of federal mandates on state Medicaid and AFDC decision-making. *Publius: The Journal of Federalism*, 29(3): 1–30.

Grogan, C. and E. Patashnik. 2003. Between welfare medicine and mainstream entitlement: Medicaid at the political crossroads. *Journal of Health Politics*, 28(1): 821–858.

Hooyman, N. R. 1999. Research on older women: Where is feminism? *The Gerontologist*, 39: 115–118.

Hospital and Health System Association of Pennsylvania (HAP). 2005. *Keystone Omnibus Survey*. Telephone survey of 804 adults in Pennsylvania. Poll conducted by Terry Madonna Opinion Research, January–February. Harrisburg: PA.

Houser, A. N. 2007. *Nursing Homes, Research Report*. Washington: AARP/Public Policy Institute.

Kaiser Commission on Medicaid and the Uninsured (Kaiser Commission). 2005. *Survey of Medicaid Officials in 50 States and D.C., States Undertaking New Medicaid*

Cost-Containment Strategies, research conducted by Health Management Associates, September–December 2003, October 2004, and October 2005. Washington: DC.

Kaiser Family Foundation (Kaiser LTC Poll). 1996. Telephone survey of 1,011 adults, nationally. Poll conducted by Princeton Survey Research Associates, June 20–July 9. Menlo Park: CA.

Kaiser Family Foundation (Kaiser Health Poll). 2005. *Health Poll Report Survey.* Telephone survey of 1,202 adults, nationally. Poll conducted by Princeton Survey Research Associates, June 2–5. Menlo Park: CA.

Kaiser Family Foundation (Kaiser Medicaid Poll). 2005. *National Survey on the Public's Views about Medicaid.* Telephone survey of 1,201 adults, nationally. Poll conducted by Princeton Survey Research Associates, April–May. Menlo Park: CA.

Kane, R. A., R. L. Kane, and R. C. Ladd. 1998. *The Heart of Long-Term Care.* New York: Oxford University Press.

Kassner, E. 2004. *Private Long-Term Care Insurance: The Medicaid Interaction*, Issue Brief No. 68: 1–8. Washington: AARP/Public Policy Institute.

Leech, B. L., F. Baumgartner, J. M. Berry, M. Hojnacki, and H. Waltzer, 2002. Organized interests and issue definition in policy debates. In A. Cigler and B. Loomis (eds.), *Interest Group Politics.* Washington: CQ Press.

Oberlander, J. 2003. *The Political Life of Medicare.* Chicago, IL: University of Chicago Press.

Olson, L. K. 2003. *The Not-So-Golden Years: Caregiving, the Frail Elderly, and The Long-Term Care Establishment.* Boulder, CO: Rowman & Littlefield.

Pew Research Center. 2006. Telephone survey of 1,405 adults, nationally. Poll conducted by Princeton Survey Research Associates, March 8–12. Washington: DC.

Quadagno, J. 1994. *The Color of Welfare: How Racism Undermined the War on Poverty.* New York: Oxford University Press.

Quadagno, J. 2005. *One Nation Uninsured: Why the U.S. Has No National Health Insurance.* New York: Oxford University Press.

Rushefsky, M. E. and K. Patel. 1998. *Politics, Power and Policy Making: The Case of Health Care Reform in the 1990s.* Armonk, NY: M. E. Sharpe.

Taylor, D., F. Sloan, and E. Norton. 1999. Formation of trusts and spend down to medicaid. *Journal of Gerontology: Social Sciences*, 54B(4): S194–S201.

Teles, S. M. 1998. *Whose Welfare?: AFDC and Elite Politics.* Lawrence, KA: University Press of Kansas.

Turiel, J. S. 2005. *Our Parents Ourselves: How American Health Care Imperils Middle Age and Beyond.* Berkeley, CA: University of California Press.

USA Today. 2005. Telephone survey of 1,000 adults nationally. Poll conducted by TNS Intersearch, October 12–16.

U.S. House, Committee on Energy and Commerce (HEC), Subcommittee on Health. 2005. *Long-Term Care Financing: Growing Demand and Cost of Services Are Straining Federal and State Budgets*, Statement of Kathryn G. Allen, Director, Health Care—Medicaid and Private Insurance Issues, Government Accounting Office (GAO), April 27. Washington: U.S. Government Printing Office.

U.S. Senate, Committee on Finance (SFC). 2005a. *Hearings on Medicaid Waste, Fraud and Abuse: Threatening the Health Care Safety Net.* Testimony of Judith Feder, Professor and Dean, Georgetown University Public Policy Institute, June 29. Washington: U.S. Government Printing Office.

U.S. Senate, Committee on Finance (SFC). 2005b. *Hearings on Medicaid Waste, Fraud and Abuse: Threatening the Health Care Safety Net.* Testimony of the American Council of Life Insurers, June 29. Washington: U.S. Government Printing Office.

U.S. Senate, Committee on Finance (SFC). 2005c. *Hearings on Medicaid Waste, Fraud and Abuse: Threatening the Health Care Safety Net.* "Medicaid Asset Transfers and Estate Planning," Testimony of Julie Stone-Axelrod, Analyst in Social Legislation, Domestic Social Policy Division, June 29. Washington: U.S. Government Printing Office.

U.S. Senate, Committee on Finance (SFC). 2005d. *Hearings on the Future of Medicaid: Strategies for Strengthening America's Vital Safety Net.* "Medicaid, Costs and Health Spending Reform." Testimony of Jeane Lambrew, Senior Fellow, Center for American Progress, June 15. Washington: U.S. Government Printing Office.

Wiener, J. M., J. Tilly, and S. M. Goldenson. 2000. Federal and state initiatives to jump start the market for private long-term care insurance. *The Elder Law Journal*, 8: 57–102.

Chapter 3

Looking for Care in All the Wrong Places

Deborah Stone

Mom was still groggy from anesthesia when we got home on a Saturday afternoon and Dad told her the visiting nurses would be coming later on. Not so groggy that she couldn't protest, though. "I don't need a nurse," she announced, and demanded to know, "*Who* asked them to come?" She hated the whole idea. I, on the other hand, was secretly titillated, for I was thick into a research project on home health-care. It took all my willpower to refrain from doing field research on my mother, but I managed to honor her privacy for the entire two hours the nurse stayed in her bedroom. The instant the nurse was out the door, I couldn't wait to ask Mom, "How was it? What did she do?"

"She didn't do a damn thing," Mom grumped. "All she did was ask questions and take notes."

Mom wasn't much help to my project, but no matter. As a researcher, I already had a good idea of what the nurse did that day. She gathered data, lots of it. The data, according to the high priests of policy, would yield better patient assessment, better outcome measures, better quality of care, and better coordination and integration of all Mom's services. (That's policy speak for what the rest of us call healing and caring.) The nurse filled out a 100-item questionnaire named OASIS that Medicare uses to classify home-care patients into payment categories. OASIS (the acronym for Outcome and Assessment Information Set) is supposed to predict "resource utilization"—in plain English, how much care someone will need. It's also supposed to help the government do "risk adjustment," which is happy talk for fixing a blatantly unfair method of compensating agencies and nursing homes for taking care of people.

The visiting nurse did some other things for my mother on that Saturday afternoon besides delivering so much Orwellian promise. She typed all the data directly into a laptop, creating an instant electronic record and enabling Medicare to keep up to the minute on Mom's case. The nurse also briefly ticked off some of the agency's rules and policies, and then, having dutifully informed Mom, secured her informed consent to treatment. I believe my mother signed four pieces of paper that day, the last of which attested that she had been given the 1-800 hotline number to the Office of the Inspector General, in case she ever suspected the visiting nurses were up to any mischief.

In short, the visiting nurse did everything that policy engineers asked of her to alleviate the nightmare of growing old and sick in America. Yet, on the day my mother came home from the hospital, the day she was most in need of reassurance, explanations about her particular condition, and a little human warmth, her first and by far longest contact with home healthcare amounted to not a damn thing. The visiting nurse massaged her laptop and never once touched Mom.

A home health aide told me that she was once reprimanded by her supervisor for taking too long with an elderly client. All the client really needed, it seems, was help putting on her elastic stockings. The aide recorded the visit as half an hour, or maybe even 45 minutes. Her supervisor said she ought to have been able to do it in ten minutes. The aide was incensed, and for her, the episode was emblematic of the trouble with home healthcare. "You can't just go in and get out. I'm sorry. You know, my grandmother had people taking care of her. I wouldn't want them to do the same—you know, just come in and wash her up and leave. They have to have some kind of relationship going."

I know what you're thinking. You're thinking, "Hey, 30 minutes to put on support hose? Damn right the woman should be reprimanded. That is exactly the sort of featherbedding government and insurance companies should snuff out." But put your grandmother in the story and suddenly this tale of petty corruption goes Dickens dark. It's far from the most egregious story of its kind I can think of, but it does nicely to outline the shadows of the industrial revolution in caregiving.

Like textile weaving, caregiving used to be done in family homes, mostly by women, using simple methods handed down through generations and learned at the hearth. Women didn't so much "provide" care, as current jargon has it; they just did it, as it was needed, as they thought best, as they were moved to do by their sense of obligation and their care—in another sense of the word—for the people around them.

Over the course of the twentieth century, a lot of caregiving moved out of homes into hospitals and institutions that were often called homes (nursing homes, congregate homes, and group homes), but that had more in common with a textile factory than any home. At the same time, a lot of caregiving was organized into occupations with formal training and licensing, and importantly, with somebody higher up calling the shots—prescribing care plans (no longer simply "care" but "care *plans*"), dictating schedules and pay scales, and generally controlling what people did when they took care of each other.

The aide's stocking story is about the Taylorization of caregiving. In the early twentieth century, an engineer named Frederick Winslow Taylor went into the factories bent on expunging inefficiency. He timed the workers at their tasks and observed them with all the stupefied intensity of Scrooge, counting and recounting his money. While the assembly line rolled on, Taylor disassembled each job into minute gestures and steps. He figured out the quickest way for workers to get their work done, and then he reconstituted their jobs, training them with a stopwatch to within an inch of their lives. Taylor meant to strip workers of all their quirks, spontaneity, and power to think, leaving nothing but pure, efficient work.

Today's home healthcare (indeed much healthcare no matter where it is offered) takes Taylor's vision one step further. Now people are disassembled into their illnesses or disabilities and chalked off on an OASIS chart. Then their illnesses are disassembled into the necessary care tasks. Somewhere in ComputerLand, Taylor's heirs model which tasks need doing for the mythical average person in each illness category. Somewhere in Washington, Thomas Gradgrind's heirs calculate how much money all this care (now called "resource utilization," lest anyone get too sentimental about it) ought to cost, or at any rate, how much the government is willing to pay for it. OASIS happens to be the system Medicare uses for home care, but virtually all public and private insurers manage their costs by transforming people into bundles of tasks, then converting the tasks into hours or dollars.

Before you know it, a woman is just a body that needs to have its elastic stockings put on. Even Minerva McGonagall, professor of transmogrification at Hogwarts, would have a hard time doing this one. But that's exactly what was going on behind the closed door of my parents' bedroom on that day of the Sabbath, and it felt to me just a mite unholy. The visiting nurse, who herself had been hauled by the hem of her long skirt out of the nineteenth century to be retrofitted with modem business methods, was hard at work transmogrifying my mother into an average, so she could be further transmogrified into a price. After all, the nurse had to know how much her agency would get paid for taking care of Mom before she could decide what to do for her. That's the magic of capitalism.

Maybe you're not so sure about the featherbedding anymore. Maybe you now understand why the extra 20 minutes that an aide wastes talking to a lady before putting on her stockings is 20 minutes well spent. Maybe those extra minutes sustain the lady's identity as something other than a body that needs fixing up, emptying, cleaning, and feeding. That would be magic worth doing.

In the course of my research, I met a physical therapist with a home care practice of mostly Medicare patients. Joanne told me about a client who had phoned, in tears, a couple of days before her next appointment because she'd just learned that her breast cancer had recurred. "I know that on my next visit we're not going to do any physical therapy," Joanne told me. "She's going to say, 'Just sit with me 'til I calm down.'"

A physical therapist can't bill Medicare for just sitting with people 'til they calm down. Nor can a physical therapist bill for just listening, holding hands, and being there to help someone face the terrors. There's no category for that sort of relationship. But patients and caregivers, even professional caregivers who have been trained not to get too close to people, believe that good care means just that sort of relationship.

"What am I going to do—say no?" Joanne continued in an assertive tone that belied her grammatical interrogative. Taking her cue, I asked her how she would bill for the visit. She was evasive, so I dropped the subject, not wanting to trap her any tighter between her ethics and the law.

My friends Susan and Bill separated for a few weeks shortly before Bill died, although they didn't call it separation. Susan called it respite. I don't know what Bill called it. Probably fear. Bill had polycystic kidney disease, had undergone three kidney transplants, and was gradually failing from a host of complications. He had severe neuropathy in his legs, walked with braces and a walker, and in his last year, fell often. His skin wounds would not heal. He would get pneumonia, get confused, go to the hospital to get pumped with antibiotics, get better, come home, get pneumonia, fall. During one of his hospital stays, Susan fled to her friends in another state, distraught because Bill refused to have ongoing home care or move to an assisted living place. No less distraught, Bill was desperate to remain independent and at home, as well as alive. Susan was undone by 24/7 caregiving, not to mention worry and heartache for the man she loved.

On the day Susan finally lost it, the day that precipitated her flight, I had phoned to talk about something else, but I began with, "How are you doing?"

"Terrible."

"Is Bill all right?" I asked.

"No, he's *not*. He's upstairs on the floor."

"Do you want me to call someone? Or I could just come over," I offered. Susan had hurt her back and I knew she was in no condition to help Bill get up.

"No, that's all right," she said, strangely calm now. "I'm getting ready to go across the street in a bit and see if Henry can help Bill get up."

Something about her lack of urgency didn't compute, so I asked, "How long has Bill been on the floor?"

"I don't know," she said. "He's . . . sort of . . . not . . . He can't really tell me."

Later I learned what had happened and why Susan was so leisurely about getting help. When she found Bill on the floor, he told her he was all right and not to call anyone. Just give him some time, and he'd get up himself—the same optimistic can-do, I-don't-need-help routine that kept him alive and at home years longer than his doctors had thought possible. Besides, the last time she had called the Visiting Nurse Association (VNA) for help, they had rebuffed her. Bill had spiked a fever and was incapable of getting out of bed. Bill's doctor told Susan he would call the VNA and order a nurse to come out and draw blood for a test to see what was going on. Susan was supposed to follow up with her own call to the VNA. When she did, the person on the other end of the phone told her, "The normal procedure is you bring the patient over for lab work." Susan thought the visiting nurses ought to understand why she couldn't follow normal procedure because they had taken care of Bill after a couple of his hospital episodes, but when she stammered out an explanation, the VNA person chastised, "Okay, but if we come out there, it'll be private pay." So this time, Susan sought help from Henry instead of the VNA. Henry is a spry 85-year-old, but he couldn't lift Bill and persuaded Susan to call 911 for an ambulance.

It is an article of faith in policy circles that home healthcare is "overutilized." Costs have skyrocketed because too many people are too quick to run for help. "There is a real problem with long-term care," explains economist Mark Pauly in *Health Affairs*. "Most of the services are not the medical services that healthy people would want to avoid but, rather, are the 'low-tech' or 'servant' services that anyone would find helpful, whether well or ill." Mr. Pauly has never met Bill.

According to the first principle of economics—the Law of Demand—people will consume more of a good if they can buy it for less, or better yet, get it for nothing. Because people on Medicare don't pay anything for home care, economic theory holds, they consume it with abandon. Co-payments would force patients and families to bear at least some of the costs of their care and that, in turn, would make them evaluate their needs with a more realistic eye. Economists speak of setting the proper incentives, but what they really mean is discouraging people like Bill and Susan from availing themselves of help.

Economic theory is right only if home care is a good in the economic sense— something that enhances people's welfare. Outside economics textbooks, care is not an unalloyed good. Like Bill, most people don't want to consume care because they desperately don't want to need it. To seek care is to ask for help and to ask for help is to admit that you need help doing things most people can do for themselves. Our culture reveres independence, and in this culture, dependence is humiliating. To accept help is to cast yourself as dependent, less than whole, and less virtuous than the independent citizen of our political rhetoric. Never mind that other people gladly make excuses for you. Shame and the loss of one's own powers are the real deterrents to using home healthcare. Money is not the half of it.

Instead of empathizing with those who need care but are too proud to ask for it, policymakers fear them as predators on the commonweal. Instead of making it easier and more dignified for them to accept help, policy erects fences to keep them away from our common care. Our public policy aims to domesticate the sick, the frail, and the elderly by turning them into judicious consumers. That is why my mother, still in her anesthesia-and-painkiller stupor, was signing all those forms on the day of her first home care visit. She had to be transmogrified into an informed consumer as well as a price. And if the economic wizards have their way, she and people like her will soon have to pay for needing care, just so that they don't forget how much they cost the rest of us.

A visiting nurse I'll call Caroline was so troubled by one case that she brought it to the agency's Ethics Committee. The client was an elderly farmer who had been paralyzed in a tractor rollover accident some years before. He needed home nursing mainly to tend his recalcitrant skin wounds. His wife had her own health problems and the nurses sometimes got pulled into helping her too, although visiting nurses are forbidden to treat anyone for whom they do not have orders. Nevertheless, what really bothered Caroline was something else. The couple's children lived nearby, the family owned a handicapped van, and often, they trundled the man out to family gatherings, church social activities, and the local Wal-Mart—a favorite spot for the mobility-impaired because it provides electric carts. And there's the rub: to be eligible for Medicare's home health benefit, a person has to be "homebound." The regulations say a person need not be literally unable to leave home to qualify as homebound, but they allow only a few limited excuses for going out. Home health nurses are supposed to police this confinement to home. Every time they visit, they are supposed to ask whether the patient has been out, and if so, for what purpose. Attending worship services or a medical appointment is okay. Most anything else is not. So the nurses told the farmer's wife that her husband was not allowed to go out and still get care.

They told her repeatedly, and she repeatedly gave them a piece of her mind: "If you make me take a choice between losing services and taking him out, I will take him out." They tried to up the ante by telling her they were sorry, but the government has these rules. She countered: "If Mr. Clinton wants to come in here and tell me I can't have services, let him come." In frustration, the nurses gave the woman to understand that if she took her husband out, they didn't want to know about it.

As the Ethics Committee deliberated (I was a fly on the wall), one point of consensus was clear: it's good for the man to get out of the house and socialize. Would that every disabled person had such loving, willing, close-by relatives, and could afford a handicapped van! So the nurses did what visiting nurses have been doing ever since the homebound requirement was introduced. They looked the other way. But they knew they were breaking the law, and they didn't feel good about it. That is why they brought the case to the Ethics Committee. They wondered whether they were unethical in caring for the couple. I wondered whether the law caused them to doubt their own compassion.

Medicare's homebound requirement comes straight out of eighteenth-century English Poor Law, whose magistrates distinguished between indoor and outdoor relief. Indoor relief meant housing people in a poor house or an orphanage, where they could be supervised and made to work before they could receive a bowl of porridge. Outdoor relief meant just giving somebody help wherever they lived—the kind of help we give when we send somebody a Social Security check or a welfare check.

In 1834, England did welfare reform in much the same way we did it in the United States in 1996. After exhaustive debate and study, reformers concluded that outdoor relief discourages industry and thrift, encourages pauperism, and incites the poor to fraud. Alexis De Tocqueville grasped the problem in his *Memoir on Pauperism*: "Nothing is so difficult to distinguish as the nuances which separate unmerited misfortune from an adversity produced by vice." How, in other words, do we tell who really deserves our help? His Majesty's Commission on the Poor Laws came up with a way: eliminate outdoor relief. Henceforth, anyone who wanted help would have to live in a workhouse—a deliberately abhorrent place—where husbands, wives, and children were separated from one another and all were forced to labor for their meager gruel. The "workhouse test" would force supplicants to show their hand. Or as His Majesty's commissioners so delicately put it, "Into such a house none will enter voluntarily; work, confinement and discipline will deter the indolent and vicious; and nothing but extreme necessity will induce any to accept the sacrifice of their accustomed habits and gratifications."

The nursing home is said by some to have the same kind of salutary deterrent effect on sick elderly people and to keep them from living off the public dole. Here is health economist Mark Pauly writing in Health Affairs in 2001: "If I have to live in a nursing home to collect benefits, and if (like most people), I would prefer not to do so unless I was so frail that I really could not do well otherwise, I am less likely to claim that my ADL score is worse than it really is." Never mind what an ADL score is. All you need to know is that the prospect of having to enter a nursing home—Pauly believes—keeps people from cheating on the admissions test. The problem with home healthcare services, Pauly explains, is that they lack such an effective deterrent. "Insurers are terrified by the thought that if people can make money from insurance and do not have to do anything that healthy people would not do, there will be very substantial (and very clever) excess claims."

This is as lucid an explanation as I have ever seen for why Medicare requires home care patients to be homebound: to be imprisoned in your own home is the next worst thing to being captive in a nursing home.

Few of us can abide the harsh wisdom of economists and royal ministers, so home care for the elderly is rife with civil disobedience. I am sure my mother was told that she had to be homebound to receive the help of the visiting nurses. I am sure that was one of the rules and policies of which she was apprised on the day she got home from the hospital and struggled to stay awake during two hours of talking head that passed for nursing. I am also sure that her surgeon encouraged her to move about as soon and as much as possible. The day after she got home from the hospital and everyday thereafter, for the ten days or so that Medicare paid for her home care, my father took her out for walks, and up to the village for lunch. They didn't think twice about it, and they told me the nurse never asked about it either.

When Bill was still well enough to drive, drive he did. He also took long walks on his braces and canes, and much impressed Henry, his walking companion, with his grit. But every time Bill went out, Susan shuddered. She wanted to cheer and wish him Godspeed, yet it crossed her mind that if the VNA found out, they would withdraw from his case, which was her case as well, for she needed their help as much as Bill did.

Joanne, the physical therapist, was helping an elderly woman learn to walk safely. The woman's husband was in a nursing home a bus ride away, and Joanne hoped to get her to the point where she could mount a bus and walk far enough to be able to visit him on her own. But Joanne also knew that Medicare's homebound rule would not countenance such frivolity. Once Joanne documented that the woman could get in and out of her home safely and walk about 25 yards—presumably to escape a fire—the case was closed as far as Medicare was concerned. I do not know whether Joanne cheated to do the humane thing. I do know that she faced a lot of these dilemmas. And I do know that many rules intended to control home care costs force otherwise law-abiding citizens to break the law or look the other way just to get the care they need or give the care someone else deserves.

A few years ago, I met with the chair of my university's politics department to discuss my future research plans. The man does meat-and-potatoes political science—presidents, political parties, elections, that kind of thing. I expected that when I told him I was studying home healthcare, he would ask what it has to do with political science. Instead, he told me a story. His mother had a home health aide for a long time before she died, he said; and at his mother's funeral, he insisted that the aide ride in the limousine with the family. "She was my mother's best friend, the most important person to her, and I wanted her to have a place of honor."

Outside the family, nobody is asking aides to ride in the limo. Home health aides typically earn seven to nine dollars an hour if they work for an agency, half again more if they work privately. A quarter to a third of them don't have health insurance. They often have a hard time keeping 40 hours of work, and their hours fluctuate with the health of their patients and the fiscal health of their employers. Welfare offices (now dubbed employment offices) steer women into home health-care by the busload, yet many aides make so little, even working full time, that they still qualify for food stamps and Medicaid.

Among the specialized occupations that produce and deliver home care these days, aides are usually the most skilled and valuable to the patient and the patient's family, but we pay them as if they were the least important. Planners, analysts, and managers—the people Robert Reich calls symbolic analysts—never wipe a tear, change a sheet, or lift a body or a spirit, but we pay them handsomely to fondle abstractions.

In the industrial world, this hierarchy makes a certain sense. Without the Brains, the Brawn might accomplish little (or at least that's the demeaning theory of industrial relations). Symbolic analysts see right through particulars and individuality and uniqueness to the generalizable essence of things. Unfortunately, when it comes to caregiving, symbolic analysts see right through the people who need to be taken care of, and you cannot take good care of somebody if you no longer see them.

A case manager may think she knows how long it takes to dress a client or give a bath; a computer model may even think it knows how long it takes an aide to dress and feed five patients. But neither the case manager nor the computer knows, or is capable of learning, what the aide knows; exactly how Mr. So-and-So's body moves and hurts, and just how to nudge his stroke-benumbed shoulder and prop his arm so that he can slide it into his shirtsleeve. Researchers invent care plans to satisfy statistical tests and cost-effectiveness standards; policymakers and care managers adopt them. But aides know the subtle arts of coaxing, joking, and soothing people into complying with the pieces of the plan. The best care plans in the world come to naught if aides are not brilliant psychologists.

By definition, home healthcare takes place in homes, out of sight of managers. Because the various nurses, therapists, aides, and case managers are rarely in somebody's home at the same time, if there is any such thing as integration of care, it happens at case conferences. They are a sort of planned substitute for chance meetings in the coffee room. One such conference took place in a spare, nondescript room, the kind with linoleum floor, fluorescent lights, a large window looking out on a parking lot, a couple of fake wood tables ringed by molded plastic chairs, and nothing but a blackboard and me, the fly, on the white walls. A physical therapist presented the case of a 49-year-old woman who had been in a car accident that had left her quadriplegic. The woman and her husband were overwhelmed by the mundane details of their new life, everything from coping with her bowels to getting her in and out of a wheelchair. They had requested more help from the agency, the physical therapist reported, but the woman had used up the three home care visits she had been allotted. When the therapist had called the insurer to get more visits authorized, the insurer denied her request, saying the woman couldn't benefit from more medical care, and anyway, "all their remaining problems are emotional, not medical." At that, the nurse on the team blurted out, "Well, I'm screwed. I'll just go see her as a friend. And if I happen to have a few things in my pocket." Another therapist cut her off. "Yeah, that's what I told 'em. I go to the market all the time. You need something? Just give me your list."

These women had been with the agency for years. Their livelihoods depended on it and on the insurers who pay its bills. They had not seen the quadriplegic woman but three times, yet they were ready to help her on their own time.

Public caregiving, the kind given by strangers trained in technique and beholden to accountants, can start out cold and distant, but it often ripens into loving, family-like relationships.

Love is not a word that rolls easily off the tongue in policy circles. Love is unprofessional. A professional does not have favorites, does not get "too attached-" and certainly does not fall in love with the clients. Most of the home care workers I have interviewed say that during their training, they were warned against getting too close and against becoming emotionally involved. They were told not to share personal information, give out their phone numbers, or get too friendly. And then they all say things like, "But you just do—if you're human, you do," and "You can't help it." Most of them, when they get going talking about the people they care for, let slip the L-word.

And notice this: at the moment when the assembled team learned that a desperately needy woman had been abandoned by her insurance plan and would now have to be abandoned by the home care agency as well, the nurse did not say, "*She's* screwed." She said, "*I'm* screwed." She felt screwed, I imagine, because she would have to violate her faith with someone she had come to care *about*, not just *for*.

The industrial system of caring forces its caregivers to break these covenants. But defiance ricochets around the system just as it erupted in the conference room. In bedrooms and living rooms all over the country, nurses and aides are making common cause with their patients. They routinely go beyond the jobs they are assigned, and the ones they are paid for. Aides who struggle to put food on their own tables buy food for their clients and slip it into their refrigerators without making a fuss. They visit their clients after hours, give out their home phone numbers, and continue providing care after the reimbursement runs out. They cook and care for clients' spouses, even though it is strictly forbidden to do anything for someone who is not a bonafide client. ("I'm not going to fix *her* dinner and just ignore *him*," one aide explained to me.) Like Joanne, they do a little creative billing to provide the care they know is right. They risk their jobs to take care of people the way their hearts tell them instead of the way the rules require.

In New York City, I asked a group of aides to talk about their work, and at the end of our meeting, I asked them to tell me about something they were especially proud of. A Guyanan woman had described a couple she cares for, ages 92 and 88. He needs a wheelchair and she uses a walker. One of the aide's jobs was getting them ready for the night and into bed. When it was her turn to tell her proud moment story, she leaned forward and whispered, as if to keep her supervisor from hearing: "Sometimes she asks me to put her in his bed, so they can . . ."—she hesitated, searching for the right words—"you know, be comfortable. I'm not supposed to. She has a hospital bed and she's supposed to sleep raised up. But I do it. I tell her I'm not supposed to, and that it's very dangerous. But then I do it."

Love is all we hope for when we are old and sick. We hope for love even more when we need others' help caring for our parents, our spouses, and our children. Yet, somehow, when we act as citizens, writing laws for Everyman and creating the constitution of our collective life, we are terrified of love. We fear that the unbounded needs of the Ailing will unleash the unbounded compassion of the Caring, and the two in cahoots will rob us blind. So we corral love into our private yards and exterminate compassion from the public lands, like so many howling coyotes.

Chapter 4

The Medicalization of Long-Term Care: Weighing the Risks

Colleen M. Grogan

Contents

Most Americans say they want to die at home, but very few do so. Although the percentage of Americans dying in hospitals has decreased since 1980, from 52 to 41 percent in 1998, the majority still die in hospitals (Pritchard et al., 1998; Blank and Merrick, 2003; Flory et al., 2004). Among Americans aged 65 and above, 50 percent die in hospitals (SUPPORT Principal Investigators, 1995; Last Acts, 2002).

Death in the hospital is usually characterized as a high-technology death, often after stays in intensive care units where the person has been hooked up to many tubes and devices in a last-ditch effort to save the individual (ibid.). Especially for older, frail elderly (those above 85 years of age), and those with terminal illnesses, such heroic efforts seem unnecessary to many and even cruel to some. Whether cruel or unnecessary, most agree that such a death is far from the ideal vision of dying in the comfort of one's own home surrounded by loved ones. Although only 25 percent of Americans die at home, more than 70 percent say that is their wish (Last Acts, 2002, p. 13).*

Apart from the place of death, it is often the case that the whole last year or two (or longer) of life is a much more medicalized experience than either the elderly or their caregivers would have wanted (ibid.). Several studies suggest that unfortunately patient preferences for death rarely dictate what actually happens. Multiple health system supply factors, such as the number of hospital beds and the availability of hospice services and nursing homes, play an important role in determining where people die (Emanuel et al., 2000; Christakis and Iwashyna, 2000; Pritchard et al., 1998). Many published memoirs of caregivers reveal their usually troubled and difficult journey with helping their elderly relative or friend in their last years of life (Callahan, 2006).† A common theme in these memoirs is the sense of loss of control—not only because the elderly care recipient's decline often goes in unanticipated directions, but because the healthcare system often takes over in ways that feel overpowering (ibid.; Gerber, 2005). The most startling memoirs come from professionals with a great deal of medical knowledge and experience with the long-term care (LTC) system, who, despite all of their know-how, often feel powerless to change the way care is provided to their elders.

A recent book by renowned gerontologist Robert Kane and his sister Joan West, for example, describe their caretaking experiences for their mother during her three-year struggle with a stroke and its aftermath. In their book, aptly titled *It Shouldn't Be This Way: The Failure of Long-Term Care*, they describe their mother's life from independent living, to a stroke, to rehabilitation, to assisted living, to a dementia unit, and finally to a nursing home, where she died (Kane and West, 2005). Another book, *My Mother's Hip*, written by a medical sociologist Margolies (2004), also describes an overmedicalized approach to caring for her mother, which often fell out of her control, again, despite her expertise. Of course, the reason such professional memoirs are troubling and surprising is that, as the professionals themselves suggest, "if the system is so difficult for them to maneuver, think of how much worse it must be for the uneducated consumer" (Callahan, 2006, p. 146).

Not only do we have the knowledge, but we also have public policies in place—advanced directives and funding for hospice and home care services—intended to

---

* Cited in 1999 Harvard opinion poll.
† In Chapter 3 of this handbook, Deborah Stone relates her parents' personal experience with long-term care.

help enable caregivers to obtain a more "ideal" death and a less medicalized dying process for their loved ones. And yet, for many this ideal remains elusive. Why? The literature offers many answers to this multifaceted question. Research tends to break down the complexity by analyzing components of the decision-making process, including whether to hire home care services or admit the individual to a nursing home for short-term rehabilitation or for LTC, or write an advanced directive. Most answers to these particular choices focus on the influence of current policy and programs, and the current healthcare infrastructure, that promote incentives or disincentives for each one (Pritchard et al., 1998; Emanuel et al., 2000).

For example, many argue that the lack of good, affordable, community-based care options contributes to the relatively high use of nursing homes that continues to persist in many areas (Gabrel, 2000). Others focusing on low utilization of hospice care services highlight both the lack of services available, and the difficulty in knowing when an elder has started on the "death trajectory" (Christakis and Iwashyna, 2000). Hospice services are often employed for those who want them, but usually very late in the dying process because providers were not absolutely sure that the patient was, in fact, on this trajectory. To explain the troubling fact that many patients with advanced directives receive aggressive medical treatment often at odds with their wishes, research points to the lack of communication between medical staff and departments about such patient wishes (SUPPORT Principal Investigators, 1995). As a case in point, emergency departments often implement very aggressive, curative medical treatments on all patients without asking whether an elder has an advanced directive. If ER-911 is called, the assumption is that aggressive curative care should be administered (Bradley et al., 2000; Cassel et al., 2000).

Although research in this vein gives us greater insights into LTC decision-making processes and is certainly helpful for guiding policy and program changes, there is an imbedded assumption that elders and their caregivers are willing to age and die in the less traveled, potentially more risky, less protective, and more uncertain world of independent living and home care. Yet what these memoirs reveal is that although caregivers and care recipients say they want a homelike environment,* they also want a low-risk, safe environment for their elders. It is exactly at those times when risk is heightened and safety threatened that caregivers are prompted to call on the healthcare system. When the care recipient is in the medical morass, caregivers often feel remorse, are conflicted, and wonder whether they "did the right thing" or not. The problem is that there is no right answer, and the conflict between risk and safety and protection versus "letting go" run deep. Indeed, the purpose of this chapter is to explicate the historical roots of this conflict.

I focus on the history of how professionals defined chronic illness and aging in the middle of the twentieth century, and show how our policy responses to that dominant definition helped to shape how Americans think about LTC today. I rely

---

* Public opinion data supports this contention (see Last Acts, 2002).

on secondary historical analyses to show how elder care has evolved over time.* I argue that this history helps to explain why Americans today are deeply conflicted between two ideals for their elders—a free, independent, and homelike environment versus a more protective, safe, and medicalized one. LTC advocates often tell us this is a false dichotomy, that we can have it both ways: an independent, healthy, safe environment in which to grow old and die. But the memoirs and research cited earlier suggest otherwise. In this chapter, I hope to shed light on this contradiction by highlighting how our approach to increasing frailty—as an agonizing choice between independence and safety—is deeply rooted in our social and political history.

The Myth of Intergenerational Family Living

> There is a myth in the American psyche that evokes a past perfection. . . .
>
> Every house is home to a large multi-generational family. . . . Grandmother lives comfortably in a sun-splashed bedroom on the first floor that is filled with her memorabilia of a productive life. She is a vision of sweetness and gentility, and her sage wisdom and placid personality are the keystones of family solidarity. At an advanced age Grandmother becomes ill with a painless but weakening disease of vague origin.
>
> The loyal family doctor . . . spends countless hours at her bedside before announcing solemnly to the family that, "She is leaving us now."
>
> The family's solicitude is boundless as they surround the deathbed. They are rewarded with a few parting gestures of love and advice as Grandmother passes from this vale surrounded by her adoring and grieving family.
>
> **Forrest et al., 1990, p. 2**

Of course, there are many problems with this picture. Set aside how very rare it is for people to die a painless death, much less to have the presence of mind to give us a few parting words or gestures of love (Nuland, 1994). Most problematic, as Forrest et al. remind us, is that "our 1900 grandmother simply wasn't there." The multigenerational caretaking family was rare for two reasons. First, simple demographic data reminds us that very little caretaking (of grandma anyway) actually needed to be done. In 1900, only 4 percent of the population reached the age of 65,

---

* Because this is only one chapter of an edited volume, and I am attempting to show broad trends over time, much of the historical detail is missing. Readers who would like more historical detail should refer to the secondary sources in the reference list, especially Haber (1983) and Haber and Gratton (1994).

and life expectancy was 47 years. Since that time, however, life expectancy has increased by 30 years and is now over 75 years of age. Since 1950, the population of Americans above the age of 65 has more than doubled, now reaching 12 percent of the U.S. population (2000 census data: www.census.gov). Even more striking are the increases of the "older-old" age brackets: "the 75–84 age group is 11 times larger than it was in 1900, while the 85+ group is 22 times larger" (Forrest et al., 1990, p. 3).

Not only were there very few family members above the age of 65 needing care, but the central characteristics that we associate with old age today—loss of control over children, household, and employment—never occurred for the majority of older people until relatively recently. For example, in preindustrial America, the old rarely experienced the empty-nest syndrome. Most older people "spent the majority of their lives with at least one child in the home" (Haber and Gratton, 1993, p. 11). Very few people approaching old age lived beyond the maturity of all their children. Moreover, most older men remained employed and heads of the household (Haber and Gratton, 1993; Chudacoff and Hareven, 1978). Even in the industrial era, when more individuals began to outlive the maturity of their offspring, the family structure of the old became increasingly complex. It did not reflect a monolithic structure where all older individuals simply moved in with one of their offspring. Rather, Haber and Gratton (1993) explain how a variety of family structures emerged during this period.

> The elderly's family varied according to locale. On the farm, in the city, and in the small villages of the United States, the elderly established distinctive types of households. In the village of the industrial era, in fact, large numbers followed a strikingly "modern" family structure. Living alone or simply with their spouse, they created the empty nest household. . . . As today, however, this arrangement did not necessarily reflect desertion by kin. Instead, during the industrial era, many older people finally had the financial capability to establish a long-preferred model of separate rather than extended or complex households. While popular beliefs consistently emphasized the importance of assisting needy family members, U.S. cultural admonitions have also stressed the primacy of the distinct nuclear family. (pp. 21–22)

Haber and Gratton's (1993) historical work helps us understand the second reason why multigenerational living was rare: contrary to popular belief, many elderly did not want to live with their children and many children did not want to live with their elders. In the cases where they cohabitated, Haber and Gratton provide numerous examples of tension in three-generational households. Diaries written by adult children from this time period express a very difficult experience sharing authority over the household with aging parents. For example, after taking her elderly mother into her home, one woman complained: "Harmony is gone.

Rest has vanished. . . . The intrusion is probably a common cause of divorce, and most certainly of marital unhappiness and problems in children" (Haber and Gratton, 1993, pp. 39–40). Haber and Gratton (1993, pp. 38–42) explain how these tensions led even "experts"—psychologists and social planners—to argue for separate living arrangements to create more family harmony. That advice, coupled with the rise in such intergenerational tensions, led to separate living arrangements increasingly becoming a part of the "American Dream." Indeed, Haber and Gratton argue that as long as family economic means were sufficient, American families strived for separate living arrangements.

> Between 1900 and 1940, the proportion of men aged sixty-five and over who lived as dependents in their children's home declined from 16 percent to 11 percent; for women the percentage fell from 34 to 23. . . . The decrease in residential dependency [was] based on rising opportunities that allowed a significant number of Americans to realize a longstanding ideal of autonomous living. Rather than exposing neglect on the part of the young or a sudden dislike of their elders, such living arrangements were largely the result of economic prosperity. Increased wages and additional wealth allowed some families to achieve an ideal of separate dwellings. . . . By 1915, in fact, a new pattern began to emerge: fewer middle-class families formed complex households while in the working-class, [extended family dwellings] became more common. (Haber and Gratton, 1993, p. 37)

This strong preference for independent living has persisted. In an advice book titled *When Our Parents Get Old*, by Metropolitan Life Insurance Company in 1959, the following was written, clearly to a middle-class audience, under the subheading Where to Live:

> Most people who have studied the problems of advancing age believe that "moving in with the children" is not necessarily the best solution. They suggest that several other possibilities be considered before setting up a three-generation family. An elderly brother or sister living alone may make an excellent partner to a parent's later years. Occasionally, elderly people who want privacy but don't want to be entirely alone rent part of their living space to another older person, or find space to share in their quarters. (pp. 4–5)

The rest of the chapter is devoted to providing advice to overcome the often difficult situation when a parent "must" move in with the child. It is important to understand this myth about the multigenerational family living together in harmony for two reasons. First, it forms the foundation of the LTC ideal. For reasons I hope to unravel, family care of our elders has been a strongly held social norm of what LTC should entail. Second, significant care of elders with chronic illness did not occur until the latter half of the twentieth century. Therefore, it was primarily perception about how to treat the elderly with chronic illness and public policy responses to these images—rather than actual caretaking experiences—that shaped how we think about eldercare today.

Chronic Illness and Aging: The Evolution of a Concept

Institutionalization of the poor began with fervor in the 1820s under the view that the causes of poverty can be located squarely within the individual (Katz, 1986; Holstein and Cole, 1996). With this outlook in hand, the philosophy of almshouse administrators was to change individual behavior through work and punishment (ibid.). Although these institutions, which housed the poor of all ages (including the sick and mentally ill), grew quite rapidly during the nineteenth century, social reformers at the turn of the century began designing institutions for certain groups in an effort to reform, rehabilitate, and educate. For example, children were sent to orphanages, the "insane" to mental institutions, and the physically disabled to special schools. Not surprisingly, the chronic, noncurable condition of most elderly individuals in almshouses did not fit well with the reform and rehabilitation rhetoric of that time (ibid.). Thus, because there was no "reform movement" for the elderly, they were simply left in the almshouses. As a result, the vast majority of "inmates" in the almshouses in the early part of the twentieth century were frail elderly persons with chronic conditions (Stewart, 1925; Haber, 1983).

This shift happened unintentionally. However, many physicians and social reformers began touting the transformation of almshouses into "old folks" homes, primarily for deserving (nonpoor) elderly needing custodial care. At the same time, most providers favored separate institutions as a solution to "caring" for elderly with chronic care needs for two reasons. First, hospitals were growing, with a new improved image as places where sicknesses could be cured. Because the elderly with chronic conditions could not be easily restored to health, there was no place for them in these new acute care institutions (Vladeck, 1980). Hospital administrators developed strong views about appropriate hospital utilization, which was generally defined as relatively short stays to treat acute care episodes of illness. Chief among their concerns was hospital overutilization, which occurred when patients would remain in hospital beds long after hospital services were necessary (Dieckmann, 1999; Sheatsley, 1962). Although medical professionals disagreed about appropriate alternative solutions to hospital overutilization (or "bed-blockers" as they were also called*), there was general agreement starting in the 1930s that a setting separate from the hospital was most appropriate.

---

* And still called today (see Mur-Veeman et al. (2005), *Hospital Intermediate Care: A Solution for the Bed-Blockers Problem?*).

The second reason why medical professionals tended to support separate elder institutional care has to do with how they defined chronic illness and aging. Actually, in the middle of the twentieth century, a debate about the concept of chronic illness emerged, but both concepts led to an institutional response. The first view, which emerged in the nineteenth century and continued to dominate in the twentieth, was that chronic illness in old age represented a deterioration of health. Therefore, it demanded a separate medical institutional model with some type of skilled nursing care to manage this decline and other associated problems of old age (ibid.; Stevens, 1971; Vladeck, 1980; Haber, 1983; Rosenberg, 1987; Haber and Gratton, 1993).

The irony of this view of care for the chronically ill is that it contributed to the hospital "overutilization problem" described in the foregoing section. Results from a survey of 50 hospital administrators across the United States, over a 12-month period from 1960 to 1961, showed that the vast majority of them attributed "inappropriate" long stays in the hospital to a lack of available skilled nursing care among family members in the community (Sheatsley, 1962). The following is an example of administrators' responses:

> In many cases, there are people who live alone or who cannot get proper care if left in their homes; the mother has too many other children to care for, or the husband cannot be trusted to provide nursing care to his wife. It is perhaps not necessary that they be hospitalized, but there are darned good reasons for doing so. (ibid., p. 34)

This statement illustrates how the idea of custodial care for the aged (as was provided in almshouse conversions to old folks homes) changed to strongly held notions that a certain level of skilled care is necessary for taking care of elders with chronic conditions.

The second view held that chronic illness and aging should be seen as similar to any other acute care condition. In other words, the chronic condition can be maintained rather than left to deteriorate, and, most importantly, can perhaps improve over time or even be cured. The strongest advocate for this view was E. M. Bluestone, who was the director of Montefiore Chronic Disease Hospital during the 1950s. He argued that caring for patients with chronic illness in institutions separate from acute care hospitals was harmful to the patient because it did not allow for restorative or curative measures. Accordingly, this view did not support the use of separate chronic disease hospitals or nursing homes. Rather, it advocated the use of hospitals, which could appropriately offer aggressive treatment to the chronically ill (Field, 1967; Fox, 1957; Dieckmann, 1999).

Note how there were no voices for viewing aging as a natural declining process that would occur over time. On the contrary, everyone supported some type of medical intervention by the middle of the twentieth century and the questions were how much, what kind, and when? Although the aging process became medically defined, treatment was not discussed extensively in the early part of the twentieth century because there were relatively few aged persons with chronic illness. In the mid-1900s, when advances in the economy, public health, and medicine created old age, it was natural to adopt the accepted medicalized view of aging to the treatment regimen; public policy responded in turn.

Public Policy Response and the Rise of Nursing Homes

In the early twentieth century, a grassroots movement and public activism converged around the idea of publicly funded old-age pensions. The explanations for passage of the Old-Age Survivors Insurance (OASI) legislation in 1935 (or Social Security, as it is more commonly referred to today) are numerous and much too complex to address in this short chapter.* Here, we focus on two reasons related to the appropriate treatment of the aged. First, when the Great Depression hit in the 1930s, there was a natural shift in public opinion regarding the causes of poverty. The predominant view emerging during this time period was that unpredictable events such as unemployment, sickness, old age, and death of a spouse had nothing to do with questionable individual behavior. Thus, the American public looked to the federal government to help solve problems of basic economic needs.

Second, the horrendous conditions of the almshouses—the institutional response to poverty—became more widely recognized, and New Deal activists argued that old-age pensions would allow elderly people to live with dignity in the community (Vladeck, 1980; Stevens and Stevens, 1974; Haber and Gratton, 1993). When Congress passed the federal-state, means-tested income program, Old-Age Assistance (OAA) for poor elderly persons, as part of OASI, it clearly stated that no assistance would be given to almshouse inmates (Vladeck, 1980; Holstein and Cole, 1996). This clause was inserted in the legislation with the intention of fostering the closure of poorhouses.

Although poorhouses did die out, institutional care for the elderly did not. From 1940 to 1950, the number of people above the age of 65 living in institutions increased at twice the rate as the elderly overall—74 percent compared to 36 percent (Fisher, 1953). This dramatic growth happened, in part, because many of the aged had disabling conditions that could not simply be addressed with the cash income derived from OASDI or OAA. It was soon obvious that significant medical care needs remained unmet for many elderly individuals. For example, a study by the Interdepartmental Committee to Coordinate Health and Welfare Activities of about 1 million people receiving OAA payments in 50 states, during 1936–1937, found that although only 2.5 percent of the elderly were bedridden, an additional 14 percent required considerable care (*Social Security Bulletin*, 1939). Most important, however, was that 22 percent of the former and 52 percent of the latter reported receiving no medical care or supervision (ibid.).

---

* See Gratton and Haber (1993) for a review of the many explanations and an extended reference list.

An interesting aspect of the study is that it does not include people living in convalescent or nursing homes because the federal government refused to provide OAA funds to people in public institutions, and a number of states did not permit any grants to residents of private institutions. But the denial of payments to elderly living in the thousands of private boarding homes—and the emerging nursing homes—would have been very difficult for states to administer. Indeed, by 1946, several states reported significant amounts of OAA funds for recipients living in such places (White, 1952a).

Actually, the amount of nursing home care covered through OAA money varied substantially across the states. For example, in a 1946 study on medical care provided to OAA recipients in 20 states, the Bureau of Public Assistance found that Connecticut and New Hampshire provided nursing home coverage for over 10 and 8 percent, respectively, of the beneficiaries whereas North and South Carolina financed only one recipient per thousand; Pennsylvania and West Virginia did not allow any OAA funded nursing home care (ibid.).

Although the cost of nursing home care also varied across the states, it is noteworthy that it was considered quite expensive even at this early period. In 1946, the average monthly cost per recipient across the 17 states that provided nursing home care was $65, an amount well over the $50 maximum the federal government allowed in OAA monthly payments (ibid.). Because the states had to pay the difference, such costs were quite burdensome for them. Among the states that provided nursing home care, institutional facilities consumed a high proportion of their total OAA medical costs. For example, although Connecticut provided nursing home care to only 10 percent of its OAA recipients, these expenditures consumed 80 percent of the state's total OAA medical outlays. This "disproportion" existed in all of the states that provided healthcare. Even in New Mexico, where less than 1 percent of OAA recipients received nursing home care, it consumed 10 percent of the state's total medical costs (White, 1952b).

Indeed, for anyone who was looking closely (and unfortunately not many were), this 1946 study made two facts—that are still with us today—crystal clear: first, quality of care varied tremendously across nursing homes and many suffered from low quality; and second, the cost of such LTC was expensive. In White's summary of the findings from the 1946 study, she wrote:

> Nursing-home care, which includes maintenance costs as well as nursing and other medical services, is expensive even in homes that do not meet high standards. Unquestionably the homes in which recipients of old-age assistance were living ranged from those of acceptable quality as nursing-care institutions to homes that were poorly equipped and operated. (White, 1952a, p. 10)

It is important to note that the increase in the number of elderly living in nursing homes from 1935 to 1950 was accompanied by the establishment and growth of proprietary facilities (Fisher, 1953). As mentioned earlier, because of provisions in the 1935 Social Security Act restricting the use of federal funds for payments to public institutions, states could only use their OAA funds to support elderly living in private places. As they started to liberalize the use of their OAA money to cover nursing home costs during the 1940s, their preference was clearly toward the private sector. Indeed, the proportion of public to private institutions in 1900 completely reversed itself: by 1950, 72 percent of institutions for the aged were composed of private for-profit establishments, up from 28 percent. Interestingly, the dominance of proprietary institutions in the nursing home industry (67 percent) is still with us today (Jones, 1999). Historians Holstein and Cole (1996, p. 29) sum up this irony nicely: "Hatred for the almshouse created a resistance to any public provision of nursing home care; thus, the almshouse . . . led to the now-dominant proprietary nursing home industry."

Medical Vendor Payments in 1950

When states realized that the elderly poor were using a large share of their OAA funds to pay for private institutional care, as well as other medical care expenses, they lobbied Congress for a separate provision to reimburse multiple providers (e.g., nursing homes, hospitals, and physicians) for medical services rendered to eligible recipients. Although the states were supposed to include the cost of medical care in their determination of OAA pension amounts, they argued that the federal maximums were too low and did not reflect the true costs of medical care. In what would become a worn argument, the states argued further that sickness and medical care expenditures often caused poverty and dependence on OAA in the first place (Altmeyer, 1950; Vladeck, 1980; Stevens and Stevens, 1974).

In an effort to address this problem, in 1950, the federal government revised the Social Security Amendments in two important ways. First, it allowed states, under the federal financial match, to pay medical providers directly for services rendered to public assistance recipients. This revision created the term "medical vendor payments" (White, 1950; Norman, 1952; Stevens and Stevens, 1974). Second, the bill lifted the prohibition against federally financed cash payments to elderly people living in public institutions. There was a growing sentiment that it was too restrictive (and perhaps unfair) to exclude them from the program. However, there was a lingering fear that these dollars would be used, yet again, to finance poorhouses. As a result, a regulatory clause was included requiring states to establish and maintain standards so that nursing homes "met the definition of a medical institution, not just the old-fashioned poorhouse" (Altmeyer, 1950, p. 60).

Thus, federally funded skilled nursing home care for the aged was born. Because of medical vendor payments, and efforts to deny any funding for poorhouses, the medicalization of institutions for the elderly became codified into public law. Medical vendor payments also created huge incentives to increase institutionalization of the aged. The medical vendor program created a new matching fund, which now reimbursed a plethora of providers for services rendered to poor, mostly the chronically ill, elderly. Because states were given the authority to set the level and terms of payments to these providers, including physicians, hospitals, and nursing homes, incentives for expanded expenditures were embedded in the legislation.

Although healthcare providers were relatively silent about medical vendor payments in the 1950 Social Security hearings, they clearly understood their significance. The Inter-Association of Health (IAH), composed of top ranking officials from six major provider groups,* submitted a statement in support of the need for earmarked funds (through medical vendor payments) to finance healthcare for public assistance recipients. The organization understood that various financing schemes would have a significant impact on its membership. Therefore, IAH's statement included "the further view that any provision to finance medical care for assistance recipients . . . should have the support of those six organizations" (statement submitted to U.S. Congress, January 23, 1950, p. 171). In a separate statement, the American Hospital Association recommended that "medical assistance include long-term care services rendered for the chronically disabled, aging population" (Hayes, 1950, p. 1073). Clearly, the group was concerned about "bed-blockers."†

As fiscal conservatives feared, public assistance programs continued to increase in large part due to the growth of medical vendor payments. Once this legislation was passed, there was a push to expand financing almost immediately. In 1953, a separate matching rate for such payments (apart from cash payments) was established; the individual medical maximums and federal matching rate subsequently rose in 1956, 1958, and 1960, culminating in the passage of Medicaid and Medicare in 1965 (Poen, 1982; Stevens and Stevens, 1974).

The Hill–Burton Act also provided funds for nursing home construction.‡ With construction funds available, and a reimbursement stream for the elderly poor needing LTC services, the number of proprietary nursing homes grew enormously. In 1957, the American Nursing Home Association conducted a survey and reported almost 400,000 beds in 17,455 nursing and convalescent homes, of which 67 percent were under proprietary auspices (Brown, 1958). Most of the latter were relatively small— an average of 23 beds per home compared with 51 beds and 83 beds per nonprofit and public nursing home, respectively (ibid.). The frail elderly quickly filled them: in just four years the percentage of persons aged 65 and above in for-profit facilities increased from only three-fourths of 1 percent (0.0075) to more than 1 percent. Not surprisingly,

---

* The six organizations are American Medicaid Association, American Hospital Association, American Nurses Association, American Dental Association, American Public Health Association, and the American Public Welfare Association.

† There are hints of a broader concern held by others in the medical and public health profession. For example, in 1952, an article published in the *New York State Journal of Medicine* argued that care for the chronically ill and aged sick persons is the number one public health problem facing the country (Merrill, 1952).

‡ See Holstein and Cole (1996) for a discussion on how Small Business Administration (SBA) and Federal Housing Authority (FHA) construction loans encouraged the building of private for-profit nursing homes.

expenditures increased commensurately: skilled nursing home costs in 1956–1957 amounted to $320 million. Approximately $125 million were paid on behalf of public assistance recipients, which amounted to almost half of all patients in skilled nursing homes receiving some public assistance support for their care (Brown, 1958).

The passage of the Kerr–Mills Act in 1960 also profoundly influenced LTC coverage and subsequent policy by including two crucial provisions in the legislation: the concept of medical indigence and comprehensive benefits. Kerr–Mills* had originally been drafted in 1959 as an alternative to the Forand bill, which proposed universal coverage for the elderly but with a restricted benefit package (Marmor, 1973). Proponents of Kerr–Mills argued that a means-tested program would be more efficient than a universal one because it offered help to the most needy. They also noted that this approach offered them more security than the Forand bill because it provided comprehensive benefits, covering not only hospital care but institutional services as well. Moreover, although Kerr–Mills was a targeted program, it was designed to be distinct from welfare; eligibility for benefits was restricted to the "medically indigent" (older people who needed assistance because they had large medical expenses relative to their income). Proponents emphasized that the "medically indigent should not be equated with the totally indigent," those who receive cash assistance (Fein, 1998, p. 311). The moral argument behind this expansion reasoned that the sick elderly—those with chronic conditions—do not have to become impoverished to have their health services expenses paid.

Despite comprehensive coverage, Kerr–Mills was largely viewed as a residual program. Although most proponents of social insurance (Medicare for the population aged 65 and above) were not in favor of Kerr–Mills, they did not spend much time fighting against it.[†] Forand sums up the view: "It will not do any harm, but it will not do any good. Personally I think it is a shame, I think it is a mirage that we are holding up to the old folks to look at and think they are going to get something" (Stevens and Stevens, 1974, p. 29).

Although it is unclear how much the elderly were helped under Kerr–Mills, it is certain that the program had a huge impact on the growth of nursing homes. From 1960 to 1965, vendor payments for institutional care increased almost ten-fold, consuming about one-third of total program expenditures (Vladeck, 1980). Given the rise in the construction of nursing homes and payments to them under medical vendor payments and Kerr–Mills, it is difficult to view these programs as residual ones that eventually would wither away after the enactment of Medicare. The latter did very little to alleviate the chronic LTC needs that these programs addressed (albeit by most accounts not very well) (see Mendelson, 1974; Vladeck, 1980).

---

* Named after its Democratic congressional sponsors, Representative Wilbur Mills and Senator Robert Kerr.

[†] Edward D. Berkowitz in his book, *Mr. Social Security*, describes how Wilbur Cohen very much wanted to please Wilbur Mills and in this sense was supportive of Kerr–Mills legislation despite his ultimate push for universal coverage for the aged under Medicare.

Medicare and Medicaid

The Social Security Amendments of 1965 (the Medicare and Medicaid legislation) combined three approaches to financing medical care into a single package. By all accounts, the creation of this massive "three-layer" cake took nearly everyone by surprise (Stevens and Stevens, 1974; Marmor, 1973; Gordon, 2003; Oberlander, 2003). The first layer was Medicare Part A, a hospital insurance program based on the Social Security contributory model. The second was Medicare Part B, a voluntary supplementary medical insurance program funded through beneficiary premiums and federal general revenues. The third and final layer was the Medical Assistance program (commonly known as the Medicaid program), which broadened the protections offered to the poor and medically indigent under Kerr–Mills and medical vendor payments. The Kerr–Mills means test was liberalized to cover additional elderly citizens, and eligibility among the indigent was broadened to include the blind, permanently disabled, and adults in (largely) single-headed families and their dependent children.

The enactment of Medicaid, in combination with Medicare, was in keeping with a pattern of adopting a limited social insurance program and "supplementing" it with public assistance. Despite Medicaid's comprehensive benefit package and the growth in the number of elderly and their chronic care needs, legislators perceived Medicaid to be a relatively minor piece of the 1965 Social Security legislation, and of much less significance than Medicare. Indeed, some thought Medicare would decrease expenditures for medical care provided to public assistance recipients because services would now be covered under Medicare (Grogan and Patashnik, 2003). Government estimates of Medicaid's future budgetary costs assumed that the program would not lead to a dramatic expansion of healthcare coverage (Stevens and Stevens, 1974). Federal officials projected that Medicaid outlays would amount to no more than $238 million per year above what was currently being spent on welfare medicine. However, it soon became clear that Medicaid was hardly "supplemental." The $238 million mark was reached only after six states had implemented their Medicaid programs. By 1967, 37 states were establishing Medicaid programs, and spending was rising by 57 percent annually (Congressional Research Service [CRS], 1993, p. 30).

The dramatic increase in Medicaid expenditures should not have come as a surprise to anyone looking closely at the earlier medical vendor payments and Kerr–Mills program. As discussed earlier, the fastest growing and most expensive component of these two public assistance programs was the cost of nursing homes for chronically ill elderly persons. By 1965, every state had medical vendor payments for public assistance recipients, and 40 states had implemented a Kerr–Mills Medical Assistance Act (MAA) program for the medically indigent that provided at least some nursing home coverage (Stevens and Stevens, 1974). Because long-term services were excluded under Medicare, the growing costs of nursing homes were simply shifted to Medicaid.

Although Medicare did not reduce Medicaid expenditures as some legislators had naively hoped, it did help to change the way the healthcare system provided services to chronically ill elderly. In 1950, the dominant view about care for the chronically ill elderly had been that they should receive skilled nursing services in an institution separate from that of a hospital. By 1965, the alternative view—that the elderly with chronic conditions should be served in the acute care hospital—became more acceptable. As Field (1967) writes:

> Neither is prolonged illness a universally hopeless, static condition. Its very nature implies a continuity of the disease, calling for continuity in treatment. Changes in the patient's condition often occur. These changes are related to the four phases of the disease: the acute phase, in which active medical care within a hospital is imperative; the convalescent stage in which the patient prepares for a return to normal or near normal health; the chronic stage in which the patient can function in his normal environment, provided he recognizes his limitations and receives continued medical and nursing supervision; and the custodial stage, in which the patient requires care with a minimum of medical attention. These steps do not necessarily follow one another in this order in the course of any one illness. The patient in the chronic stage of his illness may experience an acute exacerbation of symptoms, necessitating rehospitalization and active medical intervention. . . . *Institutional care is only part of the answer during urgent phases of illness. An overall institution for patients with prolonged illness is out of keeping with our present-day understanding of it.* (pp. 9–10; emphasis added)

Medicare's coverage of acute illnesses and rehabilitation (often called postacute care) fits in with this new emerging view. Although it did not pay for many of the associated costs of chronic illness (those described in the foregoing extract in stages three and four), such as medications and home care, Medicare's coverage of hospital and postacute care affirmed the view that institutional care is essential at times, including rehabilitation services. Yet Medicare's universal coverage of acute and postacute care, and Medicaid's separate means-tested payments for nursing homes (and subsequent community-based care options), created a fragmented LTC system; it is quite common now for the elderly to move in and out of multiple institutions during their last years of life. Although the description of the four stages of chronic illness appears logical, caring, and humane, for the elderly and their caregivers, the movement in and out of institutions can feel like a roller-coaster ride filled with confusion and displacement.

Public Policy and Questions of Family Care

By the 1970s, the foundations of our modern LTC conflict were laid: first, throughout the twentieth century, multigenerational household care of our elders, as will be documented in more detail in this section, has been a strongly held social norm of what LTC should entail, despite strong personal preferences for independent living. Second, policy responses to medicalized ideas about how to treat the elderly with chronic illness created a large supply of publicly funded institutional beds within the LTC sector. Concerns about the quality of care provided in these settings, ironically, fostered even more policies advancing medicalization. There has been a continuing evolution of these forces and ongoing attempts to reconcile the desires for independent living with those of medicalized versions of safety.

In most discussions about the provision of welfare benefits, especially in the United States, questions relating to family responsibility inevitably arise. A central concern in the Social Security debates during the early 1930s was whether benefits should be universally distributed, regardless of income, or whether they should be means-tested according to family income. Of course, the OAA program was means-tested and states were given responsibility to determine eligibility levels and other criteria for receiving benefits. Many states—some even before Social Security was passed—mandated that families should have a role in the care of their elders. For example, in 1921, Indiana enacted legislation requiring the legal responsibility of adult children for support of their parents. By 1952, 33 states had passed legislation establishing the responsibility of adult children to support OAA recipients (Schorr, 1960).

The widespread existence of these statutes attests to a strongly held norm that adult children have a moral obligation to assist their parents in times of need. Even those who advocated universal Social Security pensions and OAA believed that adult children should be required to support their parents whenever feasible (Dowdell, 1939).* Because medical vendor payments to nursing homes grew out of OAA benefits, it was perhaps a natural extension to ask about the role of family responsibility in providing care to the chronically ill elderly. As shown in the following, this issue was raised early on in hearings about medical vendor payments.

Senator Millikin: Do relatives in North Carolina show much interest in taking care of relatives?

Dr. Winston: Many relatives do. I suspect they are very much like relatives everywhere. Some do, and some do not.

U.S. Congress, January 23, 1950, p. 187

Similarly, policymakers wondered whether the increasing use of nursing homes was an indication that families were not caring for their elders. Yet, while politicians and others were questioning the appropriateness of kin sending their frail elders off to institutions, providers were encouraging them to do so. At the same time, surveys suggest that the most common reason for entering a nursing home is due to worsening health (Branch, 1982; Colerick and George, 1986; Buhr et al., 2006).

---

* Strong notions of child obligations to take care of their parents have been around for a long time (see Doty, 1986).

In the 1960s, many respondents mentioned that their physician or provider recommended such placement (Sheatsley, 1962; Townsend, 1971). When chronic illness set in, physicians clearly believed that lay family members were often ill-equipped to provide the level of skilled nursing care required (Haber, 1983).

Despite strong provider support, by the early 1970s, not long after Medicare and Medicaid were enacted, several studies of nursing home care revealed serious quality of care issues. A few exposes gave significant press to the topic. For example, a 1971 Ralph Nader report, *Old Age: The Last Segregation*, revealed a stark, inhumane portrait of nursing home care. Three years later, Mary Adelaide Mendelsohn published *Tender Loving Greed: How the Incredibly Lucrative Nursing Home Industry Is Exploiting America's Old People and Defrauding Us All*. Both books documented how nursing homes were making substantial profits although providing substandard care to their residents. They blamed the government's financial support of these poorly run institutions and, most importantly, implicated the providers' role in legitimating nursing homes for their patients.

These manuscripts, and several newspaper articles, eventually prompted the federal government to hold congressional hearings from 1976 to 1977 on the topic and eventually the legislature passed major new regulations, including certification guidelines, staffing requirements, and rules about dispensing medications and the use of restraints (Fox, 1986). Although very few nursing homes met these standards of care in the late 1970s, they added up to significant changes over time. In particular, by the 1990s, although not devoid of quality problems, nursing homes represented a medicalized and regulatory environment considered appropriate for the frailest elderly.

Nonetheless, as Congress was attempting to improve the quality of care provided by nursing homes, legislators also wondered yet again why American families were seemingly rescinding their obligations to take care of their elders (U.S. Congress, 1977; Doty, 1986).[*] A search of Congressional documents using subject heading "Medicaid" for 1976 revealed 13 hearings, 6 prints, and 4 reports all devoted to quality concerns specifically around fraud and abuse within the Medicaid program. In contrast to such views about the irresponsible American family, several researchers were documenting the high level of care actually provided. Two national surveys conducted by the Department of Health and Human Services[†] indicated that spouses and adult children spent numerous hours each week assisting nearly three-quarters of the disabled elderly living at home (Doty, 1986). Even among those who used paid help, the vast majority relied on their family to supplement their needs. The 1982 LTC survey revealed that only 5 percent of the elderly received all of their care from paid providers, and only 26 percent of it was financed by the government. By the mid-1980s, it was clear that (mostly female) family members were spending countless hours of unrecognized labor caring for their loved ones (Brody, 1981; Horowitz, 1985; Noelker and Wallace, 1985; Soldo and Myllyluoma, 1983; Abel, 1987).

---

[*] For a summary of the early findings on this question, see Doty (1986).
[†] The 1979 Health Interview Survey and the 1982 Long-Term Care Survey.

Although this helped allay concerns that families were not stepping up to the plate, it also showed how even the best intentioned family care is often overwhelming and incomplete. Terms such as "caregiver stress" and "caregiver burden" became part of the LTC lexicon; it was now openly discussed that although family care is preferred, the caregivers may simply feel too exhausted, or too frail themselves, to provide adequate skilled care for their elderly relatives (Brody, 1990; Cantor, 1983; Clipp and George, 1990; Doty, 1986; George, 1990; Montgomery et al., 1985; Zarit et al., 1980; Zarit, 1989).

Primarily in response to the high cost of nursing homes, and also in part a response to growing concerns about their poor quality of care, advocates and policymakers have been promoting alternatives to institutionalization since the early 1970s (Abdellah, 1978; Greene et al., 1993). Through existing policies and funding new programs, home care and community-based care (HCBC) options are encouraged for elderly with chronic illnesses (ibid.). Community-based care has grown enormously and, where it is offered, utilization among the elderly who need it is high.

The problem with HCBC, however, is twofold. First, for people with substantial disabilities, it can actually be more expensive than that provided by nursing homes (Weissert et al., 1988). Second, studies have also found that such care does not necessarily prevent a nursing home placement as many thought it would (Kemper et al., 1987; Kemper, 1988).* At-home care seems to be used chronologically as a care method for earlier stages of illness, whereas nursing home placement is still predominant in the last stage (ibid.). Rarely is community-based care used as a sole source of care to help the elderly die in their home (Last Acts, 2002). In our fragmented care system, community-based care tends to be a patchwork approach that assists the elderly who are moved in and out of various institutional settings: from hospital to rehabilitation to a nursing home, and—if lucky—back to the community (ibid.).

The social norms for independent living, combined with a highly medicalized LTC environment, contribute to Americans feeling deeply conflicted today between two ideals for their elders—a free, independent, homelike environment versus a protective, safe, institutionalized one. LTC advocates often tell us this is a false dichotomy, that we can have it both ways: an independent, healthy, safe environment in which to grow old (Last Acts, 2002). But the advice (or "how to") books suggest otherwise. Fox's (1982) book, *The Chronically Ill*, highlighted the conflict well:

> To go or not to go to a home? From all sides, conflicting influences tug at you. You are wise—or you are cruel—to think of such a thing; she will love, or she will hate it there. From four sides you are bombarded:
>
> ■ "Send her to a nursing home," says a doctor.
> ■ "You're just trying to duck your obligations," says the gossip.

---

* Contrary to this finding, Greene et al. (1993) found that specific community-based services targeted to specific needs can prevent nursing home entry.

- "We have the bed for her—she'll love our homelike atmosphere," says the nursing-home industry.
- "Consider alternatives to institutionalization," say citizen-action groups. (p. 14)

Recent books highlight how there are good nursing homes and that sometimes placement is necessary. Nursing homes are considered appropriate in this new vein of advice books if the at-home environment is not considered "safe." In their advice book, Forrest et al. (1990) list five classic danger signs for the frail elderly living independently: marked change in personal appearance; decrease in nutritional status; financial confusion; paranoia, hallucinations, and delusions; and falls.

The authors note that falls are the leading cause of accidental death for people above the age of 75. Indeed, falls are one of the most common triggers for nursing home placement (Doty, 1986). Even the simple fear of a fall occurring, based on an assessment that it is high risk, can often prompt a nursing home placement. Indeed, the book warns in bold that "**safety must be the prime consideration**. When the integrity of the elderly person's safety cannot be maintained, alternative living arrangements must be made immediately!" (Forrest et al., 1990, p. xx).

Conclusion: Irreconcilable Conflict?

In this chapter, I argue that the reason Americans have a much more medicalized end-of-life experience than their wishes suggest they want, may not simply be due to poorly designed public policy, but rather something that runs deeper in the American psyche. I do not mean to imply, as many others have, that American families do not care, or do not care enough. Rather, I argue that the medicalized experience may reflect a conflict deeply rooted in American social and political history, including its social conscience about successful aging: first, that independent living is preferred; and, second, that aging should be viewed as a unique form of chronic illness for which skilled and specialized health services are needed. These two paradigms suggest that we constantly trade off independence for medical safety as older people become more frail.

Three main factors have developed over time to help bolster this conflict: first, the creation of a highly medicalized environment in all the facets of LTC provision—the hospital, rehabilitation center, nursing home, and home healthcare services; second, a more fluid way to think about chronic illness—from segregated care to more integrated care, allowing movement through multiple institutions; and finally, the persistence of widespread societal expectations regarding family care obligations alongside strongly held preferences for independent living arrangements. Unfortunately, the convergence of these issues encourages families and their elders, each step along the way of increasing frailty, to confront an agonizing choice between a more free, but risky environment and a protective, institutionalized medical one.

References

Abdellah, F. G. (1978). Long-term care policy issues: Alternatives to institutional care. *Annals of the American Academy of Political and Social Science*, 438(July), 28–39.

Abel, E. K. (1987). *Love Is Not Enough: Family Care of the Frail Elderly*. Washington: American Public Health Association.

Altmeyer, A. (1950). *Social Security Revision*. Committee on Finance. Hrg., Senate, 81st Congress, second session on H.R. 6000, January 23–31, February 1–3, 6–10. Washington, DC: U.S. Government Printing Office, p. 171.

Berkowitz, E. D. (1995). *Mr. Social Security: The Life of Wilbur J. Cohen*. Lawrence, KS: University Press of Kansas.

Blank, R. H. and Merrick, J. C. (2003). *End-of-Life Decision Making: A Cross-National Study*. Cambridge, MA: Massachusetts Institute of Technology Press.

Bradley, E. H., Fried, T. R., Kasl, S. V., Cicchetti, D. V., Johnson-Hurzeler, R., and Horwitz, S. M. (2000). Referral of terminally ill patients for hospice: Frequency and correlates. *Journal of Palliative Care*, 16(4), 20–26.

Branch, L. G. and Jette, A. M. (1982). A prospective study of long-term care institutionalization among the aged. *American Journal of Public Health*, 72(12), 1373–1379.

Brody, E. M. (1981). Women in the middle: And family help to older people. *The Gerontologist*, 21, 471–479.

Brody, E. M. (1990). *Women in the Middle: Their Parent Care Years*. New York: Springer.

Brown, F. R. (1958). Nursing homes: Public and private financing of care today. *Social Security Bulletin*, 21(5), 3–8, 21.

Buhr, T. G., Kuchibhatla, M., and Clipp, E. C. (2006). Caregivers' reasons for nursing home placement: Clues for improving discussions with families prior to the transition. *The Gerontologist*, 46(1), 52–61.

Callahan, J. J. (2006). Can the family experience of long-term care be improved? *The Gerontologist*, 46(1), 144–146.

Cantor, M. (1983). Strain among caregivers: A study of experience in the United States. *The Gerontologist*, 23, 597–604.

Cassel, C. K., Ludden, J. M., and Moon, G. M. (2000). Perceptions of barriers to high-quality palliative care. *Health Affairs*, 19(5), 166–172.

Christakis, N. A. and Iwashyna, T. J. (2000). Impact of individual and market factors on the timing of initiation of hospice terminal care. *Medical Care*, 38, 528–541.

Chudacoff, H. and Hareven, T. K. (1978). Family transitions into old age. In Hareven, T. K. (Ed.), *Transitions: The Family and the Life Course in Historical Perspective*. New York: Academic Press.

Clipp, E. C. and George, L. K. (1990). Caregiver needs and patterns of social support. *Journals of Gerontology*, 46, S102–S111.

Colerick, E. J. and George, L. K. (1986). Predictors of institutionalization among caregivers of patients with Alzheimer's disease. *Journal of the American Geriatrics Society*, 34(7), 493–498.

Congressional Research Service (CRS). (1993). *Medicaid Source Book: Background Data and Analysis (1993 Update)*. Washington: U.S. Government Printing Office.

Dieckmann, J. L. (1999). *Caring for the Chronically Ill: Philadelphia, 1945–1965*. New York: Garland.

Doty, P. (1986). Family care of the elderly: The role of public policy. *The Milbank Quarterly*, 64(1), 34–75.

Dowdell, M. P. (1939). *Excerpts from Should Children be Required to Support Their Parents?* Olympia, WA: State Dept. of Social Security.

Emanuel, L. L., von Gunten, C. F., and Ferris, F. D. (2000). Gaps in end-of-life care. *Archives of Family Medicine*, 9, 1176–1180.

Fein, S. (1998). The Kerr-Mills act: Medical care for the indigent in Michigan, 1960–1965. *Journal of the History of Medicine and Allied Sciences*, 53(3), 285–316.

Field, M. (1967). *Patients Are People: A Medical-Social Approach to Prolonged Illness.* New York: Columbia University Press.

Fisher, J. (1953). Trends in institutional care of the aged. *Social Security Bulletin*, 16(10), 9–13, 19, 29.

Flory, J., Yinong Y., Gurol, I., Levinsky, N., Ash, A., and Emanuel, E. (2004). Place of death: U.S. trends since 1980. *Health Affairs*, 23(3), 194–200.

Forrest, M. B., Forrest, C. B., and Forrest, R. (1990). *Nursing Homes: The Complete Guide.* New York: Facts on File.

Fox, J. (1957). *The Chronically Ill.* New York: Philosophical Library.

Fox, N. L. (1982, 1986). *You, Your Parent, and the Nursing Home.* Buffalo, N.Y.: Prometheus Books.

Gabrel, C. S. (2000). Characteristics of elderly nursing home current residents and discharges: Data from the 1997 national nursing home survey. *Advance Data*, 312. U.S. Department of Health and Human Services: CDC, National Center for Health Statistics, p. 2.

George, L. K. (1990). Caregiver stress studies: There really is more to learn. *The Gerontologist*, 30, 580–581.

Gerber, N. (2005). *Losing a Life: A Daughter's Memoir of Caregiving.* Lanham, MD: Hamilton Books.

Gordon, C. (2003). *Dead on Arrival: The Politics of Health Care in Twentieth-Century America.* Princeton, NJ: Princeton University Press.

Greene, V. L., Lovely, M. E., and Ondrich, J. I. (1993). Do community-based, long-term care services reduce nursing home use? A transition probability analysis. *The Journal of Human Resources*, 28(2), 297–317.

Grogan, C. M. and Patashnik, E. M. (2003). Between welfare medicine and mainstream program: Medicaid at the political crossroads. *Journal of Health Politics, Policy and Law*, 28(5), 821–858.

Haber, C. (1983). *Beyond Sixty-Five: The Dilemma of Old Age in America's Past.* New York: Cambridge University Press.

Haber, C. and Gratton, B. (1993). *Old Age and the Search for Security: An American Social History.* Bloomington: Indiana University Press.

Haber, C. and Gratton, B. (1994). *Old Age and the Search for Security: An American Social History.* Indianapolis, IN: Indiana University Press.

Hayes, American Hospital Association. (1950). *Social Security Revision.* Committee on Finance. Hrg., Senate, 81st Congress, second session on H.R. 6000, January 23–31, February 1–3, 6–10. Washington, DC: U.S. Government Printing Office, p. 1073.

Holstein, M. and Cole, T. R. (1996). The evolution of long-term care in America. In Binstock, R. H., Leighton, E. C., and von Mering, O. (Eds.), *The Future of Long-Term Care: Social and Policy Issues.* Baltimore, MD: Johns Hopkins University Press, pp. 19–48.

Horowitz, A. (1985). Family caregiving to the frail elderly. In Eisdorfer, C. (Ed.), *Annual Review of Gerontology and Geriatrics*. New York: Springer, pp. 194–246.

Jones, A. (1999). *The National Nursing Home Survey: 1999 Summary*. Division of Health Care Statistics: National Center for Health Statistics, Centers for Disease Control and Prevention, Series 13, No. 152, 1–5.

Kane, R. L. and West, J. C. (2005). *It Shouldn't Be This Way: The Failure of Long-Term Care*. Nashville, TN: Vanderbilt University Press.

Katz, M. B. (1986). *In the Shadow of the Poorhouse: A Social History of Welfare in America*. New York: Basic Books.

Kemper, P. (1988). The evaluation of the national long term care demonstration. 10. Overview of the findings. *Health Services Research*, 23(1), 161–174.

Kemper, P., Applebaum, R., and Harrigan, M. (1987). Community care demonstrations: What have we learned? *Health Care Financing Review*, 8(4), 87–100.

Last Acts. (2002). *Means to a Better End: A Report on Dying in America Today*. From http://www.lastacts.org.

Margolies, L. (2004). *My Mother's Hip: Lessons from the World of Eldercare*. Philadelphia, PA: Temple University Press.

Marmor, T. R. (1973). *The Politics of Medicare*. New York: Aldine.

Mendelson, M. A. (1974). *Tender Loving Greed: How the Incredibly Lucrative Nursing Home "Industry" Is Exploiting America's Old People and Defrauding Us All*. New York: Knopf.

Merrill, A. P. (1952). Hospitals for the chronically ill. *New York State Journal of Medicine*, 52(October), 2393–2396.

Metropolitan Life Insurance Company. (1959). *When Our Parents Get Old*. San Francisco, CA: Metropolitan Life Insurance Co.

Montgomery, R. J. V., Gonyea, J. G., and Hooyman, N. R. (1985). Caregiving and the experience of subjective and objective burden. *Family Relations*, 34, 19–26.

Mur-Veeman, I., Verhoef, K., Borghans, I., and van Merode, F. (2005). *Hospital Intermediate Care: A Solution for the Bed-Blockers Problem?* Found at: http://www.integratedcarenetwork.org/publish/articles/000053/article.htm.

Noelker, L. S. and Wallace, R. W. (1985). The organization of family care for frail elderly. *Journal of Family Issues*, 6, 23–44.

Norman, V. (1952). Federal participation in vendor payments for medical care. *Social Security Bulletin*, 15(12), 8–10, 21.

Nuland, S. B. (1994). *How We Die: Reflections on Life's Final Chapter*. New York: A. A. Knopf, Distributed by Random House.

Oberlander, J. (2003). *The Political Life of Medicare*. Chicago, IL: University of Chicago Press.

Poen, M. M. (1982). The Truman legacy: Retreat to medicare. In Numbers, R. L. (Ed.), *Compulsory Health Insurance*. Westport, CT: Greenwood Press, pp. 97–114.

Pritchard, R. S., Fisher, E. S., Teno, J. M., Sharp, S. M., Reding, J. D., Knaus, W. A., Wennberg, J. E., and Lynn, J. (1998). Influences of patient preferences and local health system characteristics on the place of death. *Journal of the American Geriatrics Society*, 46(10), 1242–1250.

Rosenberg, C. E. (1987). *The Care of Strangers: The Rise of America's Hospital System*. New York: Basic Books.

Schorr, A. L. (1960). *Filial Responsibility in the Modern American Family: An Evaluation of Current Practice of Filial Responsibility in the United States and the Relationship to it of Social Security Programs.* Washington, DC: U.S. Dept. of Health, Education, and welfare, Social Security Administration, Division of Program Research.

Sheatsley, P. B. (1962). Report of a survey of hospital administrator attitudes toward use. In *Health Information Foundation. Where Is Hospital Use Headed: Proceedings of the Fifth Annual Symposium on Hospital Affairs.* Chicago: Graduate School of Business, University of Chicago, pp. 29–35.

Social Security Bulletin. (1939). Physical condition and medical care of 1,000,000 recipients of old-age assistance. *Social Security Bulletin*, 2(3), 21–27.

Soldo, B. J. and Myllyluoma, J. (1983). Caregivers who live with dependent elderly. *The Gerontologist*, 23, 605–611.

Stevens, R. (1971). *American Medicine and the Public Interest.* New Haven: Yale University Press.

Stevens, R. B. and Stevens, R. (1974). *Welfare Medicine in America: A Case Study of Medicaid.* New York: Free Press.

Stewart, E. M. (1925). *The Cost of American Almshouses.* U.S. Bureau of Labor Statistics, Bulletin No. 386. Washington: Government Printing Office.

SUPPORT Principal Investigators. (1995). A controlled trial to improve care for seriously ill hospitalized patients: The study to understand prognoses and preferences for outcomes and risks of treatment (SUPPORT). *Journal of the American Medical Association*, 274, 1591–1598.

Townsend, C. (1971). *The Nader Report. Old Age: The Last Segregation.* New York: Grossman Publishers.

U.S. Congress. (1950). *Social Security Revision.* Committee on finance. Hrg., Senate, 81st Congress, second session on H.R. 6000, January 23–31, February 1–3, 6–10. Washington: U.S. Government Printing Office.

U.S. Congress. (1977). Special Committee on Aging, Senate Hearing, Medicare and Medicaid Frauds, Parts 1–9, various dates Part 1 starting on Sept 26, 1975 through Part 9 on March 9, 1977.

Vladeck, B. C. (1980). *Unloving Care: The Nursing Home Tragedy.* New York: Basic Books.

Weissert, W., Cready, C. M., and Pawelak, J. E. (1988). The past and future of home- and community-based long-term care. *The Milbank quarterly (Milbank Q)*, 66(2), 309–388.

White, R. (1950). Vendor payments for medical assistance. *Social Security Bulletin*, 13(6), 3–11.

White, R. (1952a). Medical services in the old-age assistance program. *Social Security Bulletin*, 15(6), 3–11.

White, R. (1952b). Expenditures for medical services in public assistance, 1946. *Social Security Bulletin*, 15(8), 7–11, 20, 29.

Zarit, S. H. (1989). Do we need another "stress and caregiving" study? *The Gerontologist*, 29, 147–148.

Zarit, S. H., Reever, K. E., and Bach-Peterson, J. (1980). Relatives of the impaired elderly: Correlates of feelings of burden. *The Gerontologist*, 20, 649–655.

PROVIDING AND RECEIVING CARE

Chapter 5

Older Long-Term Care Recipients

Megan E. McCutcheon and William J. McAuley

Contents

Planning for, funding, providing, and coordinating long-term care are major concerns in the United States. Long-term care can be required at any age, and there are nearly as many people below the age of 65 who require it as there are people aged 65 and above with such needs (Feder et al., 2000). However, it is appropriate to focus specifically on long-term care for the older population because the probability of having a disability (Cohen et al., 2005) and of needing long-term care services increases substantially with age (Feder et al., 2000). This chapter describes the older population, including trends in aging, and the major factors that lead to or are

73

associated with their use of long-term care. The chapter ends with a discussion of recent trends in impairment and in technologies aimed at managing it, as well as future prospects for long-term care.

Characteristics of the Older Population

In 2003, there were 35.9 million residents aged 65 and above in the United States, representing 12.4 percent of the total population (Federal Interagency Forum on Aging-Related Statistics, 2004). Although it has been aging rapidly, the United States is not by any means the "oldest" nation, with regard to the percentage of the total population that is aged 65 and above. For example, in Italy, Japan, and Greece those aged 65 and above represent more than 18 percent of the total population. The "old-old" subgroup, those aged 85 and above—and the age group that is more likely to require assistance with long-term care—has experienced especially rapid relative growth over time. In 2000, approximately 4.2 million old-old people resided in the United States (Federal Interagency Forum on Aging-Related Statistics, 2004).

Although the figures for the United States mentioned earlier are useful for understanding aging as an important national phenomenon, it is essential to recognize that the older population is not evenly distributed across the nation's landscape. Less than 9 percent of the residents in Utah and Alaska are aged 65 or above, whereas 17.2 percent of Florida's population, and more than 15 percent of the populations of Pennsylvania and West Virginia, consist of older people. The most rural areas in the United States tend to have higher percentages of elderly people than metropolitan areas (Hawes et al., 2003). The vast majority (82.5 percent) of older persons in the United States is white, but the increase of elders in most minority populations is outpacing that of the whites. Elders who are African American, Hispanic, and Asian constitute 8.4, 5.7, and 2.7 percent, respectively, of the total older population (Federal Interagency Forum on Aging-Related Statistics, 2004).

The marital status and household composition of elders are important considerations in the assessment of long-term care because spouses and other household members tend to assist one another with long-term care. Informal caregivers generally do not relinquish their responsibility for care, even when formal services are made available to impaired older people (Li, 2005). The availability of informal care acts to limit the use of formal community-based care, and it can also delay nursing home admissions among older people (Charles and Sevak, 2005; Houtven and Norton, 2004). Because spouses often provide long-term care, it makes sense that being unmarried is a significant independent predictor of nursing home placement (Borrayo et al., 2002). Similarly, elderly long-term care users who reside in the community are far more likely than nursing home residents to be married (Spector and Fleishman, 2001). The percentage of older people who are married declines with increasing age, primarily due to widowhood, so that less than one-third of persons aged 85 and above are married. However, men who survive into old-old age are more likely to have a spouse; about 59.4 percent of men and 14 percent of women aged 85 and above are married. Only 19 percent of older men live alone as compared to 40 percent of older women (Federal Interagency Forum on Aging-Related Statistics, 2004). Half of all older women aged 75 and above live by themselves (Administration on Aging, 2004), suggesting that female elders are far less likely to have someone within the household who can provide long-term care, should they need it.

Because income can be used directly to purchase long-term care or pay for long-term care insurance, it is an important consideration in developing an overall perspective on long-term care among seniors. Income can determine the types of services that are available and accessible to elders. The older population in the United States has experienced a dramatic increase in the percentage of people having incomes above the poverty level, primarily due to Social Security. The percentage of elders living in poverty reached a low of 9.7 percent by 1999 but since then has increased slightly, reaching 10.4 percent in 2002. The rise in poverty among seniors is a serious concern, especially given the burgeoning cost of healthcare and the direct association between low income and health status (Huynh et al., 2006).

Critically, poverty levels vary dramatically by sex, race or ethnicity, and living arrangement. Elders with the highest percentages living in poverty include Hispanic (47.1 percent) and African-American women living alone (40.6 percent). In contrast, less than 4 percent of older married white men and women living with their spouses have incomes below the poverty level (Federal Interagency Forum on Aging-Related Statistics, 2004). The median income of older men exceeds that of older women by a substantial amount, $20,363 versus $11,845 in 2003 (Administration on Aging, 2004).

Among the most important contributors to the need for long-term care are chronic health problems, such as those listed in Table 5.1 (Fisher and McCabe, 2005). As shown in Table 5.1, some of the most common chronic conditions include hypertension, arthritic symptoms, heart disease, and cancer. Older men are considerably more likely than older women to report heart disease, diabetes, and cancer, although older women are much more likely to report hypertension and arthritic symptoms. Many older people have more than one chronic condition, a factor that can increase the possibility that long-term care will be required.

Cognitive and sensory limitations can also establish the need for long-term care (Gibson et al., 2004). Low cognitive capacity, especially memory impairment, is a significant risk factor for nursing home admission (Metha et al., 2002). Approximately 15 percent of older men and 11 percent of older women experience moderate to severe memory impairment. Among persons aged 85 and above, about 34 percent of men and 31 percent of women have moderate to significant memory impairment (Federal Interagency Forum on Aging-Related Statistics, 2004). Vision and hearing problems also increase with age. Approximately 47 percent of all older men and 30 percent of older women have trouble hearing without a hearing aid. However, among the old-old, 67 percent of men and 56 percent of women report

Table 5.1 Percentage of People Aged 65 and above Reporting Selected Chronic Conditions (2001–2002)

Sex	Hypertension	Arthritic Symptoms	Heart Disease	Any Cancer	Diabetes	Stroke	Asthma	Chronic Bronchitis	Emphysema
Total	50.1	35.0	31.2	20.7	15.6	8.8	8.4	6.1	5.0
Men	47.3	31.3	36.6	24.5	18.0	9.5	7.3	5.1	6.5
Women	52.2	39.3	27.1	17.9	13.9	8.2	9.2	6.8	3.8

Source: Federal Interagency Forum on Aging-Related Statistics, *Older Americans 2004: Key Indicators of Well-Being*, U.S. Government Printing Office, Washington, 2004.

problems with hearing. Similarly, there are age-related increases in the percentage of people who experience at least some problem with their vision, even when they use glasses or contact lenses. Such difficulties are reported by approximately 16 percent of older men and 19 percent of older women, and increase to 29 and 35 percent, respectively, among the old-old population (Federal Interagency Forum on Aging-Related Statistics, 2004).

When a nationally representative sample of noninstitutionalized older people was asked to report on their own health status during 2000–2002, approximately 27 percent rated it as fair or poor (Federal Interagency Forum on Aging-Related Statistics, 2004). With increasing age, people are more likely to report that their health is less than optimal. For example, among persons aged 65–74, 22.6 percent rate their health as fair or poor, but this figure increases to 34.9 percent among the old-old population. Self-ratings of health also differ significantly by the ethnicity of seniors. Among older African Americans aged 65–74, 37.6 percent rate their health as fair or poor. This percentage increases to 47.6 percent among those aged 85 and above (Federal Interagency Forum on Aging-Related Statistics, 2004).

Although there are significant differences in self-ratings of health by ethnicity, past research has suggested that older African Americans, Hispanics, and Asians are less likely than white non-Hispanics to use formal long-term care (Wallace et al., 1998). However, recent data identifies a turnaround in this trend among African Americans. Recent nursing home utilization rates have declined for whites, whereas they have increased for African Americans, so that they are now higher for the latter. Older African Americans are also more likely to use home healthcare than older whites (Pandya, 2005). Nursing home utilization, however, continues to be low for Hispanics, Asians, and Native Americans. As the United States continues to age and become more diverse, long-term care planners and policy makers must give greater attention to the mix of needs, preferences, and utilization patterns among the many segments of the older population.

Growth of the Older Population

A number of factors influence the age structure of a population, including shifts in the birth rate, life expectancy, and the numbers and age of immigrants. Life expectancy at birth has grown from approximately 49 in 1900 to 77 in 2001 (Federal Interagency Forum on Aging-Related Statistics, 2004). Both men and women have experienced improvements over this period, although the increases have been somewhat greater for women than for men. The life expectancy at older ages has also increased. In 2001, persons aged 65 years could expect to survive an average of 18 more years, and those aged 85 could anticipate living 6.5 more years. Although the life expectancy of women at age 65 continues to remain higher than that for men, there is evidence that the gap has been narrowing in recent decades (Federal Interagency Forum on Aging-Related Statistics, 2004).

Basic and Instrumental Activities of Daily Living and Other Measures of Long-Term Care Need

Long-term care is designed primarily to assist individuals in the performance of activities of daily living (ADLs) (Feder et al., 2000). ADLs are generally divided into two broad types. The basic or physical ADLs are the tasks required for self-maintenance. The usual measures include the ability to perform bathing, dressing, eating, transferring (getting in and out of bed or chairs), walking, and grooming (combing hair and shaving) (Lawton and Brody, 1969).

Instrumental ADLs (IADLs) are more complex behaviors that require substantial memory, decision making, or physical capacity. These activities make it possible to communicate with others, traverse the community, manage household and financial tasks, and self-medicate. In measuring IADLs, researchers and clinicians normally include getting to places beyond walking distance (e.g., driving, using a bus or cab), shopping (assuming that transportation is available), meal preparation, light housework, taking medications, and handling basic personal finances (Lawton and Brody, 1969).

Lower-body mobility limitations, including having difficulty lifting 10 pounds, walking up ten steps, walking a quarter of a mile, standing for 20 minutes, or bending down to pick up an object, are highly associated with the use of long-term care because they form the physical building blocks for the performance of ADLs and IADLs. Upper-body mobility limitations, such as those associated with reaching over one's head, picking up a glass, and holding a pencil, are also correlated with the use of long-term care services, although not to the same degree (Spector and Fleishman, 2001). As demonstrated in Table 5.2, there are substantial differences by sex in the ability to perform these lower- and upper-body activities among older people, with relatively more women reporting difficulty with each activity (He et al., 2005).

When people are completely unable to perform one of the ADLs or IADLs, or require supervision or direct assistance to carry them out, they are said to have a functional limitation or deficit. Because these daily living tasks are important to the health, safety, independence, and well-being of older people, some type of intervention is required when they cannot be regularly achieved without assistance. The interventions provided to address these functional limitations form the foundation of long-term care. In 2002, approximately 8.7 million people aged 65 and above residing in the community reported having one or more ADL or IADL limitations, representing 26.5 percent of all such older people. Approximately 2 million of them have three or more ADL limitations—a larger number than the 1.4–1.6 million residents of nursing homes (Johnson and Weiner, 2006; Spillman and Black, 2005). It is both surprising and distressing that a higher percentage of older people with at least one ADL or IADL limitation live alone (37.7 percent) than those without any limitation (29.7 percent). Even more alarming is the fact that 35 percent of older community residents with three or more ADL limitations, a group that has

Table 5.2 Activity Limitations among People Aged 65 and above by Sex (1998)

Activity Limitation (Very Difficult or Unable to)	Percentage of Men	Percentage of Women
Walk a quarter of a mile (about three city blocks)	16.8	28.3
Stand or be on one's feet for two hours	16.0	27.4
Climb ten steps without resting	11.9	21.8
Sit for two hours	3.8	5.8
Reach over one's head	5.5	8.3
Use one's fingers to grasp or handle small objects	3.2	4.9
Lift or carry something as heavy as 10 pounds (such as a full bag of groceries)	7.4	19.1
Push or pull large objects (such as a living room chair)	13.1	27.9
One or more of the preceding limitations	57.7	70.5

Source: He, W., Sengupta, M., Velkoff, V. A., and DeBarros, K. A., U.S. Census Bureau Current Population Reports P23–209, U.S. Government Printing Office, Washington.

considerable need for long-term care, live alone (Johnson and Weiner, 2006). Only 61.3 percent of older community residents who have an IADL or ADL limitation receive paid or unpaid help, and the vast majority (76.7 percent) of those receiving such care receive it solely from unpaid sources, especially family members (Johnson and Weiner, 2006).

In general, older people who reside in nursing homes have more ADL and IADL needs, in comparison to those who reside in the community. However, there is considerable overlap in levels of ADL and IADL deficits across the two environments, suggesting that some institutionalized individuals could appropriately reside in the community if the required resources were available (Grando et al., 2005).

When asked about their preferences, most adults indicate that they wish to receive long-term care in their homes, provided by family members or by nonkin, while relatively few prefer to receive care in nursing homes (Eckert et al., 2004; McAuley and Blieszner, 1985). As described previously, there are reasonably good estimates of the number of nursing home residents, and national surveys provide satisfactory data on the number of older community-residing residents who require long-term care. However, we have less accurate knowledge about older individuals living in alternative residential care settings, such as assisted living, group homes, and board-and-care facilities (Spillman and Black, 2005). There is good reason to believe that the number of residents in these alternative settings has grown appreciably in the past 15 years.

Recent studies suggest that there were approximately 36,000 alternative residential settings in 2002, accommodating about 800,000 residents (Spillman and Black, 2005). According to Harrington et al. (2005), residential care and assisted living increased by 97 percent from 1990 to 2002, whereas nursing home beds increased by only 7 percent over the same period. Therefore, the United States is experiencing changes in the location and type of long-term care, with increasing numbers of disabled older adults living in the community and in alternative residential settings relative to nursing homes. Although the range of disability among residents of assisted living facilities is great, those who live in these settings are generally less frail and impaired than the nursing home residents. The differences in impairment across these settings are the result of the admission and discharge criteria used by assisted living facilities. It should be noted that many of the latter are relatively new (Golant, 2004), which has limited the opportunity for residents to experience aging in place, a factor that may result in frailer, more impaired people in the future.

Sources of Payment for Long-Term Care

The costs of long-term care are paid through a variety of sources. In 1998, home care and nursing home expenditures totaled $150 billion. Of this amount, Medicaid paid approximately 40 percent, Medicare 20 percent, and private insurance 8 percent. Nearly 26 percent was paid out of pocket by recipients or their family, while the rest, 7 percent, came from all other funding sources (Feder et al., 2000). Medicaid was the primary source of nursing home care in 1998, accounting for 44 percent of all nursing home expenditures. The second largest source of payment was care recipients or their families (31 percent). The remaining payers include private insurance (7 percent) and other sources (5 percent) (Feder et al., 2000). These figures do not take into account the substantial amount of unpaid long-term care provided by family members and other informal sources of support, which has been estimated to total more than $250 billion a year (U.S. Department of Health and Human Services, 2005).

Recent Trends in Disability and Future Prospects

Data on disability among all elders in community and nursing home settings suggests that from 1984 to 1999 there was a decline in the percentage of persons who are chronically disabled with regard to ADLs or IADLs (Office of Disability, Aging and Long-Term Care, 2003). The overall decrease in this 15-year period was substantial, moving from 22.1 percent in 1984 to 19.7 percent in 1999. Because the percentage of elders in nursing homes changed little, most of the reduction in chronic disability was experienced by older people residing in the community (Office of Disability, Aging and Long-Term Care, 2003). Although fewer people require ADL or IADL assistance, some of this change can be attributed to the use of assistive devices that enable older people to manage their disability themselves and continue to function independently in the community.

The steadily increasing use of assistive equipment may be a harbinger of even larger future shifts toward the personal management of impairment without the need for human support. There is evidence that technologies such as canes, walkers, wheelchairs, bath seats, bath rails, raised toilet seats, toilet rails, portable toilets, hearing aids, and back braces are associated with reductions in requirements for informal care and can also serve to supplement formal care. Assistive technologies can be especially beneficial for those disabled elders who have sufficient cognitive abilities to effectively use them. These devices can also particularly benefit unmarried elders because they can, in some cases, provide the regular, ongoing assistance that might otherwise be available only from a spouse (Agree et al., 2005). As might be expected, current forms of assistive technology are less useful in reducing or supplementing informal and formal care among older persons with cognitive impairments (Agree et al., 2005). The development of a wide range of new assistive, housing, and medical technologies could make it possible for many of those who begin experiencing difficulty with daily living activities to maintain their independence for a longer period than is currently feasible (Wolf et al., 2005).

Because of increasing life expectancy and the fact that the first members of the baby boom generation will turn 65 in 2011, the United States will soon be experiencing a new boom in aging. Census estimates suggest that the number of Americans aged 65 and above will more than double from 35 million in 2000 to 72 million in 2030, at which point nearly 20 percent of the total population will consist of older people (He et al., 2005). Looking even further ahead, it is estimated that the older population will reach 86.7 million in 2050 (He et al., 2005).

Data also suggest very rapid growth of the old-old. Those who are aged 85 and above will more than double from 4.7 million in 2003 to 9.6 million in 2030. Furthermore, this segment of the population will increase very rapidly after 2030, when the baby boom generation joins their ranks, so that the old-old group will double again to 20.9 million in 2050 (He et al., 2005). These figures indicate that although there may be reductions in impairment among older people well into the future, they may be counterbalanced or surmounted by the substantial increases in the old-old population, who are most likely to require long-term care services. Therefore, there is little doubt that long-term care will persist as a substantial national concern. Consequently, it is important for planners, policy makers, program administrators, and researchers to improve their understanding of the issues and plan accordingly.

References

Administration on Aging (2004). *A Profile of Older Americans: 2004*. Washington: Administration on Aging, U.S. Department of Health and Human Services.

Agree, E. M., Freedman, V. A., Cornman, J. C., Wolf, D. A., and Marcotte, J. E. (2005). Reconsidering substitution in long-term care: When does assistive technology take the place of personal care? *Journal of Gerontology: Social Sciences*, *60B*, S273–S280.

Borrayo, E. A., Salmon, J. R., Polivka, L., and Dunlop, B. D. (2002). Utilization across the continuum of long-term care services. *The Gerontologist*, *42*, 603–612.

Charles, K. K. and Sevak, P. (2005). Can family caregiving substitute for nursing home care? *Journal of Health Economics*, *24*, 1174–1190.

Cohen, M. A., Weinrobe, M., Miller, J., and Ingoldsby, A. (2005). *Becoming Disabled after Age 65: The Expected Lifetime Costs of Independent Living*. Washington: AARP Public Policy Institute.

Eckert, J. K., Morgan, L. A., and Swami, N. (2004). Preferences for receipt of care among community-dwelling adults. *Journal of Aging and Social Policy*, *16*(2), 49–65.

Feder, J., Komisar, H. L., and Niefeld, M. (2000). Long-term care in the United States: An overview. *Health Affairs*, *19*, 40–56.

Federal Interagency Forum on Aging-Related Statistics. (2004). *Older Americans 2004: Key Indicators of Well-Being*. Washington: U.S. Government Printing Office.

Fisher, M. F. and McCabe, S. (2005). Managing chronic conditions for elderly adults: The VNS CHOICE model. *Health Care Financing Review*, *27*, 33–45.

Gibson, M. J., Gregory, S. R., Houser, A. N., and Fox-Grage, W. (2004). *Across the States: Profiles of Long-Term Care*. Washington: AARP Public Policy Institute.

Golant, S. M. (2004). Do impaired older persons with health care needs occupy U.S. assisted living facilities? An analysis of six national studies. *Journal of Gerontology: Social Sciences*, *59B*, S68–S79.

Grando, V. T., Rantz, M. J., Petroski, G. F., Maas, M., Popejoy, L., Conn, V., and Wipke-Teves, D. (2005). Prevalence and characteristics of nursing home residents requiring light-care. *Research in Nursing and Health*, *28*, 210–219.

Harrington, C., Chapman, S., Miller, E. M. N., and Newcomer, R. (2005). Trends in the supply of long-term-care facilities and beds in the United States. *Journal of Applied Gerontology*, *24*, 265–282.

Hawes, C., Phillips, C. D., Holan, S., and Sherman, M. (2003). *Assisted Living in Rural America: Results from a National Survey*. College Station, TX: Southwest Rural Health Research Center, Texas A&M University System Health Science Center.

He, W., Sengupta, M., Velkoff, V. A., and DeBarros, K. A. (2005). *65+ in the United States: 2005*. U.S. Census Bureau Current Population Reports P23-209. Washington: U.S. Government Printing Office.

Houtven, C. H. V. and Norton, E. C. (2004). Informal care and health care use of older adults. *Journal of Health Economics*, *23*, 1159–1180.

Huynh, P. T., Schoen, C., Osborn, R., and Holmgren, A. L. (2006). *The U.S. Health Care Divide: Disparities in Primary Care Experiences by Income*. New York: The Commonwealth Fund.

Johnson, R. W. and Weiner, J. M. (2006). *A Profile of Frail Older Americans and Their Caregivers* (Occasional Paper Number 8). Washington: Urban Institute.

Lawton, M. P. and Brody, E. M. (1969). Assessment of older people: Self-maintaining and instrumental activities of daily living. *The Gerontologist*, 9, 179–186.

Li, L. W. (2005). Longitudinal changes in the amount of informal care among publicly paid home care recipients. *The Gerontologist*, 45, 465–473.

McAuley, W. J. and Blieszner, R. (1985). Selection of long-term care arrangements by older community residents. *The Gerontologist*, 25, 188–193.

Metha, K. M., Yaffe, K., and Covinsky, K. E. (2002). Cognitive impairment, depressive symptoms, and functional decline in older people. *Journal of the American Geriatrics Society*, 50, 1045–1050.

Office of Disability, Aging and Long-Term Care. (2003). *Changes in Elderly Disability Rates and the Implications for Health Care Utilization and Cost*. Washington: U.S. Department of Health and Human Services, Assistant Secretary for Planning and Evaluation, Office of Disability, Aging and Long-term Care.

Pandya, S. M. (2005). *Racial and Ethnic Differences among Older Adults in Long-Term Care Service Use* (Fact Sheet No. 119). Washington: AARP Public Policy Institute.

Spector, W. D. and Fleishman, J. A. (2001). *The Characteristics of Long-Term Care Users* (AHRQ publication No. 00-0049). Rockville, MD: Agency for Healthcare Research and Quality.

Spillman, B. C. and Black, K. J. (2005). *The Size of the Long-Term Care Population in Residential Care: A Review of Estimates and Methodology*. Washington: Office of Disability, Aging, and Long-term Care Policy, U.S. Department of Health and Human Services.

U.S. Department of Health and Human Services. (2005). *Reauthorization of the Older Americans Act: Testimony*. Retrieved May 11 from http://www.hhs.gov/asl/testify/t970709a.html.

Wallace, S. P., Levy-Storms, L., Kingston, R. S., and Anderson, R. A. (1998). The persistence of race and ethnicity in the use of long-term care. *Journal of Gerontology: Social Sciences*, 53B, S28–S42.

Wolf, D. A., Hunt, K., and Knickman, J. (2005). Perspectives on the recent decline in disability at older ages. *The Milbank Quarterly*, 83, 365–395.

Chapter 6

Younger Individuals with Disabilities: Compatibility of Long-Term Care and Independent Living

Arthur W. Blaser

Contents

85

> Independent living is not doing things by yourself, it is being in control
> of how things are done.

> **Judy Heumann**
> *World Institute on Disability, p. 8*

Most attention to "long-term care" (LTC) is concerned with aging. As people age
the likelihood of using LTC increases, a relationship that is growing stronger. There
have always been, however, and will always be, younger individuals in the LTC system. Many of the issues confronted by younger and older individuals are the same,
whereas some others vary.

Since the 1970s, there has been an ongoing debate over whether medical professionals or users should direct LTC. The consumer-control debate is now accompanied by a new issue: which supports can best aid LTC users. This chapter focuses on
one group of LTC users—younger people with disabilities (PWDs).

Emphasis on consumer-directed LTC began with many younger users and activists, and has spread throughout the age span. Supports, necessary for complete integration in society, are also important across the age span. For those users defined as
"working age," this includes various services beyond the confines of medical care, such
as those related to employment, housing, and transportation. Ultimately, integration
requires reconceptualizing our fundamental notions about age, disability, and LTC.

Since the 1990s, LTC policy has been in crisis. As the 2005 Deficit Reduction
Act exemplifies, escalating costs are only one of the elements; limited choice and
abridgement of disability rights are critical problems as well. To address these issues
completely, we must look at the often-overlooked younger LTC users.

The "institutional bias" in LTC policy has meant that people were placed in
restrictive environments. Especially among younger residents of nursing homes and
care facilities, residents sought a role in directing their fates. Along with advocates
and surrogates (often family members making decisions to give "voice" to their kin),
younger PWDs sought to be shapers of as well as being shaped by LTC policy.

In a study that included many California LTC users, Benjamin and Matthias
(2001, p. 633) wrote that "service planners tend to equate physical limitations

with psychological and spiritual dependency among elderly people, and to focus on dependency based on functional limits in the absence of assistance, rather than on the potential for independence that may result from providing assistance." The "service planners" often ignore younger individuals altogether. The disability rights movement's major focus since the end of the twentieth century has been with creating LTC options that are consistent with, and not opposed to, independent living.

Benjamin (1996, p. 75), in his essay "Trends among Younger Persons with Disability or Chronic Disease," depicting "recent changes," indicated that "For much of the 1970s and 1980s, long-term care was considered synonymous with services for older persons, and specifically with nursing home care for older adults." He and other researchers have identified a major problem in LTC planning. Institutional facilities have been overemphasized, and the search for LTC alternatives has been underemphasized. Although he wrote in the 1990s, the issues Benjamin identified are still with us.

In the sections that follow, I will discuss key terms such as "disability," "younger," and "LTC"; identify the most common types of LTC providers and sources of information; describe younger PWDs and some historical milestones; present responses to the current LTC crisis; and assess the place of younger PWDs in the overall LTC "picture."

A "Puzzle Population": Younger People with Disabilities and Long-Term Care

This chapter concerns a population that defies precise definition. Moreover, the "disabled"/"nondisabled" borderline tends to be somewhat fuzzy (Sheets, 2005). It has become a cliché to say that "disability" is an attribute that people acquire or lose on a regular basis. However, contracting a disability is much more common than having it disappear or be cured. Increasingly, a PWD will acquire multiple disabilities over time. Similarly, application of the label "younger population" is always changing. At the same time, what qualifies as LTC may be very brief, and merely reflects an absence of support. As one can argue, there is one piece of the LTC "puzzle" that is clear: the LTC system has always had problems in satisfying users, and without significant changes such problems are likely to grow.

People with Disabilities: Patients and Long-Term Care Users

PWDs are classified as "disabled" by medical professionals, government officials, and often even themselves. Identification of a PWD as "disabled" stems from a specific approach or "model of disability." Some other common classifications are the treatment, compensation and rehabilitation, and civil rights models (Switzer, 2003, pp. 7–10); the medical or clinical model, emphasizing functional limitations, superseded by a sociopolitical or minority group model (Schriner and Scotch, pp. 164–165); and the medical, civil rights (also "social"), and cultural models (Longmore, 2003, pp. 215–224). In each case, the later approaches emphasize liberating people from their medical diagnoses. As such, LTC is addressed differently, as a means of organizing society with a wide range of supports rather than just narrowly focusing on medical treatments.

Some social scientists distinguish "impairments" usually identified in medical diagnoses (i.e., muscular dystrophy, dementia, or hemiplegia from a stroke) from "disabilities" that may be imposed by an environment that makes it difficult for the individual to function (Oliver, 1990). While bearing in mind the "disabling environments" in which LTC is often carried out, this chapter distinguishes younger PWDs by impairments that limit "major life activities" (such as walking or talking) as used in the Americans with Disabilities Act (ADA) and by the U.S. Bureau of the Census. PWDs using LTC require assistance with activities of daily living (ADLs), such as dressing or toileting, or instrumental activities of daily living (IADLs), such as using transportation or personal finance.

Policymakers and analysts label PWDs using LTC as consumers, users, clients, customers, patients, aid recipients, or rights holders. As with "care" (discussed in the following paragraphs), each of the labels may have a different implication. One may imply a hierarchy, with the PWD following the instructions of nondisabled "helpers." The term "client," for instance, is allied to a social work model, and "clients" are at the bottom of a presumed hierarchy. As Batavia (2003) argues, "patient" relegates the person who uses LTC to the "sick role"; it is closely tied to the medical model. Similarly to Batavia and others, I generally prefer "user" or "consumer" to describe the recipient of LTC services.

Similarly, policymakers and analysts may label LTC services as assistance, attendance, or caregiving. Designations may be consequential: "home health assistance" is a mandatory service under Medicaid, available to recipients in every state, whereas personal assistance is optional. Batavia and others have expressed a preference for the term "assistant" rather than "attendant" because the latter term implies the disabled person's passivity (Batavia et al., 1991). In this chapter, "personal assistance services" refer to supports that are directed by the PWD (often but not always for LTC).

Younger People

Fluidity in terms and their application are characteristic of the "younger" puzzle population of PWDs in LTC. Just as one can be a PWD (or not) in different times and places, one can be "younger" (or not) in different times and places. "Younger" is an ambiguous label: it may mean below 65, 60, 55, or even 50 years of age, the minimum age level for eligibility in the American Association of Retired Persons (AARP). The federal Older Americans Act uses eligibility thresholds of 60, whereas other laws use 62 or 65. Specific ages determine eligibility for Medicare, Social Security benefits, and age discrimination complaints.

A common age range for "younger people" is 18–64, although other breakdowns may be used. "Nonelderly" is a frequently used substitute for "younger." Batavia (2003), who wrote extensively about "independent living" and LTC, distinguishes children and "working-age adults." Similarly, some Bureau of the Census classifications categorize people below 5 or 18 years of age as "the younger" population.

Long-Term Care

LTC is a label applied or misapplied to places, policies, supports, and service users. Although PWDs often are spoken of as "in" LTC, they should be more accurately viewed as using LTC services. The former implies that a person is in an institutionalized setting, such as a nursing home. In reality, most PWDs receive LTC at home.

LTC services fall along a continuum, with degrees of hierarchy. In addition, terms such as government-run institutions, nursing homes, home healthcare, residential care, group homes, home and community-based services—sometimes supported by public authority, as in California's In-Home Supportive Services (IHSS) system—personal assistance, and independent living may overlap with each other. Some of them also serve individuals who are not LTC users.

LTC is often contrasted with acute care. The goal of acute medical services, in contrast to LTC, is to cure the person's condition. PWDs, in contrast, require long-term services. The duration of assistance is specified by some sources, such as in the National Long-Term Care Survey (NLTCS), as three months or more.

Many people attach a negative connotation to the word "care," implying that it means the provision of assistance. "Care" may suggest a hierarchy between the "caregiver" and the care user. Eustis and Fischer (1992) noted that differing attitudes toward the word "care" were one area of difference among older and younger recipients of assistance; the latter tend to be less receptive to the term. Younger users often prefer "help" or "assistance," terms that are less likely to imply dependence. Johnson (2000) argues that one could reject some uses of "care," as in "caregiver," whereas accepting others, such as "personal care attendant." She is concerned that PWDs commonly are left out of the "care equation." Although LTC transcends age classification, that fact is not always recognized.

Resources

Observers portray incomplete and inconsistent pictures of LTC resources and information sources. This is partly because of the differences in their conceptualizations of disability, age categories, and LTC itself. Regardless, as argued in this chapter, the overall availability of consumer-directed LTC and supports are inadequate.

As discussed earlier, the overwhelming majority of LTC is provided by relatives. However, PWDs may not have any family, or the latter could be unable or unwilling to provide sufficient care. As parents of younger PWDs age, they can become frail or disabled themselves. In addition, many LTC recipients view care by family members as violating their sense of independence.

For low-income older and younger LTC users, Medicaid is a common source for LTC funding. PWDs and the frail elderly may qualify for "medically necessary" LTC as long as they have income or resources at or below their state's qualifying level, which would preclude qualification for Medicaid. Individuals who are not eligible for Medicaid must purchase LTC with their own resources. Given the low employment rates for PWDs, this is only a small minority of the younger LTC population.

Although institutional care represents the largest amount of Medicaid LTC funding across age groups, the proportion going to community-based alternatives is increasing. Using Medstat data, Gold (2006) notes that by the fiscal year 2005 "63% of . . . national LTC expenditures ($59.34 [billion]) went to institutions, but 37% went to community-based services ($35.16 [billion])" (para. 8). In contrast, 12 years earlier, "84% of the . . . Medicaid national Long Term Care (LTC) expenditures ($35.4 [billion]) went to institutions (i.e., nursing facilities and ICF-MRs) and only 16% went to community-based services (i.e., Medicaid waivers, home health care, and personal care options) ($6.7 [billion])" (Gold, 2006). As discussed on pp. 97 and 98, waivers are now a major part of the Medicaid policy. Many advocates of independence and choice argue that community-based services need to become the rule, rather than the exception for LTC.

Policymakers increasingly base future LTC strategies on LTC insurance, usually marketed as protection for old age. People may be motivated to purchase it because of the fear of disability. For many younger PWDs (especially for those significantly disabled from birth), LTC insurance obviously is not an option. One company, which offers "The Maximum Lifetime Benefit Acceleration Rider (the Value Rider)," notes that it "helps Baby Boomers by increasing their long term care pool of money for use during early claims" (Business Update, 2006, para. 2). However, the rider presumes the PWD's unemployment because the policy "would allow the spouse" (not the younger disabled person) "to continue working" (para. 6). More importantly, it probably does not even attempt to provide sufficient supports so that the LTC user could participate in the workforce, if he or she so desired.

Information Sources

Information about younger PWDs using LTC can be gleaned from many places, but with each one there are caveats. Information about PWDs often will not include age breakdowns or individuals in LTC. The data usually reflects places from where it can be drawn most easily, such as the restricted environments of nursing homes. At the same time, younger persons using LTC tend to be overlooked because researchers are more interested in the elderly. Therefore, informal support recipients, especially younger PWDs, are the users least likely to be counted. As Batavia (2003) points out, no records are required under the "informal support" model. Based on estimates by the commerce department, he places the number of recipients of informal LTC at 7.2 million people. Additionally, unless personal assistance is obtained through an agency, even information on paid help is limited.

Extensive data on PWDs (most not users of LTC) is available through the Bureau of the Census, and particularly the 2003 American Community Survey (ACS) (http://www.census.gov/hhes/www/disability/2003acs.html). The latter includes extensive breakdowns by factors such as age, state of residence, and ethnicity. A major problem with the use of census data is that people in nursing homes are not included (Waldrop and Stern, 2003).

The National Organization on Disability (NOD) commissions and disseminates periodic surveys conducted by Louis Harris & Associates, an organization that uses large interview samples. It measures access to healthcare as well as political, religious, and social participation. NOD reports on a subgroup of the Harris respondents who self-identify as disabled. The first NOD survey was conducted in 1986; the fifth survey and recent data are from 2004. The latest one was based on telephone interviews "with 1,038 non-institutionalized Americans with disabilities and 988 Americans without disabilities ages 18 and over" (p. 117). Focusing only on noninstitutionalized people, it found that "19% of people with disabilities use some form of personal assistance services for help with basic needs such as getting dressed, preparing meals, or bathing" (National Organization on Disability, 2004, p. 11).

The most thorough study, and the one most germane to our inquiry, was conducted by Spector and Fleishman's (2000). Based on the 1994 Disability Supplement to the National Health Interview Survey (NHIS) (community-based users), and the 1996 Medical Expenditure Panel Survey Nursing Home Component (nursing home residents), they compare LTC consumers by age and setting.

The NHIS (http://www.cdc.gov/nchs/about/major/nhis/about200606.htm) is conducted annually by the Bureau of the Census for the National Center for Health Statistics of the Centers for Disease Control and Prevention. Sample sizes are very large (50,000–100,000 people). The 2000 NHIS was a primary basis for an analysis by the Georgetown University Long-Term Care Financing Project (2003), titled "Who Needs Long-Term Care?" The 1994 Disability Supplement to the NHIS, used by Spector and Fleishman, is also known as the NHIS-D. As with the annual NHIS, it serves as an excellent source of information on the health of noninstitutionalized Americans, but does not include many people receiving LTC services. Nor do any of its questions focus on LTC.

Extensive nursing home data is available through the National Nursing Home Survey (NNHS) (http://www.cdc.gov/nchs/nnhs.htm), although the most recent one was in 1999 (earlier surveys were taken in 1973–1974, 1977, 1985, 1995, and 1997). The NNHS, conducted by the National Center for Health Statistics, includes residents and staff from up to 1500 facilities with Medicare or Medicaid certification. The surveys offer extensive information about nursing home residents, but not about other users of LTC.

An NLTCS (http://www.nlcs.aas.duke.edu/) gathered a plethora of data on six occasions between 1992 and 2004 about Americans aged above 65 in LTC. The U.S. Bureau of the Census administers the NLTCS; funding comes from the National Institute on Aging and Duke University. The younger individuals using LTC, however, are outside the scope of NLTCS.

Medicare and Medicaid offer extensive information about certified facilities, and about the increasing number of recipients of personal care services. Prominent disability rights advocate and lawyer Steve Gold (www.stevegoldada.com) analyzes statistics related to nursing home stays of Medicaid recipients, especially through Medicaid's Minimum Data Set (MDS) (http://www.cms.hhs.gov/Minimum DataSets20/). In some cases, this data can be compared with expenditures and the use of home and community-based services. Although it offers in-depth detail about LTC expenditures, the information does not include comprehensive demographic breakdowns or include users of LTC who are not supported by Medicaid.

Completed MDS forms include data on age for every Medicaid-supported nursing home resident. But in most reports, the age data is not used. Moreover, the MDS does not provide any information on attitudes toward LTC.

Private research firms such as Medstat (http://www.medstat.com/; a prominent source in Gold's analyses) and Mathematica Policy Research (http://www.mathematica-mpr.com/health/longtermcare.asp) are increasingly generating new types of data germane to LTC, including categorization by age. Mathematica recently evaluated Arkansas (Independent Choices), Florida, and New Jersey (Money Follows the Person) programs, all designed to enhance the consumer role in LTC.

Finally, two centers evaluating LTC data are at the University of California, San Francisco: the Disability Statistics Center (http://dsc.ucsf.edu/main.php) and the Center for Personal Assistance Service (http://www.pascenter.org/home/index.php). These centers, and other similar ones, report on data gathered by many of the organizations mentioned in the "Demographics" section.

Characteristics of Younger People with Disabilities

Policymakers, scholars, and activists continuously debate similarities and differences across LTC consumer age groups, partly because circumstances are ever changing. For instance, a large generation gap in one time and location may not be present in the future ones. Many authors refer to the importance of "bridging the gap" between the aging (including LTC users, policy makers, administrators, and people who study aging) and the younger disability community (including users of LTC, policy makers, and people who study disability) (Ansello and Eustis, 1992).

Demographics

Younger individuals with disabilities are a population in flux, as is the population of PWD users of LTC, and subgroups of the PWD-LTC consumer population. The overall LTC population is a large minority of a much larger minority of the U.S. population, PWDs. In the 2000 Census, 19.4 percent of the U.S. population was disabled, or 49.7 million people aged 5 or above (Waldrop and Stern, 2003). For the 16–64 age group, the PWD percentage of the population was 18.6 percent, compared to 41.9 percent for people aged 65 and above (Waldrop and Stern, 2003). Clearly, in both age categories, there is a high percentage of disability, although the likelihood tends to rise with age.

Notwithstanding that numerically there are many younger users of LTC, they are vastly outnumbered by older users proportionally. The Georgetown University Long-Term Care Financing Project (2003) estimates that 1.4 percent of people below the age of 65 years "need" LTC, in contrast to 14 and 50 percent, of those aged above 65 and 85, respectively. Adams (2004) estimates that 4 percent of the U.S. population, about 13 million people, will need LTC at some point in their lives. About 44 percent of the LTC population, or 5,700,000 individuals will be below the age of 65 years.

Most causes of disability cross age groups, but some are more characteristic of younger PWDs. Urban gangs and international warfare are two common reasons for the young onset of disability. Obesity is another (Lakdawalla et al., 2004). Dementia, from traumatic brain injury rather than from Alzheimer's, is more likely to characterize younger than older LTC users (Beattie et al., 2002). These examples, of course, stem from social variables. In addition, better technology has meant the survival of many premature, mostly low-birth-weight babies, contributing to higher numbers of PWDs and a younger LTC population. According to a report from the National Academy of Sciences' Institute of Medicine, "In 2004, 12.5% of U.S. births were premature, a 30% increase over the rate in 1981" (Maugh, 2006, p. A18).

Just how many younger people are LTC users? Batavia (2003) has estimated that 4–5 million adults aged 65 and above were LTC users and 4 million LTC users were aged below 65. Of these, most received care in the community (3.9 million people aged 65 and above and 3.7 million were aged below 65). The 2004 Louis Harris/NOD survey confirmed that informal support is used more frequently than agency help: 77 percent of its respondents relied on family members or friends for assistance, versus 29 percent who relied on home health aides or other paid help.

There has been a major shift away from nursing homes, toward community-based services. This shift involves members of all age groups, and results from both social changes and deliberate government policy. Bernstein et al. (2003) report that the proportion of nursing home residents below 65 years of age declined from 11.6 percent in 1985 to 9.7 percent in 1999. During this time, there was a decrease in the number of people residing in nursing homes, from 6.3 to 5.9 per 1000 individuals. Surprisingly, there was also a slight increase in the number of nursing homes. These newer facilities tend to have fewer occupants than the ones they replace.

Especially for younger users, LTC is mostly received in the community. Using data from 1994 and 1996, Spector and Fleishman (2000) reported that 46.7 percent of those receiving LTC in the community (3,363,000 people) were aged 18–64, whereas 53.3 percent (3,823,000 people) were aged 65 and above. In nursing homes, 8.8 percent (138,000 people) were aged 18–64, and 91.2 percent (1,425,000 people) were aged 65 and above.

Other sources echo the results in Spector and Fleishman (2000). Pandya (2005), for instance, used 1999 NNHS data, which revealed that 18.5 percent of the black and 16.6 percent of the "other nonwhite" nursing home population was below 65 years of age. The comparable figure for white nursing home residents was 8.3 percent.

Younger Long-Term Users: Subgroups

Spector and Fleishman (2000) described certain characteristics of younger LTC users: although more are female than male, the imbalance is much less for those below than those above 65 years of age; the black proportion of the younger PWD population is much greater; younger LTC recipients are more likely to have never been married; and although all groups have very high unemployment rates, 18.7 percent of the LTC recipients of community services are employed.

Another characteristic of younger LTC users is poverty. For LTC users in the community, 26.5 percent of those aged 18–64 are in poverty, compared to 14.7 percent of those aged 65 and above. There is no comparable figure for the 18–64 years of age nursing home population. Because that group almost always relies on Medicaid funding, it is probably even poorer than those people receiving LTC in the community, regardless of age (Spector and Fleishman, 2000).

Age differences or similarities vary greatly among facilities and regions. This often reflects the widely varying LTC policies of state and local governments. Some facilities experienced great increases in younger populations. In New York City's Holly Patterson Geriatric Center, for example, by 2003, about 43 percent of the 655 residents were aged below 65 (Healy, 2003).

In California's IHSS program, there are also noticeable age differences: "Among all recipients in the IHSS program, those assessed as severely cognitively impaired represent 11.8% of those under age 65, 2.4% of those aged 65–74, and 5.4% of those aged 75 and older" (Benjamin and Matthias, 2001, p. 639). As Benjamin and Matthias (2001) recognize, age differences probably reflect the pattern of available support services.

Given a choice, however, nonelderly individuals are especially likely to choose home or community-based alternatives over institutional facilities. But choices have been greatly constrained by policymakers, by society, and sometimes by family members or the lack thereof. Demographic figures indicate only where people receive LTC; they would change with availability of new choices and supports.

Attitudes and Behavior

One of the many gaps (between disabled and nondisabled respondents) identified in the National Organization/Louis Harris survey was in a question about whether respondents worried about going to a nursing home. Thirty-six percent of respondents with disabilities were worried (somewhat worried to extremely worried) versus 23 percent of nondisabled respondents (National Organization on Disability, 2004, p. 139).

Younger PWDs in LTC are particularly concerned about and critical of the constraints that accompany institutionalization, and their complaints tend to be those that are heard. When society undergoes major changes, as it did in the United States during the 1960s and 1970s, the PWD and PWD-LTC populations were not immune. Since then, with continued change in LTC policy, their efforts to promote greater independence and control over their lives have continued.

Chroniclers of the disability rights movement have noted that initially primarily younger activists were involved; they were joined by older individuals later on. As Shapiro (1993, p. 6) wrote, "Older people have avoided affiliation with the disability rights movement. They have grown up with prejudices about a disabled life being a sad and worthless one. Many fear the same stigma will be used to take away their independence." Younger people were less inclined to accept a "sick role" that would leave them incapable of participating completely in society. The age gap has diminished over time, partly due to cooperative efforts of groups such as the National Council on Aging (www.ncoa.org) (representing many older users) and the World Institute on Disability (www.wid.org) (representing many younger users). In addition, many younger activists have grown older.

Higher education levels also lead to greater resolve to control one's medical situation. Batchelder (1999, p. 59) has observed that "Younger and more educated patients are more likely to expect to be involved in decisions about their care and to question their physician's advice." Indeed, in the Spector and Fleishman (2000) data, for both the LTC community and nursing home users, individuals aged 18–64 had received more formal education than users aged 65 and above.

LTC policy has been determined by perceptions about the wants of the elderly who are only partly grounded in reality. "The perception is that older people . . . have accommodated to nursing home placement and are 'soft' on service alternatives that support and maintain independence" (Benjamin, 1996, p. 89). Such a perception may reinforce the stance of those opposed to more home and community-based options. However, the perception may be accurate for some users regardless of age, but not for most people in need of LTC.

Age-based claims of varying validity have influenced policy in almost every subgroup of the LTC population in almost every community around the world. They sometimes foster age-based conflict. Differing perceptions are reflected in the ongoing battle over the fate of San Francisco, California's, Laguna Honda Hospital. One view, reflected in a letter to the editor of the *San Francisco Chronicle*, stated "the 'alternatives' cited by younger disabled advocates do not always work for frail

85-year-olds with multiple medical illnesses" (Palmer, 2005, p. B4). Age-based differences were also a basis of a June 2006 ballot proposition, which lost by an almost 3–1 margin. As reported in the *San Francisco Chronicle*, "Supporters of Proposition D had argued that too many beds in the skilled nursing and long-term care facility are filled by younger, violent patients who put at risk the elderly people who have traditionally been housed there" (Vega, 2006, p. B2). Similarly, three years earlier *The New York Times* had made similar charges, arguing that drug use in nursing homes is emblematic of their changing populations (Healy, 2003).

A Denver facility's experience also reveals age differences: "There are additional costs, such as higher food costs for younger adults with bigger appetites and anger-management issues that arise from having a degenerative disability" (Padilla and Gong, 2003, p. 50). As with many differences, however, the latter may not be based on age alone.

The institutional bias, inherent in LTC policy over the decades, has diminished. There is now a larger role for individual choices. This has been welcomed by members of all age groups, but particularly by younger PWDs. Despite the fatalism of many LTC users, more and more PWDs value and seek alternatives to institutional facilities. In fact, most age-based difference in attitude toward LTC is one of degree rather than of kind. Regardless, younger people tend to be given more options than older people. According to the Kane and Kane (2001, p. 115), "in decelerating order, cash, vouchers, and individually employed workers rather than packages from agencies are used to enhance control and flexibility for younger consumers." They continue, "Younger persons with disabilities reject the concept of standard home health care, which is considered a major step toward autonomy for older consumers, compared with entering a nursing home" (p. 116).

Such observations are consistent with what Walsh and LeRoy (2004, p. 134) observed in their cross-national survey of women with disabilities "aging well": "the wishes of the service recipients are too often lost in the squeeze. The rush to address half of the normalization equation (least restrictive living arrangement) runs over the other half of the equation (personal choice and self-determination)." Many LTC users, regardless of age, have commented on a lack of choice and arbitrarily restrictive settings.

In California, Benjamin and Matthias (2001) found that age made a difference in users' preferences. However, they ascribe this to more familiarity with consumer direction among younger recipients. As older recipients gain more experience with consumer direction, as community supports are developed, and as younger recipients become older, the preference gap presumably will narrow.

Changes over Time: Milestones

Younger PWDs' LTC use has adapted to changing political, economic, and social factors. Four of the more important ones have been deinstitutionalization and self-determination; the independent living movement; the ADA of 1990; and the

Olmstead Supreme Court decision in 1999. All of these drew from other, related movements in the United States, such as the fights for civil, consumer, and women's rights.

Deinstitutionalization, Self-Determination, and Independent Living

For many younger users of LTC, "top-down" and "bottom-up" approaches have been influential sources of change. The "top-down" approaches resulted in the closing and changing of large state hospitals. To proponents, the changes reflected major reform; to critics it signified the "dumping" of people into different (often privately owned) institutions.

Scala and Nerney (2000, p. 57) underscored the historical (and continued) importance of a "bottom-up" approach to LTC. They wrote that "the notion of self-direction or self-determination grew out of a recognition that, no matter the disability, having control over major aspects of one's life was just as important to those with intellectual disabilities as it was for any other person with a disability." Particularly for younger users with intellectual/developmental disabilities (ID/DD), groups such as The Arc (www.thearc.org) and People First encouraged active participation in LTC. Organizations such as the Bazelon Center (www.bazelon. org) and the Center for Self-Determination (http://www.self-determination.com/) emphasize consumer options and autonomy.

The independent living movement (http://www.ncil.org/ and http://www. independentliving.org/) is associated with Ed Roberts' activities at the University of California–Berkeley in the 1960s (Shapiro, 1993). Because "living" would be independent (while also interdependent), the centers spawned by the movement were nonresidential. From their beginning, the right of PWDs (many of whom were LTC users) to LTC choice was essential for these Centers of Independent Living (CILs). Many of them provide support services, including housing referral and vocational services, to enable LTC users to live outside of institutions.

Consumer direction of LTC is a central independent living principle. According to one source, "The idea of consumer-directed services originated over two decades ago among younger persons with disabilities in the disability rights and independent living movements" (Mahoney et al., 2002, p. 75). Batavia (2002, p. 64) argues that "Perhaps the most powerful assertion of positive autonomy in health care today is the demand by many people with disabilities to control the circumstances in which they receive their long-term care." Independent living advocates demand for "positive autonomy" in LTC has been labeled "consumer direction" (Batavia, 2002).

Batavia (1991, p. 531) has pointed out that "The need for personal assistance is not limited to any age group or any other demographic category." Yet, "Perhaps the main reason that the independent living model is largely overlooked by policymakers in this country is that long-term care policy has focused primarily on the frail elderly population." Although "independent living" is not inherently the province of younger people, the perception that it is has constrained its growth.

The Americans with Disabilities Act

The ADA, signed into law on July 26, 1990, was the result of an active social movement. The movement's goals went beyond traditional civil rights, such as rights to nondiscrimination and to participation. They included access to medical care, and to a full range of rights affected by LTC. The ADA's promise was that PWDs should no longer be segregated and subject to unequal opportunities because of a restrictive environment. The ADA involved a broader application of rights than those guaranteed through the earlier Rehabilitation Act of 1973.

Olmstead v. L.C. and E.W.

The U.S. disability rights movement has had mixed success in meeting its goals through the courts. In several court decisions, such as *Garrett v. Alabama, Toyota v. Williams,* and *Chevron v. Echazabal,* the U.S. Supreme Court interpreted the ADA narrowly, limiting the scope of disability rights. In contrast, the decision in *Olmstead v. L.C. and E.W.* (1999) was welcomed by disability rights advocates. It resulted in an integration mandate, exemplified by the specific plaintiffs and by the spate of action that followed. Implementation of *Olmstead* has become the central concern of many disability rights advocates and policy makers.

Lois Curtis and Elaine Wilson, aged 31 and 47, respectively, sought the right to live in a community setting rather than in the Georgia Regional Hospital in Atlanta. By a 6–3 margin, the Supreme Court agreed that their ability to live independently suggested that continued hospitalization was a form of discrimination prohibited by the ADA. As Justice Ruth Bader Ginsburg wrote in the majority opinion, "The ADA both requires all public entities to refrain from discrimination, . . . and specifically identifies unjustified 'segregation' of persons with disabilities as a 'form of discrimination.'" Curtis and Wilson's institutionalization, despite their wish to live in a community setting, was impermissible segregation. The "integration mandate" would soon be broadly applied to all age and disability groups.

The emphasis on positive rights was significant in the *Olmstead* decision. Georgia not only was prohibited from keeping Curtis and Wilson in a segregated setting, it was also obligated by the ADA to provide community-based alternatives. Moreover, the state could not even argue that alternatives were not available. Every state must now provide support services to enable community living.

Many disability rights groups, including NCIL, American Association of People with Disabilities (ADAPT), and The Arc, sought wide application of the *Olmstead* decision. In analyzing the positive rights guarantees within the ADA, legal scholar Weber (2004, p. 290) wrote that "Individually, the costs of service at home or in community housing is much cheaper than it is in institutions. The real difficulty is what is sometimes referred to as the woodwork problem: Making services in community settings available will bring people who need the services 'out of the woodwork.'" Enlightened LTC policy meets people's needs, and would give many younger PWDs opportunities to participate in society. Bringing people out of the "woodwork" is consistent with the *Olmstead* rationale.

Long-Term Care: Crisis and Responses

Although there is a wide agreement that there is an LTC crisis, there are disagreements about the nature of the crisis. There are more people using LTC primarily because of rising life expectancy and improved medical care. Shapiro (1993, p. 5) noted "Medicine once promised to wipe out disability by finding cures. Instead, doctors only spurred a disability population explosion by keeping people alive longer." Unfortunately, the growth in LTC has not been accompanied by supports for employment, transportation, housing alternatives, and so on. For governments, greater LTC demands may (infrequently) bring higher costs. Recipients, in contrast, are concerned with their quality of life. However, "quality of life" may be interpreted differently by different people.

Some nursing home administrators argue that quality care is possible in institutions. However, one must consider the needs of all LTC users, particularly younger people, often specifically their alienation. One way to do this is to provide separate accommodations for them. However, for many others, segregation—especially in institutions—is not the answer.

Most analysts, advocates, and policymakers worldwide extol community-based LTC alternatives, especially the ones that are consumer directed. Indeed, agency and consumer-directed services constitute a steadily growing proportion of Medicaid LTC expenditures.

Home and Community-Based Services (HCBS) grew with use of Section 1915(b) and 1915(c) waivers and Section 1115 waivers of the Social Security Act. They allow the Secretary of Health and Human Services to "waive" conditions that would otherwise limit states in their use of Medicaid funds.

Batavia (2001) describes the slow initial use of the waivers, followed by more rapid growth. By 1999, Medicaid's HCBS program was a part of every state's programs. Now it is a centerpiece of LTC strategy under U.S. President George W. Bush through his New Freedom Initiative grants. HCBS programs have been emphasized throughout the Bush presidency, and this intensified with the 2005 Deficit Reduction Act.

The Deficit Reduction Act includes a program partially implementing principles long urged by disability rights activists, "Money Follows the Person."

This suggests that the person using LTC, or a surrogate, should be able to "shop" for their LTC rather than give the initiative to providers. The "Money Follows the Person" program enables the secretary of HHS to provide grants to states to promote the availability of community-based services. Some states, such as New Mexico, have also adopted "Money Follows the Person" programs on their own.

Unlike 1915(b) (Freedom of Choice) and 1915(c) (HCBS waivers), the 1115 (Research and Demonstration) waivers are limited in time, generally up to five years. One use of the 1115 waiver was for the Cash and Counseling program, funded and promoted by the Robert Wood Johnson Foundation. It began in 1998, and extended from the initial three states (Arkansas, New Jersey, and Florida) to twelve others (as of July 12, 2006). Certain people requiring LTC are given money to purchase their own services, allowing them to live at home. They, rather than agencies, are completely responsible for their own LTC choices.

Cash and Counseling assessments indicate successes within every age group, and for every type of disability (Bunn, 2006; Cash allowance program better suits Medicaid, 2003; Dale et al., 2003). According to a study by Simon-Rusinowitz and Mahoney (2001, p. 10), "Interest peaked in the 30's–50's (about 60% of consumers), about 50% of consumers in their 60's, and about 30–40% of consumers in their 70's–90's were interested in the cash option." Interestingly, there was less (although still considerable) interest among the youngest adults, compared with those who were middle-aged.

Qualitative advantages of the "Cash and Counseling" approach may be less important to policy makers than the economic ones. Bagentsos (2004, p. 80) warns, "disability rights activists should regard the conservative agenda behind the cash-and-counseling program as a threatening one. Such a program would probably reduce the wages paid to personal assistants, as they would move from working for (frequently unionized) home health agencies to working for hard-to-unionize individual household employers." Indeed, some of the cost advantages of consumer-directed options are made possible by the low wages of personal assistants. Bagentsos' answer to the LTC crisis is not reinstitutionalization, rather it is to acknowledge a complete range of economic and human costs.

The Medicaid Community Attendant Services and Supports Act (MiCASSA) (S. 401 and H.R. 910 in the 109th Congress [2006, slightly modified as the Community Choice Act in the 110th Congress]) is a proposal to amend Title 19 of the Social Security Act. With its adoption, waivers under Medicaid would no longer have to be granted to states to make HCBS available. The latter would become the rule, rather than the exception to institutional care. Similar proposals have been in Congress since 1997.

Clearly, progress has been made. However, although younger PWDs have benefited disproportionately from all of these changes, most government resources still focus on nursing home care.

Conclusions: Integration and Long-Term Care

Attention to younger individuals using LTC enables a focus on four common assumptions, each one directing ones attention to a factor that has some influence on LTC policy. They are (1) age, (2) the nature of a PWD's disability, (3) the quantity of LTC expenditures, and (4) the power of economic and political interests. These, however, should not be a basis for unwarranted reductionism.

Age and Integration

Many examinations of age and LTC proceed from opposite assumptions: "age makes a big difference"; and "age does not make a difference." Along with the former assumption is a related claim that the aging process should be considered separately from that of disability, *per se*; what is true for younger individuals with disabilities often will not be true for older LTC users. In reality, there are often overlaps between younger and older users' needs and interests, although they are not identical. Indeed, the National Council on Disability (2004, p. 56) concluded "The studies suggest that sometimes age matters and sometimes it does not."

The most promising LTC approaches address aging issues, but do not ignore younger PWDs. Supporters of MiCASSA, for instance, include not only disability activist organizations, such as ADAPT and the World Institute on Disability, but also the Gray Panthers, the National Association of Area Agencies on Aging, and the National Council on the Aging.

Cross-Disability

Many claims that younger people with particular disabilities are poorly suited for some forms of LTC are based on unfounded stereotypes. Yet the National Council on Disability (2004, p. 10) found "The type and severity of disability do not seem to determine individuals' preferences regarding care: interest in consumer direction extends across a range of disabilities and ages." The kinds of services available tend to be more related to political and economic clout than to preferences. Although community supports will differ across a range of disabilities, the importance of consumer choice does and should not.

Quantity of Expenditures

Many accounts of the "LTC crisis" are limited to increased demand on a costly LTC system. Such financial pressures result not only from an aging population, but also from medical technology that makes it likely that younger PWDs will survive longer. However, these issues address only a part of the LTC crisis. We need to ensure that the disabled population will generally remain or become productive community members. And although enabling initiatives, such as access to assistive technology, employment, and transportation can save money over time, there could be substantial start-up costs. Moreover, the objective of containing LTC expenditures must not obscure the rights of LTC users.

Political, Social, and Economic Power

LTC policy making, which too often minimizes the consumer role, is overly influenced by the nursing home industry. We need to involve other stakeholders to a greater extent, including users and disability rights organizations. Importantly, we must empower LTC users so that they can have greater control over LTC policy and their own lives.

References

Adams, R. (2004). Medicaid reform: Will efforts to cut costs hurt the poor? *Congressional Quarterly Researcher, 14*, 589–612. Retrieved July 17, 2006 from CQ Researcher Online, http://library.cqpress.com/cqresearcher/cqresrre2004071600.

Ansello, E. and Eustis, N. (1992). A common stake?: Investigating the emerging 'intersection' of aging and disabilities. *Generations, 19*, 5–8.

Bagenstos, S. (2004). The future of disability law. *Yale Law Journal, 114*, 1–83.

Batavia, A. (2001). A right to personal assistance services: "Most integrated setting appropriate" requirements and the independent living model of long-term care. *American Journal of Law & Medicine, 27*, 17–43.

Batavia, A. (2002). The growing prominence of independent living and consumer direction as principles in long-term care: A content analysis and implications for elderly people with disabilities. *Elder Law Journal, 10*, 263–287.

Batavia, A. (2003). *Independent Living: A Viable Option for Long-Term Care*. Clearwater, FL: ABI Professional Publications.

Batavia, A., DeJong, G., and McKnew, L. (1991). Toward a national personal assistance program: The independent living model of long-term care for persons with disabilities. *Journal of Health Politics, Policy, and Law, 16*, 523–545.

Batchelder, T. (1999). Medical anthropology: Qualitative research on patient experiences and implications for long-term care facilities. *Townsend Letter for Doctors & Patients*, November, pp. 56–61.

Beattie, A. M., Daker-White, G., Gilliard, J., and Means, R. (2002). Younger people in dementia care: A review of service needs, service provision and models of good practice. *Aging & Mental Health, 6*, 205–212.

Benjamin, A. E. (1996). Trends among younger persons with disability or chronic illness. In Binstock, R., Cluff, L., and von Mering, O. (Eds.), *The Future of Long-Term Care: Social and Policy Issues*. Baltimore, MD: Johns Hopkins University Press, pp. 75–95.

Benjamin, A. E. and Matthias, R. E. (2001). Age, consumer direction, and outcomes of supportive services at home. *The Gerontologist, 41*, 632–642.

Bernstein, A., Hing, E., Moss, A., Allen, K., Siller A., and Tiggle, R. (2003). *Health Care in America: Trends in Utilization*. Hyattsville, MD: National Center for Health Statistics.

Bunn, B. (2006). A new class of employees: Family members aiding the disabled. *University of Pennsylvania Journal of Labor and Employment Law, 8*, 505–521.

Business Update (2006). New product offered for early long-term care claims. *Medicine and Law Weekly,* 149 p, June 23. Available: http://www.lexisnexis.com/universe.

Cash allowance program better suits Medicaid (2003). *Disability Compliance Bulletin, 27*(2), December 24. Available: http://www.lexisnexis.com/universe.

Dale, S., Brown, R., Phillips, B., Schore, J., and Carlson, B. (2003). The effects of Cash and Counseling on personal care services and Medicaid costs in Arkansas. *Health Affairs,* Web Exclusive, November 19.

Eustis, N. N. and Fischer, L. R. (1992). Common needs, different solutions? *Generations, 16*, 17–22.

Georgetown University Long-Term Care Financing Project. (2003). Who needs long-term care? Retrieved June 15, 2006, from http://ltc.georgetown.edu/pdfs/whois.pdf.

Gold, S. (2006). Change is happening: Look at FY 2005 MA [Medicaid] expenditures. *Information Bulletin,* 117, July 6 (E-mail newsletter and on-line at www.stevegoldada.com).

Healy, P. (2003). Nursing homes face challenge as the young fill the beds. *The New York Times,* December 10, B1, B5.

Johnson, M. (2000). The "care" juggernaut. *Ragged Edge Magazine,* November–December, 10–14.

Kane, R. and Kane, R. (2001). What older people want from long-term care, and how they can get it. *Health Affairs, 20*, 114–127.

Lakdawalla, D., Bhattacharya, J., and Goldman, D. (2004). Are the young becoming more disabled? *Health Affairs, 23*, 168–176.

Longmore, P. (2003). *Why I Burned My Book and Other Essays on Disability.* Philadelphia, PA: Temple University Press.

Mahoney, K. J., Desmond, S., Simon-Rusinowitz, L., Loughlin, D. M., and Squillace, M. R. (2002). Consumer preferences for a cash option versus traditional services: Telephone survey results for New Jersey elders and adults. *Journal of Disability Policy Studies, 13*, 74–86.

Maugh, T. H. II. (2006). Rates of prematurity, low birth weight highest ever. *Los Angeles Times,* A18.

National Council on Disability. (2004). *Consumer-Directed Health Care: How Well Does It Work?* Washington: NCD. Available: http://www.ncd.gov/newsroom/publications/2004/pdf/consumerdirected.pdf.

National Organization on Disability. (2004). *2004 N.O.D. Survey of Americans with Disabilities.* Washington: National Organization on Disability.

Oliver, M. (1990). *The Politics of Disablement.* London: Macmillan.

Olmstead v. L. C. and E. W. (1999). 527 U.S. 581. Available: http://www.lexisnexis.com/universe (online).

Padilla, P. and Gong, J. (2003). Marycrest assisted living's venture into *Olmstead* territory. *Nursing Homes Long-Term Care Management, 52*(1), 50–51.

Palmer, T. (2005). Letters to the editor: SF's elderly need full sized Laguna Honda. *San Francisco Chronicle,* B4.

Pandya, S. (2005). *Racial and Ethnic Differences among Older Adults in Long-Term Care Service Use.* Washington: American Association of Retired People. Retrieved July 14, 2006 from http://www.aarp.org/research/housing-mobility/caregiving/fs119_ltc.html.

Scala, M. and Nerney, T. (2000). People first: The consumers in consumer direction. *Generations, 24*(3), 55–59.

Schriner, K. and Scotch, R. (2003). The ADA and the meaning of disability. In Krieger, L. H. (Ed.), *Backlash against the ADA: Reinterpreting Disability Rights*. Ann Arbor, MI: University of Michigan, pp. 164–188.

Shapiro, J. (1993). *No Pity: People with Disabilities Forging a New Civil Rights Movement*. New York: Times Books.

Sheets, D. (2005). Aging with disabilities: Ageism and more. *Generations, 29*(3), 37–41.

Simon-Rusinowitz, L. and Mahoney, K. J. (2001). Preferences for consumer-directed services among different consumer groups: Cash and counseling demonstration and evaluation early findings. Presentation at Independent Choices, A National Symposium on Consumer-Direction and Self-Determination for the Elderly and Persons with Disabilities, U.S. Department of Health and Human Services. http://www.cashandcounseling.org/resources/20060126-110912/ASPEPresent.pdf.

Smart, J. (2001). *Disability, Society, and the Individual*. Gaithersburg, MD: An Aspen Publication.

Smith, M. (2004). Under the circumstances: The experiences of younger people living in residential aged care facilities. *Contemporary Nurse, 16*, 187–194.

Spector, W. and Fleishman, J. (2000). *The Characteristics of Long-Term Care Users*. Agency for Healthcare Research and Quality and the Urban Institute. http://www.ahcpr.gov/research/ltcusers/ (accessed June 21, 2006).

Switzer, J. (2003). *Disabled Rights: American Disability Policy and the Fight for Equality*. Washington: Georgetown University Press.

Tisdall, K. (2001). Failing to make the transition? Theorising the 'transition to adulthood' for young disabled people. In Priestley, M. (Ed.), *Disability and the Life Course: Global Perspectives*. Cambridge, UK: Cambridge University Press, pp. 167–178.

Vega, C. M. (2006). Proposition D: Laguna Honda Hospital measure defeated handily. *San Francisco Chronicle*, B2.

Waldrop, J. and Stern, S. (2003). *Disability Status: 2000*. Washington: Bureau of the Census, http://www.census.gov/prod/2003pubs/c2kbr-17.pdf.

Walsh, P. and LeRoy, B. (2004). *Women with Disabilities Aging Well: A Global View*. Baltimore, MD: Paul H. Brookes.

Weber, M. (2004). Home and community-based services, *Olmstead*, and positive rights: A preliminary discussion. *Wake Forest Law Review, 39*, 269–291.

Wilson, D. and Truman, C. (2004). Long-term care residents: Concerns identified by population and care trends. *Canadian Journal of Public Health, 95*, 382–386.

Chapter 7

Informal Caregivers and Caregiving: Living at Home with Personal Care

Sharon M. Keigher

Contents

Introduction: Informal Caregiving for Family and Friends Across the Life Course

"Ordinary people living out their lives and doing what needs to be done to assist family members with disabilities are hardly likely to see themselves as long-term care providers," but family, friends, and loved ones are exactly those who provide the bulk of long-term care in the United States (Kane et al., 1998, p. 14). It is estimated that 44.2 million adults in the United States—21 percent of all adults—voluntarily provide informal,* unpaid personal care and support to other adults who are ill or disabled, living at home, and who need assistance to perform the most basic activities of daily living (ADL). These caregivers represent 22.9 million, or 21 percent, of all households (National Alliance for Caregiving and American Association of Retired Persons [AARP], 2005).

These family* caregivers—spouses,† adult children, other relatives, friends, and neighbors of all ages—are the lifeline for disabled partners,† frail and aging parents, and other loved ones who cannot look after themselves. They care for the chronically ill, physically disabled, and cognitively impaired parents, as well as adult children who continue, or return home, to live with them. Some caregivers raise other people's children, or their own grandchildren, with or without the support of anyone else. Many provide such care at considerable sacrifice to themselves, continuing

---

* "Informal care" and "family care" are used interchangeably here to acknowledge the significance of both blood kinship and "families of choice." The 23 percent increase in the number of "nonfamily households" between 1990 and 2000 (from 27.4 million to 33.7 million) is suggestive of the extent to which new patterns of adult lifestyles may take on importance in an aging society.

† "Spouse" and "partner" are also used interchangeably here to acknowledge the importance of both designations in reference to caregiving situations.

to care well into their own old ages. Unfortunately, in our society, informal caregivers often go unnoticed except by those whose very lives depend upon them (ASPE and AOA, 1999, p. 2).

Informal caregivers are easily "taken for granted" by the formal health and long-term care systems, because many of the services are exactly what people provide for themselves when they can. Families "naturally" provide care without compensation, special credentials, or supervision. Often, they provide home maintenance and social and psychological support along with assistance in ADL (eating, dressing, bathing, toileting) and transportation to doctor appointments, church services, and community events. Caregivers are often the only link to social and emotional support, and the "normalcy" that most disabled and frail people of all ages experience only in their own homes and familiar communities. For persons whose medical conditions or injuries have resulted in chronic illness or disability, family and friends literally can be the foundation of healthcare, the critical safety valve in our nation's "very leaky" systems of health and long-term care. The economic value of this "free," informal care, previously estimated to be between 168 billion and 197 billion dollars annually, was reestimated in 2000 to be worth 270 billion dollars annually (Arno, 2002). This massive sum is well over twice the combined costs of nursing homes ($92 billion) and home healthcare ($32 billion).

Informal care is provided and received by people of all ages, at all stages of their life course. Among frail and disabled adults receiving long-term care, persons aged 65 years and above comprise about half, whereas those aged 18 through 64 years comprise the other half. Given the extreme heterogeneity of these care receivers, it is not surprising that their caregivers are an equally diverse group. Among all disabled adults aged 18 and above receiving care at home, 78 percent receive all of that care exclusively from informal caregivers, mostly wives and adult daughters. Another 14 percent receive a combination of informal and formal care, and only 8 percent of disabled adults living at home rely entirely on formal, paid care providers. Spillman and Black (2005) recently found that in 1999, two-thirds of older people with disabilities relied entirely on family and friends. Another 26 percent supplement their informal care with formal care, and 9 percent rely solely on formal care services.

Omitted from these caregiver estimates are children and teens below the age of 20 who, even when very young, are sometimes significant caregivers for disabled siblings, parents, or other relatives (Becker et al., 1998; Becker and Dearden, 1999; Keigher et al., 2005). Also, largely overlooked are older adults, even those in their ninth and tenth decades, who, despite their own infirmities, are primary caregivers for others. The United States has yet to recognize the significance of informal caregiving as a normative experience, which, like marriage and family policy, may be unable to sustain by itself without structural policy and financial supports.

This chapter presents a general profile of the basic *sine qua non* of family care in the United States—the unpaid, unsung individuals who provide personal assistance for disabled loved ones who depend on them to live at home. "Informal caregivers"— autonomous volunteer helpers, neither paid nor supervised, and therefore beyond the control of formal social and healthcare agencies—are the very foundation of the human capital in both the healthcare and long-term care systems in the United States. The long-term care system delivers care through organizations providing managers and direct care workers to assist individuals in their own homes and communities, in residential care, and in institutional settings, all attempting to complement the needs of disabled persons who depend on them, and hopefully in concert with their informal or family caregivers. Funded through market purchases by individuals, as well as through government programs, the amount of care delivered depends greatly on market demand and government assistance, as well as on the availability of the "no-cost" informal caregivers. Regardless of the health of the economy, government contributions, and social changes in family structures, loved ones remain the safety net, the essential foundation of modern long-term care.

After profiling America's informal caregivers, the social forces impinging on them in families and households, increasingly straining their individual capacities to provide sufficient, appropriate care will be highlighted. These societal forces raise policy concerns regarding projected declines in the availability of informal caregivers, as well as evidence of the elasticity of caregiver supply and future potential capacity. An extensive research literature has validated the stress and burden experienced by caregivers with various characteristics and in various situations, as well as their profound satisfactions and rewards.

Next, we consider some trends and public policy initiatives of the past three decades that have sought to increase both commitment of, and support for family or informal caregivers. Emerging challenges are expected to complicate informal caregiving in the next decade; thus, we conclude by calling for more meaningful partnerships between formal long-term care services, paid direct care workers, informal caregivers, and future consumers—all agents with a vital stake in strengthening our nation's capacity to care.

Profiles of Informal Care in the United States

A Profile of All Informal Caregivers

Most long-term care consists of informal assistance provided by close, unpaid family members and friends to disabled persons, enabling them to remain living at home in their own communities. They are sometimes referred to as "frontline caregivers" because of their personal or affectional relationship to the person needing assistance. Paraprofessionals or direct care workers are usually paid, trained, and supervised individuals, employed by formal agencies to provide in-home personal care and assistance. Because family caregiving work can be very isolating and difficult, formal paid caregivers are often asked to schedule their work around the needs of family caregivers, providing either respite for them or serving as extra help.

It has been estimated that as many as one in three Americans voluntarily provide unpaid informal care each year to one or more ill or disabled family members or friends above the age of 18 (ASPE and AOA, 1999). Nearly three-quarters of these caregivers assist family members and nearly one-quarter assist friends. Eight percent of the total report helping more than one care recipient over the past year.

The most common informal caregiving relationship is that of an adult assisting aging parent(s) (38 percent), whereas spouses provide 11 percent of informal care to their elderly husbands or wives. Seven percent of informal care is provided by parents to their significantly disabled children who are above the age of 18. Twenty percent is provided to other relatives—grandparents, siblings, aunts, and uncles—and about 24 percent to friends and neighbors.

At any point in time, one in five Americans is providing informal care to an ill or disabled family member, reflecting the long-term nature of such care (NAC and AARP, 2006). Although caregiving is provided by adults of all ages, the average caregiver is a 46-year-old female with some college education who is employed and spends more than 20 hours a week providing care to her mother.

Spouse caregivers tend to be older (average age 55); only 13 percent of people in their 20s and 14 percent of adults aged 70 years and above report providing any care. Caregivers in their 20s are naturally more likely to care for older family members such as grandparents, aunts, and uncles. Caregiving tends to decline as individuals take on family responsibilities, raising their own children and managing their careers, but caregiving responsibilities rise again as people reach their late 50s and 60s. Women caregivers above the age of 60 years are most frequently providing care to a partner or sibling (ASPE and AOA, 1999).

Although both women (61 percent) and men (39 percent) provide informal care, women are much more likely to be giving care throughout the entire year than men. Moreover, women provide 50 percent more hours of care than men do per week, are twice as likely to be caring for ill or disabled children, and provide care over longer periods of time, and more frequently, to two or more persons. Indeed, across the life course, male caregivers provide relatively few hours of informal care; those below the age of 64 provide 5–11 hours of care per week, whereas men in their late 60s provide about 15 hours of care per week, both typically to disabled spouses or partners. Male caregivers are more likely to be employed full- or part-time (66 percent) than female caregivers (55 percent) (National Alliance for Caregiving and AARP, 2005), whereas, overall, female caregivers provide more hours of care and a higher level of care.

These gender disparities generally persist among different ethnic and racial groups. For example, black and white Americans are equally likely to be providing informal care at any given time, but across the life course, black women do much more caregiving than white women, more frequently caring for disabled members of their extended family, and more likely to be residing with a disabled child or adult. Six percent of black women in their 50s reported caring for an ill or disabled child; and black women are more likely to be caring for grandchildren well into their 60s and 70s.

Informal caregivers report being as healthy as the general population; eight in ten report having "good or excellent" health. The 17 percent reporting "fair or poor" health are more likely to be caring for patients posing the greatest responsibility, who have lower incomes, co-reside with the care recipient, are less educated, and above the age of 50. Their caregivers are more likely to include spouses or partners. Similarly, compromised health is experienced by older grandparents with custody of minor children (Fuller-Thompson and Minkler, 2000) and older caregivers of disabled adult children.

Finally, 59 percent of informal caregivers were employed either full- or part-time during the previous year, as were 65 percent of persons caring for two or more disabled or chronically ill persons. In fact, the percentage of women caregivers who are employed closely resembles the proportion of women in the labor force generally. Women caregivers are only slightly more likely than other women to be employed part-time, and male caregivers were no more likely than other men to be working part-time.

Becoming an informal caregiver is a commonplace life course experience in the United States, particularly for women. Indeed, most females provide care to relatives or friends at more than one point in their lives. Many provide care for several care recipients, and over substantial periods of their lives.

A Profile of Informal Caregivers of Disabled Elderly Americans

Of special interest within the caregiver population described earlier are people caring for older adults sufficiently disabled enough to be eligible for nursing home placement; these caregivers are at particular risk for health, psychological, and financial stress. They are one subject of interest in the National Long-Term Care Survey (NLTCS) and the Informal Caregiver Supplement (added in 1989). Conducted in 1982, 1989, 1994, 1999, and 2004, this survey gathers data from a nationally representative sample of Medicare beneficiaries aged 65 and above on their functional limitations and receipt of formal and informal care, providing an in-depth examination of the most common form of informal caregiving—assistance provided to elderly persons living at home with significant functional impairments. Formal care is defined as "paid personal assistance provided to persons with a chronic disability living in the community," whereas informal, or family care, is defined as "unpaid personal assistance . . . ."

Rather than search for caregivers, this survey interviews Medicare beneficiaries who identify their "most" primary caregiver. It then gathers data from the primary caregivers who are doing the hands-on or supervisory caregiving. It then extrapolates from the care receiver's inability to perform, without human or mechanical assistance, one or more six basic ADLs and nine instrumental activities of daily living (IADLs), because of chronic illness or disability. ADLs include bathing, dressing, moving around indoors, transferring from bed to chair, using the toilet, and eating. The nine IADLs include light housekeeping, meal preparation, grocery shopping, laundry, taking medications, managing money, telephoning, outdoor mobility, and transportation. By focusing exclusively on elderly recipients receiving informal care, the NLTCS provides reliable and specific information about the subset of family caregivers providing the most extensive and critically important activities; it also allows identification of trends in disability and in use of formal and informal care. Unfortunately, the most recent data available, from the 1999 survey, are only partially analyzed as of this writing.

The 1999 survey identified approximately 3.7 million elders (10.7 percent) who were receiving 120 million hours of informal care from 7 million Americans each and every week (ASPE and AOA, 1999). The vast majority of these 7 million caregivers were assisting older, disabled family members, each with an average of 1.7 caregivers, with each caregiver providing almost 20 hours of unpaid help weekly. Such assistance was the primary reason why most of these older people with disabilities were able to remain in their homes and communities.

The 1999 National Long-Term care survey also found that the overwhelming majority of noninstitutionalized older adults who need long-term care—about 91.5 percent of them—were receiving some or all of it from relatives, friends, and neighbors (Spillman and Black, 2005, p. vii), a decline from 95 percent in the 1994 survey, indicating that more elders are receiving some formal services. About two-thirds use no formal care at all, relying solely on unpaid help, primarily from female partners and adult daughters or daughters-in-law. As disability increases at older ages, elders utilize increasing amounts of informal care, and become more likely to live with relatives or have a caregiver stay with them. Of all older persons with three or more ADL limitations, 86 percent reside with others and receive, on average, 60 hours of informal care per week, supplemented by slightly more than 14 hours of paid assistance (Stone, 2006, p. 406).

Most of these elders have a primary caregiver who provides the bulk of their care, and secures and coordinates help from "secondary" caregivers, paid or unpaid. Almost 75 percent of primary caregivers are women, 36 percent adult children, and 40 percent spouses; their average age is 60, and over two-thirds of them are unemployed. Two-thirds of the employed caregivers work full time, with few, if any, other income sources. The latter generally provide fewer weekly hours of assistance to elders, but still average 18 hours of care per week. Two-thirds of them had experienced conflicts between their employment and their caregiving responsibilities, and had rearranged their work schedules, reduced their work hours, or taken unpaid leaves of absence (Stone, 2006, p. 407). Many eventually will "retire early" with reluctance, usually sacrificing potential retirement income and benefits, including medical insurance, to do so.

Spillman and Black (2005) note that earlier waves of the NLTCS, between 1984 and 1994, had shown a significant decline in the number of informal caregivers and an increase in the use of formal care by paid workers for these Medicare beneficiaries. However, in the 1999 survey, the use of any formal care declined from 43 percent in 1994 to 34 percent by 1999, whereas reliance on "informal care only" had increased significantly, from 57 percent in 1994 to 66 percent by 1999.

The number and proportion of beneficiaries receiving no formal or informal help with personal care had also increased from 22 percent in 1994 to 28 percent by 1999, reflecting lower disability levels among beneficiaries in 1999, as well as greater use of assistive devices and home adaptations. Reductions in morbidity and functional decline are positive trends and good news. However, a larger proportion of informal caregivers were caring for elders with higher levels of disability in 1999 than in 1994. The population of caregivers and receivers had aged, with nearly 40 percent of caregiving children assisting parents aged 85 years and above in 1999 (increased from 34 percent in 1994). And 13 percent of caregiving children were themselves aged 65 years or above (Spillman and Black, 2005).

The Challenges, Burdens, and Rewards of Informal Caregivers in Aging Families

Contemporary Challenges to Informal Care

As the U.S. population above the age of 65 years grows from 36 million in 2007 (12 percent of the population) to 87 million (more than 20 percent) in 2050 (FIFARS, 2006), community leaders, policy makers, researchers, and especially long-term care administrators will need to be vigilant regarding the health, psychosocial, and economic well-being of not only older Americans, but their informal caregivers and direct care workers as well. This projected growth in the number and proportion of older adults reflects "societal aging"—a profound demographic age shift that is occurring in developed countries throughout the world. In the United States, the first of the postwar birth cohort, the "baby boom" generation born between 1946 and 1964, began turning 60 years of age in 2006. By 2030, over 71 million boomers will turn 65, an unprecedented increase in the U.S. population aged between 65 and 85 years. Healthier and less functionally disabled than earlier generations, many are expected to remain actively engaged in their communities, possibly providing valuable human resources to meet a vast range of human needs (Achenbaum, 2005; Morrow-Howell et al., 2001). With the right encouragement, incentives, and training, they may be the resource to provide a good deal of formal and informal care.

Longevity, Filial Bonds, and Multigenerational Families

As Americans live longer, linkages within multigenerational families are growing. Of the Americans above the age of 35 years in 2007, 80 percent are members of three-generation families, and 16 percent are of four-generation families (Bengtson, 2001; Bengtson et al., 2004). Parents and children today are likely to share five decades of life, siblings may share eight, and grandparents and grandchildren may share three or more decades—all relationships characterized by emotional closeness

(Bengtson et al., 2002). Multigenerational families today are also characterized by greater geographic distances among members, but moderate face-to-face contact is facilitated for most by increasing levels of air travel, telephone, and electronic communication. Despite occasional media images to the contrary, strong norms of filial obligation appear to be able to transcend great distances (Bengtson et al., 2002; Bengtson, 2001; Navaie-Waliser et al., 2001). Long-distance caregiving issues are of growing importance, particularly to large, multinational firms, and those that employ large number of women.

Housing Arrangements

Among other family norms that have changed dramatically since World War II is a trend at all ages toward living alone at adulthood. Multigenerational households that were previously common are rare today, except among immigrant and low-income minority populations. This "preference" for the nuclear family and privacy can be a mixed blessing for older spousal caregivers who, over time, frequently become isolated, exhausted, and depressed, needing more support, personal contact, and physical strength to continue giving care. Although older women with increasing dementia or frailty may prefer to live alone, or cannot afford to move, living alone without someone "looking after them" can place them at risk of self-neglect, exploitation, or injury.

The percentage of older adults residing with a spouse declines with age, but with a significant gender bias. Women, who comprise 58 percent of the population aged 65 years and above (FIFARS, 2004, p. xiv), are much less likely to be married at older ages than men (41.6 percent versus 72.4 percent). In 2004, of the adults aged 65–74, 79 percent of men were married, as were only 57 percent of women. By 85 years of age and above, 58 percent of men were married, as were only 15 percent of women (FIFARS, 2006, p. 8). Because men tend to marry younger women who tend to outlive them, men are much more likely to live with a wife or partner well into their ninth and tenth decades, whereas women are much more likely to become caregivers of partners before they are widowed, and more than twice as likely as men (39.7 percent versus 18.8 percent) to live alone (FIFARS, 2006, p. 8).

Minority women (Hispanic, Asian, and black) at older ages are more than twice as likely as white women to be living with their children or other relative(s) (FIFARS, 2006). For those who live independently, nearly 94 percent have living relatives (FIFARS, 2004), and two-thirds share their household with at least one family member, typically a spouse or partner or child or sibling. The 6 percent without family ties—particularly unmarried women, elders of color, and those without living children—receive support and assistance from friends, neighbors, and acquaintances (Moen et al., 2000). Some simply prefer being alone (Rubinstein, 1986).

In contrast, 80 percent of all older individuals who live alone are women, including 41 percent each of older white women and black women, and much smaller proportions of Asian and Hispanic women. Most women living alone have at least one adult child living sufficiently close to visit them regularly (AOA, 2002). Declining health, loss of a caregiver or spouse, desire for companionship, and declining income most often precipitate a move to an adult child's home (Wilmouth, 2000) or relocation to some form of congregate senior housing, assisted living, or nursing home.

For most older Americans, living longer means extended years of active healthy life followed by, for many, continuing to live with chronic illness or disability at home in the community, while receiving some assistance from family members with the tasks of everyday living. Because family and friends provide 80 percent of that assistance, having a spouse or adult daughter nearby is the factor most often credited with keeping an older adult safely at home until the end of life. The dilemma is that gradual fertility declines during the past 35 years have left the younger generations of families with fewer members available to provide older relatives with necessary personal care (Hooyman, 2006, p. xxxv).

Families generally engage in reciprocal support and assistance between older and younger members, with older adults providing support to children and grandchildren as long as they can (Silverstein et al., 2002), and children gradually providing more significant assistance to elders. Elders provide child care, advice, and financial assistance to the young, although gradually, caregiving and support flow from younger generations to elders needing care.

With increased life expectancy, these reciprocal patterns of cross-generational family support continue to be preferred, but providing care to two and even three living generations simultaneously is increasingly infeasible. As adult children with developmental disabilities or mental illnesses live longer, they also need extended care and "looking after." Some continue to live with aging parents who eventually will experience their own declining health. Grandparents caring for grandchildren have been recognized in the past two decades as a vital resource for community child welfare services that would be unable to provide sufficient foster care to children whose parents in the middle generations have been decimated by epidemics of crack cocaine, methamphetamines, violence, and HIV/AIDS (Cox, 2000; Gleeson and Hairston, 1999; Minkler and Roe, 1993; Fuller-Thompson and Minkler, 2000; Minkler et al., 2000). In 2005, 4.5 percent of all American children were living with neither parent, including 3.4 percent of white children, 5.1 percent of Hispanic children, and 9.8 percent of black children (U.S. Census, 2006); the majority of these children reside with other relatives. All these human needs converge on the complex terrain of family and informal care.

While it is estimated that by 2020 one-third of Americans will be at least aged 50 years, this "population aging" is occurring unevenly across the states, shaped by local fertility and mortality levels as well as the number of older and younger people who migrate to and from the state. In 2002, Florida had the highest proportion of persons aged 65 and above (17 percent), with Pennsylvania and West Virginia close behind, each with over 15 percent (FIFARS, 2004). Florida is expected to hold that rank in 2030, with over 27 percent of their population aged 65 and above; Maine, Wyoming and New Mexico are expected to reach 26 percent (U.S. Census Bureau, 2005). Population aging has implications for the quality of life to be enjoyed by all generations in the future.

The Heterogeneity of American Families

Powerful societal forces have precipitated these rapidly increasing variations among American families and household configurations. Increasing pluralism, ethnic and cultural diversity, growing economic uncertainties and disparities, the normalization of divorce, reconstituted and blended families, multigenerational households, and acceptance of alternative lifestyles have all challenged traditional assumptions about the capacity of families to "care for their own." Although greater numbers of people of all ages are living alone, there are more single parents raising children on their own, teen parents living with their parents, and unmarried individuals living together in various nontraditional family configurations, such as grandparents raising children, gay and lesbian couples and families, and adults of all identities adopting children and providing adult foster care. Increasingly, a family must be defined broadly to capture reality, by the strengths of its interpersonal commitments and the quality of members' relationships, rather than by blood ties, codependence, or coresidence. Having proximate, familiar, and available assistance, even just one dependable person, either sharing the household or residing nearby, is the critical ingredient of social support for most elders unable to navigate alone beyond their homes. The challenge is to facilitate these nurturing and supportive caregivers appropriately through the long-term care system.

Caregiver Stress and Burden

Caring for the frailest elders with multiple functional limitations, including dementia, can be the most difficult work people do. It can take a devastating toll on family caregivers, particularly aging partners. Faced with regularly managing a loved one's problem behaviors, caregivers frequently feel excessively burdened and develop significant depression (Greenberg et al., 2006, p. 343). Women experience more difficulties in caregiving roles than do men, with effects typically changing gradually, or "unfolding" throughout the course of a caregiving career. It is well documented that family caregivers of elders with cognitive impairments and behavior problems develop poorer mental and physical health than their age peers, and typically have the poorest caregiver outcomes (Baumgarten et al., 1992; Schultz and Williamson, 1991). Seltzer (2006) notes that "with fully 12.1 million Americans presenting such symptoms and needing such care long-term, caregiving is a major public health issue" (p. 337).

Unrelieved caregiver burden—whether the result of exhaustion, financial, or other related strains—contributes substantially to institutionalization (Feinberg et al., 2005, p. 1–2). Even if that is avoided, the financial, physical, or emotional difficulties precipitated by continuous caregiving can greatly exacerbate pressures on local healthcare systems and social services, as caregivers seek medical and psychological help for health conditions arising from isolation, poor nutrition, or injuries. If financial mismanagement, poverty, self-neglect, or elder abuse is suspected, institutionalization may become inevitable anyway, ultimately forcing public outlays for nursing home costs (U.S. Department of Health and Human Services, 2002).

Empirical research demonstrates that stress caused by the caregiving experience can have fundamentally adverse effects on the psychological, social, and physical well-being of family caregivers (Bookwala et al., 2000; McKinlay et al., 1995; Toseland et al., 1990). The sources of this stress have been identified as: the elder's challenging behavior and the caregiver's inability to manage it, the physical strain of caregiving work, its financial burden, difficult shared housing arrangements, caregiver isolation, conflicts among family members, and the specific support needs of older parents and grandparents caring for young and adult children. These are each briefly discussed in the following sections.

Alzheimer's Disease and Dementias

Caregivers of older adults suffering from significant dementia have specific support needs at different points in their "caring careers." At the time of the first diagnosis, families especially need help in planning for future care needs, locating services and public benefits, and preparing for care. Caregivers as well as elders with early dementia can benefit from education and assistance in updating a will, power of attorney documents, healthcare proxy, and advance directives. Most caregivers will also benefit from a comprehensive biopsychosocial and environmental assessment, and from individualized assistance in developing a plan of care (Adams, 2006).

Family tensions may rekindle long-standing conflicts. Frequently, the whole family system needs assistance in preparing to make decisions about the future, to solve problems, to resolve conflicts, and settle differences of opinion about care options and roles (Toseland et al., 1995). It is common for individual family members and the entire family system to struggle with emotional adjustment as dementia symptoms progress; health professionals must recognize that, for family members, understanding, accepting, and coming to terms with the situation is a long and slow process. Spousal caregivers of people with early-stage Alzheimer's disease, and often the patients themselves, can benefit greatly from psychoeducational support groups at this point (Cummings, 1999; LoboPrabhu et al., 2005).

Physical Work

Providing personal care for disabled persons requires physical strength and fitness, knowledge, and skill to avoid injuring oneself. Recently, concern has risen in the media and among healthcare professionals about the decline in physical activity and manual labor among Americans, and the resultant increase in overweight and obesity in the population. This problem has special relevance for competent performance of the basic personal care tasks required of informal, as well as formal, caregivers who are routinely lifting, transferring, and toileting disabled adults. Because of the high risk of disabling back strains and injuries, especially in the course of caring for heavy patients (Eaton, 2003), nursing and nursing assistant are among the most dangerous occupations (comparable to trucking, mining, and agriculture). Labor organizations have lobbied to restrict nurses' obligations to perform excessively strenuous, dangerous work and to require that mechanical assistance equipment be provided when appropriate.

Ironically, many family caregivers simply do such work, all the time, without insurance against occupational injury, or health insurance, and often without a salary. Indeed, government-funded programs regularly off-load certain duties onto family caregivers simply because it is too difficult and costly for formal agencies to schedule them or do them daily or at inconvenient times (e.g., administration of medications and toileting).

Although female spouses and partners provide the bulk of personal, heavy care, they are usually older themselves, lacking the physical strength to lift, pivot, and transfer "dead" weight. Male caregivers—husbands, partners, and sons—often face social mores discouraging them from what are seen as female gender roles; men often lack the personal experience, know-how, and comfort in performing certain types of personal care as well (Kramer, 2000; Kramer and Thompson, 2002). Often capable of lifting a loved one into and out of bed and dressing or bathing them, most men are not prepared to do these tasks on a daily basis. Adult sons and daughters, also unaccustomed to providing such care, often feel insecure about assisting a parent of the opposite gender. Adult children may also feel stressed and overextended trying to meet their own personal, family, or employment obligations and simultaneously caring for their parents.

Economic Imperatives and Employment Dilemmas

Persons who resign from employment to assume domestic caregiving duties usually lose more than their incomes. They often sacrifice health insurance, Social Security, other deferred retirement benefits, social contacts, and satisfying work that affirm one's identity and worth. For many, especially older workers, a temporary withdrawal from employment becomes permanent as they lose touch with professional skills and their knowledge becomes obsolete. People who "only" reduce their work hours (which rarely happens) begin making smaller pension and Social Security contributions, and typically lose their health insurance and other benefits. Now they lack insurance against an injury that could result in their own disability or unemployability.

Reluctance to work full time is often seen by managers as a lack of commitment, leading to low—or no—annual wage increases or promotions. Later in life, these partially employed caregivers suffer from reduced Social Security benefit levels. Without sufficient contributions (40 quarters of coverage in "covered employment"), some family caregivers are ineligible for any Social Security protection, except perhaps the smaller, means-tested Supplemental Security Income (SSI) benefit. In 2006, the means-tested SSI benefit amounted to only $603 per month for a person living alone and $402 if residing with others.

Labor force participation rates for older women have increased significantly since the mid-1980s, and for older men since the mid-1990s. Currently, 34 percent of men and 24 percent of women aged 65–69 years are employed. Similar growth in labor force participation occurred among women aged 62–64 years, reaching 40 percent in 2005. Even people above the age of 70 years are employed more; their employment rate has risen markedly for well over a decade to 14 percent of men and 7 percent of women (FIFARS, 2006). This steady increase in older women's workforce participation rate over the last four decades, and the more recent rise for that of older men, have resulted in fewer people available for domestic duties (FIFARS, 2006, pp. 18–19).

Caregiver Isolation

Continuous obligation in the home can quickly isolate and trap caregivers, particularly elderly spouses, leading to relinquishment of their own interests, rights, and health. Striking inequalities of resources and health status already exist between the genders, socio-income levels, and racial and ethnic groups, all of which may be exacerbated by particular types of informal caregiver situations (FIFARS, 2004). These may include caregivers without transportation resources or social supports, and who face the unique challenges of loved ones with severe mental and dementing illnesses.

Spousal or Partner Care

Aged spouses in long-term caregiving situations certainly experience particular strains. As Zarit and Zarit (1992) noted, "There is no uni-dimensional answer to the question of what helps caregivers sustain the marital bond, but clearly attention to caregiver frustration by a team of health care professionals offering consistent support facilitates ongoing commitment to caregiving." The resources available to a spousal caregiver appear to be extremely important and stronger than any particular caregiver characteristic in maintaining optimal mental health (Moritz et al., 1992).

Common predictors of spouse caregivers' emotional strain were recently identified by Kang (2006) through examination of the 1999 NLTC national survey data. A key source is the type and extent of a care receiver's disruptive behaviors. Caregivers' perceptions of feeling overloaded, experiencing limitations on his or her life, and awareness of family disagreements can also contribute to emotional strain. Other widely identified sources of emotional strain are inadequate personal coping strategies (Kang, 2006), depression (George et al., 1989; George and Gwyther, 1986), and risk of elder abuse (Paveza et al., 1992).

Parent Care by Adult Children

Among adult children providing care to parents, stress can arise from conflicts likely to represent old, unresolved sibling issues. The immediate conflicts can be about the equitable distribution of caregiving tasks or differing perceptions of the needs of a frail parent (Semple, 1992). Such family conflicts are associated with increased risk of caregiver depression. Caregivers may also experience other secondary strains such as role captivity and role overload. The full impact of caregiving cannot be understood without taking into account the proliferation of other life stressors.

Aging Adults Caring for Disabled Adult Children

Aging family members provide a significant service to society by sustaining vulnerable members, but these contributions do not come without cost. Aging parents caring for adult children with cognitive and developmental disabilities are at particular risk of mental health problems, physical illness, and social isolation (Greenberg et al., 2006, pp. 339–354). Such parents have often lived quietly for decades with the companionship of their child; making alternative care arrangements for contingencies, including one's own death, can be particularly stressful.

Comparing mothers of grown children with developmental disabilities with those of mentally ill adult children reveals both similarities and differences. According to Greenberg et al. (1993) and Seltzer (1995), mothers of the latter group show a distinct "wear and tear" pattern, being significantly more stressed, with higher levels of caregiver burden, depression, and pessimism about the future. They typically feel more distanced from the child than do similarly aged mothers of children with developmental disabilities. The researchers also note that caring for someone with Alzheimer's disease is substantially similar to caring for persons with serious and persistent mental illness. With both illnesses, there is a high degree of uncertainty regarding the illness trajectory, and unpredictable, sometimes cyclical symptoms. Needing to be constantly vigilant, most caregivers will eventually develop serious depression and declining health. The provision of respite care, social support, and assistance may alleviate some of these problems. Many research questions remain about how to mobilize external supports in strategic ways that truly maintain the perceived health of these critically important caregivers.

Caregiver Assessments and Instruments

Using appropriate, standardized assessments of caregiver burden is essential for healthcare practitioners, at a minimum to initiate early interventions and to prevent burnout. Assessment of caregiver burden is conceptualized as having three components. The first deals with impairments of the recipient, including his or her ADL deficits, sociability, disruptive behavior, and mental status. Although severity of symptoms and impairment alone are inadequate predictors of caregiver stress, they do yield useful information. Second, the tasks corresponding to the older adult's needs are rated by the caregiver as being "difficult, tiring, or upsetting." Dealing with bowel or bladder incontinence, for example, would probably be more upsetting, difficult, or tiring than assisting with meals. Third, the impact of the behaviors and the associated caregiver tasks are assessed relative to the caregiver's overall life (Gallo et al., 2000).

Administration of short screening instruments, such as the Zarit Burden Interview, can open the topic of caregiver stress for discussion. Brief depression screening instruments are useful because the prevalence of depression in caregivers is likely to be very high, and the perceived burden of care may be greater when it is present. Because perceived burden is also linked with the caregiver's sense of his or her own coping capabilities, it is useful to explore the mechanisms he or she depends on for handling stress and help him or her identify his or her own coping style. Pearlin and Scaff (1995) describe a variety of useful techniques and instruments for gathering information about coping capabilities.

The Satisfactions and Rewards of Giving Informal Care

The research literature today is rapidly expanding with "discoveries" of the rewards and satisfactions inherent in providing care for an older loved one. When asked how they felt about caregiving, even when greatly stressed, many caregivers expressed deep feelings of satisfaction, pride, and accomplishment. Some have observed that giving care is one of the few ways family members have today to demonstrate love and affection for one another in a significant way.

Adhering to ideals such as "filial piety" and "satisfying obligations," most healthy caregivers of older adults consider their work to be a privilege, a "giving back" of care that was previously given to them—genuine reciprocity. Rewards include satisfaction or pleasure in fulfilling the caregiving role, feelings of personal growth, a renewed sense of purpose in life, closer relationships with family and friends, political advocacy, and greater insight into the struggles of persons with disabilities (Harris, 2002; Kramer, 1997; Lawton et al., 1991).

In the course of providing care at home, loved ones may find room for intimacy and openness that rarely occurs in medical settings. Facilitated by focused attention to only one person, discussion of long past incidents may be reopened honestly, in the supportive context of gentle touch, quiet, and peace (Lustbader, 1991). Greenberg et al. (2006, p. 340) note that estimates of the percentage of caregivers who experience rewards from caregiving have varied widely, but range from approximately 50 to 90 percent of the caregivers sampled.

There are practical rewards to giving care as well. Many women who leave full-time employment (either temporarily or permanently) gain freedom to do meaningful things that they enjoy, may have postponed for years, or discover for the first time. A slower pace of daily life, having personal control over one's schedule, and time for intimate conversation, all are real, meaningful satisfactions for many caregivers.

Lustbader (1991) observes that caregiving experiences—feeling the wrenching helplessness of a loved one's dependence—are essential requisites that can prepare us for our own lives later. We need them to understand our own true humanness. "Prior to getting sick or reaching advanced age, we can choose to grant ourselves a close acquaintance with physical suffering and its alleviation. We can draw near to the sickbeds of friends and relatives and involve ourselves in the experience of helplessness, hoping that this foreknowledge will help us to age well" (p. 170).

An important support for many caregivers is spirituality and believing in a higher power as a means of "letting go" of feelings of frustration. Spirituality is a resource a number of caregivers credit with helping them handle multiple physical, emotional, and social demands without feeling burdened. Researchers have begun to explore the role of spirituality in helping caregivers, as well as frail older adults, cope on a daily basis. Nelson-Becker et al. (2007) identify four preliminary questions that clinicians can raise with caregivers to open discussion on spirituality that may be important to them. They also provide comprehensive guidelines for dealing with spiritual issues in professional practice, or deciding to refer the caregiver to pastoral care resources. Some caregivers use religion or spirituality to help them resolve ethical dilemmas. Spiritual assessment is another new tool under development that may be helpful to clinicians and caregivers in identifying their unresolved concerns and providing them with the language for discussing them (Nelson-Becker et al., 2007).

Trends and Policy Innovations in Support of Family Caregivers

Policy Recognition of Caregivers

Research on informal caregivers grew dramatically in the 1980s and 1990s, as did societal awareness of the importance and value of family caregivers and their needs. Bits of this recognition occasionally penetrated political arenas in Congress and state capitols. For example, the Family and Medical Leave Act, considered groundbreaking when it was introduced in Congress in the 1980s, languished there for years, although all it granted was a legal right for employees in very large corporations to take up to 12 weeks of unpaid leave from work to care for a disabled family member or a new baby. Finally, in 1992, a new Congress passed the bill again, making it the first legislation President Bill Clinton signed in 1992, immediately after taking office.

Eight years later, Clinton signed the Family Caregiver Support Act of 2000, enacted as an Amendment to the Older Americans Act. This law, which some view as the "most significant legislative amendment to the Older Americans Act in 30 years" (Hudson, 2006, p. 493), established funding within the federal Administration on Aging (AOA) for a system of caregiver resource centers throughout the aging network in each state. These centers can provide educational and program materials, referral services, and comprehensive assessments for caregivers to identify burden, stress, and unmet needs of assistance at home. They can also mobilize direct services, including limited amounts of respite care. Although this is a modest initiative overall, it is a start.

Supportive Interventions for Informal Caregivers

Finding a singular purpose for many social programs is often difficult to discern. Are services provided to help family caregivers increase and sustain their efforts, improve the quality of their care, or ensure that they are not unduly burdened by their caring work? In the United States, program goals, even when well defined, are frequently undermined because they are strictly means-tested. Services of the Older Americans Act, however, are supposedly universal, but they are especially limited by AOA's very small budget. Increasingly, income-based user copayments are being requested of participants to keep some programs viable.

Kane et al. (1998, p. 151) describe three main types of in-home services, both government and privately funded, that are aimed at supporting family caregivers. The first consists of direct services for caregivers, such as counseling, psychotherapy, training programs, and support groups, aimed at helping them adapt and cope with the demands on them. The second consists of respite programs offering caregivers some relief by providing small amounts of in-home care, day care, or periodic institutional care for the disabled person. A third type consists of payments directly to caregivers to provide partial monetary compensation for their work. Kane et al. (1998, p. 151) note that the purpose of these caregiver programs is often vague, even to the policymakers who adopt them (they result from compromise, after all), and such programs have not been well evaluated.

Programs for caregivers vary greatly and may address a variety of issues. Support and educational groups are a particularly common intervention highly valued by those who attend regularly. They tend to be most helpful when composed of caregivers assisting people with similar conditions. Some caregivers find support groups impractical, however, preferring to use their precious "free time" to do errands or to get away from their situation.

Among persons above the age of 65 years, caregivers have higher levels of depression and other health problems than noncaregivers. Consequently, some programs provide health checkups and treatment for physical and mental health problems. Others provide periodic screening and case management to support caregivers.

Training programs for caregivers tend to be the most effective when they are available "on-demand," offering the right training exactly when a caregiver needs it. For some, the right time is at the beginning stages of a condition, as part of the diagnosis; for others, it is at critical junctures in the progression of an illness (Kane et al., 1998). For caregivers, training provided by speech, occupational, and physical therapists and nurses is particularly appreciated because such professionals can offer reassurance in the course of providing very specific instruction. In all cases, training effectiveness can only be measured when its goals are clear and caregivers perceive that it meets their individual needs.

New Programs of Support for Family Caregiving

The U.S. Senate Special Commission on Long-Term Care (the "Pepper Commission") in the late 1980s is credited with originating the idea of "consumer-directed care" or "self-direction" in personal care or "personal assistance services." This concept articulated, for the first time, the commonalities among different populations of persons with disabilities needing personal assistance or community-based living arrangements to prevent institutionalization. Various terminologies emerged rapidly in the 1990s after consumer-directed care was detailed in President Clinton's massive Health Security Act of 1993 to "signify a genuine desire to put consumers in charge of their long-term care services" (Kane et al., 1998, p. 131).

Indeed, consumer control of care, or partnership between healthcare providers and patients, has been embraced actively over the last decade by different entities, including parents, advocates for persons with developmental disabilities, the Independent Living Movement of persons with physical disabilities, persons with HIV/AIDS, and the mental health club house and recovery movements.

In the mid-1990s, the federal agencies within the Department of Health and Human Services (DHHS), in collaboration with the Robert Wood Johnson Foundation, funded various demonstration projects (Independent Choices), which tested various innovations in different states. In 1997, they launched a three-state demonstration, the National Demonstration of Cash and Counseling. With nearly 100 waivers from various federal agencies, Arkansas, Florida, and New Jersey conducted randomized trials, allowing consumers the option of using traditional agency-provided personal care, or receiving a "care budget" (based on equivalent service costs) from which they could hire and manage their own personal care workers. Clients willing to try Cash and Counseling were randomly assigned to the experimental consumer choice group or the traditional service control group. By 2004, the data analysis indicated significantly better results in the consumer choice model. Cash and Counseling became a regular option in all the three demonstration states, and DHHS expanded the trial to other states.

Momentum toward consumer-directed care was already building in 1999 when the U.S. Supreme Court decided the groundbreaking case of *Olmstead v. LC*, 527 U.S. 581 (1999). To assure that people with disabilities have choices about where they will be served, and that they may live "in the least restrictive setting" possible, this ruling directed the states to develop more community-based programs for disabled persons more aggressively. To implement the *Olmstead* decision, the Centers for Medicare and Medicaid Services (CMS) have continued to encourage innovations in the states.

Conceptual development and systems thinking about long-term care have been steadily chipping away at a putative oversupply of institutional long-term care beds in the states since 1981, when the Reagan administration initiated the first in-home and community-based services (HCBS) waivers, allowing Medicaid beneficiaries who qualified for nursing home placement to be served at home with personal care and other services. However, the total package had to cost the state less than its average nursing home placement. The assumption was—and still is—that expensive nursing home beds could be replaced in most states by less costly and possibly more effective HCBS. The key to a state systems' management has been identified as finding a "proper balance" between in-home care and service-enhanced housing, specialty-built residences and nursing facilities within the states' long-term care systems. At the national level, policy research has focused on the importance of the states' allocation of resources across different care sectors and their performance (and outcomes). Greater use of federal waivers has allowed states to gradually fund more Medicaid in-home services and community-based care for disabled and frail elderly, and persons with developmental, physical, and cognitive disabilities (Stone, 2006, p. 402; Kane et al., 1998).

In the 1990s, several states (e.g., Oregon, Washington, Arkansas, and Maine) took aggressive steps toward rebalancing their long-term care systems. Oregon, using a new model of small "service-enhanced relative foster care homes," located in large, existing homes in neighborhoods, quickly and dramatically changed the balance of its LTC resources. By 1995, Oregon was serving 47 percent of its publicly funded long-term care clients with in-home services, 25 percent in new relative foster homes, and only 28 percent of the total in nursing homes. By 2005, Oregon and New Mexico were spending over two-thirds of their Medicaid LTC dollars on HCBS, whereas Washington, DC, and Mississippi were spending less than 20 percent of their Medical LTC dollars on HCBS (AARP, 2006).

Movement toward HCBS, and later consumer-directed care, was stimulated primarily by advocates of the disability rights movement, beginning in 1981 with the Reagan administration's initiatives to consolidate various health programs into block grants to the states, including the first Title XIX waivers to states under Section 2176. States had incentives to use these Medicaid waiver opportunities to consolidate programs for various constituencies. Later, the *Olmstead* decision pushed some states into deinstitutionalizing even more people with disabilities. CMS has made the Medicaid waiver process increasingly flexible, investing millions of dollars in Systems Change Grants since 2000 to assist states in these rebalancing efforts. Many states have used their own general revenues as well to strengthen their HCBS infrastructure (Stone, 2006; Kane et al., 1998).

Since the election of George W. Bush in 2000, CMS has continued granting waivers to states, as long as they control demand through the use of waiting lists, enrollment caps, service limits, and spending caps. Periodically, the White House proposes to convert Medicaid into "block grants" to the states. The Deficit Reduction Act of 2005 (discussed in Chapter 19) included additional spending for HCBS for the elderly and disabled, allowing states for the first time to offer these services as an optional benefit instead of requiring a waiver. However, unlike other optional services (e.g., rehabilitation or personal care), states are now allowed to cap the number of people eligible for the services. The Congressional Budget Office (CBO) estimated that this provision would extend additional services to about 120,000 enrollees (KCMU, 2006, p. 6).

Monitoring projects, many sponsored by advocacy organizations with the support of private foundations, have emerged to help "take the pulse" of such developments in the 50 states. The American Association of Retired Persons (AARP), for example, has published biennial reports since 1992, providing comprehensive, comparable state and national level data on 85 reliable performance indicators. The goal is to weigh each of the 50 states' (plus the District of Columbia) long-term care system "performance" relative to maintaining a "healthy balance between institutional and community care programs." These monitoring studies are a valuable resource for policymakers, researchers, consumer advocates, and others making policy decisions about the financing and delivery of long-term care, and the extant support for precious family caregivers (AARP, 2004).

The Future: Strengthened Alliances among Family Caregivers, Older Adults, Paid Care Workers, and Our Future Selves

The state of family care in the United States today seems healthy enough, until we realize how very fragile is the health of individual caregivers providing care for the most disabled and behaviorally difficult older adults. And prospects for increases in the availability of family and friends to fill these roles in the future seem remote indeed.

What can we expect to change in the coming decades? Older Americans will be healthier and living slightly longer than they do today, experience fewer functional disabilities, and require somewhat less assistance. An ever-larger proportion of younger seniors probably will be employed, continuing the trend among males, reversed in the mid-1990s, toward later retirement. In contrast, elders will still have a significant number of years in retirement, allowing at least some time for engaging in community activities, offering advice, and helping their neighbors and loved ones when needed.

Americans may also discover ways to provide for their individual selves even more effectively than they do now, by expanding the range of tools and equipment to assist older people as well as caregivers. These might include personal communications technologies, remote television monitoring of vital signs, assistive devices, and automatic bathing machines. Can long-distance virtual caregiving be far behind? Not exactly. Although technology can be helpful, it is not what most of us actually seek when sick, confused, or anxious, nor what solitary caregivers reach for if assaulted by a confused partner or parent. Caregiving is a human resource, people behaving humanely toward one another. If we can agree that family care is essentially about relationships, emotional connections, and social support, as well as meeting daily needs, we will simply need to generate more of it. Human caring is not so much a financial problem as it is one requiring creative ideas, partnerships, and social allies. Can we really stretch the supply of caregivers, considering what it takes?

Most likely we can, as the National Cash and Counseling project has demonstrated. Certainly, caregivers who do not have to maintain full-time employment elsewhere can provide more and better care for their loved ones. One approach is to extend that option to elders on Medicaid—dropping the "unpaid" prefix from informal—and family caregivers by simply compensating them. This is already possible in the 26 states covering personal care under Medicaid, in states with HCBS waivers, and potentially through the 2005 Deficit Reduction Act that expands community care if states can control enrollment of beneficiaries and spending. Such financial assistance may also allow families to purchase equipment, and hire extra human hands or skilled assistance as needed (AARP, 2006).

Being a long-term care "giver" means commitment and a sense of obligation to another person who needs personal care. These feelings mainly derive from long-standing relationships and generally have developed over time out of convenience or affection. They reflect an investment, or a sense of "giving back" for services previously received. The provision of care by family, friends, and neighbors will remain, like it or not, the most basic long-term care services we have. People do not want to relinquish the care of a loved one, but many need, desire—and deserve—more supports than they have at present. As a group, caregivers already endure too many burdens for their own health and well-being.

One way of acknowledging the caregivers' vital role in the LTC system could be to grant them legally stated rights and protections. Indeed, there are many versions of this concept posted on dozens of caregiver support group Web sites. Most of these Caregiver Bills of Rights include statements aimed directly at the isolated, burdened female caregiver, advising her to "believe in yourself," "ask for help," and "speak up," and asserting that "you have a right to take a break," all cast in terms of her "obligation to take care of herself."

But is the problem really with caregivers themselves? Another way to frame their dilemma is to address the larger issues of American society itself, the routines and policies we live by that are creating our "shortage" of caregivers. These routines and policies must change if we are to generate additional caregiving resources. In turn, this requires an honest acknowledgment that care of frail and disabled people occurs in private homes, among fragile people—the care receiver, the informal family caregiver, and an outside caregiver who is trained and paid—who must all care about and respect each other (Keigher, 1999). There will be an increasing demand for, and willingness by families, insurance companies, and government to pay for more informal and formal home care workers. As such, we must ensure that disabled persons have choices and that caregivers, both paid and unpaid, have rights of their own, including access to livable wages and affordable medical care.

The most obvious step in this direction is to assure that all three of these fragile, dedicated partners—the care receiver, informal family caregiver, and care worker—are rightfully entitled to injury protection, healthcare, and long-term care services for themselves (Keigher, 2000). Efforts to make professional nursing safer should extend to personal care work in both homes and communities. State-of-the-art, individualized training is needed so that workers and family members can both learn to properly lift, transfer, and position patients. Home assessments can help families realistically measure their needs for space adaptation, lift equipment, and alternatives to assist elders themselves, as well as those caring for them. Communities need to be retrofitted for sustainability, making it easier for citizens to stay fit, exercise, walk, and access nutritious food, promoting "mixed neighborhoods" of all ages and incomes, sustaining the availability of potential caregiving friends for older residents, who may remain valued neighborhood assets.

The second need is a "no-brainer": Everyone must be entitled to healthcare as a right. Today, an appallingly high proportion of nursing assistants, home care workers, and family caregivers are without health insurance—the very people likely to be injured, and when ill, likely to jeopardize a fragile older patient and, in turn, the family caregiver. We need to implore all of these fragile stakeholders to be as conscientious as possible about maintaining their health and assure that care is available to them, because others depend on them so much.

The third need is long-term care now for today's disabled Americans of all ages, and in future for all of us. This is the provision we all will be fortunate to have at some later date. Perhaps family and home care workers should be allowed to "earn" home care credits toward their own care in the future, by providing care today. Like Social Security itself, only an intergenerational compact secured by the government could assure this.

Our country could greatly strengthen the fragile caregiving arrangements in the homes of millions of Americans by making a commitment to healthcare for all. That is the first step, and it is high time that we took it.

References

AARP. (2004). *Across the States: Profiles of Long-Term Care*. Washington: American Association of Retired Persons, Public Policy Institute.

AARP. (2006). *Fact Sheet: Rebalancing: Ensuring Greater Access to Home and Community-Based Services*. Washington: American Association of Retired Persons, Public Policy Institute. Online at www.aarp.org.

Achenbaum, A. (2005). *Older Americans, Vital Communities: A Bold Vision for Societal Aging*. Baltimore, MD: Johns Hopkins Press.

Adams, K.B. (2006). The transition to caregiving: The experience of family members embarking on the dementia caregiving career. *Journal of Gerontological Social Work*, 47(3/4), 3–29.

AOA (Administration on Aging). (2002). *A Profile of Older Americans*. Washington: U.S. Department of Health and Human Services.

Arno, P. (2002). Well-being of caregivers: The economic issues of caregivers. In T. McRae (Chair), *New Caregiver Research*. Symposium conducted at the annual meeting of the American Association of Geriatric Psychiatry, Orlando, FL.

ASPE and AOA (Assistant Secretary for Planning and Evaluation and Administration on Aging). (n.d. ca. 1999). *Informal Caregiving: Compassion in Action*. Washington: U.S. Department of Health and Human Services.

Baumgarten, M., Batista, R.N., Infante-Rivard, C., Hanley, J.A., Becker, R., and Gauthier, S. (1992). The physiological and physical health of family members caring for an elderly person with dementia. *Journal of Clinical Epidemiology, 45*, 61–70.

Becker, S., Aldridge, J., and Dearden, C. (1998). *Young Carers and Their Families*. Oxford: Blackwell Science.

Becker, S. and Dearden, C. (1999). Children as carers: The experiences of young carers in the U.K., the mental health issues. *Mental Health, 21*, 273–275.

Bengtson, V.L. (2001). Beyond the nuclear family: The increasing importance of multigenerational relationships in American society. The 1998 Burgess Award Lecture. *Journal of Marriage and the Family, 63*, 1–16.

Bengtson, V.L., Biblarz, T.J., and Roberts, R.E.L. (2002). *How Families Still Matter: A Longitudinal Study of Youth in Two Generations*. New York: Cambridge University Press.

Bengtson, V.L., Putney, N.M., and Wakeman, M.A. (2004). The family and the future: Challenges, prospects and resilience. Paper presented at Conference on Public Policy and Responsibility Across Generations, Boston College, Boston.

Bookwala, J., Yee, J.L., and Schulz, R. (2000). Caregiving and detrimental mental and physical health outcomes. In P.A. Williamson, P.A. Parmelee, and D.R. Shaffer (Eds.), *Physical Illness and Depression in Older Adults: A Handbook of Theory, Research and Practice* (pp. 93–131). New York: Plenum Press.

Cox, C.B. (Ed.). (2000). *To Grandmother's House We Go and Stay: Perspectives on Custodial Grandparents*. New York: Springer.

Cummings, S. (1999). Spousal caregivers of early stage Alzheimer's patients: A psychoeducational support group model. *Journal of Gerontological Social Work, 26*(3/4), 83–98.

Eaton, S.C. (2003). Frontline caregivers in nursing facilities: Can policy help in the recruitment and retention crisis? *Public Policy & Aging Report, 13*(2), 8–11.

Feinberg, L.F., Wolkwitz, K., and Goldstein, C. (2005). *Ahead of the Curve: Emerging Trends and Practices in Family Caregiver Support*. Washington: National Center for Caregiving, Family Caregiver Alliance, American Association of Retired Persons.

FIFARS (Federal Interagency Forum on Aging-Related Statistics). (2004). *Older Americans 2004: Key Indicators of Well-Being*. Federal Interagency Forum on Aging-Related Statistics. Washington: U.S. Government Printing Office.

FIFARS (Federal Interagency Forum on Aging-Related Statistics). (2006). *Older Americans Update 2006: Key Indicators of Well-Being*. Federal Interagency Forum on Aging-Related Statistics. Washington, DC: U.S. Government Printing Office.

Fuller-Thompson, E. and Minkler, M. (2000). African American grandparents raising grandchildren: A national profile and health characteristics, *Health and Social Work, 25*(2), 109–118.

Gallo, J.J., Fulmer, T., Paveza, G.J., and Reichel, W. (2000). *Handbook of Geriatric Assessment* (3rd ed.). Gaithersburg, MD: Aspen Publishers.

George, L.K., Blazer, D.G., Hughes, D.C., and Fowler, N. (1989). Social support and the outcome of major depression. *British Journal of Psychiatry, 154,* 478–485.

George, L.K. and Gwyther, L.P. (1986). Caregiver wellbeing: A multidimensional examination of family caregivers of demented adults. *The Gerontologist, 26,* 253–259.

Gleeson, J.P. and Hairston, C.F. (Eds.). (1999). *Kinship Care: Improving Practice through Research.* Arlington, VA: Child Welfare League of America.

Greenberg, J., Seltzer, M., and Brewer, E. (2006). Caregivers to older adults. In B. Berkman and S. D'Ambruoso (Eds.), *Handbook of Social Work in Health and Aging* (pp. 339–354). New York: Oxford University Press.

Greenberg, J.S., Seltzer, M.M., and Greenley, J.S. (1993). Aging parents of adults with disabilities: The gratifications and frustrations of later-life caregiving, *The Gerontologist, 33,* 542–550.

Harris, B.P. (2002). The voices of husbands and sons caring for a family member with dementia. In B.J. Kramer and E.H. Thompson Jr. (Eds.), *Men as Caregivers: Theory, Research, and Service Implications* (pp. 213–233). Berlin: Springer.

Hooyman, N. (2006). Introduction: Our aging society. Demography and aging. In B. Berkman and S. D'Ambruoso (Eds.), *Handbook of Social Work in Health and Aging.* (pp. xxxi–xl). New York: Oxford University Press.

Hudson, R. (2006). Social services and health planning agencies. In B. Berkman and S. D'Ambruoso (Eds.), *Handbook of Social Work in Health and Aging* (pp. 493–498). New York: Oxford University Press.

Kane, R.A., Kane, R., and Ladd, R. (1998). *The Heart of Long-Term Care.* New York: Oxford University Press.

Kang, S.-Y. (2006). Predictors of emotional strain among spouse and adult child caregivers. *Journal of Gerontological Social Work, 47*(1/2), 107–131.

KCMU. (2006). *Deficit Reduction Act of 2005: Implications for Medicaid.* Washington: Kaiser Commission on Medicaid and the Uninsured. Online: www.KFF.org/kcmu.

Keigher, S. (1999). *Handle with Care: Fragile Elders and Caregivers in the Milwaukee Community Options Program.* School of Social Welfare, UW-Milwaukee and the Faye McBeath Foundation, Milwaukee. Available at: http://www.uwm.edu/Dept/SSW/facstaff/bio/keigher/handle_with_care.pdf.

Keigher, S. (2000). The interests of three stakeholders in independent personal care for disabled elders. *Journal of Health and Human Services Administration, 23*(2), 136–160.

Keigher, S., Zabler, B., Robinson, N., and Fernandez, A. (2005). Children as caregivers of mothers with HIV. *Child and Youth Services Review, 27*(8), 881–904.

Kramer, B.J. (1997). Gain in the caregiving experience: Where are we? What next? *The Gerontologist, 37,* 218–232.

Kramer, B.J. (2000). Husbands caring for wives with dementia: A longitudinal study of continuity and change. *Health and Social Work, 25*(2), 97–107.

Kramer, B.J. and Thompson, E.H. (Eds.). (2002). *Men as Caregivers: Theory, Research, and Service Implications.* Berlin: Springer.

Lawton, M.P., Moss, M., Kleban, M.H., Glicksman, A., and Rovine, M. (1991). A two-factor model of caregiving appraisal and psychological well-being. *Journals of Gerontology, 56,* P181–P189.

LoboPrabhu, S., Molinari, V., Arlingaus, K., Barr, E., and Lomax, J. (2005). Spouses of patients with dementia: How do they stay together "till death do us part"? *Journal of Gerontological Social Work, 44*(3/4), 161–174.

Lustbader, W. (1991). *Counting on Kindness: The Dilemmas of Dependency*. New York: Free Press.

McKinlay, J., Crawford, S., and Tennstedt, S. (1995). The everyday impacts of providing informal care to dependent elders and their consequences for the care recipients. *Journal of Aging and Health, 7*(4), 497–528.

Minkler, M., Fuller-Thomson, E., Miller, D., and Driver, D. (2000). Grandparent caregiving and depression. In B. Hayslip Jr. and R. Goldberg-Glen (Eds.), *Grandparents Raising Grandchildren: Theoretical, Empirical, and Clinical Perspectives* (pp. 207–220). New York: Springer.

Minkler, M. and Roe, K.M. (1993). *Grandmothers as Caregivers: Raising Children of the Crack Cocaine Epidemic*. Newbury Park, CA: Sage.

Moen, P., Erickson, M.A., and Dempster-McClain, D. (2000). Social role identities among older adults in a continuing care retirement community. *Research on Aging, 22,* 559–579.

Moritz, D.J., Kasl, S.V., and Ostfeld, A.M. (1992). The health impact of living with a cognitively impaired elderly spouse. *Journal of Aging and Health, 4,* 244–267.

Morrow-Howell, N., Hinterlong, J., and Sherraden, M. (2001). *Productive Aging: Concepts and Challenges*. Baltimore, MD: Johns Hopkins Press.

National Alliance for Caregiving and American Association of Retired Persons (AARP). (2005). *Caregiving in the United States*. Washington, DC: AARP (www.caregiving. org/data/04 execsumm.pdf).

Navaie-Waliser, M., Feldman, P.H., Gould, D.A., Levine, C., Kuerbis, A.N., and Doneland, K. (2001). The experiences and challenges of informal caregivers: Common themes and differences among whites, blacks and Hispanics. *The Gerontologist, 41,* 733–741.

Nelson-Becker, H.B., Nakashima, M., and Canda, E.R. (2007). Spiritual assessment in aging: A framework for clinicians. *Journal of Gerontological Social Work, 48*(3), 331–347.

Paveza, G.J., Cohen, D., Eisdorfer, C., et al. (1992). Severe family violence and Alzheimer's disease: Prevalence and risk factors. *The Gerontologist, 32*(4), 493–497.

Pearlin, L.I. and Scaff, M.M. (1995). Stressors and adaptation in late life. In M. Gatz (Ed.), *Emerging Issues in Mental Health and Aging* (pp. 87–123). Washington: American Psychological Association.

Rubinstein, R.L. (1986). *Singular Paths: Old Men Living Alone*. New York: Columbia University Press.

Schultz, R. and Williamson, G.M. (1991). A 2-year longitudinal study of depression among Alzheimer's caregivers. *Psychology and Aging, 6,* 569–578.

Seltzer, M.M. (1995). The life course impacts of parenting a child with a disability. *American Journal of Mental Retardation, 106,* 265–286.

Seltzer, M. (2006). Overview: Special caregiving situations. In B. Berkman and S. D'Ambruoso (Eds.), *Handbook of Social Work in Health and Aging* (pp. 337–338). New York: Oxford University Press.

Semple, S.J. (1992). Conflict in Alzheimer's families: Its dimensions and consequences. *The Gerontologist, 32,* 648–655.

Silverstein, M., Conroy, S.J., Wang, H., Giarrusso, R., and Bengtson, V.L. (2002). Reciprocity in parent–child relations over the adult life course. *Journals of Gerontology, 57*(1), S3–S13.

Spillman, B.C. and Black, K.J. (2005). *Staying the Course: Trends in Family Caregiving (Issue Brief #2005–7)*. Washington: AARP Public Policy Institute.

Stone, R.I. (2006). Emerging issues in long term care. In R. Binstock and L. George (Eds.), *Handbook of Aging and the Social Sciences* (6th ed., pp. 397–419). San Diego, CA: Elsevier Academic Press.

Toseland, R.W., Rossiter, C.M., Peak, T., and Smith, G. (1990). Comparative effectiveness of individual and group interventions to support family caregivers. *Social Work 35*, 209–217.

Toseland, R., Smith, G., and McCallion, P. (1995). Supporting the family in elder care. In G. Smith, S. Tobin, E. Robertson-Tchabo, and P. Power (Eds.), *Strengthening Aging Families: Diversity in Practice and Policy* (pp. 3–24). Newbury Park, CA: Sage.

U.S. Census Bureau. (2005). Table 3. Interim projections: Ranking of states by projected percent of population age 65 and above, 2000, 2010, 2030. *Population Division, Interim State Population Projections*. www.census.gov/populations/www/projections/projectionsage-sex.html.

U.S. Census Bureau. (2006). Table 64. Children under 18 years by presence of parents: 1970 to 2005. *America's Families and Living Arrangements: 2005*. http://www.census.gov/population/www/.

U.S. Department of Health and Human Services. (2002). *Delivering on the Promise: U.S. Department of Health and Human Services Self-Evaluation to Promote Community Living for People with Disabilities*. Washington.

Wilmouth, J.M. (2000). Unbalanced social exchanges and living arrangement transitions among older adults. *The Gerontologist. 40*(1), 64–75.

Zarit, S.H. and Zarit, J.M. (1992). Families under stress: Interventions for caregivers of senile dementia patients. *Psychotherapy: Theory, Research and Practice, 19*, 461–471.

Chapter 8

Trends and Challenges in Building a Twenty-First Century Long-Term Care Workforce

Edward Alan Miller and Vincent Mor

Contents

I began my career in long-term care as a dishwasher, later becoming a nursing assistant for seven years, followed by nearly seven more years as a licensed nursing home administrator. I grew up in the poultry capital of America—southwest Missouri—where most of my friends ended up working on a production line. I found myself at a local nursing home washing dishes and being made fun of by my chicken processing friends for working at the "old folk's home." At first, I have to admit that I agreed with them. I thought it was more prestigious to work at the chicken plant and was very upset that my mother forced me to work at the nursing home.

All of us here know it takes a special person to be a good CNA and I knew that there was nothing special about me. I reluctantly became a nurse assistant and learned a valuable lesson—I am special. . . .

Lori Porter
National Association of Geriatric Nursing Assistants, 2005

A well-trained, stable workforce—with well-trained professionals and paraprofessionals such as certified nurse assistants, home health aides, personal assistants, licensed practical nurses, registered nurses, nurse supervisors, physicians, social workers, pharmacists, administrators, and therapists specializing in care for the chronically ill and disabled—is a necessary prerequisite for quality long-term care. But for every Lori Porter, who enthusiastically embraces a rewarding career in long-term care, there are countless others who lack the necessary incentives and opportunities to do so. Although this is especially true of lesser-skilled workers, as the combination of low wages, insufficient benefits, inadequate training, heavy workloads, and associated stigma conspires to make recruitment and retention a challenge; it is also true of nurses, physicians, and others who prescribe services and supervise direct-care staff. Promoting better compensation, career advancement, and improved work environments for caregivers at all levels is the major challenge facing development of an adequate twenty-first century long-term care workforce in the United States.

Who Provides Formal Long-Term Care?

According to the U.S. Bureau of Labor Statistics (USBLS), there were 3.85 million individuals employed in long-term care in 2003, 57 percent of whom delivered direct care, including 545,690 registered nurses (RNs) and licensed practical nurses (LPNs), and 1.65 million nurse aides, home health aides, and personal care workers (American Health Care Association, 2004). Compared to the workforce in general, nurse aides working in long-term care (nursing homes, home health) are more likely to be female (90.9 percent, 89.2 percent), nonwhite (43.3, 51.4), unmarried (60.6, 56.4), have a high school education or less (72.6, 62.1), and have children at home (56.3, 51.1). Nearly 50 percent have incomes below 200 percent of the federal poverty level. Approximately half are between the ages of 25 and 44 years (United States General Accounting Office, 2001). On average, home care aides tend to be older than nursing homes aides (46.2 versus 38.0). Compared to nursing home aides, home care aides are also more likely to be Hispanic or Latino (15.9 versus 7.8 percent) and to be foreign-born or non-U.S. citizens (23.7 versus 13.8 percent).

The USBLS estimates that in 2003 there were 170,880 RNs and LPNs and 567,150 paraprofessional staff, including 255,370 home health aides and 269,860 personal and home care aides, employed in home-based service (American Health Care Association, 2004). Because a significant proportion of home-based aides are hired privately, however, USBLS estimates likely underestimate the number of home care workers (Stone, 2004). This explains, in part, why one recently pub-lished study using data from the 2000 Census and including workers employed by both private households and home care agencies, resulted in a value, 788,149, significantly higher than those previously published (Montgomery et al., 2005). Regardless of the exact number, however, the demand for home care workers has grown in light of consumer preferences for increased public funding for home-and-community based services (HCBS) and socioeconomic and demographic trends that favor a more consumer-driven market (Wright, 2005). At an estimated growth rate of 56 percent, the USBLS (2005) projects that, between 2004 and 2014, home health aides will be the fastest growing U.S. occupation, with personal and home care aides, at 41 percent, being the fourth fastest. This is in contrast to registered nurses and nursing aides, orderlies, or attendants, who are expected to grow by 29.4 and 22.3 percent, respectively, during the same time period.

In contrast to home care, more comprehensive data exists on staffing in nursing homes, where 80–90 percent of hands-on care is provided by nurse aides. Although analysis of data from the Online Survey, Certification, and Reporting (OSCAR) system indicates that the number of RNs and LPNs working in nursing homes remained steady at about 100,000 and 200,000 full-time equivalent employees (FTEs), respectively, between 1992 and 2004, the number of certified nurse assistants (CNAs) declined from 700,000 to 600,000 FTEs. This is in contrast to the number of residents, which increased from 1.28 to 1.63 million between 1977 and 1999, and the number of beds per facility, which increased from 79 to 105 during the same time period (Decker, 2005). This growth in utilization has been accompanied by greater acuity among residents, with the proportion of residents aged 85 and above increasing from 34.8 to 46.5 percent between 1977 and 1999, and the proportion able to independently perform basic life activities (eating, walk-ing, dressing, and bathing) declining during these years (from 66.8 to 52.8, 32.9

to 21.1, 29.6 to 12.9, and 13.0 to 5.6 percent, respectively) (Decker, 2005). Thus, as the number of CNAs has declined, workloads and the social and medical complexity of residents cared for have grown significantly.

Are Staffing Levels Sufficient to Ensure Quality?

Clearly, long-term care providers must have enough well-trained staff to perform the tasks necessary to respond to every client's needs. Analysis of OSCAR indicates that total staff hours per resident per day in 2004 averaged 3.6, ranging from approximately 0.5 for RNs to 0.8 for LPNs and 2.3 for CNAs. Federal law requires a minimum of eight hours per day of RN services and twenty-four hours per day of licensed nursing service. Although 36 states have adopted their own nursing facility staffing levels, no staff-to-resident ratios or hours per resident per day have been established by the federal government (Tilly et al., 2003).

Total staff hours in many nursing homes are below recommended levels (see Figure 8.1). Nearly 30 percent average fewer than 2.75 nursing hours per patient per day, the minimum recommended by the Centers for Medicare and Medicaid Services (CMS) (2002). Less than 10 percent average more than 4.55 hours per patient per day, the level favored by many experts in the field (Harrington et al., 2000). There is also dramatic interstate variation in staffing levels. According to OSCAR, more than half the nursing homes in seven states—Missouri, Oklahoma, Kansas, Iowa, Illinois, Texas, and New Mexico—do not meet minimum federally

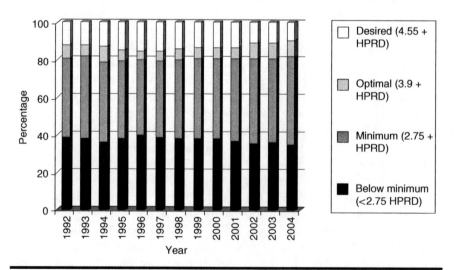

Figure 8.1 Percentage of nursing homes meeting various recommended minimum total staff levels, hours per resident per day (HPRD), 1992–2004. (Brown University analysis of Online Survey, Certification, and Reporting [OSCAR], 1992–2004.)

recommended standards. Whereas 40 percent of nursing homes would need to increase total staffing levels to meet CMS' preferred minimum standards, 95 percent would need to increase total staffing levels to meet the levels preferred by advocates. Currently, the federal government lacks a process for collecting and monitoring accurate staffing data in nursing homes, let alone among home care providers. Furthermore, because there is considerable heterogeneity in residents' social and clinical needs for care from facility to facility, uniform staffing ratios might not be appropriate without taking this into consideration.

Research has consistently demonstrated a relationship between staffing and the quality of care in nursing homes. Higher staffing has been associated with resident survival, functional status, fewer pressure sores and infections, less physical restraint use, catheterization, weight loss, dehydration, and lower hospitalization rates. Better staffing also leads to lower worker injury and litigation rates, as well as less stressful conditions, so that physical and psychological abuse may also be less likely (Centers for Medicare and Medicaid Services, 2002; Institute of Medicine, 2001, 2003). One recent study of California nursing homes found that facilities with higher staffing (>4.1 hours per resident per day) performed better on 12 of the 16 process of care measures, including getting residents out of bed, engaging in activities, and providing feeding assistance and incontinence care. It also found that staffing proved to be a better predictor of quality than eight separate clinical indicators currently used by the federal government (Schnelle et al., 2004). This is also true of another recent study, which examined the relationship between staffing and quality in four states and found reductions in quality associated with increases in both RN and NA/LPN turnover (Castle and Engberg, 2005).

Although there is little empirical evidence on the relationship between staffing and quality of care in home care, Stone (2004, p. 525) observes that "anecdotes and qualitative studies suggest that problems with attracting and retaining direct care workers translate into poorer quality and/or unsafe care, major disruptions in continuity of care, and reduced access to care." Without sufficient staff, home care agencies may not have enough aides to send out, let alone be able to provide clients with the same good worker day in and day out. This increases pressure on family caregivers, who already provide most care to frail and disabled individuals living in the community (Stone, 2004). It may also lead individuals and families to choose residential care options even though these options may not be among their preferred choices.

Not only does available evidence indicate that staffing levels affect quality, but it also suggests that the mix of staff available may affect quality as well. Elderly patients treated by advanced practice geriatric nurse specialists experience fewer hospital readmissions and nursing home-to-hospital transfers (Intrator et al., 2004). However, these staff resources are relatively rare. Indeed, the nursing shortage has translated to increased use of contract nurses, which undermines continuity of patient care. Analysis of OSCAR indicates that the percentage of nursing homes using 5 percent or more contract nurses doubled between 1997 and 2004, from

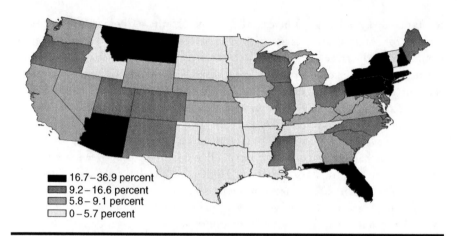

Figure 8.2 Percentage of freestanding nursing homes employing 5% or more contact nurses, 2004. (Brown University analysis of Online Survey, Certification, and Reporting [OSCAR] data, 2004.)

5 to 10 percent for RNs and 7 to 14 percent for LPNs, respectively (see Figure 8.2). There is evidence to suggest that this level of use of contract nurses is associated with poorer care. There is also limited evidence to suggest that a relationship may exist between the quality of home care workers and clinical, functional, and lifestyle outcomes of consumers (Stone, 2004). Leadership with special training and certification might make a difference as well. Although there are currently only 500 active certified nursing home administrators, facilities administered by them perform better in terms of the number and severity of deficiencies than facilities without a certified administrator (American College of Health Care Administrators, 2005).

Staff turnover in long-term care is particularly problematic. Annual turnover rates in home care range from 40 to 60 percent (Paraprofessional Healthcare Institute, 2005). Annual turnover rates in nursing homes approach 50 percent for most staff categories and, depending on the tightness of the labor market, may exceed 100 percent in certain areas as positions must often be filled multiple times during the course of a year. At 71.1 percent in 2002, turnover is especially high among CNAs (Decker et al., 2003). Turnover in nursing home leadership is equally problematic; nearly half of Directors of Nursing (DONs), staff RNs, and LPNs were replaced in 2002 and 35.5 percent of administrative RNs. Recent estimates also place turnover among nursing home administrators at somewhere between 40 and 43 percent (Castle, 2005).

Turnover is quite varied across regions. In New Jersey, New York, and Pennsylvania, CNA turnover was estimated to be 45.7 percent in 2002, whereas in Arkansas, Louisiana, Oklahoma, and Texas this rate exceeded 100 percent (Decker et al., 2003). The volume of vacancies in nursing homes is also high, with an estimated 96,000 FTEs in vacant positions in 2002 (Decker et al., 2003). Approximately 52,000 of these vacancies were for CNA positions, with an additional 13,900 and

25,100 for RN and LPN positions, respectively. Vacancy rates were especially high among staff RNs (15.0 percent) and LPNs (13.2 percent) and somewhat lower for CNAs (8.5 percent) and other positions. Bowers et al. (2000) suggest that turnover affects quality, in part, by causing disruptions in care continuity and resident–caregiver relationships, which, in turn, reduce the chances that care will be provided in ways that satisfy residents' needs and preferences. By promoting instability and turnover among direct care staff, turnover among administrators has been shown to compromise quality as well (Castle, 2001, 2005).

What Does the Future Hold for Long-Term Care Staffing?

Staff shortages in long-term care will become even more significant in the future. The number of Americans needing long-term care is projected to increase from 13 to 27 million between 2000 and 2050, with the number of elderly individuals needing such care increasing from 8 to 19 million (United States Department of Health and Human Services, 2003). Consequently, the USBLS projects that an additional 1.9 million direct care workers will be needed in long-term care settings between 2000 and 2010 alone (United States Department of Health and Human Services, 2003). But although the need for long-term care services is expected to increase greatly over the coming decades, the supply of workers is not expected to keep up with the resulting demand due to reductions in the number of people who have traditionally filled these jobs. The Health Resources and Services Administration (HRSA, 2002), for example, has projected that the current RN deficit is likely to increase from 6 to 29 percent between 2000 and 2020. Thus, medical advances and the graying of the population will result in a marked increase in the demand for nursing services, whereas the number of nurses leaving the profession due to attrition and retirement will exceed the number entering the field. This growing gap in "caring capacity" will be apparent at all levels of staffing in every long-term care organization. This is because the nation is training fewer and fewer geriatric specialists, including doctors, nurses, CNAs, home health aides, and advance practice nurses—at a time—given the demographics—when we should be training more.

Thirty percent of the nation's 670 baccalaureate nursing programs satisfy criteria for exemplary geriatrics education. However, less than 23 percent of these require a stand-alone geriatrics course. Only three of the nation's 145 medical schools have geriatric departments, and less than 10 percent of these require a course in geriatrics. Given limited capacity to produce geriatric specialists, it should not be surprising that only 21,500 of the nation's 2.2 million practicing RNs are certified in geriatrics, while only 6,600 of the nation's 650,000 physicians are certified in this area, although projections suggest that 36,000 geriatricians will be needed by 2030 (Kovner et al., 2002). Although 91 percent of nursing home residents have a significant mental disorder, only 1.7 percent of general psychiatrists provide services in nursing homes, with only 2600 having received subspecialty certification in geriatric psychiatry since 1991. Training in geriatric mental health is similarly lacking among psychologists and social workers (American Geriatrics Society and American Association of Geriatric Psychiatry, 2003). Most direct care staff have little or no training specific to geriatric care as well.

Why Is There Difficulty in Recruiting and Retaining Staff?

There are several reasons why many find long-term care unattractive, or choose not to stay after entering the field. Part of the explanation has to do with the "second-rate" status associated with working in this area, whether as a physician or hourly employee making minimum wage. This stems, in part, from the widespread public perception that caring for the elderly is unpleasant and unappealing, along with media portrayals of some long-term care providers as profiteers more interested in making money than ensuring high-quality patient care. Based on a recent Kaiser Family Foundation (2005) national survey of the public, nursing homes, at 35 percent, rank below pharmaceutical manufacturers (43 percent) and just above health insurers (34 percent) and managed care plans (30 percent) in the share of adults who believe that they are doing a "good job" meeting the country's need. This is in contrast to nurses (94 percent), doctors (69 percent), and hospitals (64 percent). Although 69 percent of respondents agree that nursing homes provide frail and disabled people a safe environment they could not have at home, twice as many believe that nursing homes make people worse rather than better off (see Figure 8.3). Furthermore, 74 percent believe that nursing homes do not have enough

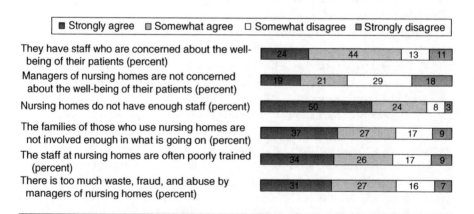

Figure 8.3 Views of nursing home management, percent who agree. (From Kaiser Family Foundation [2005] Health Poll Report Survey [conducted June 2–5, 2005].)

staff. Sixty percent believe that staff at nursing homes are often poorly trained, and 58 percent believe that there is too much waste, fraud, and abuse by managers.

Despite public perceptions, providing direct care is physically and emotionally demanding, with injury rates exceeding those for almost any other profession. In 2003, workplace injuries in nursing homes and residential care facilities averaged 10.1 per 100 full-time workers, compared to 6.8 per 100 construction workers and 5.0 per 100 workers in all private workplaces (Wright, 2005). There are also a high number of assaults on direct care staff, with 59 percent of nursing assistants in one study reporting being assaulted by residents at least once a week and 16 percent daily (Gates et al., 2002). Injury rates and assaults may be especially high in less well-staffed facilities, with heavy caseloads being cited as one of the major reasons why CNAs leave long-term care and why retention is higher in facilities with more staff (Centers for Medicare and Medicaid Services, 2002; Mickus et al., 2004; Trinkoff et al., 2005). Ensuring safety is also a concern among home care workers, who may, in fact, be at greater risk as they venture out into the community (Sylvester and Reisener, 2002).

Other frequently cited factors contributing to turnover include inadequate initial training and continuing education, rotating assignments and limited involvement in decision making, perceived lack of value and respect on the part of supervisors, and little or no opportunities for professional growth and career advancement (Eaton, 2002; Mickus et al., 2004). Rotating assignments make CNAs feel unappreciated because it demonstrates a lack of value for their skills and knowledge, and prevents the development of ongoing caregiving relationships with residents, which compromises their ability to provide quality care (Bowers, 2003).

Another frequently cited reason for turnover is low wages (Eaton, 2002; Mickus et al., 2004). The long-term care workforce is among the lowest paid in the nation. This is especially true of paraprofessional direct care workers, who, with a median hourly wage of $9.20 in 2003, earned nearly 33 percent less than all U.S. workers (American Health Care Association, 2004). Furthermore, only 48.3 percent of nursing home aides engage in year-round, full-time employment. Even fewer home care aides—34.3 percent—do so (Montgomery et al., 2005). In part because a significant portion work only part-time, at $13,287 and $12,265, respectively, in 2002, the median annual incomes for nursing home and home care aides were barely above the federal poverty line of $11,060 for a family of two and well below that of $16,700 for a family of four (Paraprofessional Healthcare Institute, 2003a). Direct care workers are also less likely to receive benefits, including health insurance, vacation time, tuition assistance, pension coverage, and child care (Fishman et al., 2004). This is especially true in home care where agencies often "fill their rosters with as many part-time aides as they can hire, train them to minimum required standards, and assign work with little regard for the aides' need for full-time hours or other professional treatment. As a result, turnover in the industry is high, care provided is erratic, and both home care aides and home care clients suffer" (University of Wisconsin Center for Cooperatives, 2006, p. 1).

What Strategies Might Promote Greater Recruitment and Retention?

Recruitment and retention represent significant costs, both for long-term care providers and the quality of care that they provide. Direct costs, including administrative costs, overtime pay, temporary staffing and advertising, screening, interviewing, and training (Seavey, 2004), range from $2500 for aides to $7000 for RNs (Castle and Engberg, 2005; National Commission on Nursing Workforce for Long-Term Care, 2005). The indirect costs are also substantial and include lost productivity, reduced admissions, deterioration in employee morale, and reductions in service quality (Seavey, 2004). The presence of significant costs, both direct and indirect, implies that successful efforts to reduce turnover will have a significant return on investment. Consequently, several strategies have been adopted to improve workforce recruitment and retention in long-term care. The most prominent have been attempts to change the workplace environment, increase wages and benefits, and create opportunities for career advancement and training.

Work-Oriented Redesign

A number of initiatives promote systematic work-oriented redesign that eschews hierarchical management structures in favor of strategies that enhance worker autonomy and involvement in decision making (National Commission on Nursing Workforce for Long-Term Care, 2005). These include several management practices shown to distinguish the culture of nursing homes with lower turnover and higher-quality care from those with higher turnover and lower-quality care. This is reflected in several studies which found that in comparison to the latter, the former had more effective leadership and management offering caregivers recognition, meaning, feedback, and opportunity; an organizational culture valuing and respecting both caregivers and residents; positive human resource policies in the areas of compensation, training, career ladders, and scheduling; thoughtful and motivational organization and care practices such as consistent assignment, individualized care planning, and the use of team and group processes; implementation of active quality improvement programs; and adequate staff ratios and support (Barry et al., 2005; Eaton, 2002; Grant, 2004; Mor, 1995; Rantz et al., 2004). There is also evidence that smaller facilities have better outcomes than larger facilities (Grant, 2004; Rantz et al., 2004).

Frequently highlighted are the benefits of primary assignment in which the staff work consistently with the same residents. Ninety percent of nursing homes rotate staff from one group of residents to another after a period of time (Farrell, 2005). This promotes instability in caregiver–resident relationships, thereby making it difficult for staff to honor and anticipate residents' needs and personal preferences. In contrast, primary assignment promotes greater resident–caregiver bonding, and as such, increases caregiver satisfaction while providing the foundations for resident-centered care, with positive implications for quality of life and resident outcomes, such as personal appearance and hygiene; pressure ulcers and ambulation; and greater sense of security, comfort, control, choice, and well-being (Burgio et al., 2004; Campbell, 1985; Caudill, 1991–1992; Cox et al., 1991; Goldman, 1998). There is also considerable interest in self-managed work teams, which have been shown to lower absenteeism and turnover and improve decision making, job satisfaction, and performance in manufacturer settings (Yeats et al., 2004).

Wages and Benefits

Given lower wages and benefits and fewer advancement opportunities than in other industries, long-term care providers have difficulty competing with employers offering less physically and emotionally demanding low-pay jobs (Paraprofessional Healthcare Institute, 2003a). This is reflected in one study, which found that inactive nurse aide registrants in North Carolina who left long-term care earned more income, experienced less unemployment, and cycled through fewer positions each year than active registrants still employed in long-term care (Konrad et al., 2003). In addition to other low-wage industries, long-term care providers have a difficult time competing with hospitals, where wages and benefits for RNs and paraprofessionals workers are considerably higher (United States Department of Health and Human Services, 2003). For example, the average annual salary for RNs and nurse aides are 17.0 and 9.4 percent lower, respectively, in nursing homes than in hospitals. Additionally, nurse aides are nearly twice as likely to receive health insurance and pension coverage in hospitals as under nursing home employment. In 2001, $2.7 billion would have been needed to increase wages and benefits to achieve parity in compensation among hospital and nursing home staff (Decker et al., 2001), a value that would be considerably higher if accounting for even the lower wages and fewer benefits in home care. This competition for staff is likely to increase as acute care hospitals' demands for workers specially trained in geriatrics rise along with those of nursing homes and home care providers.

As of 2003, 26 states have sought to increase compensation through wage pass-through policies in which a reimbursement increase from a public source—usually Medicaid—is directed toward increased wages and benefits for direct care workers (Harmuth and Dyson, 2004). Between 1999 and 2002, average CPI-adjusted Medicaid *per diem* rates increased by a modest 3.8 percent, from $105.80 to $117.73 (Grabowski et al., 2004). Most state Medicaid programs reimburse nursing homes on the basis of cost centers where a certain amount of payment is directed toward nursing, capital, administration, housekeeping, and other areas. Those who wish to direct more money into staffing set higher limits on how much they pay for nursing than for other areas. According to one survey, nine states extended pass-throughs to nursing home workers only, whereas four extended them exclusively to home care workers and eight to both nursing home and home care workers (Paraprofessional Healthcare Institute, 2003a).

The purpose of wage pass-through programs is to ensure that increases in payments show up as higher wages and more generous benefits for direct care workers. However, there has been little systematic evaluation of wage pass-through programs. Of the twelve wage pass-through states responding to a 1999 survey, four reported that they had a positive impact on recruitment and retention, three reported that they had no impact, and three said the impact was unknown (North Carolina Division of Facility Services, 2000). Results from four unsophisticated evaluations performed have been mixed; Michigan experienced a 61 percent increase in CNA wages and 21 percent decline in turnover over the 13 years of its wage pass-through program, whereas wages for nurse aides in Massachusetts increased by 8.7 percent during the first year of that program and vacancy rates stabilized. After one year of implementation, turnover in Kansas nursing homes declined from 111 to 101 percent following implementation, whereas total compensation for direct care workers in Wyoming increased from $9.08 to $13.74 per hour and turnover declined from 52 to 37 percent over the first three months for that state's wage pass-through (Harris-Kojetin et al., 2004; Paraprofessional Healthcare Institute, 2003a). Although the efficacy of wage pass-through programs has yet to be fully examined, most agree that low wages contribute to high turnover, especially among direct care workers.

Because wage pass-throughs provide a mechanism to attract and retain a higher-quality workforce, they have garnered support from both industry and resident advocates. Given widespread support for programs such as these, there is a greater need to rigorously evaluate the staff and wage pass-through policies that are in place. There is also a need for more effective auditing and enforcement procedures to ensure that additional funding is going where it is supposed to go. This process of ensuring provider accountability is critical, although it can be potentially burdensome for states.

Training, Career Ladders, Loan Forgiveness, and Scholarships

Training

The federal government requires that CNAs and home health aides work under the supervision of an RN and receive at least 75 hours of minimum training. This includes 16 hours of clinical training in addition to 59 hours in the classroom learning basic caregiving skills. Within four months of employment, these workers must pass a state-sanctioned competency test to work for a Medicare- or Medicaid-certified nursing home or certified home health agency, and must receive an additional 12 hours of training annually to maintain certification (Paraprofessional Healthcare Institute, 2005). This is in contrast to home care aides or personal care workers hired by state, local, or nonprofit agencies and independent providers hired directly by consumers. These individuals may or may not be subject to training requirements and may or may not work under the supervision of an RN (Stone, 2004).

Because of rising acuity and frailty, especially in nursing homes, there is a growing concern that current training requirements do not adequately prepare direct care workers for their positions (Salsberg, 2003). This has spurred 26 states to extend mandatory CNA training beyond the 75 hours required by the federal law, including 15 states that require 100 or more hours (Office of Inspector General, 2002). CNAs working in Missouri must receive at least 175 hours of training. Virginia recently expanded its minimum number of training hours from 80 to 120. Ohio, New Mexico, and Florida have developed new rules standardizing training CNAs and other direct care workers throughout their states (Harmuth and Dyson, 2005; Office of Inspector General, 2002).

A number of states have also extended training requirements for home health aides. Wyoming requires 91 hours of training and Washington 105 hours. Several require home health aides to be certified as CNAs with, perhaps, additional training on topics related specifically to home care. Although Maryland has no training requirements for personal care aides, home health aides must receive CNA certification in addition to 12 hours of in-service training. However, many states require training for personal assistance workers. Maine requires 40 hours of training for all personal care assistants. Other states require personal care assistants to complete the same training as home health aides, whereas some require only a few hours of in-service training (Harmuth and Dyson, 2005; Paraprofessional Healthcare Institute, 2005). There is also a growing awareness of the need to support self-directed consumers who hire and train their own workers (Paraprofessional Healthcare Institute, 2004).

Recently, there has been interest in providing new workers with more intensive and structured orientation, with some state and provider initiatives adopting peer-mentoring systems for new employees (Paraprofessional Healthcare Institute, 2003b). An example is New York's "Growing Strong Roots" peer-mentoring program, which pairs new employees with exemplary and experienced CNAs who acquaint them with the customs, resources, and values of their facilities. Both mentors and mentees receive additional training. Mentors also receive formal recognition and a bonus or increase in salary. Retention among new CNAs and their mentors increased by an average of 17 and 21 percent, respectively, in six nursing homes participating in the program's initial evaluation. No significant increases were identified in comparison homes. The program has therefore added an additional 22 facilities to its roster (Harris-Kojetin et al., 2004).

Another initiative that promotes a more nurturing approach is the Learn, Empower, Achieve, and Produce (LEAP) program developed by Mather Lifeways, a long-term care provider in Illinois. The goal is to develop leadership, mentoring, teamwork, and communication skills among all staff. Nurse managers, RNs, and LPNs participate in a six-week workshop to develop leadership, role model, clinical gerontological, and team-building skills. CNAs participate in a fourteen-hour, seven-week workshop that focuses on career and skill development in a variety of areas, including person-centered care, communication, care team building, and mentoring. CNAs that complete this training become level 2 CNAs and receive salary increases ranging from $0.50 to $1 per hour. LEAP was piloted in 1999 and replicated at three other sites between 2000 and 2002. Both nurse and CNA turnover declined among participating facilities. Both nurses' and CNAs' perceptions regarding their work empowerment, job satisfaction, and organization communication improved significantly, with improvement on these variables being associated with fewer health deficiencies cited on state inspections. More than 400 "specialists" from 26 states have been trained to replicate LEAP in their own facilities (Hollinger-Smith, 2002; National Clearinghouse on the Direct Care Workforce, 2005).

Career Ladders

Both Growing Strong Roots and LEAP incorporate career ladders, which allow workers to acquire skills that enable them to grow professionally and advance through a progression of better paying jobs. There are several basic types of career ladders: those that provide workers with opportunities for higher pay and greater professionalization within the context of their current positions, and those that provide staff with financial incentives to participate in supplemental "job-enhancement" training programs. The latter includes programs that create formal tiers within the same occupation. It also includes programs that enable workers to move progressively from one occupation to another, for example, from being CNAs or home health aides to LPNs or RNs.

Several states have encouraged career enhancement within the context of current positions. One example is "Growing Strong Roots" in New York. Another example is North Carolina's "WIN A STEP UP" program, which provides nurse aides with financial incentives in the way of bonuses and higher wages to complete 11 training sessions over 16 weeks focusing on clinical proficiency, interpersonal skills, and communication. Before the start of the program, supervisors in participating facilities receive training in the "coaching style" of mentoring, whereas nurse aides commit to continuing employment for at least three months. Compared to nonparticipants, participating nurse aides demonstrate better retention and job satisfaction (WIN A STEP UP, 2005). Other states have developed more targeted programs that enable CNAs to acquire skills for performing specific additional tasks. Examples include Maine, which has developed a 24-hour medication administration course and South Dakota, which allows CNAs who have completed basic training to specialize in a particular clinical area such as dementia or wound care (Harmuth and Dyson, 2005; National Commission on Nursing Workforce for Long-Term Care, 2005).

A second type of career ladder program creates formal tiers within the same occupation, the gradual assumption of which provides workers with increases in pay and responsibility (Fitzgerald and Carlson, 2000). Although programs such as LEAP have only two tiers, several similar initiatives have three or more. Johns Hopkins Geriatric Center, a 218-bed facility in Baltimore, Maryland, has established a three-level career ladder in which entry-level staff begin as geriatric nurse aides (GNAs), but with subsequent classroom and clinical education and training, gradually move to geriatric patient aide (GPA) and patient care technician (PCT) positions. GNAs provide basic care mandated by federal and state law; GPAs perform several additional procedures such as ostomy care, pulse oximetry, and blood sugar monitoring; and PCTs acquire more advanced acute care skills necessary to care for certain patient populations (Harris-Kojetin et al., 2004). Through its Performance Improvement and Quality Improvement program, Ararat Nursing Home, a 200-bed facility in Mission Hill, California, has established a five-tier career ladder, with increases in responsibility and pay of 25–50 cents per hour as CNAs move from level to level (National Commission on Nursing Workforce for Long-Term Care, 2005). States such as Delaware and North Carolina have also created new job levels for CNAs referred to as "senior CNAs" and "GNAs," respectively (Harmuth and Venkatraman, 2001).

A third type of career ladder provides direct care workers with the education and training opportunities necessary for them to move progressively to better paying occupations; for example, from CNAs to LPNs and RNs. Under its PRIDE program, New Courtland Elder Services, a subsidiary of the Presbyterian Foundation of Philadelphia, adopted a career ladder program consisting of three CNA levels as well as in-house preparation courses and scholarships encouraging nurse aides to earn their General Educational Development (GED) diplomas or to become LPNs and RNs (National Commission on Nursing Workforce for Long-Term Care, 2005). Cooperative Home Care Associates (CHCA), a worker-owned home health agency in New York's South Bronx, provides its workers with opportunities for career advancement, leadership development, and working participation in agency decisions. CHCA has established three levels of home health aides, with each successive level associated with additional training and higher wages. There are also opportunities to advance to positions within administration and training, and several programs have been established to help aides advance beyond home health to other occupations (e.g., nursing). Approximately 80 percent of CHCA's employees share ownership, with the majority of board members being elected from among direct care staff (Inserra, 2002; Powell, 2006; Stone, 2004).

Effective career ladder programs do their best to seamlessly integrate training with the work and personal lives of employees by offering courses at convenient times and providing students with access to the financial assistance necessary to pay for tuition, books, and other expenses. Furthermore, several successful programs have formed partnerships with local workforce investment agencies, community-based organizations, unions, community colleges, and other educational institutions to design and implement appropriate training programs and career advancement opportunities (Fishman et al., 2004). In fact, community colleges throughout the country report collaborative efforts with healthcare providers to address nursing shortages in their areas (National Commission on Nursing Workforce for Long-Term Care, 2005). Joining forces with a local community college, for example, five Genesis ElderCare facilities located on the same campus in rural Massachusetts provide entry-level employees with formal career ladder classes and college courses, including an on-site evening LPN program. This program has been funded, in part, by the State of Massachusetts Extended Care Career Ladder Initiative, which supports several organizations' efforts to develop opportunities for direct care workers to increase their skills to reduce turnover and vacancies in long-term care. Although originally targeted at CNAs, Massachusetts Extended Care program has since been expanded to home care (National Commission on Nursing Workforce for Long-Term Care, 2005).

On a larger scale, the provider–educational institution approach has been used by both private foundations and public agencies as they seek to encourage more health workers to enter geriatrics. For example, states match HSRA grants to fund regionally based Geriatric Education Centers (GECs), which are accredited health profession schools that foster collaborative relationships among educators to improve health professional training in geriatrics and to provide clinical experiences in geriatrics in nursing homes and other long-term care settings (United States Department of Health and Human Services, 2003). Similarly, the American Association of Colleges of Nursing has joined forces with the John A. Hartford Foundation to establish the Geriatric Nursing Education Project to support curriculum development and new clinical experiences in geriatric settings by forging partnerships between schools of nursing and long-term care organizations.

Online Training

Online training and the Internet are playing a major role in seamlessly integrating health professional training to people's work and personal lives, and encouraging low-income individuals who have families and other full-time obligations to pursue more advanced careers in long-term care. There are several examples that illustrate how computer-assisted learning can be used to promote career mobility in this area. Indeed, were it not for online resources, many facilities might not be able to comply with regulatory requirements for continuing education. This has helped spur the creation of Web sites such as www.myziva.com, which provides nursing home operators with a comprehensive array of management tools and resources, including 100 continuously updated online courses, education materials, and other resources. There has also been a growing proliferation of Web-based continuing medical education sites more generally, including those sponsored by the American Medical Association, which has produced its own resources on pain management and osteoporosis while endorsing online systems created by others. Furthermore, online training now constitutes 10 percent of all higher education, among the most prominent areas of which is healthcare. These include bachelor's, master's, and doctorate programs in health administration and nursing, in addition to certification programs for medical and nurse assistants (eLearners, 2005; OnlineCareers.com, 2005). It has been suggested that funding for expanded online programs be provided through state and federal grants (National Commission on Nursing Workforce for Long-Term Care, 2005; Salsberg, 2003). For example, North Carolina and Minnesota have designated funding to support on-site online training for CNAs in nursing homes.

Loan Forgiveness and Scholarships

Financial incentives may prove to be an especially attractive means of spurring people to pursue educational opportunities in long-term care. This is not only true for CNAs, home health aides, and LPNs looking to advance their careers, but also for physicians, nurses, and others who may not otherwise choose careers in this area. Indeed, there has been growing interest among state and federal officials in directing scholarships and loan forgiveness programs toward both the professional and paraprofessional segments of the long-term care workforce. Scholarships provide support for tuition and other expenses incurred by students as they pursue their education, whereas loan forgiveness pays off educational debt after students complete their programs. Although both approaches may be effective in encouraging financially better-off individuals to pursue careers in targeted specialties, scholarships may be more effective than loan forgiveness in stimulating financially disadvantaged students to do so, as they may not have the money for tuition even though it may be reimbursed after graduation. This is especially true when tuition is high, education takes several years, and loan repayment is competitive or uncertain. Loan forgiveness, however, may be more easily connected to service obligation in a particular geographic area, facility, or field (Salsberg, 2003). For example, medical students will sometimes receive scholarships, fulfill their obligation, and then immediately move on. This is in contrast to loan forgiveness programs, which, because they do not require individuals to sign up for service years in advance, but instead after their education has been completed, allows them to choose the areas within which to work, thereby increasing the likelihood that they will stay for longer periods of time.

There are several state and federal programs that provide loan forgiveness and tuition assistance. Among a multitude of federal programs, the Health Resources and Services Administration provided $15 million in loan repayment under its Nursing Education Loan Repayment programs to nurses who agree to serve at least two years in designated facilities (United States Department of Health and Human Services, 2003). At the state level, the Michigan Nursing Scholarship program offered $4 million in scholarships to RN and LPN students in exchange for a commitment to work in a Michigan healthcare facility after graduation (National Commission on Nursing Workforce for Long-Term Care, 2005). Minnesota established a program to fund scholarships to nonadministrative workers looking to advance their careers in long-term care, whereas Virginia implemented a scholarship and loan repayment program for students who agree to work in this area for a specified period of time. Not only does New York's Workforce Retraining Initiative provide support to workers in meeting the requirements of existing positions, but it also assists eligible workers as they transition to new jobs within healthcare (Harmuth and Dyson, 2005). Several government programs also provide low-income or unemployed individuals opportunities to pursue employment in the health field. The federal Work Investment Act (WIA) has funds that can be used to give low-income or unemployed individuals paid work experience and on-the-job training to help them become more employable, and the Welfare-to-Work program helps welfare recipients and low-income noncustodial parents in high-poverty areas obtain jobs in the public- or private-sector (Salsberg, 2003; Stone and Wiener, 2001). A number of states such as Arkansas, Montana, New Jersey, and South Carolina have explicitly sought to recruit Welfare-to-Work recipients to nursing homes (Harmuth and Dyson, 2005).

What Are the Roles of Unions in Long-Term Care?

Strategies to improve recruitment and retention in the long-term care workforce derive from several sources. These include key stakeholders such as individual providers and provider networks, federal and state officials, and organizations such as the Association of Homes and Services for the Aging and the National Association of Geriatric Nursing Assistants. Another key and increasingly important player in promoting higher wages, career advancement, and workplace redesign has been the remarkable growth in unionized long-term care workers. Today, the largest long-term care union, Service Employees International Union (SEIU), includes 440,000 home care workers and 160,000 nursing home employees. With 110,000 nurses and 40,000 doctors, SEIU is also the largest union of healthcare workers. Furthermore, the ranks of SEIU continue to swell. In 2005, for example, 41,000 home care workers in Michigan voted to join the union. Overall, SEIU membership increased from 625,000 to 1.8 million between 1980 and 2005. Currently, there are more than 300 SEIU local union affiliates and 25 state councils in North America (Service Employees International Union, 2006).

SEIU has proven highly successful in garnering higher wages and benefits for its members. In California, SEIU-affiliated home care workers received wage increases of $2 per hour over two years in addition to comprehensive health coverage. Home care workers in New York have also secured comprehensive coverage in addition to paid vacation and sick days, a pension, and training and education opportunities. SEIU has also worked with public authorities, advocates, and clients to pass legislation, creating quality home care councils in several states. The purposes of these councils are to promote consumer direction, create registries of carefully screened attendants to make it easier for clients to find reliable workers, provide emergency backup services when regular caregivers become unavailable, recruit new workers to the field, and allow attendants to collectively bargain for better wages and benefits (Service Employees International Union, 2006).

The healthcare industry is one of the few sectors of the economy in which unions have won more than 50 percent of their certification elections. In nursing facilities, unions prevailed in 60 percent of elections conducted by the National Labor Relations Board between 1999 and 2001. The two most active unions were SEIU and the Teamsters, which were involved in 42 and 13 percent of elections, respectively. However, significantly fewer elections were held in the south and west, regions that have traditionally proven to be less union friendly than the northeast and midwest (Palthe and Deshpande, 2003). Some providers have sought to develop collaborative relationships with unions, whereas others have proved to be much more resistant (Stone and Wiener, 2001). In a qualitative study of 20 California and Pennsylvania nursing homes, Eaton (2000) found that in contrast to lower-quality facilities, which were mostly nonunion and actively discouraged worker input, higher-quality homes were mostly unionized and welcomed and solicited systematic worker input.

Conclusion

Although there are federal and state programs and other efforts targeted at stimulating the supply of nurses and other healthcare workers, shortages are more acute and the work is generally considered less desirable in the long-term care sector. Consequently, there is widespread agreement that key stakeholders could do much more in targeting loan forgiveness, scholarship, wage enhancement, training, career ladder, and other programs to recruit individuals at all levels to long-term care specifically. The long-term care workforce, including CNAs, home health aides, personal care assistants, LPNs, RNs, advanced practice nurses, administrators, and geriatricians, must be expanded, supported, and trained for the multiplicity of tasks and responsibilities necessary to deliver high-quality care to frail and chronically disabled individuals in both residential and home- and community-based settings. This is true both in the context of current workforce deficits and in the context of even greater deficits to come if administrators do not join with workers in engaging public policy makers in solving the workforce crisis in long-term care.

References

American College of Health Care Administrators. 2005. *Long-Term Care Administrator Certification and Its Impact on Quality of Long-Term Care Services*. Alexandria, VA: American College of Health Care Administrators.

American Geriatrics Society and American Association of Geriatric Psychiatry. 2003. The American Geriatrics Society and American Association for Geriatric Psychiatry recommendations for policies in support of quality mental health care in U.S. nursing homes. *Journal of the American Geriatrics Society* 51(9): 1299–1304.

American Health Care Association. 2004. *Estimates of Current Employment in the Long-Term Care Delivery System*. Washington: American Health Care Association.

Barry, T., D. Brannon, and V. Mor. 2005. Nurse aide empowerment strategies and staff stability: effect on nursing home resident outcomes. *The Gerontologist* 45(3): 309–317.

Bowers, B.J. 2003. Turnover reinterpreted: CNAs talk about why they leave. *Journal of Gerontological Nursing* 29(3): 36–44.

Bowers, B.J., S. Esmond, and N. Jacobson. 2000. The relationship between staffing and quality in long-term care facilities: exploring the views of nurse aides. *Journal of Nursing Care Quality* 14(4): 55–64.

Burgio, L.D., S.E. Fisher, J.K. Fairchild, K. Scilley, and M. Hardin. 2004. Quality of care in the nursing home: effects of staff assignment and work shift. *The Gerontologist* 44(3): 368–377.

Campbell, S. 1985. Primary nursing: it works in long-term care. *Journal of Gerontological Nursing* 8: 12–16.

Castle, N.G. 2001. Administrator turnover and quality of care in nursing homes. *The Gerontologist* 41(6): 757–767.

Castle, N.G. 2005. Turnover begets turnover. *The Gerontologist* 45(2): 186–195.

Castle, N.G. and J. Engberg. 2005. Staff turnover and quality of care in nursing homes. *Medical Care* 43(6): 616–626.

Caudill, M.E. and M. Patrick. 1991–1992. Turnover among nursing assistants: why they leave and why they stay. *The Journal of Long-Term Care Administration* 19(4): 29–32.

Centers for Medicare and Medicaid Services. 2002. *Appropriateness of Minimum Nurse Staffing Ratios in Nursing Homes, Phase II Final Report*. Baltimore, MD: Centers for Medicare and Medicaid Services.

Cox, C.L., L. Kaeser, A.C. Mongomery, and L.H. Marion. 1991. Quality of life nursing care: an experimental trial in long-term care. *Journal of Gerontological Nursing* 17: 6–11.

Decker, F. 2005. *Nursing Homes, 1977–99: What Has Changed, What Has Not?* Hyattsville, MD: National Center for Health Statistics.

Decker, F.H., K.J. Dollard, and K.R. Kraditor. 2001. Staffing of nursing services in nursing homes: present issues and prospects for the future. *Seniors Housing and Care Journal* 9(1): 3–26.

Decker, F.H., P. Gruhn, L. Matthews-Martin, K. Jeanine Dollard, A.M. Tucker, and L. Bizette. 2003. *Results of the 2002 AHCA Survey of Nursing Staff Vacancy and Turnover in Nursing Homes*. Washington: American Health Care Association.

Eaton, S.C. 2000. Beyond "unloving care": linking human resource management and patient care in nursing homes. *International Journal of Human Resource Management* 11(3): 591–616.

Eaton, S.C. 2002. What a difference management makes! Nursing staff turnover variation within a single labor market. *Appropriateness of Minimum Nurse Staffing Ratios in Nursing Homes, Phase II Final Report*, pp. 5.1–5.64. Washington: U.S. Department of Health and Human Services.

eLearners.com. 2005. *Online Health & Medicine Training Programs,* http://www.elearners. com/programs/training/health.htm (accessed October 7, 2005).

Farrell, D. 2005. *Consistent Assignment.* Providence, RI: Quality Partners of Rhode Island.

Fishman, M.F., B. Barnow, A. Glosser, and K. Gardiner. 2004. *Recruiting and Retaining a Quality Paraprofessional Long-Term Care Workforce: Building Collaboratives with the Nation's Workforce Investment System.* Washington: U.S. Department of Health and Human Services.

Fitzgerald, J. and V. Carlson. 2000. Ladders to better life. *The American Prospect* 11(15): 54–60.

Gates, D., E. Fitzwater, S. Telintelo, P. Succop, and M.S. Sommers. 2002. Preventing assaults by nursing home residents: nursing assistants' knowledge and confidence— a pilot study. *Journal of the American Medical Directors Association* 3(6): 366–370.

Goldman, B.D. 1998. Nontraditional staffing models in long-term care. *Journal of Gerontological Nursing* 24: 29–34.

Grabowski, D.C., Z. Feng, O. Intrator, and V. Mor. 2004. Recent trends in state nursing home payment policies. *Health Affairs* W4(Suppl Web-Exclusive): 363–373.

Grant, L.A. 2004. Family and employee satisfaction in nursing homes. *Seniors Housing and Care Journal* 12(1): 3–13.

Harmuth, S. and S. Dyson. 2004. *Results of the 2004 National Survey of State Initiatives on the Long-Term Care Direct-Care Workforce.* Bronx, NY: The National Clearinghouse on the Direct Care Workforce and the Direct Care Workers Association of North Carolina.

Harmuth, S. and S. Dyson. 2005. *Results of the 2005 National Survey of State Initiatives on the Long-Term Care Direct-Care Workforce.* Bronx, NY: The National Clearinghouse on the Direct Care Workforce and the Direct Care Workers Association of North Carolina.

Harmuth, S. and A. Venkatraman. 2001. *Results of a Follow-Up Survey to States on Career Ladder and Other Initiatives to Address Aide Recruitment and Retention in Long-Term Care Settings.* Raleigh, NC: North Carolina Division of Facility Services.

Harrington, C., C. Kovner, M. Mezey, J. Kayser-Jones, S. Burger, M. Mohler, R. Burke, and D. Zimmerman. 2000. Experts recommend minimum nurse staffing standards for nursing facilities in the United States. *The Gerontologist* 40(1): 5–16.

Harris-Kojetin, L., D. Lipson, J. Fielding, K. Kiefer, and R.I. Stone. 2004. *Recent Findings on Frontline Long-Term Care Workers: A Research Synthesis 1999–2003.* Washington: U.S. Department of Health and Human Services.

Health Resources and Services Administration. 2002. *Projected Supply, Demand, and Shortages of Registered Nurses: 2000–2020.* Washington: U.S. Department of Health and Human Services.

Hollinger-Smith, L. 2002. *Evaluation of the LEAP Replication Study.* Unpublished.

Inserra, A., M. Conway, and J. Rodat. 2002. *The Cooperative Home Care Associates: A Case Study of a Sectoral Employment Development Approach.* Washington: The Aspen Institute.

Institute of Medicine. 2001. *Improving the Quality of Long-Term Care.* Washington: National Academy Press.

Institute of Medicine. 2003. *Keeping Patients Safe: Transforming the Work Environment of Nurses.* Washington: National Academy Press.

Intrator, O., J. Zinn, and V. Mor. 2004. Nursing home characteristics and potentially preventable hospitalizations of long stay residents. *Journal of the American Geriatrics Society* 52(10): 1730–1736.

Kaiser Family Foundation. 2005. *The Public's View on Long-Term Care*, http://www.kff. org/healthpollreport/june_2005/index.cfm (accessed October 22, 2005).

Kaiser Family Foundation Health Poll Report Survey (conducted June 2–5, 2005).

Konrad, T.R., J.C. Morgan, and S. Haviland. 2003. *Where Have All the Nurse Aides Gone? Part III*. Chapel Hill, NC: North Carolina Institute on Aging.

Kovner, C.T., M. Mezey, and C. Harrington. 2002. Who cares for older adults? Workforce implications of an aging society. *Health Affairs* 21(5): 78–89.

Mickus, M., C.C. Luz, and A. Hogan. 2004. *Voices from the Front: Recruitment and Retention of Direct Care Workers in Long Term Care across Michigan*. Lansing, MI: Michigan State University.

Montgomery, R.J., L. Holley, J. Deichert, and K. Kosloski. 2005. A profile of home care workers from the 2000 census: how it changes what we know. *The Gerontologist* 45(5): 593–600.

Mor, V. 1995. Invest in your frontline worker: commentary. *The Brown University Long-Term Care Quality Newsletter* 7(1): 4–5.

National Clearinghouse on the Direct Care Workforce. 2005. *Mather LifeWays: LEAP for a 21st Century Workforce*, http://www.directcareclearinghouse.org/practices/r_pp_det. jsp?res_id=47610 (accessed November 9, 2005). Bronx, NY: National Clearinghouse on the Direct Care Workforce.

National Commission on Nursing Workforce for Long-Term Care. 2005. *ACT NOW for Your Tomorrow*. Washington: National Commission on Nursing Workforce for Long-Term Care.

North Carolina Division of Facility Services. 2000. *Results of a Follow-Up Survey to States on Wage Supplements for Medicaid and Other Public Funding to Address Aide Recruitment and Retention in Long-Term Care Settings*. Raleigh, NC: North Carolina Division of Facility Services.

Office of Inspector General. 2002. *Nurse Aide Training, OE-05-01-00030*. Washington: U.S. Department of Health and Human Services.

OnlineCareers.com. 2005. *Online Health Care Degrees*, http://www.onlinecareers.com/ programs/health-care/ (accessed October 7, 2005).

Online Survey, Certification, and Reporting (OSCAR), 1992–2004.

Online Survey, Certification, and Reporting (OSCAR), 2004.

Palthe, J. and S.P. Deshpande. 2003. Union certification elections in nursing care facilities. *The Health Care Manager* 22(4): 311–317.

Paraprofessional Healthcare Institute. 2003a. State wage pass-through legislation: an analysis. *Workforce Strategies, No. 1*. Bronx, NY: Paraprofessional Healthcare Institute and Institute for the Future of Aging Studies.

Paraprofessional Healthcare Institute. 2003b. Introducing peer mentoring in long-term care settings. *Workforce Strategies, No. 1*. Bronx, NY: Paraprofessional Healthcare Institute.

Paraprofessional Healthcare Institute. 2004. *Workforce Tools, Number 2*. Baltimore, MD: Centers for Medicare and Medicaid Services.

Paraprofessional Healthcare Institute. 2005. The role of training in improving the recruitment and retention of direct-care workers in long-term care. *Workforce Strategies, No. 3.* Bronx, NY: Paraprofessional Healthcare Institute.

Porter, L. 2005. *Testimony Before the National Commission for Quality Long-Term Care.* Joplin, MO: National Association of Geriatric Nursing Assistants.

Powell, P. 2006. *Cooperative Home Care Associates: Integrated Model for Recruitment, Training, and Retention.* Bronx, NY: National Clearinghouse on the Direct Care Workforce, http://www.directcareclearinghouse.org/practices/r_pp_det.jsp?res_id=48910 (accessed January 7, 2006).

Rantz, M.J., L. Hicks, V. Grando, G.F. Petroski, R.W. Madsen, D.R. Mehr, V. Conn, M. Zwgart-Staffacher, J. Scott, M. Flesner, J. Bostick, R. Porter, and M. Maas. 2004. Nursing home quality, cost, staffing, and staff mix. *The Gerontologist* 44(1): 24–38.

Salsberg, E. 2003. *Making Sense of the System: How States Can Use Health Workforce Policies to Increase Access and Improve Quality of Care.* New York, NY: Milbank Memorial Fund.

Schnelle, J.F., S.F. Simmons, C. Harrington, M. Cadogan, E. Garcia, and B. Bates-Jenson. 2004. Relationship of nursing home staffing to quality of care. *Health Services Research* 39(2): 225–250.

Seavey, D. 2004. *The Cost of Frontline Turnover in Long-Term Care.* Washington: Institute for the Future of Aging Services, America Association of Homes and Services for the Aging.

Service Employees International Union. 2006. *SEIU Stronger Together,* http://www.seiu.org (accessed February 10, 2006).

Stone, R.I. 2004. The direct care worker: the third rail of home care policy. *Annual Review of Public Health* 25: 521–537.

Stone, R.I. and J.M. Wiener. 2001. *Who Will Care for US?: Addressing the Long-Term Care Workforce Crisis.* Washington: The Urban Institute and the American Association of Homes and Services for the Aging.

Sylvester, B.J. and L. Reisener. 2002. Scared to go to work: a home care performance improvement initiative. *Journal of Nursing Care Quality* 17(1): 75–87.

Tilly, J., K. Black, B. Ormond, and J. Harvell. 2003. *State Experiences with Minimum Nursing Staff Ratios for Nursing Facilities: Findings from the Research to Date and a Case Study Proposal.* Washington: U.S. Department of Health and Human Services.

Trinkoff, A., M. Johantgen, C. Muntaner, and R. Le. 2005. Staffing and worker injury in nursing homes. *American Journal of Public Health* 95(7): 1220–1225.

United States Bureau of Labor Statistics. 2005. *Occupations with the Largest Job Growth, 2004–14,* http://www.bls.gov/emp/emptab3.htm (accessed January 9, 2006).

United States Department of Health and Human Services. 2003. *The Future Supply of Long-Term Care Workers in Relation to the Aging Baby Boom Generation, Report to Congress.* Washington: U.S. Department of Health and Human Services.

United States General Accounting Office. 2001. *Nursing Workforce: Recruitment and Retention of Nurses and Nurse Aides Is a Growing Concern, GAO-01-750T.* Washington: U.S. General Accounting Office.

University of Wisconsin Center for Cooperatives. 2006. *Cooperative Home Care Associates.* Madison, WI: University of Wisconsin Center for Cooperatives, www.uwcc.wisc. edu/info/i-pag/chca.html.

WIN A STEP UP. 2005. *Is NA Turnover a Problem? We've Got a Solution. . . .* Chapel Hill, NC: University of North Carolina Institute of Aging and North Carolina Department of Health and Human Services.

Wright, B. 2005. *Direct Care Workers in Long-Term Care.* Washington: AARP Public Policy Institute.

Yeats, D.E., C. Cready, B. Ray, A. DeWitt, and C. Queen. 2004. Self-managed work teams in nursing homes: implementing and empowering nurse aide teams. *The Gerontologist* 44(2): 256–261.

Chapter 9

The Role and Responsibilities of the Medical Director and the Attending Physician in Long-Term Care Facilities

Daniel Swagerty

Contents

Introduction

In 1974, in response to perceived quality of care problems, Medicare regulations, for the first time, required a physician to serve as the medical director in skilled nursing facilities and be responsible for the medical care provided in those facilities [1–4]. Since 1991, the long-term care field has undergone fundamental changes in medical knowledge, clinical complexity, societal and legal attitudes, demographics and patient mix, and reimbursement and care settings [5–7]. Increasingly, medical directors are held accountable by state legislators, regulators, and the judicial system for their clinical and administrative roles in facilities of all kinds [7–9]. At least one state, Maryland, has enacted legislation outlining the specific regulatory responsibilities and educational prerequisites for medical directors, and other states may follow its lead [9–10].

The 2001 Institute of Medicine report *Improving the Quality of Long-Term Care* urged facilities to give medical directors greater authority and hold them more accountable for medical services. The report further states, "Nursing homes should develop structures and processes that enable and require a more focused and dedicated medical staff responsible for patient care. These organizational structures should include credentialing, peer review, and accountability to the medical director" [11].

In April 2002, the American Medical Directors Association (AMDA) convened an expert panel to review its position statement in the context of the evolution that is occurring within long-term care [12]. Their work product outlined the medical director's major roles in the facility and was geared toward ensuring that appropriate care is provided to an increasingly complex, frail, and medically challenging population (Table 9.1) [12]. These concepts were considered when the Center for Medicare and Medicaid Services revised the Surveyor Guidance related to F Tag 501 for medical direction in 2005 [13].

Regulatory Oversight

Although the federal regulation F Tag 501 for medical direction remained the same, the Guidance to Surveyors was entirely replaced [13]. The regulation requires each facility to have a medical director who is responsible for the implementation of resident care policies and the coordination of medical care. These two roles provide the basis for the functions and tasks required of medical directors in long-term care facilities.

The regulation is as follows:

§483.75(i) Medical Director
  1. The facility must designate a physician to serve as medical director
  2. The medical director is responsible for
     i. Implementation of resident care policies
     ii. The coordination of medical care in the facility

Table 9.1   Roles and Responsibilities of the Medical Director in the Nursing Home

Role and responsibilities
It is the AMDA's view that the roles and responsibilities of the medical director in the nursing home can be divided into four areas: physician leadership, patient care—clinical leadership, quality of care, and education

Physician leadership
Help the facility ensure that patients have appropriate physician coverage and ensure the provision of physician and healthcare practitioner services
Help the facility develop a process for reviewing physician and healthcare practitioner credentials
Provide specific guidance for physician performance expectations
Help the facility ensure that a system is in place for monitoring the performance of healthcare practitioners
Facilitate feedback to physicians and other healthcare practitioners on performance and practices

Patient care—clinical leadership
Participate in administrative decision-making and the development of policies and procedures related to patient care
Help develop, approve, and implement specific clinical practices for the facility to incorporate into its care-related policies and procedures, including areas required by laws and regulations
Develop procedures and guidance for facility staff regarding contacting practitioners, including information gathering and presentation, change in condition assessment, and when to contact the medical director
Review, consider, and/or act upon consultant recommendations, as appropriate, that affect the facility's resident care policies and procedures or the care of an individual resident
Review, respond to and participate in federal, state, local, and other external surveys and inspections
Help review policies and procedures regarding the adequate protection of patients' rights, advance care planning, and other ethical issues

Quality of care
Help the facility establish systems and methods for reviewing the quality and appropriateness of clinical care and other health-related services and provide appropriate feedback
Participate in the facility's quality improvement process
Advise on infection control issues and approve specific infection control policies to be incorporated into facility policies and procedures
Help the facility provide a safe and caring environment
Help promote employee health and safety
Assist in the development and implementation of employee health policies and programs

(*continued*)

Table 9.1 Continued

Education, information, and communication

Promote a learning culture within the facility by educating, informing, and communicating

Provide information to help the facility provide care consistent with current standards of practice (defined as "approaches to care, procedures, techniques, and treatments that are based on research and/or expert consensus and that are contained in current manuals textbooks and or publications, or that are accepted, adopted or promulgated by recognized organizations or national bodies.")

Help the facility develop medical information and communication systems with staff, patients, and families and others

Represent the facility to the professional and lay community on medical and patient care issues

Maintain knowledge of the changing social, regulatory, political, and economic factors that affect medical and health services of long-term care patients

Help establish appropriate relationships with other healthcare organizations

Source: Adopted from American Medical Directors Association, *Roles and Respon-sibilities of the Medical Director in the Nursing Home*, Position Statement A06, March 2006.

The intent of this requirement is that

- The facility has a licensed physician who serves as the medical director to coordinate medical care in the facility and provides clinical guidance and oversight regarding the implementation of resident care policies.
- The medical director collaborates with the facility leadership, staff, and other practitioners and consultants to help develop, implement, and evaluate resident care policies and procedures that reflect current standards of practice.
- The medical director helps the facility identify, evaluate, and address and resolve medical and clinical concerns and issues that
  - Affect resident care, medical care, or quality of life.
  - Are related to the provision of services by physicians and other licensed healthcare practitioners.

Although many medical directors also serve as attending physicians, the roles and functions of a medical director are separate from those of an attending physician. The medical director's role involves the coordination of facility-wide medical care, whereas the attending physician's role involves primary responsibility for the medical care of individual residents [14–15].

The medical director's roles and functions require the physician serving in that capacity to be knowledgeable about current standards of practice in caring for long-term care residents, and about how to coordinate and oversee related practitioners

[16–18]. As a clinician, the medical director plays a pivotal role in providing clinical leadership regarding application of current standards of practice for resident care and new or proposed treatments, practices, and approaches to care. The medical director's input promotes the attainment of optimal resident outcomes, which may also be influenced by many other factors, such as resident characteristics and preferences, individual attending physician actions, and facility support. The 2001 Institute of Medicine report states, "nursing homes should develop structures and processes that enable and require a more focused and dedicated medical staff responsible for patient care" [11]. The medical director is in a position, because of his or her role and function, to impact the overall quality of care provided in a nursing facility, address individual resident's clinical issues, and supervise the quality of medical provided. The text *Medical Direction in Long-Term Care* [15] asserts that "The Medical Director has an important role in helping the facility deal with regulatory and survey issues . . . the medical director can help ensure that appropriate systems exist to facilitate good medical care, establish and apply good monitoring systems and effective documentation and follow up of findings, and help improve physician compliance with regulations, including required visits. During and after the survey process, the medical director can clarify for the surveyor's clinical questions or information about the care of specific residents, request surveyor clarification of citations on clinical care, attend the exit conference to demonstrate physician interest and help in understanding the nature and scope of the facility's deficiencies, and help the facility draft corrective actions."

The Attending Physician's Role

Attending physician involvement in long-term care is essential to the delivery of quality long-term care [19–23]. Attending physicians should lead the clinical decision making for patients under their care. They can provide a high level of knowledge, skill, and experience needed in caring for a medically complex population in a climate of high public expectations and stringent regulatory requirements. In 2001, AMDA developed a policy statement outlining the role and responsibilities of the attending physician in long-term care [24]. Physicians need clearly stated expectations to fulfill their attending responsibilities. They need a set of essential functions and tasks that should be performed by them and cannot be delegated to others (Table 9.2) [24]. Although various factors make physician adherence challenging, attending physicians should work with medical directors to address the obstacles, not cite them as a reason to avoid responsibility.

Medical Direction

Nationally accepted statements concerning the roles, responsibilities, and functions of a medical director can be found at the AMDS web site [24]. The facility is responsible for designating a medical director, who is currently licensed as

Table 9.2   Role of the Attending Physician in the Nursing Home

Responsibility for Initial Patient Care. The attending physician should

Assess a new admission in a timely fashion (based on a joint physician–facilitydeveloped protocol, and depending on the individual's medical stability, recent and previous medical history, presence of significant or previously unidentified medical conditions, or problems that cannot be handled readily by phone)

Seek, provide, and analyze needed information regarding a patient's current status, recent history, and medications and treatments, to enable safe, effective continuing care, and appropriate regulatory compliance

Provide appropriate information and documentation to support the facility in determining the level of care for a new admission

Authorize admission orders in a timely manner, based on a joint physician–facility-developed protocol, to enable the nursing facility to provide safe, appropriate, and timely care

For a patient who is to be transferred to the care of another healthcare practitioner, continue to provide all necessary medical care and services pending transfer until another physician has accepted responsibility for the patient

Support patient discharges and transfers. The attending physician should

Follow up with a physician or another healthcare practitioner at a receiving hospital as needed after the transfer of an acutely ill or unstable patient

Provide whatever documentation or other information may be needed at the time of transfer to enable care continuity at a receiving facility and to allow the nursing facility to meet its legal, regulatory, and clinical responsibilities for a discharged individual

Provide pertinent medical discharge information within 30 days of discharge or transfer of the patient

Make periodic, pertinent on-site visits to patients. The attending physician should

Visit patients in a timely fashion, based on a joint physician–facility-developed protocol, consistent with applicable state and federal regulations, depending on the patient's medical stability, recent and previous medical history, presence of significant or previously unidentified medical conditions, or problems that cannot be handled readily by phone

Maintain progress notes that cover pertinent aspects of the patient's condition and current status and goals. Periodically, the physician's documentation should review and approve a patient's program of care

Determine progress of each patient's condition at the time of a visit by evaluating the patient, talking with staff as needed, talking with responsible parties/family as indicated, and reviewing relevant information, as needed

Respond to issues requiring a physician's expertise, including the patient's current condition, the status of any acute episodes of illness since the last visit, test results, other actual or high-risk potential medical problems that are affecting the individual's functional, physical, or cognitive status, and staff, patient, or family questions regarding the individual's care and treatments

Table 9.2   Continued

At each visit, provide a legible progress note in a timely manner for placement on the chart (timely to be defined by a joint physician–facility protocol). Over time, these progress notes should address relevant information about significant ongoing, active, or potential problems, including reasons for changing or maintaining current treatments or medications, and a plan to address relevant medical issues

Ensure adequate ongoing coverage. The attending physician should
Designate an alternate physician or appropriately supervised midlevel practitioner who will respond in an appropriate, timely manner in case the attending physician is unavailable
Update the facility about his or her current office address, phone, fax, and pager numbers to enable appropriate, timely communications, as well as the current office address, phone, fax, and pager numbers of designated alternate physicians or an appropriately supervised midlevel practitioner
Help ensure that alternate covering practitioners provide adequate, timely support while covering and intervene with them when informed of problems regarding such coverage
Adequately notify the facility of extended periods of being unavailable and of coverage arranged during such periods
Adequately inform alternate covering practitioners about patients with active acute conditions or potential problems that may need medical follow-up during their on-call time

Provide appropriate care to patients. The attending physician should
Perform accurate, timely, relevant medical assessments
Properly define and describe patient symptoms and problems, clarify and verify diagnoses, relate diagnoses to patient problems, and help establish a realistic prognosis and care goals
In consultation with the facility's staff, determine appropriate services and programs for a patient, consistent with diagnoses, condition, prognosis, and patient wishes, focusing on helping patients attain their highest practicable level of functioning in the least restrictive environment
In consultation with facility staff, ensure that treatments, including rehabilitative efforts, are medically necessary and appropriate in accordance with relevant medical principles and regulatory requirements
Respond in an appropriate timeframe (based on a joint physician–facility-developed protocol) to emergency and routine notification, to enable the facility to meet its clinical and regulatory obligations
Respond to notification of laboratory and other diagnostic test results in a timely manner, based on a protocol developed jointly by the physicians and the facility, considering the patient's condition and the clinical significance of the results
Analyze the significance of abnormal test results that may reflect important changes in the patient's status and explain the medical rationale for subsequent interventions or decisions not to intervene based on those results when the basis for such decisions is not otherwise readily apparent
Respond promptly to notification of, and assess and manage adequately, reported acute and other significant clinical condition changes in patients

(continued)

Table 9.2 Continued

In consultation with the facility staff, manage and document ethics issues consistent with relevant laws and regulations and with patients' wishes, including advising patients and families about formulating advance directives or other care instructions and helping identify individuals for whom aggressive medical interventions may not be indicated

Provide orders that ensure individuals have appropriate comfort and supportive care measures as needed, for example, when experiencing significant pain or in palliative or end-of-life situations

Periodically review all medications and monitor both for continued need based on validated diagnosis or problems and for possible adverse drug reactions. The medication review should consider observations and concerns offered by nurses, consultant pharmacists, and others regarding beneficial and possible adverse impacts of medications on the patient

Provide appropriate, timely medical orders and documentation. The attending physician should

Provide timely medical orders based on an appropriate patient assessment, review of relevant pre- and postadmission information, and age-related and other pertinent risks of various medications and treatments

Provide sufficiently clear, legibly written medication orders to avoid misinterpretation and potential medication errors, such orders to include pertinent information such as the medication strength and formulation (if alternate forms available), route of administration, frequency and, if applicable, timing of administration, and the reason for which the medication is being given

Verify the accuracy of verbal orders at the time they are given and authenticate, sign, and date them in a timely fashion, no later than the next visit to the patient

Provide documentation required to explain medical decisions, that promotes effective care, and allows a nursing facility to comply with relevant legal and regulatory requirements

Complete death certificates in a timely fashion, including all information required of a physician

Follow other principles of appropriate conduct. The attending physician should
Abide by pertinent facility and medical policies and procedures

Maintain a courteous and professional level of interaction with facility staff, patients, family/significant others, facility employees, and management

Work with the medical director to help the facility provide high-quality care

Keep the well-being of patients or residents as the principal consideration in all activities and interactions

Be alert to, and report to the medical director—and other appropriate individuals as named through facility protocol—any observed or suspected violations of patient or resident rights, including abuse or neglect, in accordance with facility policies and procedures

Source: Adopted from American Medical Directors Association, *Role of the Attending Physician in the Nursing Home*, Position Statement E03, American Medical Directors Association, March 2003.

a physician in the state in which the facility he or she serves is located. The facility may provide for this service through any of several methods, such as direct employment, contractual arrangements, or another type of agreement. Whatever the arrangement or method employed, the facility and the medical director should identify the expectations for how the medical director will work with the facility to effectively implement resident care policies and coordinate medical care.

Implementation of Resident Care Policies and Procedures

The facility is responsible for obtaining the medical director's ongoing guidance in the development and implementation of resident care policies, including review and revision of existing policies. The medical director's role involves collaborating with the facility regarding the policies and protocols that guide clinical decision making (e.g., interpretation of clinical information, treatment selection, and monitoring of risks and benefits of interventions) by any of the following: facility staff; licensed physicians; nurse practitioners; physician assistants; clinical nurse specialists; and licensed, certified, or registered healthcare professionals such as nurses, therapists, dieticians, pharmacists, social workers, and other healthcare workers.

The medical director has a key role in helping the facility to incorporate current standards of practice into resident care policies and procedures or guidelines to help assure that they address the needs of the residents. Although regulations do not require the medical director to sign the policies or procedures, the facility should be able to show that its development, review, and approval of resident care policies include the medical director's input.

This requirement does not imply that the medical director must carry out the policies and procedures or supervise staff performance directly, but rather must guide, approve, and help oversee the implementation of the policies and procedures. Examples of resident care policies include, but are not limited to

- Admission policies and care practices that address the types of residents that may be admitted and retained based on the ability of the facility to provide the services and care to meet their needs
- The integrated delivery of care and services, such as medical, nursing, pharmacy, social, rehabilitative, and dietary services, which includes clinical assessments, analysis of assessment findings, care planning including preventive care, care plan monitoring and modification, infection control (including isolation or special care), transfers to other settings, and discharge planning
- The use and availability of ancillary services such as x-ray and laboratory

- The availability, qualifications, and clinical functions of staff necessary to meet resident care needs
- Resident formulation and facility implementation of advance directives (in accordance with the state law) and end-of-life care
- Provisions that enhance resident decision making, including choice regarding medical care options
- Mechanisms for communicating and resolving issues related to medical care.
- Conduct of research, if allowed, within the facility
- Provision of physician services, including (but not limited to)
  - Availability of physician services 24 hours a day in case of emergency
  - Review of the residents' overall condition and program of care at each visit, including medications and treatments
  - Documentation of progress notes with signatures
  - Frequency of visits, as required
  - Signing and dating all orders, such as medications, admission orders, and readmission orders
  - Review of and response to consultant recommendations
- Systems to ensure that other licensed practitioners (e.g., nurse practitioners) who may perform physician-delegated tasks act within the regulatory requirements and within the scope of practice as defined by the state law
- Procedures and general clinical guidance for facility staff regarding when to contact a practitioner, including information that should be gathered before contacting the practitioner regarding a clinical issue or question or change in condition

Coordination of Medical Care

The medical director is responsible for the coordination of medical care in the facility. The coordination of medical care means that the medical director helps the facility obtain and maintain timely and appropriate medical care that supports the healthcare needs of the residents, is consistent with current standards of practice, and helps the facility meet its regulatory requirements. In light of the extensive medical needs of the long-term care population, physicians have an important role both in providing direct care and in influencing care quality. The medical director helps coordinate and evaluate the medical care within the facility by reviewing and evaluating aspects of physician care and practitioner services, and helping the facility identify, evaluate, and address healthcare issues related to the quality of care and quality of life of residents. "A medical director should establish a framework for physician participation, and physicians should believe that they are accountable for their actions and their care" [16].

The medical director addresses issues related to the coordination of medical care identified through the facility's quality assessment and assurance committee and quality assurance program, and other activities related to the coordination of care [25–28]. This includes, but is not limited to, helping the facility

- Ensure that residents have primary attending and backup physician coverage
- Ensure that physician and healthcare practitioner services are available to help residents attain and maintain their highest practicable level of functioning, consistent with regulatory requirements
- Develop a process to review basic physician and healthcare practitioner credentials (e.g., licensure and pertinent background)
- Address and resolve concerns and issues among the physicians, healthcare practitioners, and facility staff
- Resolve issues related to continuity of care and transfer of medical information between the facility and other care settings

A response from a physician implies appropriate communication, review, and resident management, but does not imply that the physician must necessarily order tests or treatments recommended or requested by the staff, unless the physician agrees that those are medically valid and indicated.

In addition, other areas for medical director input to the facility may include

- Facilitating feedback to physicians and other healthcare practitioners about their performance and practices
- Reviewing individual resident cases as requested or as indicated
- Reviewing consultant recommendations
- Discussing and intervening (as appropriate) with a healthcare practitioner about medical care that is inconsistent with applicable current standards of care
- Assuring that a system exists to monitor the performance of the healthcare practitioners
- Guiding physicians regarding specific performance expectations
- Identifying facility or practitioner educational and informational needs
- Providing information to the facility practitioners from sources such as nationally recognized medical care societies and organizations where current clinical information can be obtained
- Helping educate and provide information to staff, practitioners, residents, families, and others

Critical Investments to the Medical Directorship

The most important investment to the medical director position is dedicated time devoted by the physician. Performing administrative duties should be kept separate from clinical time spent caring for residents as their attending physician. Although contractual duties of the medical director may require only several hours per month, it is vitally important for the medical director to invest the time to become involved in the fabric of the facility, to identify problems, and to participate in solutions. This type of involvement usually requires at least eight hours per week for a 100-bed facility. The time requirement for these administrative tasks would vary only slightly in smaller or larger facilities. Each task requires a certain amount of time to develop and implement, which is fairly fixed regardless of the number of the beds.

A second critical investment is adequate staff support. Many nursing facilities have been highly successful in dedicating a physician assistant or advanced practice nurse to a part- or full-time position in assisting the medical director. This individual would investigate clinical situations, organize and conduct quality management monitors, review charts for compliance with resident care policies, and represent the medical director when absent. This position can be vitally important in assisting the medical director to provide 24-hour coverage of resident care and administrative problems. Although all attending physicians should have 24-hour coverage for the residents in their practice, if the system fails, emergency coverage for those residents falls to the medical director or his or her surrogate.

Adequate financial resources must be allocated by the nursing facility as a third critical investment. The medical director should receive adequate support for their administrative time. Physicians have often been willing to assume the medical directorship to supplement their income with nursing facility resident care visits and by the revenues generated by hospital admissions from the facility. Basing the medical director position on a salary and not on resident care revenue should enable the medical director to devote the time required to effectively perform their administrative duties. The long-term care facility and medical director should delineate the financial arrangement and responsibilities of each party in a written contract. Adequate financial resources would also be required if a physician assistant or advanced practice nurse is employed. Medical staff liaison activities, staff assistants, the quality management program, and education activities all require financial support by the facility.

Education is the fourth critical investment that must be made by both the nursing facility and the medical director. Education for all nursing facility employees enhances quality of care and employee satisfaction, and may increase employee retention. In-service sessions and teaching rounds help motivate the staff to do a good job and increase their morale. Integrating the nursing facility into geriatric medical and nursing education is imperative for providing quality care now and in the future. The teaching nursing home develops great pride in the staff and residents of the facility.

Conclusion

The medical director of a long-term care facility is of vital importance in the management and provision of quality care. Excellence in nursing facility care will never be achieved until the medical director plays a truly meaningful role in the operations of the facility through an integral involvement, appropriate organizational position, and adequate financial support. The position of medical director should be nurtured and enhanced by the medical community and long-term care industry. Only then will society be assured of the highest quality in nursing facility care.

References

1. Gruber, H. W. The medical director in the nursing home—a catalyst for quality care. *Journal of the American Geriatrics Society.* 1977; (November)11: 497–499.
2. Pattee, J. J. Role of medical director in a nursing home. *Minnesota Medicine.* 1977; (February): 107–108.
3. Lawson, I. R., et al. Medical director in long-term care. *Journal of the American Geriatrics Society.* 1978; (April): 157–166.
4. Fanale, J. E. The nursing home medical director. *Journal of the American Geriatrics Society.* 1989; (April): 369–375.
5. Elon, R. The nursing home medical director role in transition. *Journal of the American Geriatrics Society.* 1993; (February)2: 131–135.
6. Levenson, S. A. The new OBRA enforcement rule: Implications for medical directors and attending physicians (7 parts). *Nursing Home Medicine* 1995; 3: 32–34, 45–48, 83–85, 122–126, 150–154, 195–199, 214–216.
7. Levenson, S. A. Bridge building, not rain dancing: A medical director's core management responsibilities. *Journal of the American Medical Directors Association.* 2001; (May/June)3: 125–133. http://www.jamda.com/article/PIIS1525861004701814/fulltext.
8. Levenson, S. A. The impact of laws and regulations in improving physician performance and care processes in long-term care. *Journal of the American Medical Directors Association.* 2004; 5(4): 268–277. http://www.jamda.com/article/PIIS1525861004701358/fulltext.
9. Levenson, S. A. The Maryland regulations: Rethinking physician and medical director accountability in nursing homes. *Journal of the American Medical Directors Association.* 2002; (March/April)2: 79–94.
10. Boyce, B. F., Bob, H., Levenson, S. A. The preliminary impact of Maryland's medical director and attending physician regulations. *Journal of the American Medical Directors Association.* 2003; 4: 157–163.
11. Institute of Medicine. *Improving the Quality of Long-Term Care.* Washington: National Academy Press; 2001, p. 201.
12. American Medical Directors Association. *Roles and Responsibilities of the Medical Director in the Nursing Home,* Position Statement A06, March 2006.
13. CMS Manual System Pub. 100–07. *State Operations Provider Certification,* Transmittal 15. Tag F501, Medical Director—Guidance to Surveyors. November 28, 2005.
14. Levenson, S. A. The nursing home medical director: A new era. *Journal of Long-Term Care Administration.* 1989; 17(1): 6–9.
15. Pattee, J. J., Otteson, O. J. *Medical Direction in the Nursing Home—Principles and Concepts for Physician Administrators.* Minneapolis, MN: Northridge Press; 1991, p. 5.
16. Levenson, S. A. Medical direction in long-term care. *A Guidebook for the Future,* 2nd ed. Durham, NC: Carolina Academic Press; 1993, p. 135.
17. Zimmer, J. G., Watson, N. M., Levenson, S. A. Nursing home medical directors: Ideals and realities. *Journal of the American Geriatrics Society.* 1993; 2: 127–130.

18. Pattee, J. J. History and evolution of the role of the medical director. *Clinical Geriatric Medicine.* 1995; (August): 331–341.

19. Dimant, J. Roles and responsibilities of attending physicians in skilled nursing facilities. *Journal of the American Medical Directors Association.* 2003; (July/August)4: 231–243. http://www.jamda.com/article/PIIS1525861004703552/fulltext.

20. Levenson, S. A. *Medical Director and Attending Physicians Policy and Procedure Manual for Long-term Care.* Dayton, OH: MedPass; 2005.

21. Swagerty, D. L., Rigler, S. The physician's role in directing long-term care: Understanding the rules is important for protecting your patients and your practice. *Postgraduate Medicine.* 2000; (February)2: 217–227.

22. Winn, P., et al. Improving communication among attending physicians, long-term care facilities, residents and residents' families. *Journal of the American Medical Directors Association.* 2004; 5(2): 114–122. http://www.jamda.com/article/PIIS1525861004700663/fulltext.

23. American Medical Directors Association. *Role of the Attending Physician in the Nursing Home, Position Statement E03.* March 2003.

24. www.amda.com.

25. Levenson, S. A. A medical quality assurance and improvement program: The essentials for a medical director. *Journal of Medical Direction.* 1993; 3: 20–27.

26. Levenson, S. A. The knowledge base of long-term care medical direction: Guidelines for contributors and continuing education planners. *Journal of Medical Direction.* 1992; 2: 12–15.

27. Levenson, S. A. The medical director and continuous quality improvement. *Journal of Medical Direction.* 1992; 2: 67–75.

28. Wilson, K., et al. Facility investigations: Medical directors should know the rules. *Journal of the American Medical Directors Association.* 2002; 2(4 Supplement): H38–H39. http://www.jamda.com/article/PIIS1525861004705162/fulltext.

FOCUSING ON SERVICES

Chapter 10

Long-Term Care Services, Care Coordination, and the Continuum of Care

Megan E. McCutcheon and William J. McAuley

Contents

The Care Continuum

The 35-year-old concept of a continuum of care continues to play an important role in the conceptualization, design, and implementation of programs and services that address the growing needs of the aging population. Liebowitz and Brody introduced the term "continuum of care" in 1970, developed through the collaboration of research and practice, to describe a concept of care for older individuals within acute, intermediate, and independent living environments (Liebowitz and Brody, 1970). Ideally, a continuum of care consists of a wide variety of services and appropriate providers that deliver assistance and support, which address the diverse and changing needs of older people (Liebowitz and Brody, 1970). A true continuum of care would involve episodic healthcare visits that occur, along with required continuing care, as the client progresses through various care environments as he or she becomes less capable of living independently (McBryde-Foster and Allen, 2005). The care continuum should range from services for active seniors (such as those provided through senior centers and area agencies on aging) and assistive community services (home health, personal care, and nutrition services) to facility admissions due to unstable or declining health conditions. Palliative care and hospice, interspersed with occasional, unpredictable outpatient and hospital visits, should be available for end-of-life needs (Dyeson, 2004).

Clearly, certain groups of younger people experience chronic disabilities and would also benefit from care coordination. For example, children with developmental disabilities or complex medical needs may experience frequent transitions of care from hospitalizations to specialists' community offices. Not only can coordinated care positively affect the status of children and young adults by improving access to services, decreasing hospitalizations, and assuring comprehensive care, but it can also limit the negative effects of illnesses and disabilities on their parents (i.e., parents' work schedules) (Palfrey et al., 2004). Pediatric cancer patients are another population that may require shared management of care so that services and treatments are provided effectively and efficiently (Kisker et al., 1997).

The medical home model designed for youth highlights communication, collaboration, and integration as integral parts for the continuity of coordinated care (Kelly et al., 2002). The American Academy of Pediatrics and the U.S. Department of Health and Human Services identified several important steps for successful transitions of child care to adult-oriented care. These steps strongly emphasize care coordination and the various elements involved with the delivery of comprehensive care, which will be discussed throughout this chapter (Rosen et al., 2003). It is clear that coordinated care is applicable to many different populations in need of continuing medical attention; however, this chapter focuses on the older population, which is more likely to require such supportive services.

Three important points should be made about the continuum of care at the outset. First, the use of the term "continuum" may suggest that older people move along a steady progression from independence to greater dependence and death in a consistent, predictable manner. This is not at all the case for most elderly people. Instead, there may be many declines and improvements in health status and functional capacity as people experience short-term shifts in chronic diseases, contract acute illnesses, and are treated and cured or receive rehabilitation and restorative services. Given these continually shifting circumstances, programs and services must be nimble and responsive to change. Those responsible for organizing and providing long-term and acute care to the aged must keep in mind that such clients have the capacity to rebound if they receive appropriate treatments and services. Therefore, when assessing the requirements of older individuals, care coordinators should consider whether rehabilitation and restorative services would be beneficial.

Second, it is too easy to reify the continuum of care—to think of it as the prevalent state of affairs, rather than as an ideal concept against which current conditions should be measured. In only rare cases are there medical and long-term care services and programs, funding sources, and coordination personnel in place to constitute a true continuum of care for older people. In most cases, what currently exists is, at best, cobbled together, incomplete, and inadequate for the vast majority of individuals in need. Therefore, priority should be placed on policies that facilitate the actualization of a continuum of care model—with the full range of programs and services—to more elders (Gross et al., 2004; Palley, 2003).

Third, the term "continuum" suggests a beginning and endpoint, with movement in one direction. In reality, older people experience dramatic change in functional capacity and acuity over time, with periods of improvement as well as decline. Therefore, we should be careful when referring to a continuum of care not to suggest one-way movement toward more impairment and more intensive service needs. Kane (1993) has suggested that we use the term "repertoire" of services to emphasize that there should be a variety of available services that elders can utilize as they need them, where they need them. Although we agree with her goal, and terminology can definitely make a difference in our perceptions, we will use the term continuum because it is generally accepted.

Depending on the needs and conditions of the older adult, multiple professionals may be involved with the provision of care at any point. Therefore, it is important for care coordinators to understand the extensive variety of services that may be available in any area. Their responsibilities include assessing the needs of their clients as well as helping them negotiate the service system miasma caused by the complexities of applications, eligibility determinations, multiple service agencies, scheduling issues, and other factors that are required to assure that the elders receive the care when and where they need it. As the central communicator among the client, healthcare and long-term care providers, payers, and other family and community resources, the care coordinator is the individual who can best optimize the older person's health and functional outcomes (McBryde-Foster and Allen, 2005).

Ideal Continuum of Long-Term Care Compared with Current Reality

Ideally, a continuum of long-term healthcare and social services would consist of the early recognition and management of each health event, change in condition, medical procedure, or other issues affecting an individual's health or function. It would entail a seamless coordination of complete healthcare and social services across settings and across changes in health status (The Care Coordination Coalition, 2005). It would take into account available informal supports and client choice (Stone, 2000). It would also be setting-independent, as much as possible, so that older people are not forced to change residence to receive the types of services they need. The care would be provided by a multidisciplinary team of professionals who know the client's health history and are aware of current ailments, medication regimens, recent procedures, test results, and ongoing social and medical services. Such knowledge could only be achieved through complete and accurate record keeping and a commitment to information sharing across all providers. To establish an ideal continuum of care within a community, there should be a skillful collaboration among the various providers in the locale, so that information is readily exchanged and services can be effectively and efficiently coordinated (Stefanacci and Podrazik, 2005).

Unfortunately, this ideal is not met in most cases. One problem in establishing a proficient continuum of care for elders is the diverse funding streams that have some responsibility for long-term care and healthcare and that utilize very different eligibility criteria. The current financing of healthcare, which is varied and disjointed, does not meet the needs of this aging population (Gross et al., 2004; Miller and Weissert, 2004).

Medicaid is a welfare program that merges federal and state funds for people with very limited financial resources (Palley, 2003). States have considerable leeway in determining who is eligible and what services are available, fostering large differences among the states in the types of assistance provided and who can receive them.

Medicaid is the primary funding source for nursing home care, primarily because a large number of residents "spend down" to Medicaid eligibility levels while in the facilities (Stefanacci and Podrazik, 2005).

Medicare, however, is a completely federal program that subsidizes a variety of healthcare services for the elderly and disabled, including physician, hospital, rehabilitation, hospice, and home healthcare; recently Congress added a prescription drug benefit. Although Medicare reimburses for some nursing home days following acute episodes, it does not pay for long-term nursing home care (Centers for Medicare & Medicaid Services, 2002).

Some older individuals have private health insurance or private long-term care insurance. In 2003, approximately 61 percent of noninstitutionalized persons aged 65 years and above had some form of private health insurance, with 35 percent obtained through an employer or employment-based retirement plan and 29 percent purchased directly by the recipient; a small minority obviously received health insurance through both sources (Administration on Aging, 2004b). In contrast, the growth of private long-term care insurance has been relatively slow, and it is not currently a major payment source for such care. Currently, only about 7 percent of long-term care spending is financed by private insurance (Feder et al., 2000). Many of these privately paid policies cover health services not supported by Medicare.

There are many gaps and redundancies in the services available through these funding streams and, with the exception of some special circumstances described in the following section, they do not "work together" very well. The limited opportunity to craft a reasonable set of services for an individual across these and other health financing sources is a substantial impediment to a continuum of care for older people.

Access to a continuum of care is especially a concern for rural elders who need medical and social assistance but have limited access to the necessary services and programs. One-fifth of the country's older population resides in rural areas; such residents are more likely to be older and in poorer health and have more functional impairments than urban older adults (National PACE Association, 2002a). Rural and small town elders also tend to have lower incomes by nearly 20 percent than their urban counterparts (Ritchie et al., 2002). The limited housing, health, and social support options available for both low-income and rural seniors suggest that those who are in the greatest need of services may also be the most likely to experience an inadequate continuum of care (Stefanacci and Podrazik, 2005).

Long-Term Care Services

Informal Care: The Backbone of Long-Term Care

It has been estimated that up to 85 percent of elder care in the United States is "informal" care provided by family, or in some cases, friends or neighbors (Lubben and Damron-Rodriguez, 2003). Because most "formal" services (those provided for pay) are available only intermittently, on a limited schedule, or for short periods; the help provided by informal caregivers is crucial. It has been estimated that the dollar value of informal care provided to older people is approximately $257 billion per year (Pandya, 2005; United States Department of Health and Human Services, 2005). Because the assistance provided through informal sources is so important to continuity, any approach to care coordination should take the availability of informal caregivers into account, including the types of care they can provide, their expertise for providing it, their physical and psychosocial needs, the level of burden they experience, and the potential for burnout (Dyeson, 2004). Furthermore, because these caregivers often take on the role of care coordinator as well, they should be continually involved and consulted as decisions are made regarding the types and scheduling of formal services (Coleman and Boult, 2003; Craig and Jones, 2005; Stille et al., 2005).

Home- and Community-Based Care

Home- and community-based care consists of services provided to older community residents in their homes or in community settings outside their homes. Such assistance includes social and medical care services, case management, home-delivered meals, transportation, senior center programs, adult day care centers, and respite services. Several studies have suggested that the care provided through home- and community-based services can delay or limit the need for institutional care (Palley, 2003). Continual management of follow-up visits and assessments in home- and community-based programs can potentially decrease mortality, delay functional deterioration, and prevent the need for high-cost institutional facilities (Ritchie et al., 2002). Clients and relevant family members should be informed of the various service options so they can be involved in decision making. They should be closely linked with the care team that completes assessments so they can be directly involved in care planning as well (American Geriatrics Society, 2000).

Home health services funded by Medicare provide nursing, rehabilitation, and assistive care. Social workers maintain contact with recipients and providers and coordinate this care (Dyeson, 2004). Recently, however, the program has substantially reduced home health services and has instituted policies that curtail long-term care (Herd, 2001; McCall et al., 2003).

Aimed at limiting the utilization of institutional facilities, Medicaid-waiver (Section 1115) programs establish home and community services for frail older adults (Palley, 2003). These Medicaid-funded services are generally less medically oriented than those offered through Medicare and tend to emphasize personal care and homemaker assistance. As noted earlier, many older individuals are not eligible for such services due to strict income and asset limitations.

Many community-based services are available through area agencies on aging, established through the Older Americans Act, to address the well-being and independence of older adults. Some of the programs available include senior centers, adult day services, nutrition services, and transportation. These various services address the multiple needs of the growing older adult population and allow many older individuals the opportunity to remain in the community. However, although these services are potentially available to all elders, because of limited dollars, area agencies on aging are expected to target those with the greatest social and economic needs (Administration on Aging, 2000, 2004a; United States Department of Health and Human Services, 2005).

Senior centers offer social, physical, educational, and recreational activities to community-dwelling older adults. For those who are less independent and have additional care needs, adult day centers may be more appropriate. The latter address the needs of older adults with functional or cognitive impairments while providing respite care to their caregivers as well (National Association of Area Agencies on Aging, 2006). The variety of care offered may include personal assistance, therapeutic services, meals, caregiver support groups, social services, and health-related services (Pandya, 2004). The majority of adult day services are private pay because only limited public funding has been available. Greater access to adult day care would allow more older individuals to remain in the community and potentially avoid costly institutionalization (Pandya, 2004).

Congregate meal sites can be found at senior centers as well as at other facilities within the community. Through congregate meal programs, seniors receive a nutritional lunch within a social setting (National Association of Area Agencies on Aging, 2006). Older individuals who have mobility problems and are unable to shop or prepare their own food can also receive nutritious meals without leaving their home through home-delivered meal programs, such as meals-on-wheels (National Association of Area Agencies on Aging, 2006).

There are also programs that provide transportation services to older adults who have difficulty traveling to medical offices, meal sites, or other critical locations (National Association of Area Agencies on Aging, 2006). Although often limited in schedule and coverage area, transportation services can often facilitate service coordination by providing clients crucial access to a wider variety of service locations.

Area agencies on aging not only offer programs that can help older individuals remain in their homes, but they also seek to coordinate the comprehensive delivery of care either directly or through the collaboration with other community providers (National Association of Area Agencies on Aging, 2006). Unfortunately, their low level of funding and lack of direct control over agencies with which they do not have service contracts limit their ability to coordinate services effectively.

Nursing Home Care

Individuals who require ongoing skilled nursing services, substantial assistance with basic activities of daily living (ADL), or rehabilitation services may be admitted to nursing homes. Approximately 1.6 million people reside in approximately 17,000 facilities in the United States (Katz and Karuza, 2005). It has been estimated that by the year 2030, 5.3 million older adults will be receiving care in nursing homes (Malench, 2004).

Because Medicare policies regarding the funding of hospital-based acute care have led to reduced hospital stays of older people, they tend to be admitted to nursing homes "quicker and sicker" than they were in the past. This transition toward providing care in facilities and settings traditionally used for long-term care has obscured the unclear distinction between acute and long-term care (Stone, 2000). Furthermore, nursing homes and acute care hospitals tend to have very different goals and care standards (Katz and Karuza, 2005): Acute care hospitals emphasize a disease-focused medical model; nursing homes stress a maintenance and quality-of-life model. Recently, due to the reductions in length of hospital stays, more nursing homes have also established a rehabilitation mission. These differing approaches to care can result in substantial problems in transition and unique case management issues (Katz and Karuza, 2005).

Through a special Medicare program, rural hospitals can define a certain number of their acute care beds as swing beds, which can switch from acute to skilled nursing beds, as needed (Dalton et al., 2005). This program is especially valuable in supporting older people in the transition from acute to rehabilitation or recuperation care because they can make the switch without moving to a new setting. In fact, they often can stay in place, receiving much or all of their care from the same staff. Moreover, swing beds are helpful to rural hospitals, many of which are experiencing financial woes, because they can discharge patients from acute care while retaining them as skilled care. In many very rural counties, the only available skilled nursing beds are hospital swing beds. In general, the stays of people in rural hospital swing beds are considerably shorter than those in freestanding skilled nursing facilities or in hospital-based skilled care units (Dalton et al., 2005).

Assisted Living Facilities

Assisted living facilities have been developed with a consumer focus and are typically private-pay facilities. They offer homelike environments, and tend to operate on more of a hospitality model than a healthcare or long-term care model (Mollica, 2003). Although state and local regulations for assisted living facilities differ considerably, thereby limiting standardization, requirements generally include the provision or coordination of several services that include round-the-clock staff, health and social services, housekeeping, laundry, activities, meals, and transportation (Stefanacci and Podrazik, 2005).

Assisted living facilities appeal to older individuals interested in more options for later life living, especially those elders with limited function or cognitive decline and complex medical conditions, because they can age in a homelike environment while maintaining more of their independence (Stefanacci and Podrazik, 2005). However, due to the diverse care needs of this population, and the generally limited on-site services available, it can be difficult to maintain a balance of independence with the need for assistance as elders become frailer. Therefore, it is important for these facilities to acknowledge that they are often serving a vulnerable population, and to be vigilant about exceeding the facility's ability to address their special and wide-ranging care needs (Stefanacci and Podrazik, 2005). Approximately 900,000 residents are living in more than 36,000 assisted living facilities in the United Sates. More than half of the residents are aged 85 years or above, and a relatively large percentage needs at least some assistance with ADL and medication management (Stefanacci and Podrazik, 2005).

Personal Care Settings

Board and care homes are residential facilities that provide supervision and personal care assistance to a relatively small number of older people who can no longer live alone and do not require skilled nursing care (Benedictis et al., 2005; Medicare, 2005b; Perkins et al., 2004). They are also referred to as adult foster or family care homes, residential care facilities, adult group homes, personal care facilities, and sometimes even assisted living facilities. Board and care homes often provide services to low-income residents who generally pay for their care with their supplemental security income (SSI) benefits (Herd, 2001; Perkins et al., 2004). Some of the services provided include a private or shared room, meals, assistance with ADL, and staff oversight (Benedictis et al., 2005; Castle, 2004; Perkins et al., 2004). Although board and care homes are an important component within the aging network, there are significant issues related to the regulation of these facilities. Licensing of these settings depends on state and local laws and, due to the lack of consistent monitoring, the quality of care provided to residents is of some concern (Benedictis et al., 2005; Castle, 2004; Medicare, 2006).

Continuing Care Retirement Communities

Continuing care retirement communities (CCRCs), also referred to as life care communities, generally include independent, assisted, and nursing home settings on a single campus. Usually, individuals enter the CCRC once and can transition from setting to setting as warranted by their needs and health status (AARP, 2004). CCRCs are chiefly private-pay environments, with entrance fees ranging from $20,000 to $400,000 in addition to monthly payments. Residents may either own their units or rent them (AARP, 2004). The three most commonly available contracts for CCRCs include "extensive contracts" that permit unlimited long-term nursing care for either a small increase in monthly payments or at no additional cost; "modified contracts" that provide long-term nursing care for a specified time and cost; and "fee-for-service contracts," in which long-term nursing care is paid in full by the resident at the daily rate (AARP, 2004). The flexibility of receiving care outside of the community may be limited by the requirements in the CCRC contract (Centers for Medicare & Medicaid Services, 2005). Although many of these communities assure care for the remainder of an individual's life, the high costs of CCRCs often make them unaffordable options for those with lower incomes.

Care Coordination Models

Because of the many complications and disjunctions within long-term care and between acute care and long-term care, and because the ideal continuum is extremely rare in any community, coordination is a key component of long-term care for the older population. The characteristics of effective care coordination include diagnosis and assessment, eligibility determination, support with applications and enrollment, communication with formal organizations and informal caregivers, development of all-inclusive plans, and maintenance and sharing of accurate records (Aliotta, 2003; Burton et al., 2004; Coleman, 2003). Such coordination is essential for enhancing the delivery of quality care and quality outcomes, especially for older people who are frail and have complex needs (Aliotta, 2003; Chumbler et al., 2005; Gittell and Weiss, 2004; Mollica, 2003; Temkin-Greener et al., 2004). In the following sections, we describe models of care coordination, beginning with case management, the most common approach.

Long-Term Care Case Management

Case management, a professional approach to coordination, aims to facilitate the appropriate delivery of informal, self, and agency care to older people (Lubben and Damron-Rodriguez, 2003). It is an essential component of care coordination. Those older people receiving home- and community-based care tend to benefit from this approach by experiencing an increase in services, life satisfaction, and care confidence, as well as a reduction in unmet needs (American Geriatrics Society, 2000).

Quality case management depends on a case manager who is experienced and educated about the aged, especially their complex medical, functional, and social problems, and the services that can address their special needs (American Geriatrics Society, 2000). The case manager identifies a frail elder's special requirements and coordinates the services provided by multiple practitioners and across settings. At the same time, he or she seeks to optimize client autonomy and function (American Geriatrics Society, 2000; Tahan, 2005). In addition to coordinating services, case managers must also manage the funding sources of these services, including multiple public and private sources (Lubben and Damron-Rodriguez, 2003).

In fact, because of differing client needs, funding streams, and eligibility requirements, advocacy is a crucial activity in assuring that clients and family members can successfully negotiate the maze of items that comprise any local "system" of care (Tahan, 2005). Case managers must advocate for the client's best interest while coordinating the range of required services, to assure that elders achieve their optimum functioning or return to their previous health status (Tahan, 2005). Owing to the multifaceted responsibilities involved with numerous providers and payers, case managers face enormous challenges (Mollica, 2003). They must therefore understand the complex reimbursement policies of various public and private agencies and be knowledgeable of other available resources, including informal caregiver support (American Geriatrics Society, 2000).

Monitoring services to assure that the quality and quantity of care is another important responsibility of care coordinators. In addition to coordinating formal services and informal supports, social workers or nurse case managers can also provide direct services along with other team members such as home health professionals (Lubben and Damron-Rodriguez, 2003).

Although case managers are often paid by an organization that is responsible for funding part or all of the community services, some families and older individuals use private case managers for this purpose (Lubben and Damron-Rodriguez, 2003). In addition, some case management models involve agencies that are responsible for both the management and delivery of care (Lubben and Damron-Rodriguez, 2003).

Healthcare Coordination

Any effort to coordinate long-term care successfully must also include acute health services and transitions from acute to other forms of care. Older individuals may be served by several physicians and from multiple providers who address their various health conditions, functional impairments, and social needs. Because many elders have comorbidities, they often receive care from multiple specialists (Gittell and Weiss, 2004). In fact, about 15 percent of Medicare clients receive care only from specialists (Koopman and May, 2004). The use of so many different doctors can result in limited communication among them as well as a lack of complete knowledge of their clients' health history, health conditions, or treatments (Coleman and Bout, 2003).

Such isolated healthcare can lead to adverse effects, including the replication of services or medications, conflicting and confusing care instructions, avoidable hospital and emergency room utilization, and higher overall costs (Aliotta, 2003; Burton et al., 2004; Parry et al., 2003; Temkin-Greener et al., 2004). It can also result in medication errors, overmedication, and adverse drug reactions (Burton et al., 2004; Coleman and Bout, 2003; Koopman and May, 2004; Parry et al., 2003). Interdisciplinary care teams that address communication and coordination across providers and settings can help avoid these potentially serious problems and improve the efficacy of acute and long-term care (Parry et al., 2003; Temkin-Greener et al., 2004).

Collaborative efforts to provide continuous care coordination across acute and chronic health conditions will most likely require organizational change. One approach should include the involvement of clients and their families in care planning, which would lead to more informed, confident, and prepared recipients and caregivers. The shared management of care can be enhanced through education aimed at providing clients and their families with the skills necessary to assist with the maintenance of medication schedules and the promotion of healthy behaviors (Harrison and Verhoef, 2002).

Additionally, procedures must be established to facilitate the sharing of client information among providers. Such efforts are complicated by unlinked record systems, the transmission of noncoded clinical data, and complex administrative information that includes various insurances and relevant social information (Gittell and Weiss, 2004; Miller and Weissert, 2004). The sharing of comprehensive care plans that can be understood across settings is one strategy for improving communication and coordination (Schrag, 2005).

Rewards have generally been lacking for professionals who participate in shared decision making for treatments as well as those involved in the development of comprehensive healthcare plans (Schrag, 2005). However, financing strategies have been used by some payers to motivate and promote healthcare coordination. One example is the provision of fixed monthly payments to the hospital and its physicians that include the various forms of required follow-up care in addition to their usual fees (Gittell and Weiss, 2004).

Transitional Care and Care Coordination

Many older adults experience numerous care transitions due to shifts in chronic conditions and hasty hospital discharges promoted by financial requirements (Parry et al., 2003). Transitional care consists of coordinated and continuous care provided to clients during these periods, sub- and postacute nursing settings, services provided in the client's home- or community-based services, assisted living settings, or nursing homes (Coleman and Boult, 2003; Parry et al., 2003). It should include a comprehensive plan that takes into account the current objectives, preferences, and health status of the client (Coleman and Boult, 2003).

Older individuals moving to and from various health and long-term care settings are at risk for disjointed care due to the independent operation of provider organizations (Coleman et al., 2004; Parry et al., 2003). The resulting fragmentation of services may lead to conflicting care recommendations and medication regimens, deficient follow-up, care disruption, risks of care disparities and replication, and limited planning for the future (Coleman et al., 2004; McBryde-Foster and Allen, 2005). Inadequate transitional care can also increase the unnecessary use of hospitals and emergency rooms, thus increasing costs (Coleman et al., 2004; Moore et al., 2003).

Hospital discharge staff members often do not have adequate time to organize efficient or effective transfers due to financial pressures (Parry et al., 2003). Other barriers include the lack of financial incentives, inadequate quality measures, limited formal relationships between and among sites, and untimely management of client data transmission, which is often complicated by the Health Insurance Portability and Accountability Act (HIPAA) (Coleman, 2003). As a result, service providers in the next setting may not receive complete information about a client's condition, prognosis, or type of care required (Parry et al., 2003). Clearly, transitional care planning and coordination must be improved so that providers across settings can minimize adverse outcomes, promote care continuity, and plan and deliver quality care that is appropriate for meeting the needs of older people (Coleman and Bout, 2003; McBryde-Foster and Allen, 2005; Moore et al., 2003).

It is particularly important for clients and their family caregivers to be part of the development of transitional care plans (Coleman, 2003; Malench, 2004; Parry et al., 2003). This involvement should include the education of the client and family about the care to be delivered and the creation of clear and realistic expectations, thus increasing client confidence and generating the empowerment needed for successful progression through the health and long-term care systems (Harrison and Verhoef, 2002). It is particularly important to discuss new care settings with care recipients and their families. They should also receive guidance on managing the client's condition; addressing modified medication and activity regimens; identifying adverse symptoms or regressions and appropriate contact persons for further questions or concerns; and assuring the timely initiation of care (Coleman, 2003; Craig and Jones, 2005).

About 30 percent of clients who experience care transitions within the final 30 days of their lives are transferred at least three times. Because of the lack of information and limited attention given to the preferences of the client and family, caregivers experience a high level of dissatisfaction with the care provided (Craig and Jones, 2005). The evidence suggests, then, that providers are often not aware of client or family care preferences or do not have access to a plan indicating the preferences.

One example of an effort to coordinate care transitions is the Care Transitions Intervention model, which focuses on client education and supports for active involvement in the transition process. It addresses four critical areas of transitional care, including self-directed medication safety, communication of health records, follow-up care, and symptom management. These objectives correspond with national efforts to support client-centered care, collaborative planning, coordinated care, drug safety, and lower healthcare costs (Coleman et al., 2004; Parry et al., 2003). The design of the intervention, although standardized, is sufficiently flexible to mold around a client's individual needs and chronic conditions. Importantly, intervention recipients were less likely to have subsequent hospitalization (Coleman et al., 2004).

Chronic Care Model

The chronic care model was designed to address and improve assistance for individuals with ongoing conditions. Six important elements of the chronic care model include (a) developing provider and community resource relationships; (b) implementing complete organizational support of chronic care delivery; (c) empowering clients and families and promoting self-care management; (d) defining team responsibilities and care structures; (e) incorporating chronic care guidelines into daily practice; and (f) utilizing electronic information systems for reminders, tracking client status, and accessing client registries. These model components have been found to decrease costs and increase the quality of such care (Bodenheimer et al., 2002).

The senior health center model is a primary care clinic for older clients that is based on the former model. It provides care coordination and access to qualified health workers from various disciplines. The senior health center supports self-care management and the use of electronic health records (EHRs), which have been found to improve client health communication across settings, including nursing homes and home health agencies (Stock et al., 2004). The organization of comprehensive service sites for multiple conditions, each requiring specialized resources, serves to promote holistic care while minimizing overhead costs. Although this approach should enhance access to care, to date there is little research comparing its outcomes with those of more traditional care (Stock et al., 2004).

Disease Management Model

The disease management model is a client-centered coordinated care model designed to (a) assure the continuous quality improvement of care through a primary care coordinator, regardless of client care setting and (b) identify both effective and ineffective methods of care as determined through treatment outcomes (Claiborne and Vandenburgh, 2001). This model has evolved from both population-based care for chronic conditions and evidence-based medical outcome models that promote interdisciplinary approaches to disease intervention. In addition to the objectives of providing evidence-based health promotion and quality-of-life improvements, prevention, comprehensive care assessments, and early treatments, the disease management model also strives to reduce the length of episodic care, provide disease-specific treatments, and encourage the self-management of illness. The delivery of disease management care involves a shift from professionals providing episode-specific care to an interdisciplinary team approach that facilitates access to services, client education, and assessment of psychosocial issues (Claiborne and Vandenburgh, 2001).

Care Coordination Programs

Demonstration programs are being conducted in several states to improve the coordination of care within and across long-term and acute care settings. Some of the program goals include restructuring of the health delivery systems, minimizing episodic and intermittent care, creating easier access to services, and establishing interdisciplinary coordination teams. One of the first programs that embraced the joint health and functional approach to aging care was the federal Program of All-Inclusive Care for the Elderly (PACE) (Mollica, 2003).

Program of All-Inclusive Care for the Elderly

PACE, developed as an alternative to long-term care, addresses the functional independence of low-income seniors who are nursing home certifiable but want to remain in the community as long as possible (Friedman et al., 2005; Gross et al., 2004; Lynch et al., 2005; Mollica, 2003; Palley, 2003). PACE enrollees must also be at least 55 years old and live within the program service area.

The program provides individualized care by a team of professionals at day health centers, where a primary care clinic is housed (Coleman, 2003; Friedman et al., 2005; Lynch et al., 2005). The multidisciplinary team consists of a physician (often a geriatrician), nurse, social worker, and ancillary therapists, as well as additional professional and nonprofessional staff (Lynch et al., 2005). PACE staff members monitor their clients across primary, acute, and long-term care settings, and are involved with the planning of the client's discharge in each place (Coleman, 2003; Gross et al., 2004; Lynch et al., 2005; McBryde-Foster and Allen, 2005; Temkin-Greener et al., 2004). This approach to care can address and limit the risks associated with uncoordinated care as the client's needs change. The programs usually contract with medical providers but retain responsibility for the management of services and reimbursements (Lynch et al., 2005).

PACE advanced from a demonstration project in 1986 to a recognized managed care provider through the Balanced Budget Act of 1997. The PACE program receives capitated funds from Medicare and Medicaid, which helps overcome problems with differing funding streams. It serves over 9000 participants at the 28 PACE location sites in 17 states (Friedman et al., 2005; Lynch et al., 2005). The average participant is 80 years of age, with 7.9 medical conditions and three ADL limitations (National PACE Association, 2002b). Although program recipients tend to have serious ADL limitations and medical problems, with slightly less than half having a diagnosis of dementia, they experience reduced utilization of nursing homes (Friedman et al., 2005; National PACE Association, 2002b), fewer hospitalizations, relatively limited physical decline, greater use of ambulatory services, and better reported quality of life and health status than similarly situated nonrecipients (Lynch et al., 2005). Assessments of PACE programs have demonstrated that they are an efficacious and cost-effective model of quality care for this vulnerable and potentially costly aging population, and a valuable option for coordinating long-term and acute care (Gross et al., 2004; Palley, 2003). In general, PACE tends to be less costly than traditional fee-for-services care (Gross et al., 2004).

Because the programs depend on adult day health centers and require participants to be nursing home eligible, state agencies do not focus exclusively on this care coordination program (Mollica, 2003). Some other barriers that might affect the growth of PACE include the limited ability of enrollees to use outside care providers, high costs for non-Medicare eligible participants, state and local financial restrictions, staffing shortages, and unsupportive state policies (Gross et al., 2004). Additionally, considerable effort is required to establish a PACE site, including the time and costs for the modifications of information systems for processing claims or reports, establishing program criteria and rates, managing quality assurance efforts, and processing PACE application approvals, as well as for the operation of the program and its facilities (Gross et al., 2004).

Rural Program of All-Inclusive Care for the Elderly

The provision of PACE services to rural elders is needed to address the needs of this isolated and aging population (National PACE Association, 2002a). However, due to the limited number of healthcare sites and the access problems that rural older adults experience, alternative approaches to service delivery are needed. Some potential methods for expanding PACE-type programs for rural elders include use of mobile sites or outreach centers housed with other units that can deliver services to participants, application of technological approaches that can support team coordination and delivery of care, identification and recruitment of nontraditional transportation providers, implementation of contractual community partnerships with diversified providers, and the expansion of services to other populations requiring extensive care coordination (National PACE Association, 2002a).

Rural PACE programs can be created using a network model that includes team members from various organizations and locations, shares network facilities and equipment, and assists with enrollment (National PACE Association, 2002a). Another model is the rural–urban linkage approach: It extends existing PACE programs to neighboring or nearby rural areas or joins existing rural and urban providers to create a new PACE program for rural older adults that can provide specialized services, which would otherwise not be available; spreads administrative costs and financial risks across a larger group of participants; and utilizes familiar rural community resources (National PACE Association, 2002a).

Web-Based Care Coordination

Because provider communication and client outcomes have been found to be positively associated, the application of information technology systems can be a useful method for enhancing the current problematic communication and care coordination that too frequently exists between and among physicians and care settings (Burton et al., 2004; Coleman, 2003). The secure transmission of electronic data for clients with multiple chronic conditions can minimize the negative outcomes of uncoordinated care (Burton et al., 2004). According to the Institute of Medicine, EHRs can enable clinicians to update, exchange, and access complete and current client data easily across a variety of settings (Burton et al., 2004). The Institute of Medicine encourages the use of EHRs to minimize the uncoordinated care and medical errors that may otherwise result from incomplete or broken information sharing (Koopman and May, 2004). Another advantage of EHRs is that it eliminates paper records that are difficult to update and standardize for cross-setting use (Coleman, 2003).

There are several feasible options to achieving the benefits of EHRs, including Web-based interfaces to access data, smart cards containing a computer microchip with client health and demographic information, and personal data assistants managed by clients or family members with information provided at all healthcare or long-term care sites (Burton et al., 2004; Coleman, 2003).

Although EHRs can improve the communication of clients' records and facilitate the coordination of care, different health systems may utilize separate, incompatible EHR systems, thereby limiting their effectiveness (Koopman and May, 2004). Other barriers include the lack of standardized records, high start-up and maintenance costs, the lack of clinical or financial support, client privacy concerns, and the legal liability of physicians. Also, some disadvantages of the smart card system have been identified, such as lost cards, inconsistent updates by providers, and the need for universal readers at all provider locations (Burton et al., 2004; Coleman, 2003).

The San Francisco Department of Aging and Adult Services has developed a program that uses an Internet-based care management tool that allows agencies to share client information and manage their care. The online consumer assessment, referral, and enrollment standard instrument, used to access all services, creates referrals to applicable services within the aging system, and allows cross-communication of program participants (Coleman, 2003).

The Department of Veterans Affairs (VA) has implemented a client-centered care coordination/home-telehealth program (CC/HT) to address the self-care needs of chronically impaired older individuals living in the community (Chumbler et al., 2005). CC/HT enhances self-monitoring of health status and allows direct client/provider communication through the use of such data and communication technologies. Using four of the six elements (discussed in the section titled Chronic Care Model) of the chronic care model, CC/HT sends data daily over the Internet to the care coordinator to determine if a follow-up contact is necessary. This thoroughness can assist in the early detection of additional problems (Chumbler et al., 2005). An increase in primary care visits among diabetic veterans using CC/HT suggests that the program and care coordinators were effective in monitoring clients, ensuring that their needs were addressed before any decline in health status (Chumbler et al., 2005). Research findings suggest that the program potentially could limit future diabetic problems and improve symptom management, as well as save costs, primarily due to a decrease in hospitalizations (Chumbler et al., 2005). Furthermore, CC/HT was found to enhance the quality of care by educating the client and strengthening client/provider communication through the use of telecommunication technologies (Chumbler et al., 2005).

Health Maintenance Organizations

There are several managed care plans available through Medicare, including health maintenance organizations (HMOs), preferred provider organizations (PPOs), and private fee-for-service plans. HMOs contract with the federal government to provide health coverage to Medicare eligible individuals who choose to enroll in this type of health plan. The percentage of participating providers has been decreasing steadily due to capitation rates that they deem to be inadequate (Evashwick, 2001). Among other measures, the Medicare Modernization Act of 2003 has attempted to increase the number of network providers by raising these payments (MCOL, 2005).

In addition to the regular services covered by Medicare, individuals enrolled in a Medicare HMO may also receive benefits such as vision, hearing, dental, prescription drug coverage, and extended days in the hospital (Centers for Medicare & Medicaid Services, 2006). Enrollees are assigned a care manager who assesses and monitors the services delivered by network providers (Evashwick, 2001). Participants must also choose a primary care physician within the HMO network. Although some might view this as a negative requirement of the plan, it can also be potentially beneficial as a means for effective care coordination. The roles of both the care manager and primary care physician, for example, can potentially curtail the duplication of services, conflicting care recommendation by multiple providers, and negative polypharmacy effects (Evashwick, 2001).

Social Health Maintenance Organization

The Social Health Maintenance Organization (SHMO) is a demonstration project aimed at providing care to individuals enrolled in Medicare (Gross et al., 2004). Although it has been operating for 20 years, there are only four functioning programs to date (Gross et al., 2004; Medicare, 2005a). Supported by the federal government, SHMOs include coverage of home- and community-based services for the chronically disabled (Lynch et al., 2005). SHMO I sites (currently three) utilize care coordination to manage and individualize home- and community-based care. SHMO II (currently one) alters the payment methods to include risk adjustments, thereby addressing concerns about selective enrollments as well as attempting to incorporate geriatricians more directly into the development of care plans (Lynch et al., 2005). Unfortunately, there are very limited findings supporting positive outcomes for these demonstrations or suggesting the improvement of enrollee health and quality of care as compared to other Medicare HMO or fee-for-service recipients (Lynch et al., 2005).

Coordination and Advocacy for Rural Elders

In 1997, the Coordination and Advocacy for Rural Elders (CARE) program was initiated to extend and improve community services and chronic care for frail aging rural veterans. Its goal was to support their health and function by increasing access to community-based and VA facility-based health and social services, promoting preventive and self-care education, and offering care coordination and advocacy. This program, which began as a pilot, educates clients and caregivers, provides client advocacy, arranges services, and follows client progress. CARE has been found to be a useful model of rural care for vulnerable older veterans residing at home. Over the years, many unaddressed client needs have been detected by CARE staff and almost two-thirds of the clients have been referred to service providers (Ritchie et al., 2002).

Future Directions

Home- and community-based services can play an important role in establishing and maintaining a successful continuum of acute and long-term care for the frail older population. As discussed throughout this chapter, they can promote independent living, assist with transitions, and delay institutionalization. However, we have also described how various healthcare systems and insurance plans can contribute to the fragmentation of care delivered to the older adult population. One approach for the future provision of comprehensive and coordinated care to the chronically ill aging population includes the development of home-based managed care organizations. Such programs can address the growing need for home care services overall as well as meet the specific needs and preferences of older and other chronically ill populations. Consumer choice within managed care has become a real concern for disabled people because of the direct relationship between quality of care and quality of life (Kodner and Kyriacou, 2003). The current lack of consumer-directed care in many managed care programs means limited involvement by clients and family members in the decision-making process regarding health-related services, treatments, or care sites. Because these decisions are controlled most often by the managed care organizations, recipients, and caregivers alike are deprived of the knowledge, confidence, and empowerment needed for the successful coordination of services and smooth progression through the long-term care system (Harrison and Verhoef, 2002; Kodner and Kyriacou, 2003).

Seven recommendations by the Care Coordination Coalition (2005) to the White House Conference on Aging Policy Committee offer a view toward the future directions that should be undertaken to improve the coordination of care for older Americans. The Coalition's recommendations include (a) reimbursement levels based on the provision of coordinated and comprehensive care; (b) requirements for quality coordinated care, such as multidisciplinary services and management across settings, advance care planning, continuing education and training for client self-management, and round-the-clock contacts; (c) standardized electronic client care records accessible by multiple providers; (d) finance demonstration projects for optimal care planning and delivery; (e) long-term care annual workforce reports that include policy effects; (f) annual reports on the status of coordinated care system development; and (g) stimulation of aging care through a national agenda.

Conclusion

Clearly, the much ballyhooed continuum of care for older adults remains a hollow concept for most older recipients of long-term care. It is also evident that care coordination can dramatically and positively affect the health and well-being of older adults. Service development, communication, collaboration, and care coordination must be improved to properly address the complex care needs of the aging population. Without these improvements, older adults will continue to experience medication errors, service duplication, fragmented and inadequate care, and unnecessary hospitalizations and nursing home admissions. Such problems foster a sicker and more disabled population who require even greater and more expensive care. Along with the rapidly increasing older population, healthcare costs are also growing at a fast pace. These expenses can be constrained and care can be improved through the provision and maintenance of effective care coordination and communication.

This chapter has identified problems with care coordination and some potential solutions for rectifying them. However, we must explore further ways of improving current healthcare and long-term care and promoting successful coordination to enhance the well-being of our frail older population.

References

AARP (2004). *Continuing Care Retirement Communities (CCRC)*. Retrieved October 13, 2005, from http://www.aarp.org/families/housing_choices/other_options/a2004-02-26-reitrementcommunity.html.

Administration on Aging (2000). *Full Text of Older Americans Act Amendments of 2000* (amendments only). Retrieved April 3, 2006, from http://www.aoa.gov/ABOUT/legbudg/oaa/legbudg_oaa_fulltext_pf.asp.

Administration on Aging (2004a). *Older Americans Act: Summary of Key Changes in the 2000 Amendments.* Retrieved April 6, 2006, from http://www.aoa.gov/about/ledbudg/oaa/legbudg_oaa_summary.asp.

Administration on Aging (2004b). *A Profile of Older Americans: 2004.* Washington: U.S. Department of Health and Human Services, Administration on Aging.

Aliotta, S. (2003). Coordination of care: The council for case management accountability's third state of the science paper. *Case Manager, 14(2),* 49–52.

American Geriatrics Society (2000). Care management position statement. *Journal of the American Geriatrics Society, 48,* 1338–1339.

Benedictis, T., Modnick, T., and Segal, R. (2005). *Board and Care Homes for Seniors.* Retrieved March 29, 2006, from http://www.helpguide.org/elder/board_care_homes_seniors_residential.htm.

Bodenheimer, T., Wagner, E., and Grumbach, K. (2002). Improving primary care for clients with chronic illness. *The Journal of the American Medical Association, 288(14),* 1775–1779.

Burton, L.C., Anderson, G.F., and Kues, I.W. (2004). Using electronic health records to help coordinate care. *Milbank Quarterly, 82(3),* 457–481.

Castle, N.G. (2004). Facility charter and quality of care for board and care residents. *Journal of Health & Social Policy, 20,* 23–42.

Centers for Medicare & Medicaid Services (2002). *Medicare Coverage of Skilled Nursing Facility Care.* Retrieved April 17, 2006, from http://www.medicare.gov/Publications/Pubs/pdf/snf.pdf.

Centers for Medicare & Medicaid Services (2005). *Types of Long-Term Care.* Retrieved August 14, 2006, from http://www.medicare.gov/LongTermCare/Static/CCRC.asp.

Centers for Medicare & Medicaid Services (2006). *Medicare & You 2006.* Retrieved April 17, 2006, from http://www.medicare.gov/publications/pubs/pdf/10050.pdf.

Chumbler, N.R., Vogel, W.B., Garel, M., Qin, H., Kobb, R., and Ryan, P. (2005). Health services utilization of a care coordination/home-telehealth program for veterans with diabetes: A matched-cohort study. *Journal of Ambulatory Care Management, 28(3),* 230–240.

Claiborne, N. and Vandenburgh, H. (2001). Social worker's role in disease management. *Health & Social Work, 26(4),* 217–225.

Coleman, E.A. (2003). Falling through the cracks: Challenges and opportunities for improving transitional care for persons with continuous complex care needs. *Journal of the American Geriatrics Society, 51,* 549–555.

Coleman, E.A. and Boult, C. (2003). Improving the quality of transitional care for persons with complex care needs. *Journal of the American Geriatrics Society, 51,* 556–557.

Coleman, E.A., Smith, J.D., Frank, J.C., Min, S., Parry, C., and Kramer, A.M. (2004). Preparing clients and caregivers to participate in care delivered across settings: The care transitions intervention. *Journal of the American Geriatrics Society, 52,* 1817–1825.

Craig, J. and Jones, W.J. (2005). End-of-life care. *Journal of Nursing Administration, 35(4),* 158–160.

Dalton, K., Park, J., Howard, A., and Slifkin, R. (2005). *Trends in Skilled Nursing and Swing-Bed Use in Rural Areas, 1996–2003.* Working paper # 83. Chapel Hill, NC: The University of North Carolina at Chapel Hill, North Carolina Rural Health Research and Policy Analysis Center, Cecil G. Sheps Center for Health Services Research.

Dyeson, T. (2004). The home health care social worker: A conduit in the care continuum for older adults. *Home Health Care Management & Practice, 16(4),* 290–292.

Evashwick, C.J. (2001). *The Continuum of Long-Term Care* (2nd ed.). Stamford, CT: Thomson Learning.

Feder, J., Komisar, H.L., and Niefeld, M. (2000). Long-term care in the United States: An overview. *Health Affairs, 19,* 40–56.

Friedman, S.M., Steinwachs, D.M., Rathouz, P.J., Burton, L.C., and Mukamel, D.B. (2005). Characteristics predicting nursing home admission in the program of all-inclusive care for elderly people. *The Gerontologist, 45(2),* 157–166.

Gittell, J.H. and Weiss, L. (2004). Coordination networks within and across organizations: A multi-level framework. *Journal of Management Studies, 41,* 127–153.

Gross, D.L., Temkin-Greener, H., Kunitz, S., and Mukamel, D.B. (2004). The growing pains of integrated health care for the elderly: Lessons from the expansion of PACE. *The Milbank Quarterly, 82(2),* 257–282.

Harrison, A. and Verhoef, M. (2002). Understanding coordination of care from the consumer's perspective in a regional health system. *Health Services Research, 37(4),* 1031–1054.

Herd, P. (2001). Vertical axes on the long-term care continuum: A comparison of board and care and assisted living. *Journal of Aging & Social Policy, 13,* 37–56.

Kane, R.A. (1993). Dangers lurking in the "continuum of care." *Journal of Aging & Social Policy, 5(4),* 1–7.

Katz, P.R. and Karuza, J. (2005). Physician practice in the nursing home: Missing in action or misunderstood. *Journal of the American Geriatrics Society, 53(10),* 1826–1828.

Kelly, A.M., Kratz, B., Bielski, M., and Rinehard, P.M. (2002). Implementing transitions for young with complex chronic conditions using the medical home model. *Pediatrics, 110,* 1322–1327.

Kisker, C.T., Fethke, C.C., and Tannouos, R. (1997). Shared management of children with cancer. *Archives of Pediatrics & Adolescent Medicine, 151,* 1008–1013.

Kodner, D.L. and Kyriacou, C.K. (2003). Bring managed care home to people with chronic, disabling conditions: Prospects and challenges for policy, practice, and research. *Journal of Aging and Health, 15,* 189–222.

Koopman, R.J. and May, K.M. (2004). Specialist management and coordination of "out-of-domain care." *Family Medicine, 36,* 46–50.

Liebowitz, B. and Brody, E.M. (1970). Integration of research and practice in creating a continuum of care for the elderly. *The Gerontologist, 10,* 11–17.

Lubben, J.E. and Damron-Rodriguez, J. (2003). An international approach to community health care for older adults. *Family & Community Health, 26(4),* 338–349.

Lynch, M., Estes, C.L., and Hernandez, M. (2005). Chronic care initiatives for the elderly: Can they bridge the gerontology-medicine gap? *The Journal of Applied Gerontology, 24(2),* 108–124.

Malench, S.S. (2004). Family and social work roles in the long-term care facility. *Journal of Gerontological Social Work, 43*, 49–60.

McBryde-Foster, M. and Allen, T. (2005). The continuum of care: a concept development study. *Journal of Advanced Nursing, 50(6)*, 624–632.

McCall, N., Petersons, A., Moore, S., and Korb, J. (2003). Utilization of home health services before and after the Balanced Budget Act of 1997: What were the initial effects? *Health Services Research, 38*, 85–106.

MCOL (2005). *Medicare Modernization Act*. Retrieved April 20, 2006, from http://www.medicarehmo.com/mchmmma.htm.

Medicare (2005a). *Alternatives to Nursing Home Care: Social Managed Care Plan*. Retrieved March 29, 2006, from http://www.medicare.gov/Nursing/Alternatives/SHMO.asp.

Medicare (2005b). *Types of Long-Term Care: Board and Care Homes*. Retrieved March 29, 2006, from http://www.medicare.gov/LongTermCare/Static/BoardCareHome.asp.

Miller, E.A. and Weissert, W.G. (2004). Managed care for Medicare-Medicaid dual eligibles: Appropriateness, availability, payment, and policy. *The Journal of Applied Gerontology, 23(4)*, 333–348.

Mollica, R. (2003). Coordinating services across the continuum of health, housing, and supportive services. *Journal of Aging and Health, 15*, 165–188.

Moore, C., Wisnivesky, J., Williams, S., and McGinn, T. (2003). Medical errors related to discontinuity of care from an inpatient to an outpatient setting. *Journal of General Internal Medicine, 18(8)*, 646–651.

National Association of Area Agencies on Aging (2006). *Area Agencies on Aging: A Link to Services for Older Adults and Their Caregivers*. Retrieved April 5, 2006, from http://www.n4a.org/aboutaaas.cfm.

National PACE Association (2002a). *Setting the PACE for Rural Elder Care: A Framework for Action*. Retrieved October 12, 2005, from http://www.nrharural.org/pubs/pdf/PACEbrch.pdf.

National PACE Association (2002b). *Who Does PACE Serve?* Retrieved November 8, 2005, from http://www.npaonline.org/webiste/article.asp?id=50.

Palfrey, J.S., Sofis, L.A., Davidson, E.J., Liu, J., Freeman, L., and Ganz, M.L. (2004). The pediatric alliance for coordinated care: Evaluation of a medical home model. *Pediatrics, 113(5)*, 1507–1516.

Palley, H.A. (2003). Long-term care policy for older Americans: Building a continuum of care. *Journal of Health & Social Policy, 16(3)*, 7–18.

Pandya, S.M. (2004). *Adult Day Services: AARP Public Policy Institute Fact Sheet*. Retrieved April 3, 2006, from http://www.aarp.org/research/housing-mobility/homecare/aresearch-import-839.html.

Pandya, S.M. (2005). *Caregiving in the United States. AARP Public Policy Institute Fact Sheet*. Retrieved March 27, 2006, from http://www.aarp.org/research/housing-mobility/caregiving/fs111_caregiving.html.

Parry, C., Coleman, E.A., Smith, J.D., Frank, J., and Kramer, A.M. (2003). The care transitions intervention: A client-centered approach to ensuring effective transfers between sites of geriatric care. *Home Health Care Services Quarterly, 22(3)*, 1–17.

Perkins, M.M., Ball, M.M., Whittington, F.J., and Combs, B.L. (2004). Managing the care needs of low-income board-and-care home residents: A process of negotiating risks. *Qualitative Health Research, 14(4)*, 478–495.

Ritchie, C., Wieland, D., Tully, C., Rowe, J., Sims, R., and Bodner, E. (2002). Coordination and advocacy for rural elders (CARE): A model of rural case management of veterans. *The Gerontologist, 42*, 399–405.

Rosen, D.S., Blum, R.W., Britto, M., Sawyer, S.M., and Siegel, D.M. (2003). Transition to adult health care for adolescents and young adults with chronic conditions. *Journal of Adolescent Health, 33*, 309–311.

Schrag, D. (2005). Communication and coordination: The keys to quality. *Journal of Clinical Oncology, 23(27)*, 6452–6455.

Stefanacci, R.G. and Podrazik, P.M. (2005). Assisted living facilities: Optimizing outcomes. *Journal of the American Geriatrics Society, 53(3)*, 538–540.

Stille, C.J., Jerant, A., Bell, D., Meltzer, D., and Elmore, J.G. (2005). Coordinating care across diseases, settings, and clinicians: A key role for the generalist in practice. *Annals of Internal Medicine, 142*, 700–708.

Stock, R.D., Reece, D., and Cesario, L. (2004). Developing a comprehensive interdisciplinary senior health care practice. *Journal of the American Geriatrics Society, 52*, 2128–2133.

Stone, R.I. (2000). *Long-Term Care for the Elderly with Disabilities: Current Policy, Emerging Trends, and Implications for the Twenty-First Century.* New York: Milbank Memorial Fund.

Tahan, H.A. (2005). Essentials of advocacy in case management. *Lippincott's Case Management, 10(3)*, 136–145.

Temkin-Greener, H., Gross, D., Kunitz, S.J., and Mukamel, D. (2004). Measuring interdisciplinary team performance in a long-term care setting. *Medical Care, 42(5)*, 472–481.

The Care Coordination Coalition (2005). *Care Coordination Across the Continuum Policy Recommendations: White House Conference on Aging Policy Solutions Forum.* Retrieved December 5, 2005, from http://www.whcoa.gov/about/policy/meetings/Sol_forum_agenda/2005_July/07_19_05.pdf.

United States Department of Health and Human Services (2005). *Reauthorization of the Older Americans Act: Testimony.* Retrieved April 6, 2006, from http://www.hhs.gov/asl/testify/t050517a.html.

Chapter 11

Legal Issues Related to Long-Term Care: Elder Law, Estate Planning, and Asset Protection

Jan L. Brown

Contents

Introduction

Many of us think about legal issues, litigation, and using lawyers only when our rights have been violated and we now need to correct the wrongdoing or defend ourselves. However, when working with persons who are impaired, either physically, mentally, or diagnosed with a debilitating illness or disease, it is important to understand that there are laws in effect that serve to protect such persons, their choices, and their desires. When someone is incompetent or mentally impaired, it is especially vital to understand the specific legal issues involved and the legal needs that must be addressed to provide for the incompetent or impaired individual.

This chapter is divided into three sections: legal documents specific to persons who require long-term care, the legal strategies concerning asset protection for persons requiring long-term care, and scams and financial exploitation situations which specifically target seniors or persons who are impaired in some way.

This chapter is written to provide general information to the reader, not to provide legal advice. Unlike many professions, law is vastly different from state to state. Cases which result from litigation provide standards and interpretations of the laws in each state. Therefore, it is vital that anyone seeking particular legal information seek advice from a licensed attorney in the state involved in the action.

Legal Documents

Estate Planning

There are four legal documents recommended for adults, regardless of their health situation or status. The word "adult" in this case is defined as an individual above 18 years of age and of sound mind. These documents, which are extremely important for persons requiring long-term care or with debilitating illnesses, are Financial Power of Attorney, Healthcare Power of Attorney, Advanced Directive, a.k.a. Living Will, and a Last Will and Testament or, if appropriate, a Revocable Living Trust.

Capacity Issues

It is important to understand the capacity-level requirement for the person who is signing the document. "Capacity," the term used to determine if someone has the ability to process information correctly and make decisions for themselves, is defined by the law in the state where the person is residing or domiciled. The general view is that an individual who is impaired may still have the capacity to sign legal documents depending upon the level of impairment. For example, someone with Alzheimer's disease normally has the capacity to sign legal documents throughout the early stages and often into the mid-stages of the disease. In the later stage of the disease, capacity is often in question or nonexistent because an individual normally can no longer process the information he or she is receiving or cannot evaluate it and, therefore, is unable to make decisions based on understanding of the issue(s). Legal capacity is not to be confused with a physician's determination of his or her patient's medical abilities. Legal capacity is defined by state laws and cases, although often a physician's evaluation is helpful or even required if court involvement is necessary. The capacity level required to sign certain papers also varies from one document to another as well as from one state to another. For example, the capacity required to sign a Last Will and Testament is likely different from that of a real estate contract, deed, or a Power of Attorney document.

The impaired or ill person's attorney who is drafting the document is able to determine if his or her client has the legal capacity to sign it or not. If an individual does not have the legal capacity necessary to sign a specific document, the document should not be signed, and often court involvement is required (see the section on Guardianship or Conservatorship).

Powers of Attorney

For anyone who is suffering from health issues, whether a physical ailment or a mental impairment, an advocate is beneficial and often required to ensure that proper care and treatment are available. Although this section is addressing the legal documents for persons who require long-term care services or medical care, the reader should remember that anyone 18 years of age or older, if impaired, will need someone to act for them, and very possibly make many important decisions on their behalf. These decisions include medical treatments, choice of physicians, second opinions, placement in a rehabilitation or nursing home facility, financial decisions, paying of bills, filing insurance claims, and obtaining available benefits.

It is this author's view that the most important legal document people above 18 years of age can have is one that appoints someone or an organization (i.e., an agency) to act for them in the event that they are unable to act for themselves. This may mean that someone is unconscious, heavily medicated, or incapable of communicating his or her wishes and desires. The document that appoints someone to act for another is called a "Power of Attorney."

The purpose and function of a Power of Attorney document is to appoint another person to act for the signer of the document and provide the "power" or action that can be taken on behalf of the incapacitated individual. The person making the appointment is generally called the "principal"; the person appointed is called the "agent," "surrogate," "attorney-in-fact," or "power of attorney," depending upon the state where the document is drafted.

The agent must act in the best interest of the impaired or incapacitated person. "Best interests" may be defined broadly depending upon the action and again, the state's statutes governing the activities of the agent. Sometimes, the term is defined as "substituted judgment," meaning agents apply their best judgment to making decisions on behalf of the principal or impaired person. In a number of states, criminal as well as civil charges can be brought against agents who have not acted in the best interest of their clients and such actions have harmed them or were contrary to their wishes and goals.

What power or authority is given to the agent depends on the document itself and the way in which the power or authority is interpreted by the courts in the state where the incapacitated or incompetent person resides. Some states allow agents to make any and all decisions for their clients, whereas others restrict the authority to specific types of decisions that are listed in the document itself. For example, in some states, the agent has the power to gift or transfer monies (normally used to reduce death taxes or to qualify for benefits) without requiring specific language authorizing it, whereas other states require very specific language in the Power of

Attorney document detailing the amounts that can be transferred and to whom the gifts can be made. In these states, the agent cannot engage in an action unless it is specifically authorized in the document.

In some states a Power of Attorney document is able to address both financial and healthcare issues, whereas in other states separate Power of Attorney documents are required. The former is normally a great convenience for the agent. However, sometimes clients want different agents for their financial and healthcare decisions; in this case, two separate documents are required.

Financial Power of Attorney normally allows the agent to manage bank accounts, stocks and bonds, savings bonds, investments, real estate, loans, mortgages, notes, retirement accounts (including IRAs, SEPs, 401(k), 403(b), and pensions), life insurance, personal property, business interests, execute contracts, register property, and pay taxes. The purpose of the Financial Power of Attorney is to allow the agent to continue the financial transactions that the incapacitated person would normally handle or attend to new issues that need to be addressed. This can include paying bills (including rent and mortgages), collecting rents or account receivables, dealing with investments, paying taxes and, of course, the normally pressing issue of filing insurance claims. Without Financial Power of Attorney, the agent cannot take such actions and bills can go unpaid, notes uncollected, insurance claims go unfilled, etc. To act, the agent generally must present an original or a certified copy of the Financial Power of Attorney to the bank, investment company, life insurance company, and the like. Some financial institutions will send the document to their internal legal counsel for review, whereas others require only a bank clerk to register the document by noting the agent's name and the existence of the document in the incompetent or impaired person's bank records.

As stated earlier, each state has its own laws and cases which dictate the use of the Financial Power of Attorney. It is interesting and sometimes frustrating to learn that many financial institutions also have their own requirements, often which directly conflict with state law (such as not recognizing Power of Attorney unless it is the financial company's Power of Attorney document). Lastly, locale can also make a difference. Small banks or small towns normally are less strict with the agents or with their review of the documents.

A Healthcare Power of Attorney document provides the agent with the authority to act on such issues as choosing or refusing medical treatments, including surgeries; hiring medical staff, including nursing home aides and other caregivers; selecting doctors, hospitals, rehabilitation centers, nursing homes, and other housing options; reviewing medical instructions; planning for ongoing care, burial (including religious services, if desired), filing medical insurance claims; enrolling in medical plans and services; and generally communicating with all healthcare providers and providing them with directions on behalf of their clients. Generally, a Healthcare Power of Attorney does not provide the agent with the authority to make end-of-life care decisions.

The agent is often the advocate for the impaired principal. Normally a spouse, child, or other relative is the appointed agent. When there is not a relative available, oftentimes a close friend or agency will act as healthcare power of attorney. Additionally, there are more and more "geriatric case management" businesses and many of them are willing to serve as the healthcare agent.

Living Wills

Also known as declarations or advanced healthcare directives or end-of-life directives, Living Wills are legal documents that provide an individual's wishes regarding end-of-life care, including instructions to doctors, hospitals, and family members. Generally, the Living Will states that an individual does not want any treatment that prolongs the dying process. Definitions for end-of-life care, which are state-specific, may include a medical condition which is "terminal," the individual is in a "state of permanent unconsciousness," or he or she enters into a vegetative state.

"Terminal" generally is defined as a condition that is incurable and is likely to cause death within a relatively short period of time. Treatment to cure or reverse the condition is not available. "Permanent unconsciousness" signifies a condition where the upper portion of the brain is no longer functioning and the condition is irreversible.

Terminal or state of permanent unconsciousness is determined by a physician (a number of states require two physicians). If the dying individual is able to communicate and has the capacity, his or her wishes will be followed, regardless of any Living Will.

The Living Will document addresses life support, medical treatment, palliative care, and pain care and appoints a surrogate or agent to enforce its instructions. This person is the advocate for the individual and has the authority to enforce the individual's written wishes. Specifically, most states' Living Will statutes address the following treatments:

■ *Cardiac resuscitation.* A group of treatments used when someone's heart and breathing stops. CPR is used in an attempt to restart the heart and breathing. It may consist of mouth-to-mouth breathing or it can include pressing or pounding on the chest to mimic the heart's function and cause blood to circulate. Electric shock and drugs also are used frequently to stimulate the heart.

■ *Mechanical respiration.* Used to support or replace the function of the lungs. A machine called a ventilator (or respirator) forces air into the lungs. The ventilator is attached to a tube inserted into the nose or mouth and down into the windpipe (or trachea). Mechanical ventilation often is used to assist a person through a short-term problem or for prolonged periods in which irreversible respiratory failure exists due to injuries to the upper spinal cord or a progressive neurological disease.

■ *Tube feeding.* The provision of artificial nutrition and hydration or any other artificial or invasive form of nutrition (food) or hydration (water) supplements or replaces ordinary eating and drinking by giving a chemically balanced mix of nutrients and fluids through a tube placed directly into the stomach, the upper intestine, or a vein.

■ *Blood transfusion.* The transfer of blood or blood products from one person (donor) into another person's bloodstream (recipient).

■ *Forms of surgery or invasive diagnostic tests.* Surgery is the branch of medicine concerned with diseases and conditions which require or are amenable to operative procedures. Surgery is the work done by a surgeon. Invasive procedure is a medical procedure which penetrates or breaks the skin or a body cavity, that is, it requires a perforation, an incision, a catheterization, etc. into the body; a diagnostic test is a procedure which gives a rapid, convenient, and inexpensive indication of whether a patient has a certain disease.

■ *Kidney dialysis machine.* A machine that filters a patient's blood to remove excess water and waste products when the kidneys are damaged, dysfunctional, or missing. Blood is drawn through a specially created vein in the forearm, which is called an arteriovenous (AV) fistula. From the AV fistula, blood is taken to the dialysis machine through plastic tubing. The dialysis machine itself can be thought of as an artificial kidney which acts to filter the blood removal. Once the filtration process is complete, the cleansed blood is returned to the patient. Most patients using dialysis due to kidney impairment or failure use a dialysis machine at a special dialysis clinic. Most sessions take about four hours, and typically patients visit the clinic one to three times per week.

■ *Hemodialysis.* A procedure that cleans and filters blood. It rids the body of harmful wastes and extra salt and fluids. It also controls blood pressure and helps the body keep the proper balance of chemicals such as potassium, sodium, and chloride.

■ *Peritoneal dialysis.* Another procedure that replaces the work of the kidneys. It removes extra water, wastes, and chemicals from the body. This type of dialysis uses the lining of the abdomen, the peritoneal membrane, to filter the blood.

■ *Antibiotics.* A drug used to treat infections caused by bacteria and certain other microorganisms (National Hospice and Palliative Care Organization, 2004; MedicineNet.com, 2004).

It is vital to take into account an individual's religious affiliation when discussing a Living Will and Advanced Directive. Even different segments in the same religious group often have different views on appropriate life support and treatments for end-of-life situations.*

The need for a Living Will was emphasized by the 2005 Florida case of *Schiavo v. Schiavo*. Terri Schiavo, residing in a nursing home and receiving life-support treatments, was in a permanently unconscious state for 15 years (The New York Times, 2005). She did not have a written directive regarding her end-of-life choices. After years of her having received life-support treatment, her husband sought to remove her from life support. Terri Schiavo's parents and sibling disagreed, generating a very long, well-publicized, and difficult fight. Her situation touched off a national religious and political battle that eventually reached and involved not just the state legislature, but the governor, the White House, and numerous levels of the judicial system. After years of legal and political maneuvering, and several court decisions, the feeding tubes were removed and Mrs. Schiavo died 14 days later (The New York Times, 2005).

The Schiavo case reinforces the need to have written, legal, and effective documents concerning individual desires for end-of-life care. Because a Living Will is a legal document, this author recommends that it be state-specific to ensure its effectiveness and enforceability. Although a Living Will often is described as a simple document, it is not simple to make choices regarding one's end-of-life care and to ensure that they will be honored. The best time to prepare and sign a Living Will is prior to a life-threatening time or event, so these important desires can be made with clear thinking and time given to the choices chosen.

Guardianship or Conservatorship

If an individual is impaired and has not signed a Financial Power of Attorney or Healthcare Power of Attorney and no longer has the capacity to sign these documents, court involvement may become necessary. Again, each state's laws determine the action necessary to have an individual or agency appointed or to provide healthcare and financial agency assistance to the incapacitated person.

To appoint an individual or agency, a formal court proceeding is required (called a guardianship or conservatorship, depending upon the state). In these hearings, the alleged incapable or incompetent person must be adjudicated as such and an individual or agency (a guardian or conservator depending upon the state laws) must be approved and appointed by the court. Medical testimony is required to allow the court to determine if the alleged incapacitated person is incapacitated, in part or in whole.

If the person is found to be incapacitated in part, the court may allow the individual to continue certain decision making on his or her own behalf. However, if

---

* For a comparison on religious affiliations and their impact on end-of-life decisions, see http://www.dickinson.edu/endoflife/bio.htm, a Web site by James M. Hoefler, Ph.D., professor at Dickinson College in Carlisle, Pennsylvania, titled Tube Feeding Options at the End of Life.

he or she is deemed fully incapacitated, then the person can no longer be involved in decision making, including choices about his or her end-of-life care. Decisions, of course, should always be in the "best interest" of the incapacitated person. When a guardianship or conservatorship exist, the court supervises the appointed person's actions to ensure that the "best interests" rule is followed. Depending upon the state, either a simple form or a very detailed report is required to indicate the steps that have been taken.

The appointment of a guardianship or conservatorship by the court can take anywhere from a few days to six months or longer, depending upon the urgency of the situation and the state laws. This author encourages persons to sign Power of Attorney and Living Will documents so as to choose their own agents and eliminate the need for court involvement.

Last Will and Testament

A Last Will and Testament is a legal document that defines how and what happens to an individual's estate after he or she dies. It includes issues such as who will receive assets, how they will be distributed, and the name of the executor (the person in charge of handling the estate).

If a person dies without a Will (dying intestate), the laws of the decedent's state are the determining factor regarding the decedent's property. State intestate laws vary greatly. In some states, the surviving spouse receives the majority of his or her spouse's assets, whereas in others states the surviving spouse may receive a very small share of the estate.

Depending upon state law, a Will may be valid and operational if it is written and signed (holographic) by the individual. However, most individuals choose to have an attorney draft it to ensure the Will's effectiveness. If there are specific issues (i.e., large estates with federal estate tax issues or "special needs" spouse or children), they should be included and addressed appropriately in the Will's drafting and design.

Inheritance Taxes

Entire volumes can be written on the taxes associated with estates and, in fact, the IRS has detailed its opinions extensively. For this chapter, I will present only a brief overview of state inheritance taxes and federal estate taxes. The former vary greatly among the 50 states. Many states, including Pennsylvania, impose an inheritance tax which is a tax on the right to inherit property. Other states, for example, Florida, do not have an inheritance tax at all. For those states with an inheritance tax, the rate varies. The rate also can depend on the relationship of the beneficiary to the decedent. Tax rates are susceptible to frequent changes, often based upon federal tax law changes.

Under the current federal law (2006), estates valued at $2,000,000 or less do not incur a federal estate tax. For estates with $2,000,000 or more, federal estate tax is an issue. The federal tax rate incrementally increases to a maximum 46 percent tax rate. These tax rates are subject to frequent changes which occur with nearly every rewrite or amendment of the tax laws.

For individuals with larger estates or estates that will incur federal taxes, special tax planning language can be included in their Will which will minimize and may eliminate any federal estate tax. Federal tax law is complicated; any estate that is subject to federal estate tax should be reviewed carefully with an attorney to plan any necessary steps to minimize the tax due upon the estate. Proper estate planning for sizeable estates can save hundreds of thousands of dollars and sometimes millions of dollars.

Probate

Probate is generally the legal process required to administer an estate when someone dies and has assets titled and owned in his or her name alone. To probate an estate, an individual's assets are collected, final debts settled, necessary taxes paid, then property is transferred from the decedent to his or her heirs. State-specific requirements also must be fulfilled throughout the process, which can take anywhere from three months to one year, or beyond, depending upon the complexity of the estate and the state's probate system.

The first step in the probate process is to determine whether or not the decedent left a Will. If there is one, the executor and his or her legal counsel take the Will to the courthouse in the locale where the decedent lived and present it to the Register of Wills (or court) with a Petition for Probate, or similar document. Normally, the executor named in the Will is the spouse or adult child. If the executor named in the Will is not available, or is unwilling to act and there is no other available successor, an interested party will need to step forward and petition the court to be appointed administrator of the estate.

If there is no Will or if the original copy of the Will cannot be found, again someone, normally the spouse or a child, will need to step forward. If there is no disagreement as to who will serve, the Register of Wills or court will make the appointment. If, however, there is disagreement among family members, a hearing may be required.

Once the estate is opened, and an executor is appointed by the court, the actual administration of the estate can begin. Creditors are normally put on notice to submit claims against the estate. Beneficiaries or individuals with an interest in the estate should be notified as well. All of the assets of the decedent are collected by the executor or administrator and an inventory is taken listing them. A prepayment of inheritance taxes may be appropriate, depending on the state's law. If an inheritance tax return is due and the inheritance tax is not paid, penalties and interest will begin to accrue.

Other issues which must be handled by the executor may include the selling of real and personal property, liquidating stocks and other assets, resolving disputes with creditors, paying debts, establishing an account, applying for an employer identification number, and preparing and filing of the required tax returns. When all outstanding matters have been resolved, the estate is finalized in a manner determined by state law. This may require preparing an accounting of the estate administration and receiving court approval before making final distribution of the remaining assets in accordance with the Will, or if there is no Will, in accordance with the laws of the state where the decedent lived. Final settlement of the estate is done (either informally or formally) depending upon the state's requirements. Probate can be involved and time-consuming or less involved, with minimal time requirements, depending upon the estate itself and the state's laws which apply.

Revocable Living Trusts or Intervivo's Trust

In some states, the process by which an estate is administered (probate) is fairly simple and can be completed within three to nine months. However, there are other states where the probate process is tedious, lengthy, and requires court involvement and high fees. For those states, a Revocable Living Trust (hereinafter referred to as a Living Trust) may be a better document than a Will to deal with one's estate.

A Living Trust is a legal document created during a person's lifetime that establishes a new entity, a trust, to handle one's estate. The trust document itself is created and designed according to specific situations and needs of the individual. Once the trust is created, certain assets are transferred or retitled into the trust, which now becomes the legal owner of the assets.

The trust document itself specifies how these assets are managed during one's lifetime and distributed upon one's death. Because a Living Trust is a revocable instrument, it can be changed or modified during the trustee's lifetime just like a Will. The creator of the trust (the trustor) normally has the power to make changes to the trust such as adding and deleting beneficiaries, changing the terms of their estate or distribution of assets, and even terminating the trust itself.

A properly drafted, executed, and funded Living Trust will avoid probate and, instead, a process called trust administration is required. In states which have a simple probate process, trust administration can be very similar to probate. It typically takes the same period of time to administer a trust as to probate a Will, and the costs are generally the same. However, in states that have a burdensome, lengthy probate process, trust administration may be easier and faster than probate.

If the trust is not funded or drafted properly, then trust administration can actually take longer and cost more than normal probate costs as both probate and trust administration can be required. A Living Trust may be advisable if an individual desires professional management of his or her funds or if real property is located outside of the individual's state of residence.

Asset Protection Planning: Protecting Assets from Nursing Home Costs

Nursing Home Care: Its Costs and Affordability

The costs of nursing home care, which vary state by state, depend upon geographic location. In some states (Alabama, Arkansas, Kansas, Indiana, Kentucky, and Oklahoma), the charges are below $4,000 per month (or $48,000 per year), whereas in other states (Connecticut, Hawaii, and New York) they average $7,000 a month (or $84,000 per year) but can be as high as $9,000 a month (or $108,000 a year). Costs can also vary within the state, depending upon such factors as small town versus metropolitan area. For example, in New York, the average monthly cost in the center of the state, Long Island, Rochester, and New York City is $6232, $9842, $7375, and $9132, respectively (New York State Department of Health, 2006).

Nursing homes are expensive and most people cannot pay the costs, beyond a very limited time, on their own. For instance, a 2005 study by Kaiser on the percentage of elderly living in the community with assets equal to or greater than three years of nursing homes costs found that only 8 percent of widows and divorced or never married persons had sufficient assets to pay for their nursing home care for a period of three years or more. The percentage declined as the population aged, to the point that only 12 percent of persons aged 85 years and older had assets equal to or greater than three years of nursing homes costs. Not surprising, a higher percentage of males (23 percent) than females (16 percent) had assets sufficient to cover such nursing home costs (Kaiser Commission on Medicaid and the Uninsured, 2005).

The majority of persons entering nursing homes have no long-term care insurance. It was not an option for many seniors, often due to such factors as the high costs of the premiums or the inability of the individual to meet the medical underwriting restrictions. Thus, the majority of seniors most often pay privately for their nursing home care until they are impoverished, at which time Medicaid provides coverage.

Because so many people exhaust their assets quickly, a number of elders began to seek out ways to shelter or protect their resources. This is especially important for the noninstitutionalized spouse, families with disabled children, and those who wish to leave an inheritance to their children.

Asset Protection: Case Study

The following case, which is typical of those that elder law attorneys deal with on a daily basis, shows why individuals may desire or need to protect their assets. Situation: a woman (aged 78), whose husband (aged 81) has progressive Alzheimer's or a dementia-type disease, has taken care of him at home but finds herself less capable of providing for him as the disease progresses. He begins to wander, becomes very agitated, sometimes physically aggressive, is incontinent, and no longer sleeps through the night. Their total assets include a home, a vehicle, and $250,000 in investments and savings. During the marriage, she had stayed at home raising the children, and he worked to support them until he retired at age 65. Her income from Social Security is $430 a month; he receives $1097 from Social Security and $640 monthly from a pension each month. When he passes away, her Social Security income will increase to $1,097, but she will not receive any of his pension. If nursing home placement is required, two-thirds of their investments will be spent on his care; with no planning, she will be allowed to keep only about $101,000 to provide for her needs during the rest of her life. Her life expectancy is approximately ten years (according to Social Security actuarial tables for 2006), although her family has a history of much longer longevity, with many of them living into their 90s.

If she is frail and requires in-home care assistance she will likely not have sufficient assets to remain at home for the duration of her life. Nor will she have sufficient income or assets to cover her costs for an assisted living facility. It may also become very difficult and possibly impossible for her to pay her health insurance premiums (Medicare Part B, medical supplements and Medicare Part D, prescription cost premiums), prescriptions, taxes, utilities, and other bills that would allow her to maintain her house.

In this case, if the woman was able to shelter an additional one-third of the family's investments, she would be able to avoid impoverishment, have sufficient means to pay for her healthcare needs as they arise, and likely be able to remain in her home or afford an assisted living facility. Indeed, the development of legal strategies and applications to protect assets from nursing home costs was based on the need to assist persons who otherwise would have insufficient means to care for themselves as they age and as their healthcare needs increase. The goal is to allow the institutionalized spouse to qualify for Medicaid, which pays the nursing home costs while protecting or sheltering assets for the spouse at home (hereinafter called the community spouse). Protecting assets allows the institutionalized spouse to qualify for Medicaid earlier than if no asset protection planning had been done.

Asset Planning: Methods Used for Protecting Assets

Gifting funds to children or a relative to remove funds from the institutionalized spouse and community spouse's name is one method of protecting assets. Such gifts must be very carefully calculated and thought out, and issues such as trustworthiness of children, marital status, and ability to manage money and liability issues must all be completely and thoroughly addressed.

Gifting or transferring funds to an irrevocable trust is another method of protecting assets. The funds in the trust, which can be made unavailable for nursing home costs, may be used by the community spouse. Because the trust is extremely restricted and irrevocable, the assets transferred and the legal document itself must be carefully scrutinized. Transferring assets into such a trust results in a penalty period which, in the past, has been extended beyond the penalty period timeframe for outright gifts to children or relatives.

The amount of money transferred to a family member or trust must be carefully analyzed and calculated. Important factors for consideration are income, cost of care, asset values and growth expectancy, state and federal taxes, health needs of the parties, family dynamics, federal and state laws, and the period of ineligibility of benefits which results from such transfers.

Each state has created exceptions that allow specific instances or transfers to be acceptable without resulting in a period of ineligibility or penalty period. Some of the exceptions are included in the regulations themselves, whereas others are the results of appeals or fair hearings. The latter are not published, so few people beyond those who were involved in the actions are aware of them.

Annuities

In some states, an immediate annuity can be purchased with the institutionalized spouse's money to reduce the funds available for nursing home costs. In the states that allow it, the purchase of an annuity is not considered a transfer, thereby avoiding any period of ineligibility. In this situation, the income generated will go to the purchaser of the annuity (either the institutionalized person or community spouse). The total amount allowed for the purchase of an annuity is state-specific. In some states, the beneficiary of the annuity, after the institutionalized spouse or community spouse, must be the state, allowing the state to recover any remaining assets.

Personal Care Contract

In a few states, personal care contracts are an acceptable way to protect assets from nursing home costs. In it, a child or other relative receives a sum of money or property in exchange for lifetime care. They do not need to provide the daily care themselves but can oversee or supervise it.

In some states, the department administering medical assistance has repeatedly rejected the personal care contract if the provider or supervisor of care is a family member. These states have yet to be swayed by the argument that a child who gives up his or her job and income to care for a parent should be allowed to be reimbursed in this manner for those years of care or supervision.

Spousal Refusal

In some states, a spouse may assign his or her support rights to the state; the community spouse can then refuse to pay for the institutionalized spouse's care.

Spousal refusals allow the community spouse to keep all of the marital assets and his or her own income. Only the institutionalized spouse's income will be available for the nursing home care. Although federal law permits this process, only one state, New York, has adopted the federal law regarding spousal refusal.

Divorce

If a person divorces his or her institutionalized spouse, the state often reviews the situation to ensure that the distribution of assets is fair or that any prenuptial agreement is accurately followed. However, until recently, divorce has not been a method generally utilized to protect assets from nursing home costs. With the passage of the Deficit Reduction Act of 2005 (DRA of 2005), it may be used more often.

Spend Down

The laws governing Medicaid do not penalize the spending of the institutionalized or community spouse's funds as long as fair market value is received for what is purchased. Spending assets to pay off debt (also known as spend down) can be used when qualifying for Medicaid benefits. Some of the ways in which spend down funds can be used are mortgage payments; prepay health insurance premiums; pay off credit card debt; purchase a vehicle; make "acceptable" improvements to their residence, such as updating or remodeling the bathroom with safety features; home improvements; and prepay taxes. The idea of using the spend down strategy is to provide greater value to the community spouse's property, something he or she may not be able to afford otherwise.

Opposition to Asset Protection Planning

The Medicaid program is funded by tax dollars and many persons and organizations, such as the insurance industry, strongly oppose asset protection planning. The insurance industry has lobbied successfully to limit asset protection methods. Insurance representatives prefer that people purchase long-term care insurance policies to cover some of their nursing home costs. Unfortunately, the vast majority of seniors cannot afford or do not qualify for long-term care insurance, due to the very strict medical underwriting requirements.

Some people who oppose asset protection planning argue that millionaires give away their assets to qualify for Medicaid. However, this is not the case: under the law, there are penalties and restrictions if large amounts of money are given away. Such arguments, however false, have been persuasive to Congress and asset protection planning has been restricted legislatively.

Jurisdiction: Laws That Apply to Asset Protection Planning

Medicaid (also known as medical assistance) is a federally funded program which is administered by the states. Although federal law regulates Medicaid, state laws are a very important component to understanding the eligibility requirements for Medicaid benefits. Both state-specific regulations and federal law must be utilized and adhered to when qualifying an individual for Medicaid. This chapter is not meant to discuss the specifics of the Medicare or Medicaid programs, but to present some of the laws, rules, and regulations applicable to both the programs.

To qualify for Medicaid benefits, the applicant must meet two major requirements: medical necessity and financial eligibility levels (asset limits of $2000–$2400 or less for a one-person household). The latter clearly illustrates that people must impoverish themselves before they can receive Medicaid benefits. Some assets are considered "exempt" or not counted when qualifying for medical assistance benefits. Examples of resources not counted in determining eligibility include the following:

- Your personal home
- $1000–$1500 in life insurance
- Revocable and irrevocable burial reserves subject to specified limits, which is based on the average amount of a funeral in a county
- Burial space and marker
- One motor vehicle (Pennsylvania Department of Public Welfare, 2007)

The Look Back Period

The look back period is part of the medical assistance application procedure that is conducted by the state agency administering the medical assistance program. This administrative procedure will review, or look back, for any transfers of property for less than fair market value. Any transfer of property during the look back period of time, transferred for less than fair market value, could affect the applicant's eligibility for medical assistance. During the look back period of time, the reviewing organization notes any gifts or distribution of funds that have been made by the applicant or the applicant's spouse to determine if any penalty is to be imposed on these transfers before receiving medical assistance benefits.

The current look back period is 36 months for gifts and 60 months for trusts from the date of the medical assistance application. Therefore, if someone enters a nursing home and had made a gift of $32,000 to her children 37 months prior to the institutionalization, this money would be beyond the look back period and no penalty would be imposed. However, if the person had made the gift 16 months before going into the facility, there would be a period of ineligibility during which time the resident would have to pay the bill on her own. Moreover, under recent law changes, the look back period has been changed dramatically: the DRA of 2005 extends it to 60 months, from the date of application for Medicaid long-term care benefits.

Thus, if a person who gave away his assets within the five-year period and applies for medical assistance benefits, he or she will either have to return the gift or use his or her spouse's protected share throughout the penalty period. At the time of this publication, the DRA of 2005 has yet to be fully implemented by the states and federal government.

It is important to remember that to qualify for medical assistance, the community spouse can have only a small amount of assets (the statutory protected share) and the institutionalized spouse must be impoverished. Generally, the latter can only have $2000–$2400 or less.

Transfers and Gifts: Fair Market Value

When the state agency reviews the applicant and his or her spouse's assets during the look back period, the agent determines if any of the gifts or transfers made were at fair market value or not. Fair market value is defined as the true and appropriate value assigned to the object or property transferred. For instance, if a house is appraised and valued at $140,000, that is considered the fair market value. Therefore, if the parties sell the house to a child for $140,000, it does not result in a period of ineligibility. If it is sold for anything less, a period of ineligibility will be imposed.

Estate Recovery

Estate recovery programs, required by federal law, are administered by the states (Omnibus Budget Reconciliation Act, 1993). Their purpose is to recover any medical expenses from a Medicaid recipient's estate. Estate recovery was a monumental change in the law. Until 1993, Medicaid was an entitlement program, like Medicare and Social Security, and required no repayment. However, the Omnibus Budget Reconciliation Act of 1993 (OBRA 1993) changed medical assistance, requiring the state to recoup the costs of the applicant's care after he or she dies, using liens or collection of debt methods.

Each state has defined its own estate recovery program's parameters and they vary considerably. Some states restrict their recovery to "probatable" assets (assets titled in the recipients name alone). However, others have become increasingly expansive in recent years in their definition of estate recovery property to collect more funds.

The estate recovery program includes the following parameters: only persons aged 55 years or older are subject to its provisions; the executors of the estate are legally responsible for the repayment of medical assistance benefits; states are able to place liens on estate property so as to receive repayment prior to other claimants; states do not need to seek repayment until the community spouse has passed away; and states are prohibited from recovery against the estate if disabled or blind children reside in the deceased institutionalized person's home.

Legislative History Regarding Asset Protection Planning

Prior to 1988, if a married person needed nursing home care, the couple's assets had to be depleted before he or she could receive any Medicaid benefits. The community spouse was thus impoverished, and had a difficult time providing for his or her basic needs. The Medicare Catastrophic Coverage Act of 1988 (MCCA 1988) allows the community spouse to keep a portion of the married couple's assets to meet a minimum monthly maintenance amount. This was the only part of the MCCA that was not repealed.

Additionally, the MCCA also created a look back period of 30 months, preceding the application for Medicaid, for any transfer of assets. The period of ineligibility for benefits was computed using a formula based on the value of the transfer (gift) and the average monthly costs of nursing home care in the state. The maximum period of ineligibility was 30 months.

Additional restrictions related to qualifying for medical assistance were included in OBRA 1993. The bill altered asset protection planning by extending the look back period to 36 months from the transfer of the gift. For certain trust assets, the look back period was extended to 60 months. Moreover, a new exception for the transfer rules was created to provide for special needs or disabled individuals under the age of 65 years.

As stated earlier, OBRA 1993 also established the estate recovery program, mandating the states to create and implement them. If the state did not do so within the timeframe of the law, federal funding was to be withheld.

In 1996, another restriction regarding asset protection planning and transferring assets was written into law with the passage of the Kassebaum–Kennedy bill, which was renamed as the Health Insurance Portability and Accountability Act (1996). In this bill, a section was inserted to prohibit the transferring of assets to qualify for medical assistance benefits and such transfers were defined as a criminal act. The law was dubbed "Granny Goes to Jail" because nearly all individuals making transfers to qualify for medical assistance benefits were senior citizens. This criminalization of asset protection planning was highly criticized by senior groups. In 1997, the "Granny Goes to Jail" law was repealed. However, it was replaced with a new restriction on the "advisor" who provides advice on how to transfer assets to qualify for medical assistance benefits: that person was now guilty of committing a criminal act. This law was dubbed "Granny's Attorney Goes to Jail." In 1998, the attorney general of the United States held the "Granny's Attorney Goes to Jail" law to be unconstitutional as it violated the First Amendment right of free speech.

In 2005, the most restrictive law to date, the DRA of 2005, was passed by the Senate with a one-vote margin. At the time of this writing, it has neither been fully implemented, nor have federal rules and state regulations been published. Additionally, there are at least six lawsuits pending, all challenging the constitutionality of the law. Therefore, it is uncertain if DRA of 2005 will ever be fully implemented.

The DRA of 2005 extends the look back period for all transfers or gifts (except to disabled children below 65 years of age) from 36 to 60 months. The period of ineligibility is calculated with similar formulas to earlier laws, but the start of the look back period now begins at the time of the medical assistance application rather than the date of transfer. It is possible that this requirement will require individuals to transfer assets five years prior to nursing home placement to protect their resources.

DRA of 2005 also addresses the use of annuities which, in some states, have been utilized to protect assets. Under the legislation, if an immediate annuity is purchased to shelter assets from nursing home costs, the state must be named the remainderment beneficiary. This allows the state to recover some or all of its costs for the owner's medical assistance benefits.

The DRA of 2005 also requires, in an effort to stop undocumented immigrants from receiving Medicaid, proof of citizenship (i.e., birth certificate and passport) to qualify for the program. This has become an enormous concern as many persons in nursing homes have Alzheimer's disease and may not be able to locate a birth certificate. Additionally, many African Americans in the south during segregation were not issued birth certificates as they were denied access to hospital maternity wards. It is estimated that 3–5 million low-income citizens may lose medical assistance benefits because they will not be able to provide proof of citizenship. The intent of the laws previously discussed in this section has been to restrict or eliminate sheltering of assets from nursing home costs.

Scams: Exploitation of Seniors

Seniors are specifically targeted by individuals and companies that run fraudulent schemes. A senior may receive 15–20 telephone calls per day by persons soliciting money, selling low-value products for high prices, promising a lottery prize, or playing on sympathies in hopes of obtaining credit card information or selling a product. Every day, unscrupulous sales people knock on the doors of older people, often using high-pressure sales techniques, even threats, to convince them to buy products, make house repairs, or to purchase unwarranted and nonbeneficial insurance or financial products. Many seniors make such purchases based upon the sales agent's friendliness, honest looking face, or sad stories. Many people have fallen victim to scam artists who present themselves as sincere and reputable individuals, sometimes with fake identification and employment history. There are countless examples of seniors being scammed by sales people who remind them of their grandchild, who indicate that they would like to be their friend, or threaten to harm them if a purchase is not made. Persons who fraudulently misrepresent themselves, a product, or a benefit are often very good at what they do, and scam operations make billions of dollars every year.

Many seniors are embarrassed and will not report an abuse or fraudulent occurrence, oftentimes not even telling their families. It is hoped by including the following in this chapter, that persons who work with older persons will be aware of some of the issues surrounding such scams and, if suspected, can assist seniors and possibly recover some of their money.

Home Improvements or Household Repairs

The typical scenario is a "knock on the door" approach. The scam artist "contractor" will knock on the senior's door with a story about the person's roof, siding, gutter, driveway, or windows needing repair. He or she will convincingly point out the areas of repair, appear very knowledgeable, and present the situation to the homeowner as dire. Payment of 50 percent down, usually in cash, will be requested and then a future date will be made to replace the item(s). Oftentimes the senior does not have a receipt or cancelled check to track down or trace the "contractor" who generally does not ever return.

Telephone Scams

Telephone scams are widespread, ranging from winning lotteries and helping charities to winning a free vacation and Medicare financial abuse. Telescams are a $40 billion per year business. Recently, there are the "Australian" and "New Zealand" lottery scams where the caller excitedly announces to the senior that he or she has a winning ticket for millions of dollars. They are told that they need to pay only a small fee to receive the million dollar prize. The convincing telephone scammer provides a telephone number for the senior to call to verify the company, along with his name and title. Victims are asked to provide their Social Security number to verify their identification, and credit card number to cover the small fee that is required before any lottery winnings can be distributed. The big "win," of course, is never received. Many of these telephone lottery scam businesses are based outside the United States and therefore it is nearly impossible to stop them, recover lost funds, or indict the individuals involved.

Government Agency Misrepresentation

Scam organizations representing themselves as federal, state, and government employees call seniors to obtain their Social Security and credit card information. There are countless scams targeting Social Security and Medicare beneficiaries in this manner. Numerous scams include persons who identify themselves as agents of the federal government, or from the Medicare office, to discuss benefits. The caller attempts to obtain Social Security numbers, credit card information, or bank account numbers on the pretext that such information is required to process a Medicare claim or enroll the senior in a Medicare benefit (such as free medical equipment).

Direct Mail Solicitation

Thousands of pieces of mail are delivered to seniors daily which misrepresent products, issues, laws, and benefits. They range from "estate planning" and "tax savings" methods to a chance of purchasing "limited time only" trinkets at a high, inflated cost.

Financial Scams

There are numerous scams which target seniors with the goal of selling financial and insurance products which offer no benefit to the senior. Disreputable individuals often sell long-term annuities guaranteeing high interest returns, tax-free interest, and other false benefits. The sales agents present themselves as people who have special information that is not easily obtained or known and which can greatly benefit the senior. Once these agents have the older person's confidence, they will then convince the victim to purchase expensive investment products, which can result in restricting the victim's access to his or her money and may offer no real benefit to the victim in her lifetime. Unfortunately, it is not unusual to find that an 85-year-old who cashed out her stocks, certificates of deposit, or sometimes her entire investment portfolio to purchase a long-term annuity with a ten- or fifteen-year term without understanding the purchase or restrictions. These purchases often leave seniors without ample income or assets, placing them in a precarious financial situation for the rest of their lives.

Many states, most notably New York, have taken action to halt the fraudulent sales of annuities. Because the commissions on annuities are some of the highest paid to insurance agents, some states have requested that the sales commission paid by the insurance company to the sales agent be reduced in an effort to halt aggressive, inappropriate practices.

Estate Planning and Living Trust Scams

Sometimes the benefits of certain legal documents are misrepresented by unscrupulous insurance agents who wish to handle a senior's investments. Recently, "Living Trust Mills" have gained attention in many states as one such estate planning scheme. In some states, Living Trusts offer little or no benefit to a senior. An insurance agent or company normally partners with unethical attorneys to misrepresent the benefits of Living Trusts and annuities. The sales agents normally act as "front" men and will contact the senior either via telephone, direct mail, or seminar, to discuss "new laws," "ways to save taxes," or "probate avoidance schemes," often representing themselves as employees of the attorney. The insurance agent attempts to convince the senior that a Living Trust is cheaper and better than a Last Will and Testament, that it saves taxes or shelters assets from nursing home costs, none of which is true in certain states. Oftentimes, the attorney never meets with the senior, and will draft the legal documents based on the sales agent's representation of the person's circumstances and needs.

As previously stated, in many states, Living Trusts offer minimal or no benefit yet may cost ten times more than a Will. The sale is made on the personality and supposed expertise of the agent. The discovery of the lack of benefits and other misrepresentations are often discovered by family members only after the victim passes away.

Sweepstakes

As has been discussed, legitimate services, products, and methods of marketing can be converted or altered to create a scam or fraudulent scheme. Sweepstakes are another example. There are numerous legitimate sweepstakes, but there are also now a number of fraudulent schemes. The typical scenario is where seniors are contacted and told they have won a prize. They may even receive confirmation of the prize in the mail, and are then told to wire funds to pay the taxes due, or a "release fee" that can range from $100 to $10,000. The prize either is never received or is of a much lower value than the money paid. Because of the way the companies are created, it is difficult to locate, sue, or recover any of the fraudulently sent cash.

Laws and Enforcement Agencies to Protect against Scams, Fraud, and Telemarketing Fraud

There are laws specifically created to reduce or eliminate such scams against persons, particularly seniors. Theft, larceny, theft by deception, and fraud are all crimes that can be prosecuted by filing criminal complaints. Working with the police or the local district attorney, the senior can report the crime and aid in prosecuting the person who stole their money or made misrepresentations to them. Cases where an individual has been a victim of fraud can also be addressed by filing civil lawsuits against the perpetrators. Such civil action may become a class action lawsuit to try to recover the money or provide some restitution for many of the persons who were victimized.

There are also legal agencies and authorities who can act and may possibly recover the fees. Each state's Area Agency on Aging (AAA) (under the state's Department of Aging) has enforcement powers as defined under the Older American's Act. The protective services department of the AAA can institute an investigation based on anonymous callers and bring criminal charges against perpetrators of fraud. Local District Attorney Offices often work together with the AAA to pursue and file criminal charges.

States' Attorney General Offices have the authority to pursue civil or criminal actions against perpetrators of fraud, including levying large fines and injunctions, which can prevent a company from "doing business" in the state. The consumer fraud or consumer protection division in the Attorney General's Office will accept complaints and investigate them. Oftentimes, companies are more responsive to a complaint investigation by the Attorney General's Office than an individual.

In addition, each state's Department of Insurance has regulating authority over insurance companies and their agents doing business in their states. The department can levy a fine, cancel an agent's license, or restrict the agent(s) and companies involved in fraudulent sales practices. Similar to the Attorney General's Office, the Insurance Departments have consumer protection departments where complaints can be filed and investigated. A complaint investigated by the Department of Insurance Office oftentimes also carries more weight and influence than an individual action.

The United States Post Office, specifically the United States Postal Inspector's Office, will investigate and prosecute mail fraud. It has the authority to prosecute, as a criminal action, individuals and companies who use the United States postal mail service in conjunction with committing a crime such as fraud.

The Federal Bureau of Investigation has the authority to investigate interstate fraud. Ponzi or pyramid schemes often involve numerous locales and persons working and selling in many states. In a scam involving large investments, it is not uncommon to find a number of local and federal agencies investigating and working together to stop the illegal scheme, prosecute the wrongdoers and recover funds for the victims.

The Securities and Exchange Commission, another federal agency which works to bring justice to securities fraud situations, has investigative and prosecution powers against securities misrepresentation. Aside from the federal agency, each state has a banking or securities exchange department which also has investigation and prosecution powers.

In an attempt to regulate and reduce misrepresentation, the federal government in 1996 enacted a law specifically addressing telemarketing. It restricts the hours of telemarketing calling and prohibits telemarketers from providing misleading information about the services or products being offered. It requires firms to maintain a "Do Not Call" list, which includes persons who have either registered with the federal "Do Not Call Registry" or have told the company to add their name to the list themselves. Violations result in the telemarketing firm being subject to a $10,000 fine for each offense. Many states have their own "Do Not Call" registry as well as additional fines levied against offenders.

Finally, the Direct Marketing Association maintains a list of persons who do not want to receive direct mailings from any organization. To remove their name from company mailing lists, individuals can send the request to

Mail Preference Service
Direct Marketing Association
PO Box 643
Carmel, NY 10512

Conclusion

There are numerous legal issues that pertain to all seniors. Creating legal documents such as a Will, Power of Attorney, Living Will, or Healthcare Power of Attorney are essential for the senior, especially one who is facing long-term care needs. The laws surrounding estate planning change and it is important to have legal documents drafted and reviewed by an attorney to ensure estate planning needs will be met.

In some cases, the senior and family may benefit from nursing home planning and asset protection plans, especially if nursing home placement is anticipated and there is a special needs child or community spouse involved. The laws pertaining to Medicaid benefits also change frequently and often dramatically. It is vital to obtain expert legal advice for this type of situation to ensure rights are protected and impoverishment is avoided.

References

Deficit Reduction Act. (2005). Senate Bill 1932, 42 USC §1396p and §1396r-5.

Health Insurance Portability and Accountability Act. (1996).

Kaiser Commission on Medicaid and the Uninsured. (2005). *The Distribution of Assets in the Elderly Population Living in the Community, June 2005*. Washington, DC: The Henry J. Kaiser Family Foundation.

MedicineNet.com. (2004). Definition of terms, retrieved on September 8, 2004, http://www.medterms.com.

National Hospice and Palliative Care Organization. (2004). Definition of terms, retrieved on September 8, 2004, http://www.nhpco.org.

New York State Department of Health. (2006). Office of Medicaid Management, January, Albany, New York.

Omnibus Budget Reconciliation Act. (1993).

Pennsylvania Department of Public Welfare. (2007). *Medicaid—General Eligibility Requirements*, retrieved on April 26, 2007, http://www.dpw.state.pa.us/servicesprograms/medicalassistance/003670296.htm.

The Medicare Catastrophic Coverage Act. (1988). 42 USC §1396r.

The New York Times. (2005). Week in review, retrieved July 2006, http://www.nytimes.com/2005/06/19/weekinreview.

Chapter 12

Long-Term Care Housing Trends: Past and Present

Shannon M. Chance

Contents

The United States faces a pressing need for more and better housing to sustain its aging population. As waves of baby boomers reach retirement age, our deficit of supportive housing begs society to focus its attention on filling the gap. A variety of disciplines—including healthcare, design, and policy—must lend their talents toward crafting solutions to meet America's imminent housing needs. The impending wave of housing construction for long-term care prompts us to evaluate the history of housing for the aging as well as the features that contribute to quality accommodations for elderly and frail people.

Almshouse Tradition in the United States

Institutional long-term care had its humble beginnings in the early American almshouses and rural "poor farms" that were developed by local societies and churches. They were unspecialized institutions that offered welfare service to dependent persons of all ages, which only incidentally provided some medical care for sick residents (Malone, 1998; Starr, 1982). Being located in buildings originally constructed as private houses (Pratt, 1999; Shore, 1994), colonial American almshouses maintained a residential appearance as well as a communal nature (Starr, 1982). Nonprofit community groups, societies, or church organizations often converted existing homes into almshouse facilities, and they incorporated rules and ways of interacting that were developed in Europe (Shore, 1994).

Almshouses sponsored by county or municipal governments also emerged to serve individuals who were unaffiliated with any of the private societies (Shore, 1994). Publicly funded city almshouses were constructed—dating back to 1622 in Boston, 1713 in Philadelphia, and 1736 in New York—and they provided communal facilities to care for sick, elderly, orphaned, lame, or blind persons (Shore, 1994).

Publicly funded institutions gave way to the first nonprofit hospital built in the United States, the Pennsylvania Hospital of Philadelphia, which opened in 1756 (Goldsmith, 2005). It was followed by privately financed hospitals in New York (chartered in 1791 and opened two decades later) and Boston (in 1821). These private hospitals are notable because they were the first permanent facilities in the United States that were specifically developed to provide care for the sick, and to serve all social classes (Starr, 1982).

Despite the advent of the medical hospital, the almshouse continued to provide a mainstay of care in the United States. The almshouse actually increased in importance in the 1800s, often duplicating services found in hospitals (Malone, 1998; Starr, 1982). Starr (1982) explains that the need for almshouses increased in 1828 when the U.S. government ended "home relief" programs that had been financing in-home care for the needy during difficult economic times. He states

> By making the almshouse the only source of governmental aid to the poor, legislatures hoped to restrict expenditures for public assistance.

Often squalid and over-crowded, a place of shame and indignity, the almshouse offered a minimal level of support—its function as a deterrent to poverty and public assistance ruled out any amenities. Deterioration and neglect were common. (Starr, 1982, p. 150)

Differentiation of Specialized Groups

Following the Civil War, reformers wanted to dismantle the ill-reputed almshouse; residents were often sent to other facilities that were being created specifically to house the sick, the orphaned, the "insane," and the blind (Starr, 1982). McArthur (1970) notes that other specialized facilities were created for widows, seamen, and military veterans and that this trend directly influenced long-term care by distinguishing aged individuals as a need-specific group. According to him, by the early 1930s the elderly were almost entirely separated from other need groups.

At the same time, public hospitals enjoyed improved public perception—especially because their mortality rates were decreasing. For one, operators began the practice of moving contagious and other undesirable patients to "pesthouses," remaining almshouses, or specialized institutions. These new medically oriented facilities often also excluded people with incurable conditions, sending them to long-term care facilities (Starr, 1982). Asylums and similar long-term care institutions were developed on large rural tracts of public land in remote areas, further reflecting a desire to separate the general population from those with the most stigmatized conditions (Pratt, 1999).

Medical Model Formalizes

Interest in the layout and design of hospital facilities gained attention, and in 1858, Florence Nightingale introduced a new ward design (Purves, 2002; Thompson and Goldin, 1975). The Crimean War had precipitated Nightingale's work to improve hospital ward layout and efficiency, as well as hygiene and ventilation (Starr, 1982; Thompson and Goldin, 1975). Nightingale's open-ward floor plan provided efficient ventilation and nurse stationing at the ward entrance (Bobrow and Thomas, 2000). The Crimean War also prompted Isambard Brunel's civil engineering designs for mobile and rapid-deployment hospitals that could easily be extended at the ends; this open-ended scheme is still in use today (Bobrow and Thomas, 2000; Thompson and Goldin, 1975). American colonists borrowed plan layouts such as these from Europe, as well as an English system of laws and values that mandated self-reliance for the able-bodied (Shore, 1994).

Architectural Developments and Changing Public Perceptions

European precedents—regarding design and social values—have tremendously influenced American attitudes toward healthcare as well as the physical form of long-term and acute care facilities. With the emergence of the public hospital, the general tone of hospital architecture shifted to reflect an increasingly bureaucratic organization, serve a changing user group, and render new medical services. The hospital's interior and exterior features shed their residential nuances in favor of a more public style influenced by an increasingly business-like, paternalistic structure (Starr, 1982).

According to Bobrow and Thomas (2000), nursing units that house patients for long periods have historically formed the core of hospitals. Before 1200, nursing units used the same type of open bay structure as church naves. In fact, the first hospital nursing units were often part of an abbey and their form remained relatively unchanged through the 1800s (Bobrow and Thomas, 2000; Thompson and Goldin, 1975). Although construction methods of the time did not allow the long spans possible today, the narrow form, typical of both nursing units and Gothic church naves, provided ample day lighting. The rows of beds aligned along exterior walls of the narrow space also benefited from natural cross-ventilation. This was important because electric lighting and mechanical systems (to heat, cool, and clean the air) had not yet been developed.

The character and number of hospitals changed markedly following the Civil War. The open bay form dominated for many centuries, but studies conducted at the Johns Hopkins University hospital in 1875 identified problems inherent in these large, open nursing wards (Bobrow and Thomas, 2000; Thompson and Goldin, 1975). They recommended alternative models that could decrease noise, distribute heat more evenly, increase patient privacy, and allow for isolating infected patients (Bobrow and Thomas, 2000; Thompson and Goldin, 1975). Open wards disappeared as smaller patient rooms (arranged along double-loaded corridors) gained popularity (Bobrow and Thomas, 2000).

Acute Care Takes Center Stage

Following the Civil War, acute care provided by hospitals became the dominant concern in healthcare; long-term care did not receive the same proactive concern and development. The advent of both antiseptic surgery and nursing as a profession reinforced the systems of order and cleanliness that characterized medical care of the late 1800s (Starr, 1982). Although hospitals came to be seen as places where people went to recover, long-term care facilities acquired a negative stigma. In addition, hospitals developed programs for research and teaching (Shore, 1994), but this sort of inquiry and invention and hope and optimism did not transfer to long-term care.

The standard home for long-term care at that time provided meager services to collections of elderly, orphans, disabled, and mentally ill people, and was viewed as a last resort (Shore, 1994). The types of social support and services previously available through the almshouse (such as companionship, meals, and basic personal care assistance to people of all ages who could not provide these for themselves) became increasingly less accessible. Malone (1998, p. 798) claims that between the early and mid-twentieth century, the "almshouses disappeared, sometimes through being transformed into other institutions (such as long-term care facilities)." Some social welfare programs were developed (independent of care facilities) in the first-half of the 1900s, but many of the services previously available at almshouses were never replaced.

Starr (1982) indicates that need for almshouse-type care did not diminish with the inception of the medical hospital. Migration to cities—such as that following the American Civil War—actually increased the demand for both acute and long-term care. These influxes changed the structure of the American family, detaching people from their familial support systems.

Residential Model Differentiates Long-Term Care

As hospitals dedicated more of their beds to surgery and acute care, they discharged patients earlier to private homes or newly emerging convalescent homes. The line between patients and staff formalized, with care increasingly administered by professional nurses rather than by the residents or live-in caregivers who had historically provided care in the almshouses and early hospitals (Starr, 1982). This formalization affected both the structure of, and life within, both long-term care facilities and acute care hospitals. The facilities for long-term care took two primary forms (Shore, 1994).

According to Shore (1994, p. 5), the "voluntary, philanthropic, fraternal, ethnic, church-related home was the primary type of facility providing services throughout the 19th century and up to the early 1920s." Such places served retired missionaries, poor people, and those abandoned or without families (Gordon, 1998), including the elderly, orphaned, physically or mentally ill, or disabled.

For instance, during the late 1800s nonprofit groups such as the "Ladies Sheltering Aid Society" organized homes that Shore (1994) describes as communal "collection pots." He states that this form of housing represented a "feared and dreaded fate [that] was accepted only when there was no other alternative" (p. 5). Residents were referred to as "inmates" and a quarter of people either in or waiting to get into these homes died of pneumonia each year. Some organizations running these facilities asked residents to turn over their remaining assets in exchange for the assurance of life-long accommodation, meals, and care. These organizations became known as "life-care facilities" and gradually evolved into a much more acceptable form of care known as the continuing care retirement community (CCRC) (Gordon, 1998). This method of pooled-risk (using a communal collection pot that financially supported care for life) was carried over from Eastern Europe (Shore, 1994).

The financial incentive presented by housing wealthier people spurred the growth of the second major form of accommodations that was in use between the Civil War and World War II (WWII) specifically for seniors. According to Shore (1994), this reputable type of housing emerged in the late 1800s, created by German and Scandinavian immigrants familiar with the European *Altenheim*. Such homes offered a clublike atmosphere and were unaffordable to most people who needed long-term care.

Shore (1994, p. 5) states that these "two distinctly different types of facilities coexisted until virtually the end of World War II." Although post-Depression policies would discourage these types of housing for a time, aspects of these two models would eventually reemerge in the 1970s and 1980s. Aspects such as the clublike atmosphere and life-care assurance in exchange for prepaid assets would provide precedent for long-term care development after a period of dormancy. The intervening years reflected a marked influence by the federal government, and far-reaching national policies were often designed in response to shifting economic conditions. Improvements in medical care between the Civil War and World War I required ever-increasing amounts of funding that immediately affected the design of acute care facilities.

Cost Concerns Dominate

Starr (1982) notes that the issue of funding hospital care reached crisis proportions in 1904. In New York City, government and private charities could no longer meet the hospitals' financial needs, and their focus turned to efficiency and business management. Starr (1982, pp. 160–161) describes an increased "demand for more careful accounting, more specialized labor, and better coordination of the various auxiliary hotel, restaurant, and laboratory services that a hospital maintained."

Old charitable hospitals and almshouses had been managed informally. However, the large new hospital organizations made efficiency paramount and managed their affairs in a scientific way. Although the hospital quickly adopted a very bureaucratic and institutional-feeling environment, the charitable retirement home did not fall under the same regulations. Long-term care facilities did not shift in this manner until later; rather, they faced a period of neglect as the existing system was disassembled and replaced with unregulated private homes. Eventually, however, both long-term and acute care saw technology and institutionalization prioritized, and these trends had both positive and negative consequences.

Construction Technologies Evolve

The scientific discoveries that followed the Civil War celebrated order and efficiency, as did the technical construction-related discoveries of the Industrial Revolution, which was underway. Medical science and construction technology both tremendously affected healthcare. New construction methods changed the look and feel of acute care facilities, and eventually of long-term care facilities.

Modern materials and techniques allowed for buildings that were bigger and taller than ever before. The development of long-span steel construction, elevators, and air-conditioning prompted completely new building forms (Bobrow and Thomas, 2000). After 1900, mechanical air-conditioning provided the means to create wider buildings that no longer had to be oriented with regard to prevailing breezes or natural convection (Bobrow and Thomas, 2000; Schiller, 2004). The development of the flush-type toilet in 1870 (Pathak, 1995) and the subsequent installation of bathroom facilities also had important effects on the layout of healthcare facilities.

National Policy

The marked change in building technologies and in healthcare systems, and the emphasis on order and efficiency prevalent throughout the twentieth century, are also reflected in government policies. The Great Depression of 1929 precipitated federal government involvement in social welfare for the first time. To meet the tremendous demand for services that was precipitated by soaring unemployment, the government provided income assistance so that needy individuals could live in privately owned homes. The Social Security Act of 1935 granted federal relief to the aged, the blind, and to needy families with dependent children. This is considered by most experts to be the beginning of the nursing home industry in America, the growth of which spawned many other types of facilities for long-term care (Pratt, 1999; Shore, 1994).

The Social Security Act of 1935 and its associated welfare programs were developed as a way to extend economic relief to the general community. The Act provided a system of "old age and survivors insurance" through which qualified individuals could receive federal funds to assist in paying for their own care (Shore, 1994, p. 6). Ordinary homeowners began to provide housing and care to the elderly, and a haphazard cottage industry of privately owned rest homes emerged (McArthur, 1970; Shore, 1994).

Since the 1935 Act denied financial assistance to those living in government or local "county" homes, many publicly run facilities closed, transferring their residents to private homes where these individuals would be eligible to receive Social Security benefits (McArthur, 1970; Shore, 1994). The legislation also denied financial assistance to those who contracted for life care, thus limiting such assistance through organized, not-for-profit charities (Shore, 1994). It forced the closure of existing life-care facilities as well as any remaining almshouses (McArthur, 1970).

Unlike the charitable almshouse, the emerging cottage industry of nursing care represented a source of profit, and private owner-operators sometimes abused their unregulated status. McArthur (1970) explains that the care provided by these places proved insufficient, especially as their residents aged and needed increasing levels of attention. However, because payment for services was now channeled through individual residents, users came to be seen as "residents" rather than indigent "wards" as viewed previously (Shore, 1994).

The Rise and Decline of Nursing Homes

Federal policies such as these fostered the private, unregulated nursing home as the dominant provider of long-term care in the United States for several decades—the institutional alternative to expensive extended hospitalization (Pratt, 1999; Scaggs and Hawkins, 1994). These policies also dictated the quality and type of services rendered, but declining quality led to negative public perception of the facilities. Deteriorating through the 1970s, these facilities became notorious for fraud, abuse, and deadly fires. Federal legislation, eventually enacted in 1965 and 1975, mandated only limited state regulations (Gordon, 1998).

The need for extended care continued to increase throughout the twentieth century, however, and nursing home waiting lists grew despite their growing stigma (Shore, 1994). The number of elderly citizens needing care inflated, as general improvements in living conditions extended the average life expectancy. Progress included better water delivery and sanitation systems, the advent of antibiotics (and a resulting reduction of pneumonia and many other infectious diseases), advances in medical science, and increased accessibility to primary healthcare (Cox and Groves, 1990; Shore, 1994).

Public housing programs developed by the federal government following the Depression and WWII provided some housing for senior citizens. They were, however, geared toward the active and healthy elderly, and offered only the most basic amenities (Pynoos and Matsuoka, 1996). Public housing was one component of a vast construction boom following WWII that failed to provide infrastructure, both in terms of physical design and service offerings, to accommodate the long-term needs of residents. Postwar houses and apartments were designed and constructed to accommodate the stereotypical young American family, without regard for how the structures would function for an aging population. Much of this new housing was located in suburbs with no public transportation, and with features such as steps at the entrance and narrow bathroom doors that restrict mobility (Pynoos and Matsuoka, 1996; Smith, 2003). Indeed, the typical housing stock has proven to be quite ineffective at supporting an aging population, and has exacerbated the current need for formal housing solutions.

The tremendous need for housing that followed WWII also led to the 1948 Hill–Burton Act, which in turn generated improvements in hospital facilities and their nursing units (Bobrow and Thomas, 2000). The legislation funded two decades of hospital construction in underserved areas (Goldsmith, 2005; Pratt, 1999). It also promoted experimentation by giving communities the capability to develop local hospitals "that reflected the latest trends" and it prompted innovation, especially within nursing units (Bobrow and Thomas, 2000). The boom of post-WWII health care construction was fueled by the development of private insurance for hospital and medical care (Goldsmith, 2005). These postwar changes had consequences for long-term care. In addition, a 1954 amendment to the Hill–Burton Act extended financing for a limited number of not-for-profit long-term care facilities (Pratt, 1999).

The enactment of Medicare and Medicaid in 1965, stimulated the growth of nursing homes and their emergence as corporate entities (Pratt, 1999; Shore, 1994). Through a 1967 congressional mandate, licensing boards were created in all states to regulate facilities providing various types of medical and healthcare. This federal legislation required that by 1970 each state would have a licensing board to oversee nursing homes in its jurisdiction (Shore, 1994). At the same time, the national and state governments were attempting to control the escalating costs of these facilities. Private insurance companies, as well as corporate and private purchasers of insurance and healthcare, also pushed for increased cost effectiveness (Pratt, 1999).

Financial support to nursing homes did not keep pace with the expectations placed on them, and the long-term care industry struggled to balance service with funding (Scaggs and Hawkins, 1994). Pressure to cut costs and produce profits, in the face of strict funding limitations, contributed once again to inadequate conditions and poor public perceptions (Pratt, 1999).

The deinstitutionalization of many mentally ill persons throughout the 1960 and 1970s produced another need that remains inadequately addressed. Pynoos and Matsuoka (1996, p. 116) assert that this movement "placed many people with mental health problems in the community. This shift to community-based care led to the growth of special needs housing for people with developmental disabilities, substance abuse problems, and a variety of mental health problems." These programs have received very little funding, have faced tremendous neighborhood opposition, and have rarely succeeded in meeting needs—as reflected in the numbers of mentally ill people living on American city streets today (Pynoos and Matsuoka, 1996).

Regulations at the federal and state levels have also been used to control the locations of healthcare facilities, including those for long-term care. The National Health Planning and Resource Development Act of 1974 required states to institute "Certificate of Need" reviews to control the geographic distribution of such facilities, specifically including nursing homes. Pratt (1999) explains that although the Medical Facilities Survey and Construction Act (sponsored by Hill and Burton in 1946) had encouraged construction of healthcare facilities, this new policy was designed to do the opposite. It controlled competition, regulating and often discouraging new construction. Although the Certificate of Need system was dismantled in most states during the 1980s, this short-lived national policy had direct and lasting effects on the distribution of long-term care facilities (Pratt, 1999).

Public awareness of the need for more long-term housing and services rose during the 1970s. Waves of retirees, who could not obtain the support they required to continue living in their existing homes, discovered that their main alternative was to move into nursing homes or other "board-and-care" facilities. Pynoos and Matsuoka (1996, p. 116) explain that "frail older people, especially those with low incomes, had few residential options available." Yet institutional facilities provided higher levels of care than most seniors and other people with disabilities needed.

In response to growing needs, some new services were developed to help people stay in their private homes or in other residential-model facilities. One example of such a program was created through the 1978 Congregate Housing Services Act, which funded meals and other services for low-income seniors who lived in federally subsidized housing (Gordon, 1998). Residentially based "congregate housing" gained acceptance and popularity throughout the 1980s. This type of housing was constructed at a range of affordability levels and was available to those who required government assistance as well as to those who did not (Gordon, 1998).

Largely due to wider housing offerings and declining levels of disability among seniors, utilization of nursing homes has drastically declined since its height in the mid-1970s. Only about 4 percent of the elderly reside in nursing homes at present, in contrast to a figure of nearly 6 percent in the early 1970s (Vierck and Hodges, 2003).

Through various legislative measures, housing for long-term care began to fall into three basic categories based on the level of dependence: housing for well and independent seniors, housing for moderately impaired or semi-independent individuals, and housing for frail and dependent people (Pynoos, 1987). People living in nursing facilities today are generally more vulnerable, weak, and cognitively impaired than elders living in other settings (Mollica and Johnson-Lamarche, 2005).

The nursing home has continued to evolve and expand its range of services, often being combined with other levels of care to create new hybrid forms. Stand-alone nursing homes are increasingly rare today; traditional facilities now usually constitute one component of a larger system, such as a CCRC. Contemporary nursing facilities may also combine traditional in-patient services with many out-patient and outreach offerings, including research and public education programs (Shore, 1994).

Consumer Market Drives Change

Over the past three decades, an incredible range of housing types has emerged to serve our aging population. Change has often been precipitated by the desires expressed through market forces. Since the mid-1980s, for-profit real estate developers have become increasingly active in the construction and administration of long-term care facilities, and an emphasis on customer service has developed under the capitalist model. The call for more affordable options and services—and for arrangements that ensure long-term security and provision for one's increasing needs for care over time—has spurred housing suppliers to develop a wide assortment of products (Gordon, 1998).

In general, providers have developed creative ways to improve the quality and types of services to attract more clients (Pratt, 1999). They have developed a wide array of optional services, ranging from modest to luxurious (Gordon, 1998). Some hospital operators have capitalized on underused wings by converting them into nursing care or other types of long-term care facilities (Pratt, 1999; Scaggs and Hawkins, 1994). Nursing homes have become highly efficient with regard to scheduling and cost (Shore, 1994). Nursing home and hospital operators have branched out, offering services such as home healthcare (Pratt, 1999). It is likely that this diversification will continue as the number of retirees grows, becomes increasingly affluent, and represents a larger portion of the overall consumer market in America (Gordon, 1998).

Services represent the characteristic that most distinguishes senior housing from all other types; the physical features and the amount of amenities provided differentiate "luxury" facilities from those tailored to elders of low- to middle-economic status. According to Gordon (1998, pp. 25–26), such services "may include restaurants, . . . periodic housekeeping and flat laundry services, game rooms, fitness centers, tennis, golf and pool facilities, barber shops and beauty salons, on-site banks, convenience stores and gift shops, concierge or activity director services, [and] local minibus transportation."

Breaking from more than a century of American tradition that required moving people to new locations as their level of dependency increased, the idea of "aging in place" reemerged. Although this concept is generally described as a new innovation, it actually reflects an approach used across the globe where necessary care is provided within a single community throughout one's life. People, like plants, tend to thrive in a stable setting; they tend to suffer when they are transplanted at their frailest. The United States is now moving toward an arrangement that provides greater flexibility to accommodate people's changing needs for assistance and care. These include two major hybrid models for long-term care and housing that emerged (or re-emerged) toward the end of the twentieth century: assisted living and continuing care. Each of these housing types is described in detail in Chapter 15 on housing types and design.

The very nature of "aging in place" necessitates having qualified caregivers and support services available to meet increasing medical needs. Gordon (1998) raises concern that government regulations, which segregate housing from care, are often overly restrictive. He notes that under current guidelines, many aging residents living in residentially focused facilities who require increasing levels of service, will be forced to move into more supportive facilities.

Trends for the Future

Today, there are growing efforts to create a more comfortable, responsive, and welcoming environment that still honors the quantitative constraints of codes, cost, and profitability. Over the past three decades, a new human-centered approach has gradually re-emerged, in contrast to the economic and functionalist priorities shaping so many existing healthcare facilities.

With thoughtful consideration, good design can actually increase profits and save money while simultaneously addressing the vast array of legal stipulations and functional needs. Building programs must convey pragmatic requirements, but these written documents used to guide design decisions must also enumerate qualitative aspirations for the facility. Facility planners can ensure higher quality of life for a facility's users by stating minimum standards for personal control, privacy and dignity, light and color, heating and ventilation, and for supporting specific needs of patients, visitors, and staff. The people who are planning and designing facilities must shift their emphasis from the procedure to the person, from functionality to flexibility (Kobus, 2000; Purves, 2002).

Architectural and healthcare consultants working together—studying, analyzing, and developing new solutions—have already produced many convincing results. Kobus (2000) states that these two groups of consultants must lead the way in keeping the healthcare housing industry focused on the patient and the patient's family. At the same time, experts in healthcare, design, and policymaking should work to correct past deficiencies regarding physical facilities as well as the overall healthcare system.

Indeed, the United States is finally shifting to a more patient-oriented system of medical and long-term care. Holistic approaches to both medicine and architecture are emerging, such as those that incorporate alternative therapies as well as environmentally sustainable building systems (Purves, 2002). The contemporary obsession with health and safety requirements (developed to create risk-averse environments) is being tempered (Parker et al., 2004). Technology is increasingly seen as assistive, rather than central to healing (Purves, 2002). These changes foster life quality in a broader sense by protecting the dignity, identity, and independence of frail people in addition to satisfying their safety and hygiene needs (Cox and Groves, 1990). In this pursuit, Purves insists that researchers should develop ways to measure emotional responses to, and ephemeral qualities of, environments created for healthcare.

To correct past deficiencies, increased attention must be given to bridging social disparities; citizens of all economic levels should be able to obtain adequate long-term care. Although problems with housing have been "especially severe for minorities, renters, and older persons living in rural areas" (Pynoos, 1987, p. 40), there is evidence of a shift as "[s]ome developers are beginning to change their focus and to develop projects that are affordable to middle-income seniors" (Gordon, 1998, p. 49). Shifting priorities must continually inform the evolution of long-term care facilities and the services they offer.

Features and Qualities to Include

Architectural features that should be taken into account when planning, constructing, or renovating a long-term care facility vary drastically in size and scope.

Long-term care facilities must be organized in a logical way, so that users can easily locate rooms and services, differentiate public and private spaces, and quickly establish a sense of familiarity and community (Goodman and Smith, 1992).

The physical environment can have powerful effects in the lives of its users. A well-designed facility promotes a sense of comfort, safety, and meaning; it aids staff in performing duties and tasks; and it also facilitates and encourages family visits (Sloane et al., 2001). Parker et al. (2004, p. 956) explain that life quality is "multidimensional" and combines "diverse attributes such as physical health, psychological state, level of independence and social relationships."

Connectedness and companionship are critical aspects for quality of life that can be enhanced or hampered by the place's architecture, policies, recreational offerings, and overall culture (Thomas, 1998a; Eckert et al., 2001). Given conscientious coordination throughout design and operation, long-term care facilities can provide spaces that foster a sense of belonging and tranquility. The number of one's human contacts and the control one has over these interactions influence one's level of happiness, sense of personal identity, and satisfaction with life (Eckert et al., 2001; Regnier, 2002).

Residents should have many spaces available for engaging with groups of people as well as a range of places that provide a sense of privacy. The individual residential unit constitutes the most intimate space within a long-term care environment. The psychological aspects of control, ownership, and freedom provided by having one's own space hold deep symbolic meaning for people raised in Western societies, as so eloquently expressed in Woolf's (1929) essay *A Room of One's Own*. The desire for individual space carries into American healthcare, which has emphasized privacy in many forms . . . from individual experience, to facility ownership and doctor's employment, to the architectural spaces designed for patient care (Starr, 1982).

Private dwelling units for long-term accommodation are on the rise in America. Privacy also remains a central concern for people who must share their living unit with another person (Scaggs and Hawkins, 1994). Designers of shared or "semiprivate" rooms should take care to provide a sense of control and privacy for each resident. Sloane et al. (2001) recommend that each individual should have his or her own storage place, window, television, and telephone, and there should be a solid (perhaps movable) barrier between individuals' spaces. Sloane et al. (2001, p. 184) also note that "the ability to control who exits and enters" greatly influences privacy. The primary aspect of perceived privacy, however, is having a private toilet area (Gordon, 1998). Although sharing bathing facilities is often considered acceptable, people generally desire a sink and toilet for their use alone (Gordon, 1998; Sloane et al., 2001).

Residents often experience a sense of alienation in arrangements where there is inadequate delineation between public and private spaces, such as an insufficient buffer between the corridor and the resident's bed. Individual spaces that are out of scale also feel repressive. Providing spatial variety and individual spaces that have human, homelike scale can foster an overall sense of belonging and a noninstitutional feel (Childs et al., 1997).

Positive morale among residents and staff who believe they are in a good place can go a long way toward maintaining health; it can support healing and growth as well. The suffering and boredom so often associated with long-term care facilities can be mitigated by healing forces such as light, plants, and animals (Bobrow and Thomas, 2000; Thomas, 1998b).

As stated by Eckert et al. (2001, p. 3), one study found that there are three aspects shaping life quality in long-term care facilities: "the ability to communicate with other residents and staff within the facility, the ability to care for oneself, and the ability to care for and help others in more need than themselves." Opportunities to give care to people, pets, or even plants provide the type of "positive distraction" that keep residents from feeling helpless and lonely (Purves, 2002; Thomas, 1998a). Music, art, laughter, and nature have all been shown to produce measurable and therapeutic benefits as well (Purves, 2002).

Some of the most important quality of life factors—choice and positive stimulation—are closely related. Personal control of temperature, lighting, sound, and odor are very important in long-term care facilities, especially because sensory tolerance for extremes tends to decline with age (Gordon, 1998; Regnier, 2002; Sloane et al., 2001). Operable windows allow personal control of natural light and ventilation. These features can also positively influence the operating costs of a facility.

Other, more practical design considerations involve safety, security, cleanliness, and maintenance. A built or social environment that takes a heavy-handed approach to these, however, will feel stifling and oppressive, especially to residents with low levels of dependency (Parker et al., 2004). Facility designers and operators must work to strike a careful balance between risk aversion and freedom.

Another practical consideration involves the high percentage of "service spaces" necessary to support living and working within a long-term care facility. These include nursing stations, medical care rooms, administrative offices, and break rooms for staff as well as sufficient spaces for cooking and bathing facilities, janitorial closets, and storage of equipment.

Of all the service spaces required in a long-term care facility, however, circulation can present the biggest design challenges and opportunities; it must be integrated with the utmost sensitivity if it is to support the resident's sense of orientation. The flow of circulation around the site and through the building should be clear and convenient, and must accommodate persons with varying levels of mobility. Wayfinding is important for all users, and especially for people experiencing memory loss. Color, material, décor, and signage can help differentiate otherwise similar wings of corridors and rooms (Scaggs and Hawkins, 1994). Creating a variety of spaces within a facility that have their own distinct characteristics can also help residents determine their location and distinguish the appropriate use of each space.

Special Care Facilities

Features that enhance way-finding are especially critical for residents suffering from Alzheimer's disease because their desire to wander increases as their disease progresses. Because such patients share similar characteristics, many special wards have been developed to provide care specific to their common symptoms and needs.

Specially designed wards have also been created to care for people who have various developmental disabilities.

Wards for residents with Alzheimer's disease usually incorporate increased security measures, including key-coded doors and provisions for higher levels of observation to compensate for the tendency of these residents to wander (Scaggs and Hawkins, 1994). It is important to provide outdoor spaces, but they must be easily observable by staff and be designed to keep residents from leaving the premises (Regnier, 2002).

Design features that aid in "place recognition" are especially important for residents who are cognitively impaired. Giving each space a distinct character that clearly indicates its use can help orient such elders (Childs et al., 1997). Toilets must also be very easy to locate; placing them within the sight line of beds, or providing an easily recognizable symbol on nearby bathroom doors, can aid orientation measurably (Sloane et al., 2001).

Regnier (2002, p. 268) explains that care for those "with memory loss often requires a smaller, self-contained setting with fewer residents and a carefully trained staff." Special care facilities often subdivide cognitively impaired residents into groups of four to fifteen, with small sleeping rooms clustered around living spaces that are shared by individuals in each section (Childs et al., 1997). As cited in Eckert et al. (2001, p. 298), one researcher found that, this arrangement fosters a "small-group effect" and facilitates "high levels of communication, emotional involvement, sharing, and commitment." The type of care provided in special units is changing as new diseases are identified and as new medications and treatments are developed to address them (Regnier, 2002).

Researchers note that many smaller residential facilities naturally support place recognition. Many large existing facilities are converting portions of their complexes to special-care wards and integrating condition-specific support features. States are increasingly involved in regulating facilities that provide care to special user groups. As of 2005, 44 states had requirements regarding facilities for residents with Alzheimer's disease and other forms of dementia (Mollica and Johnson-Lamarche, 2005).

Conclusion

Although the earliest facilities for healthcare supported recuperation and fostered health in a holistic sense, history shows a subsequent decline in concern for these aspects of well-being as medical technologies took center stage. As a result, the institutionalized settings that came to typify the healthcare of twentieth-century America failed to capture society's imagination or endearment. Long-term care facilities garnered particularly strong public disdain. Today, the general population demands a change that will foster higher quality of life for users of long-term care facilities. More and more people recognize that a well-designed facility can increase a resident's feelings of independence and autonomy, sense of belonging, satisfaction, contentment, pride, and dignity.

The emerging market of baby boomers, in particular, seeks a more comprehensive and considered approach to the design, development, and operation of healthcare facilities. They are researching their options, asking questions, and spurring change. As a result, housing providers are developing creative responses that include various sets of services and features that create more pleasant and supportive environments.

Functional features are far less likely than qualitative features to get lost among the complexities of the design process. It is crucial for those involved in the development of long-term care facilities to understand—and be able to identify and specify—attributes that contribute to a healthful, pleasant, and inspiring environment for living and healing. We must prepare ourselves to address imminent needs as well as make lasting contributions toward the improvement of housing for long-term care.

References

Bobrow, M. and Thomas, J. (2000). Inpatient care facilities. In Kilment, S. A. (Ed.), *Building Type Basics for Healthcare Facilities*. New York: Wiley, pp. 131–191.

Childs, M., Grape, T. H., Webb-Johnson, A., and Wojciechowski, A. (1997). Long-term care design: What you need to know about life-enhancing environments. *Journal of Healthcare Design, IX*, 121–124.

Cox, A. and Groves, P. (1990). *Hospitals and Health Care Facilities: A Design and Development Guide* (2nd ed.). Boston, MA: Butterworth Architecture.

Eckert, K., Zimmerman, S., and Morgan, L. A. (2001). Connectedness in residential care: A qualitative perspective in the changing health care environment. In Zimmerman, S., Sloane, P. D. and Eckert, J. K. (Eds.), *Assisted Living: Needs, Practices, and Policies in Residential Care for the Elderly*. Baltimore, MD: Johns Hopkins University, pp. 292–313.

Goldsmith, S. (2005). *Principle of Health Management Care: Compliance, Consumerism, and Accountability in the 21st Century*. Boston, MA: Jones and Bartlett.

Goodman, R. J. and Smith, D. G. (1992). *Retirement Facilities: Planning, Design, and Marketing*. New York: Whitney Library of Design.

Gordon, P. A. (1998). *Seniors' Housing and Care Facilities: Development, Business, and Operations*. Washington: Urban Land Institute.

Kobus, R. L. (2000). Perspective. In Kilment, S. A. (Ed.), *Building Type Basics for Healthcare Facilities*. New York: Wiley, pp. 1–7.

Malone, R. E. (1998). Whither the almshouse? Overutilization and the role of the emergency department. *Journal of Health Politics, Policy and Law, 23*(5), 795–832.

McArthur, R. F. (1970). The historical evolution from almshouse to EFC. 2. A three part discussion. *Nursing Homes, 19*(6), 26–27, 45.

Mollica, R. and Johnson-Lamarche, H. (2005). *State Residential Care and Assisted Living Policy: 2004*. National Academy for State Health Policy of the United States Department of Health and Human Services. Retrieved August 10, 2006, from http://aspe.hhs.gov/daltcp/reports/04alcom1.pdf.

Parker, C., Barnes, S., McKee, K., Morgan, K., Torrington, J., and Tregenza, P. (2004). Quality of life and building design in residential and nursing homes for older people. *Aging and Society*, *24*, 941–962.

Pathak, B. (1995). *History of Toilets*. Paper presented at the International Symposium on Public Toilets, Hong Kong. Retrieved August 14, 2006, from http://www.sulabhtoiletmuseum.org/pg02.htm.

Pratt, J. R. (1999). *Long-Term Care: Management across the Continuum*. Gaithersburg, MD: Aspen Publishers.

Purves, G. (2002). *Healthy Living Centers: A Guide to Primary Health Care Design*. New York: Architectural Press.

Pynoos, J. (1987). Housing the aged: Public policy at the crossroads. In Regnier, V. and Pynoos, J. (Eds.), *Housing the Aged: Design Directives and Policy Considerations*. New York: Elsevier Science, pp. 25–40.

Pynoos, J. and Matsuoka, C. E. (1996). Housing. In Evashwick, C. J. (Ed.), *The Continuum of Long-Term Care: An Integrated Systems Approach*. New York: Delmar Publishers.

Regnier, V. (2002). *Designing for Assisted Living: Guidelines for Housing the Physically and Mentally Frail*. New York: Wiley.

Scaggs, R. L. and Hawkins, H. R. (1994). Architecture for long-term care facilities. In Goldsmith, S. B. (Ed.), *Essentials of Long-Term Care Administration*. Gaithersburg, MD: Aspen Publishers, pp. 254–280.

Schiller, M. (2004). *Mechanical and Electrical Systems*. Chicago, IL: Kaplan AEC Architecture.

Shore, H. H. (1994). History of long-term care. In Goldsmith, S. B. (Ed.), *Essentials of Long-Term Care Administration*. Gaithersburg, MD: Aspen Publishers, pp. 1–10.

Sloane, P. D., Zimmerman, S., and Walsh, J. F. (2001). The physical environment. In Zimmerman, S., Sloane, P. D. and Eckert, J. K. (Eds.), *Assisted Living: Needs, Practices, and Policies in Residential Care for the Elderly*. Baltimore, MD: Johns Hopkins University, pp. 173–197.

Smith, E. (2003). *Visitability Defined 2003*. Disability Rights Action Coalition for Housing document. Retrieved August 20, 2006, from http://www.concretechange.org/Definition_of_Visitability.htm.

Starr, P. (1982). *The Social Transformation of American Medicine: The Rise of a Sovereign Profession and the Making of a Vast Industry*. New York: Basic Books.

Thomas, W. H. (1998a). Building home-ness into existing long-term care facilities. *Journal of Healthcare Design*, *X*, 57–61.

Thomas, W. H. (1998b). Cultural expectations and locale—creating the eldergarden. *Journal of Healthcare Design*, *X*, 63–66.

Thompson, J. D. and Goldin, G. (1975). *The Hospital: A Social and Architectural History*. New Haven, CT: Yale University.

Vierck, E. and Hodges, K. (2003). *Aging: Demographics, Health, and Health Services*. Westport, CT: Greenwood.

Woolf, V. (1929). *A Room of One's Own*. New York: Harcourt, Brace & Co.

ADMINISTERING CARE

Chapter 13

Long-Term Care Governance and Administration: A Historical Perspective

---

Stephen E. Proctor

Contents

Introduction

This chapter is intended to acquaint the reader with the development of effective governance and administration in long-term care organizations. Its historical perspective takes the reader through the changes in board functioning as long-term care organizations moved from a charity focus to more of a business orientation. It also includes recent trends that are likely to shape long-term care board and staff roles in the future. Presbyterian Homes Inc. (PHI), with its 80-year history, is a leading provider of long-term healthcare and housing. In this chapter, PHI serves as an example of the dynamic environment in which changes in the governance of long-term care organizations are taking place. This example demonstrates the need for creative and energetic leadership to meet the challenges ahead.

The development of governance models in the for-profit long-term care sector has, for the most part, paralleled that of publicly traded companies and other private business ventures. These for-profit models, from large publicly traded companies to small family businesses, are well documented in business literature, and are beyond the scope of this chapter. Rather, our discussion of governance and administration focuses on the unique blend of public expectations and relationships in the not-for-profit sector.

The Development of Governance

The development of boards in the not-for-profit long-term care sector is rooted in the charitable intentions of community, fraternal, and religious groups. Not-for-profit healthcare providers have a long and distinguished history. Emerging from the almshouses of the past, these entities housed people thought to be "undesirables," including those needing long-term care. Facility names such as The Home for Incurables, The Home for the Friendless, and sponsoring groups such as the Humane Impartial Society and Women's Aid and Relief Society clearly communicated that long-term care was something other than a business venture (United States Bureau of Labor Statistics, 1941).

A few of these organizations date back to the early 1800s, with a larger group established before the Depression of the 1930s. By 1939, the Bureau of Labor Statistics identified 1,543 not-for-profit facilities with a capacity of 92,592 people (United States Bureau of Labor Statistics, 1941). Nearly all these institutions were founded before the advent of Social Security and the subsequent additions to the publicly funded safety net for seniors. These not-for-profit organizations were relatively small and unsophisticated, averaging approximately 60 residents per location. They reflected the personality of the sponsoring group. The concept of governing an organization was understood in traditional terms: "to exercise continuous sovereign authority over the organization" (Merriam-Webster's Dictionary).

Boards were focused on the essential aspects of doing good and were particularly concerned with the organization's operating details. Many times the founders of the organization established defined areas of responsibility. Women, who were often the driving force behind the charitable intentions of the organization, were given certain responsibilities. They provided oversight of facilities and staff, and even interviewed prospective residents. They often divided the responsibilities of oversight and service delivery among board members. Specific assignments included visiting residents and maintaining the gardens. In this division of labor, the male counterparts were usually charged with financial responsibilities such as those related to the investment portfolio and major capital expenditures (Swaim, 1961).

The minutes of the meetings of these boards were rich in detail due to the nature of their work. These included reports on the health status of individual residents, the hiring and firing of staff, and the establishment of salary levels, as well as other day-to-day business decisions. Being a board member of a not-for-profit long-term care facility could be an intensely personal experience, consuming a tremendous amount of time and attention. It was a calling that could last for a lifetime.

With the advent of Medicare and Medicaid in the 1960s, the nature of not-for-profit organizations, even those with a long history of providing charitable care, began to change rapidly. The opportunity to serve a larger, publicly funded population of older persons required staff and board members to adapt to the regulations and accountability that accompanies governmental support. The nature of these organizations was also in transition in other ways, with a significant number of them being formed to serve an older population not in need of charitable assistance. In these situations, a more corporate model of governance was adopted as the most appropriate fit for the changing organization. In some respects, many of these not-for-profit entities were hard to distinguish from proprietary organizations, creating confusion in terms of tax exemption, and public perception of the nature of not-for-profit organizations and their role in the community.

As the services offered by not-for-profit long-term care providers expanded from "homes for the aging" to an array of services, including postacute healthcare and rehabilitation as well as a variety of housing options and community services, each additional type of service brought added regulation and consumer expectations that changed the role of board and staff. Regulations were developed that codified public expectations for board oversight of quality and effective management of the facility. The legal liability for failing to measure up to these standards became clear. In addition, the consumer movement, which emerged in the 1960s and 1970s, embraced long-term care; family groups and independent living residents became more vocal. Some of them began demanding a seat on the governing board as a way for their voice to be heard in the delivery of care and services.

As not-for-profit organizations became more complex, their governance began to evolve into a more business-focused model. Still, they retained many of the underlying principles of public accountability that were historically a part of the not-for-profit environment. Primary influences in this transition included a wider range of health services, staff with greater professional and technical expertise, increased government regulation, larger capital expenditures that required increases in debt financing, and a more adversarial legal environment. The necessity for a different relationship between board and paid staff emerged, as well as the need for board members with a different skill set. As the business side of the enterprise grew, in addition to religious personnel and persons from the community who were focused almost solely on the charitable mission of the organization, there were now a growing number of laypersons with financial acumen. Correspondingly, the expectations of staff in not-for-profit organizations changed, and the relationship between boards and staff assumed a more corporate flavor.

Even in this newly evolved state, many of the traditional responsibilities of boards remained intact. Delegating day-to-day operations to paid staff, boards retained many oversight functions. In a significant number of organizations, board members continued to be called trustees, highlighting the board's fiduciary role of holding the institution in trust for the public interest. In recent years, the Enron scandal and the aftermath have highlighted the fiduciary responsibility of board oversight in protecting the public interest (Ivanovich, 2006). Interestingly enough, the concept of stewardship, which has historically been at the center of not-for-profit governance, is now being embraced by the for-profit sector in the post-Enron environment.

These traditional oversight responsibilities continue to be carried out with a renewed enthusiasm.

- Maintaining the ethical standards of the organization
- Assuring that the organization meets all legal requirements and is operating in accordance with its mission and purpose, including adherence to the organization's bylaws and articles of incorporation
- Assessing the effectiveness of staff in carrying out the mission of the organization on a daily basis
- Protecting the organization's assets and managing the resources of the organization effectively
- Representing the organization to the public and constituent groups, and playing a central role in fund-raising.

The influx of more business-focused board members added a number of performance expectations.

- A more deliberate organizational planning process
- A more proactive role and strategic outlook in assessing alternatives facing the organization
- A more financially oriented decision-making process, weighing risk and reward while maintaining consistency with the organization's mission and purpose
- Accountability for financial performance that is measured against financial forecasts and the comparative results of other, similar organizations
- A less insular view of the organization and the way it functions, including how it competes for human resources in the marketplace.

These new types of board members also brought with them the perspective of a wider world in terms of changes in technology, expectations of growth, and needs of the community.

These adaptations have created a challenging situation for individuals who have chosen to work in the not-for-profit sector. High ethical standards and a tradition of care and compassion have been combined with an expectation of measurable results that is more characteristic of the business sector. This evolution has created a confusing and contradictory set of expectations that is more sharply defined than is normally experienced in the for-profit world. The terms "mission" and "margin" are often used in the same sentence, as are the terms "marketing" and "ministry." This intermingling of language, used in board discussions, has been a source of individual and organizational stress. Those members who are focused on ministry may question what marketing has to do with the mission of the organization.

The need to maintain close and supportive relationships with sponsoring organizations, such as churches and other sources of public support, continues to be required, although now with an increased expectation of professional business management. Not-for-profit boards and staff who were once focused almost solely on raising funds for the support of charity are now expected to be business strategists and decision makers. Changes in board composition that spring from this development have created profound alterations in the governance of long-term care organizations.

Development of Professional Leadership in Long-Term Care

With its beginnings as a charitable enterprise, long-term care organizations attracted staff that felt a calling to ministry and were focused on serving the underserved in society. It is not surprising that the long-term care field tended to attract clergy, often people who were in second careers.

As the for-profit sector emerged, it was essentially a family-driven business model, usually sole proprietors or partnerships with strong connections with the local community. The environment changed, however, with the flood of federal and state funds that accompanied the Medicare and Medicaid programs. The number of nursing home beds doubled between 1963 and 1973 (Johnson and Grant, 1985). The development of investor-owned regional corporations and publicly traded corporations grew. By 1972, it was estimated that there were at least 70 nursing home chains, and by 1974, 106 publicly held corporations controlled 18 percent of nursing home beds and one-third of the industry revenue (Butler, 1975).

The demand increased in the mid- to late 1950s and early 1960s for more professional leadership for long-term care. Organizations such as PHI were pioneers in the effort to provide educational opportunities; its initial programs attracted people from 30 states and a number of foreign countries. Offered as "short courses," they were among the first halting steps toward creating a more professional administration in long-term care. Later in the 1960s, university-based programs were established (Friedsam, 2006). People from social services, business administration, nursing, and a host of other backgrounds began to migrate to long-term care as a profession.

The advent of Medicare also brought long-term care closer to the mainstream of medical care offered in hospitals and other community settings. Although Medicare did not develop into the predominant payer source for long-term care services, it changed admission patterns, with transfers from hospitals assuming a more important role as an entry point for older persons receiving long-term care services. A posthospital focus for long-term care inspired the need to plan for ongoing rehabilitative programs to assure continuity of care.

Public payment for long-term care services through Medicare and Medicaid brought a heightened level of public scrutiny. A number of authors, such as Mendelson (1975), in her book *Tender Loving Greed*, exposed poor care and called for more regulations and stronger enforcement. Another author, Vladeck (1980), later assumed a role as enforcer of national nursing home regulations.

In the early 1970s, the licensure of long-term care administrators became a requirement in every state. The then current nursing home administrators were "grandfathered" in, waiving the new eligibility rules as a prerequisite for taking standardized tests. Future generations of administrators, however, faced educational and relevant experience requirements, including a certain period of time to be served as an administrator-in-training. Only on completion of these conditions could an individual sit for the licensure exam. This situation resulted in an interesting anomaly when persons with responsible positions in acute care chose to work in long-term care. In spite of their education and healthcare experience, they were required to serve as an administrator-in-training under a licensed administrator for approximately six months before they could occupy a comparable position in a nursing home (The Pennsylvania Code, Chapter 39, amended 2006).

Boards of Directors

Looking at the expanded expectations of board members, one might ask, "What attracts people to serve on governing boards in this environment?" Many people historically volunteered to serve primarily because being a board member of the governing board of a not-for-profit organization was easy. It also enhanced their social status in the community. These individuals opted out when faced with heavier workloads and additional risks. Those who remained began to ask themselves a different question, "If I am going to have to work harder, give more time, and place myself at greater personal and professional risk, does the good I can achieve outweigh the difficulties?" Understanding this question is critical for long-term care organizations. It has shaped the role of boards, including their relationship with the organization's paid staff.

The Work of Boards

The governing board has the ultimate power and responsibility to direct the organization in the achievement of its mission. However, the power of board members is collective, not individual. Individual board members are not given the authority to act independently of the rest of the board in governance or in day-to-day operations. When board members gather in a meeting, however, they have the authority to make decisions that shape the organization in numerous ways. They establish policies and guidelines that limit or empower paid staff in the performance of their duties, write bylaws that may permit committees of the board to make decisions or perform functions on their behalf between board meetings, and form *ad hoc* committees to carry out specified duties and present recommendations for action. An understanding of the principle of collective action is at the heart of every effective board. It gives staff the confidence that, to the maximum extent possible, the board speaks with one voice in providing direction to them, and that all board members are included in the discussions surrounding important policy questions.

The board primarily relates to the staff through the chief executive officer (CEO), with other staff relationships of secondary importance. In some organizations, a strict line of communication causes information to be funneled solely through the CEO. This approach can result in clear communication to the board from the staff. In organizations where various staff members communicate directly with the board, lobbying of board members to favor one department over others can result. In these cases, control of communication between board and staff may be necessary. However, in a complex environment where the organization is committed to transparency in the way it deals with board members, such constraint may not be the best approach. It may create other problems in the relationship between board and staff members as they pursue the mission of the organization. If the senior staff of an organization is secure and committed to fostering a collegial environment, directing communication through various points of the organization has many advantages. It avoids the problem of the board receiving a steady diet of carefully filtered information, and may expose the board to important issues in their decision-making process.

Before it begins to recruit members, the board leadership must reflect on its priorities and expectations of them. For example, does the board exist primarily for interpreting the mission of the organization to the wider community and raising financial support for the organization and its charitable mission? This purpose is expressed in the oft-repeated axiom to "give, get, or get off," when the subject of fund-raising is addressed. From this point of view, the reputation of board members is a critical asset when it is used to promote the organization's mission, gain access to foundations and other funding sources, and inspire the confidence of existing and potential donors.

Conversely, the board may focus its attention primarily on the effective operation of the organization and the way in which it strategically fulfills its mission in a highly competitive and regulated environment. In this case, the level of expertise that a board member brings to the table is of paramount consideration, not necessarily his or her capacity to provide financial support. In most organizations, both tasks are essential and require attention from the governing board. The range of expertise and financial resources needed will influence the size and structure of the board.

A large board of more socially prominent community members is very important if the goal is to increase public awareness of the organization and raise financial support. Having more people involved in the organization's decision-making processes can foster a feeling of community ownership and affinity that will enhance fund-raising efforts. However, a board that is too big and cumbersome may be unable to make decisions on a timely basis, an essential ingredient in the modern long-term care organization. A smaller board may be more conducive to efficient decision making, but may lack the cross section of community members needed to understand and support decisions when they are implemented.

One solution to meeting these varying needs is to form a charitable foundation that assumes the first set of responsibilities, with oversight provided by the governing board. Another may be for the parent corporation to focus on charitable support, with a subgroup of the board or a separate corporate entity offering strategic direction and oversight of the activities of the organization. Combinations of these approaches can provide additional options.

Another structural issue involves the extent to which the whole board delegates its work to committees or functions as a board of the whole. The days of board committees providing reports that are automatically approved by governing boards has ended. Their members correctly understand that approval of a committee recommendation when there is incomplete understanding of the relevant issues can result in substantial risk to the organization, and potentially to them personally. Given these dangers, there is a trend toward smaller boards with fewer committees to preprocess their work. Moreover, committees now have more sharply defined roles and, in many cases, meet more often. A recent example is the more intensive work of audit committees that do more than just play a part in selecting the auditor and receiving the results. They are now charged with assuring the integrity of the financial systems of the organization by meeting throughout the year to oversee its internal audit functions.

Governance Activities

The responsibility to maintain the ethical standards of the organization is greatest at the highest level of governance. Much of this leadership is carried out by example, by keeping the conduct of the board above reproach, and communicating to staff that anything less than the highest ethical standards will not be tolerated at any level of the organization. This process often begins with lofty pronouncements in the mission, vision, and values statements. It continues in the way conflicts of interest are handled at the board level and the behavior of paid staff is monitored.

Certain aspects of establishing the tone or culture of the organization are distinctive for not-for-profit organizations. The expectations of boards in a for-profit long-term care organization are relatively straightforward, with a primary focus on maximizing profitability and shareholder value. Measurements of profitability and growth are well-established and targets are relatively easy to define. Other variables enter into the picture, but often to a lesser degree.

As in for-profit organizations, expectations of financial performance of not-for-profit long-term care organizations can be strongly influenced by lending institutions or outside rating agencies (such as Moody's or Standard & Poor's) if they have outstanding debt which requires it. Other important expectations that come into play in the not-for-profit environment are based on the ethical standards of the organization, as expressed by the board. Community values and other less quantifiable aspects of performance, often focused on process, can be equal to or greater than measurable financial outcomes. The importance of identifying and monitoring key quality indicators has become a critical board activity focused on protecting the public interest.

Meeting Legal Requirements

Assuring that the organization meets all legal requirements and is operating in accordance with its mission and purpose, including adherence to its bylaws and articles of incorporation, is a relatively straightforward function of the board of trustees. These endeavors involve monitoring compliance with the various state and federal inspection agencies as well as with accreditation processes of outside organizations. They also entail establishing effective compliance programs and monitoring compliance efforts in ongoing operations, billing, and financial practices. The potential for compliance problems with the development of new ventures and business relationships has added a new dimension in board legal oversight in the current business and healthcare environment.

Protecting Organizational Assets

Both the board and staff are responsible for protecting organizational assets. This is not simply directed at making a maximum profit and saving large sums of money for some future catastrophic event. Boards are often engaged in a debate over applying balance among providing charity care, improving quality, investing in physical plant and new programs, and assuring the future financial security of the organization. The expectation of long-term care residents and their families is that the organization will be there for as long as they need care. When people enter a long-term care continuum as independent living residents, this expectation may have a 20-year horizon.

Developing a Strategic Plan

From rather simple beginnings, strategic plans for long-term care organizations grew into lengthy, formal documents, which attempted to forecast five years into the future, melding environmental conditions with program development, growth, operating budgets, and capital needs. In the past, strategic plans were reviewed and updated by the board on an annual basis, and were often left on the shelf for the remainder of the year. Given the constraints of time and the limited attention span of board and staff, it is not surprising that they did not occupy a central role in the organizations' daily functioning. These plans also outlined the tactical steps that would be required to execute them and contained a significant amount of sensitive, proprietary information. Their distribution was on a "need-to-know basis," which tended to obscure the focus of the organization from the very people who were charged with implementing the plan. It was not surprising that the subsequent lack of clarity regarding the direction of the organization made the board slow to react to the surrounding environment (Mintzberg, 1994; Kim and Mauborgne, 2005, pp. 81–82).

The increasing rate of change in the healthcare and housing components of long-term care and the desire for an increasing number of people to understand the strategic direction of the organization have caused the planning approach to evolve into a more focused and concise format. At PHI, the strategic plan has been reduced to seven pages, from the 200-page document of 20 years ago. This change has made it easier for the board to be engaged in the most critical issues facing the organization, and to have a greater influence on the direction of the organization. Staff members are also forced to simplify their approach to planning by stripping away the reams of supporting information that tended to be more tactical than strategic. A shorter, more focused scheme invites a different strategy for its utilization by staff and board members. At PHI, distribution of strategic plans is relatively wide. They are used as communication tools with the board, staff, and the wider community, and as a basic building block in creating a transparent environment.

Although most organizations have retained a formal strategic planning process, some have moved even further, abandoning it in favor of "strategic thinking" that places a higher value on flexibility and speed than on predicting the future. The thought behind this approach is that the surrounding environment is so unpredictable and fluid that formal strategic plans quickly become obsolete and tend to make the organization less adaptable to the environment. Regardless of the specific approach to formulating the strategy of the organization, it is an essential element in effective governance.

In either case, once consensus is reached on the strategic plan, effective boards constantly measure the performance of the staff against it. At PHI, the board affirms the strategic plan for the organization, which is followed by six- and twelve-month updates during the year. The performance of staff is measured by how effectively their activities result in achieving the mission of the organization, as defined in the strategic plan. Other organizations use differing approaches, but the result is always the creation of a feedback loop by which the board is able to hold the staff accountable for connecting their day-to-day activities with the board's expectations.

Assessing Risk and Reward

One of the key fiduciary and strategic roles of boards is the assessment of risk and reward. This extends beyond the financial calculations that are commonly understood in a business context. As with the case of many not-for-profit providers of housing and healthcare, PHI has a healthy tension between providing for a short- and long-term social return of accomplishing its mission, and short- and long-term financial gains. Risk and return for PHI has been as much about serving others and, in effect, achieving a greater social return, as it has been about economic matters. That being said, every board grapples with mission, financial constraints, and the need to secure the future of the institution in the face of external threats to the organization. Boards must assure that the level of risk of every new undertaking (or the risk of doing nothing) is commensurate with the rewards to be achieved—strategic advantage, financial payback, and/or social good. These are essential mission questions that the board cannot delegate to any other group.

Creating Strong Voluntary Board Leadership

Given the challenges facing not-for-profit organizations today, it is more important than ever to secure talented individuals to serve on the governing board and to mold them into a cohesive, high performing team. Because these individuals are not compensated for the hours they spend on the organization's behalf, creating strong voluntary board leadership can be a challenge. Attracting intelligent and creative individuals to serve is often a function of their perception of the organization and their ability to make a difference in the way the organization's mission is implemented. A set of formal selection criteria, designed to facilitate identification of and outreach to a diverse group of individuals, is a solid starting point. Diversity within a board can and should take many forms—racial, ethnic, age, gender, and other commonly understood definitions of diversity are a beginning. Differences in life experience and expertise are equally important. Not-for-profit organizations must reach out to embrace people with know-how and skills demonstrated in other areas and educate them on the particular issues of long-term care. It is also important to create a climate in which the experience the board members bring to the table benefits the organization, especially in areas where there are common issues and solutions that are transferable to the long-term care environment. Expertise in areas such as human resources, financial measurement and benchmarking, investment performance, forging relationships with rating agencies, application of technology, and staff education are just a few of the most obvious areas where staff of long-term care organizations can benefit from the knowledge and wisdom of board members.

The orientation and ongoing education of board members is critical to an effective board. At PHI, a parent corporation with a series of affiliate and subsidiary boards exists to cover the range of activities of the organization. A standard orientation process for all new board members and trustees that serves a number of purposes has been developed.

- It provides an understanding of the mission and culture of the organization.
- It acquaints board members with the various components of the organization that are connected by a common mission.
- It outlines the expectations of board members—specific tasks and duties, ethical standards, and the relationship between board and staff.
- It fosters the development of relationships among board members so they gain a better appreciation of their collective wisdom.
- It provides a safe environment to ask questions so new board members spend less time as observers in their first board meetings, and become active participants in organizational affairs more quickly.

This orientation, taught by current and former board leadership and staff, is seen as the first investment in the education of board members. Ongoing education is undertaken using a variety of approaches, including selected readings, e-mails, formal sessions as a part of retreats and regular meetings, and encouragement and reimbursement to attend outside educational programs related to long-term care. Ongoing staff support is provided to individual board members in areas where they may find the terrain unfamiliar. This effort ranges from providing them with a glossary of terms that is used in the field to presenting more detailed explanations of specific financial issues. In the final analysis, investing in the intellectual capital and wisdom of board members may provide the highest return a not-for-profit long-term care provider can make.

Current Expectations and Trends

The public expectation for oversight of the mission and financial affairs rests heavily on the minds of governing boards. They have the primary responsibility for shaping the ethical climate of the organization and assuring that the financial condition of the organization is disclosed to all interested parties. In the not-for-profit long-term care organization, there are several other factors that enter into the equation to heighten sensitivity to the governing board's fiduciary role.

- The volume of government dollars in the form of Medicare, Medicaid, state and federal rent subsidies, and other types of public sector reimbursement programs requires the highest level of accountability. Strict adherence to the spirit and the letter of the laws and regulations that govern these programs is essential.
- Organizations with a significant charitable mission that depend on the generosity of donors and constituent groups (religious, fraternal, and community sources) require a public perception of trustworthiness as the foundation of this support.
- There is no tolerance for the well intentioned but inept not-for-profit organization. The board must ensure that the organization has sound business practices, including a compliance program that is able to identify and prevent potential problems in a systematic way.
- Not-for-profit staff compensation is under close scrutiny, and boards are being held responsible for documenting wage levels that are considered reasonable in the marketplace.
- Sarbanes-Oxley, although initially focused on abuses in the for-profit sector, has become the measuring stick in the not-for-profit sector as well. Many organizations such as PHI that have been following aspects of Sarbanes-Oxley for many years are now tightening these efforts to mirror public corporation's expectations.

In recent years, the trend in the fiduciary work of boards and staff has been moving toward a stewardship model. This concept is based on an idea, with ancient roots, clearly understood in the Judeo-Christian tradition. Some of the recent works on the subject of stewardship (Block, 1993) are quite provocative and challenging to the *status quo*. In the wider business environment, shareholders, employees, and the general public have begun to embrace the concept of stewardship as a way to look beyond the present to achieve the best long-term results for the organization and contribute to the greater good of society. This emerging view is that each of us holds the resources of the world (and of the individual organizations to which we relate) in trust for future generations. At the core, there is the recognition that as human beings, we have relatively short personal and professional lives, and that we have a responsibility to leave something of value behind—a legacy that will enable future generations to have a better life. This elevates and ennobles the concept of board governance, and bodes well for the future of not-for-profit long-term care organizations.

In my view, the most exciting development in terms of board governance is the trend toward engaging boards in a pre-strategic discussion of what is important to the organization (Chait et al., 2005). In addition to discussing the fiduciary and strategic roles of boards, Chait et al. outline what they call the "generative process," where boards are involved in a process that precedes strategy—a place normally occupied by the senior staff of the organization. They use terms such as "deciding what to decide, problem framing, engaging in sense making, discovering emergent strategies, and promoting robust discourse" as they explain how boards get involved in thinking that "makes sense out of circumstances." This may be the new frontier of governance that will inspire and engage the best and the brightest of society to volunteer to serve on boards where they know they can make a difference. Long-term care organizations that embrace this approach will discover an important advantage over their counterparts in an increasingly competitive environment.

Consumer Activism on Governance of Long-Term Care Facilities

With the advent of the consumer movement throughout society, there have been increased expectations that the governance process will reach out to engage residents and family members in a meaningful way. Greater involvement of the consumer in care planning and other similar activities is common to other components of the healthcare environment.

The emergence of consumer activism in continuing care retirement communities (CCRCs) has been a growing phenomenon for the past 20 years. A 2002 survey conducted by the American Association of Homes and Services for the Aging illustrates its current status, with more than 35 percent of responding organizations indicating that they had resident board members (AAHSA Leadership Development Survey, 2002). In many parts of the country, CCRC residents have banded together to lobby for laws requiring such membership on the CCRC board of directors, and have formed statewide groups to exchange information and pursue their common interests. Groups associated with nursing homes, such as the National Citizens' Coalition for Nursing Home Reform, are primarily driven by family members due to the high prevalence of physical and cognitive impairments among patients.

Some of the expectations placed on long-term care providers have created a number of tension points that impact current and future organizational operations. Because long-term care involves a range of services, engaging residents, family members, and other interested parties is a multidimensional effort that takes into account the following:

- Nature of the relationship between provider and consumer, including the financial relationship with consumer—entry fee models, co-op models, third-party payers—and anticipated length of relationship
- Physical or cognitive limitations of residents
- Family role as direct or indirect consumers

Each type of service provided within the long-term care spectrum must respond to these factors in a different way, utilizing a variety of approaches that can range from formal or informal advisory groups of residents and family members to full board participation. In general, the increased frailty of assisted living or skilled nursing residents will result in a higher likelihood that formal governance structures will involve family members. Also, the shorter the anticipated relationship with residents, the more likely that engagement of these residents will be of a more informal nature and less likely to be invested in governance structures.

Skilled Nursing: Assisted Living

All long-term care facilities are required to have a mechanism for residents to gather, expressing their needs and desires collectively. Typically these are called "residents councils" or "associations." They were originally formed at a time when lengths of stay in long-term care facilities were much longer, and residents generally possessed better physical health and cognitive abilities. As long-term care residents have become frailer, increased attention has been given to family and friends' councils to elicit the consumer point of view and provide an outlet for the needs and concerns of families who take an active part in the care of their elders. In recent years, as the lines between skilled nursing and assisted living residents have become more blurred, resident involvement has become more limited. Despite these difficulties, there should be strong efforts to engage residents and their families. Regular meeting times, bylaws, and election of officers may vary significantly and must be tailored to the persons being served.

Independent Living

With independent living residents, whether in a purely housing environment or on a multilevel campus of care, consumer involvement can assume an entirely different dimension. Typically, these residents are younger, and more physically and cognitively able to express themselves. They expect to be treated as customers. They may also look askance at a family member who presumes to speak on their behalf. Structures to engage independent living residents tend to be much more formal and self-sustaining. On state and federal levels, regulations often require the governing body to have a mechanism for residents to express their needs, independent of the facility management. In most independent living environments, it is customary to have a resident representative on the board of the facility, at least in an advisory capacity.

The most complicated of these relationships is found in the CCRC. In addition to being younger and healthier, such residents have typically had higher incomes and are more likely to have occupied decision-making positions throughout their work life. If they paid an entry fee, they may regard themselves as owners or investors rather than as customers, and expect to have a formal position on the governing board.

There are a variety of potential problems associated with having residents on the governing board. The two most frequently cited concerns are the ability to set rates and advocate spending policies focused on the long-term good of the organization rather than the short-term advantage of current residents. However, it is PHI's experience that, when handled properly, these generally do not turn out to be major problems. This conclusion has been confirmed by other continuing care providers (Van Ryzin, 2004).

From PHI's perspective, the key to successful relationships with CCRC residents is the latter's trust that the governance structure permits them to communicate their needs and desires effectively, and that the organization will respond promptly to their concerns. The presence of a resident or two on the governing board will not be a substitute for establishing this level of responsiveness between residents and the governing board.

Residents as Board Members

With a parent corporation and several operating subsidiaries, PHI has ample opportunity for resident involvement in decision making. Elected resident association officers may serve as advisors or as voting members of a governing board. There are no automatic positions reserved for residents by virtue of election or holding an office in the resident association. Rather, PHI has established guiding principles for the selection of board members who have worked well in engaging residents in governance.

- A focus on temperament, experience, and a forward-looking approach is important in all board positions.
- Family members of residents (past or present) have represented a strong pool of board talent.
- The nominating process for residents is the same as for all other potential board members; residents are never tokens, but are regarded as equal to every other board member.
- Resident board members are expected to meet the same expectations as other individuals on the board. In PHI's case, this may include travel to other PHI facilities for meetings.
- As a not-for-profit organization, PHI has no owners. All board members are stewards of the public trust. Residents may have made a financial investment in their living accommodations, but that is not the equivalent of ownership.
- As with all members, the power of the board occurs when it is in session. Board members will not attempt to exercise power as individuals.

There are a few practical considerations that enter into a resident's decision to serve on the governing board. Besides devoting the needed time and attention to board responsibilities, the resident may be lobbied by other residents to bring a special issue before the board, or to vote a certain way on a matter under board consideration. If residents are able to maintain a normal lifestyle between board meetings, they are usually willing and able to serve with distinction.

Occasionally, due to illness of a spouse or other relative, a board member may also serve as an advocate for a family member. Staff may respond to the board member in a different way than they do to other family members. On these rare occasions, staff education is critical to ensure that the board member is free to take on this role without having his or her suggestions or concerns being treated as new policy positions.

Effective Administration

Establishing a Climate of Transparency

In the wake of WorldCom and Enron, transparency has become a popular topic, belying the reality that many effective leaders have successfully practiced it for decades (Baum, 2004). The benefits of transparency in long-term care administration are significant. The creation of such an environment demands integrity from everyone in the organization. It inspires confidence and invites the commitment of stakeholders and, when combined with effective measurement tools, can focus the attention of employees more successfully.

At its very core, transparency involves establishing a climate that is open and honest in all of its internal and external relationships. A consistent matching of the behavior of the organization's leadership with the values espoused in the mission statement and other corporate publications is essential. Transparency plays out in many ways in the work of a not-for-profit long-term care organization. At the most basic level, transparency creates the trust that is at the heart of every important internal and external organizational relationship. Some key applications of transparency are outlined in the following sections.

Staff and Governing Board Roles

The ethical tone of the organization is established by the governing board's standards related to conflict of interest. Such disclosure assures the public that no individuals associated with the organization will place their personal needs ahead of the interests of the organization. One might call this paving the ethical high road on which everyone must travel. Staff and board relationships are based on the confidence that both give first priority to organizational requirements in every deliberation. A lack of hidden motives does not preclude honest disagreement, which is, of course, desirable for organizational growth.

It is the duty of staff to ensure that board members are given all the information they need to make informed decisions, without swamping them with data that can lead to confusion. Staff must distill the material in such a way as to make it understandable and clear. They should take great care not to slant reports or board discussion toward a predetermined outcome. Board members must be certain that they are receiving the whole story. This confidence will enable board members to take the kind of calculated risks that are required in the fast-moving long-term care environment. In addition to having the facts associated with a particular issue, the board must be privy to the debate, and even be informed of any staff conflict regarding the subject. A high degree of trust among staff and willingness of the governing board to value dissent are essential. Moreover, it must be understood that when a decision is reached, the period of dissent is over; at that point, the organization should be single-minded in the pursuit of the agreed upon action.

There are many methods for giving the board needed information. Once a solid background has been established regarding the underlying issues facing the board, a primary responsibility of the paid leadership is to provide ongoing data about the state of the organization and its environment. A popular tool used at PHI is a periodic narrative update that calls attention to the various organizational activities. Typically less than six pages, it also includes regulatory and legislative changes that will have an impact on the field of long-term care. A constant stream of such essentials serves as education for the board, and provides a context for current and future issues.

At PHI, a "dashboard" has been created to provide board members with details related to the organization's health. This approach facilitates identification of the most critical elements in the organization's success and of the best ways to measure performance in those areas. Debate over critical indicators or predictors of future success is in itself an illuminating experience.

Although the dashboard contains a number of key financial ratios, there are many other measures of the organization's health—human resources, quality of care, fund-raising, etc. The most critical part of this process is the periodic review of what should be measured, to make sure the board not only understands the information, but can also add or delete items as needed.

Once the elements of the dashboard have been identified, the method and frequency of distribution are established. With the advent of technology, the possibilities are almost endless. At PHI, in addition to providing this information at every board meeting, the data is also put on the board's Web site for easy and timely access by board members. By the 15th of the month, they can check all of the predetermined key performance metrics of the earlier month, and if they notice anything that requires further study, they can contact the administration for referral to the appropriate department.

This kind of transparency is also helpful in terms of outlining board expectations of staff performance. The primary means of clarifying these performance objectives is a well-written strategic plan and the tactical steps that spring from it. Setting goals for achieving the organization's mission and targets for growth in volume, program variety, and financial performance are all key to giving the staff direction and freedom to apply their collective energy toward a common purpose. Whereas the strategic plan is the starting point for establishing expectations, the dashboard provides clear measurements and targets for improvement.

Staff

Transparency also means that leaders continually reinforce the value of employees' contributions to achieving the mission of the organization. Moreover, employees should be given information needed for their work, praised for outstanding effort, and informed when they fall short of expectations so they have an opportunity for improvement. Finally, employees must be able to count on openness and even-handedness in the application of policies related to employment, compensation, and discipline.

Unity of purpose is the hallmark of a successful staff. A first step is to convey the larger picture of the organization's mission and how staff efforts in various parts of the enterprise contribute to its success. As a result, each employee knows performance measures and why they are important. Annual performance reviews provide a minimal type of feedback, which must be supported by open and frequent, informal, and sincere communication that constantly reinforces what is most important.

Those We Serve

The people we have been called to serve need to be aware of their financial obligations and to have access to financial information both before and after the decision is made to become a resident. Such access can assure clients that the organization is fiscally secure and will be there for them in the future. In addition, residents are engaged in the annual budget process and the regular disclosure of financial information. In this way, they can evaluate the effectiveness of leadership in fulfilling its stewardship responsibility. Although there are always consumers who focus on providing services for the lowest possible cost, on balance they are also concerned about the larger picture—the ability to attract and retain qualified staff by providing a fair wage and an advantageous benefit package, and assuring the financial strength of the organization well into the future.

Transparency also means that residents and their family members will be given all the information they need to make informed decisions about their medical care and end-of-life decisions. Engaging consumers and family members early and often is not an option but an essential method of operation for every long-term care provider.

Constituent Groups

The way leadership articulates the organization's values and holds itself accountable assures constituent groups that leadership will remain faithful to the mission. Regular reporting of the extent of the organization's charitable care to those who cannot pay for services and the ongoing need for financial support is essential. If the organization's sponsor is a community or religious group, the integrity and openness of the long-term care organization have a direct impact on the reputation of the sponsoring group. This holds even if there are no legal ties to convey legal responsibility or liability. A scandal (real or perceived) at PHI would have a negative effect on the reputation of the Presbyterian Church as a whole, as well as of nearby Presbyterian congregations. This would severely impair the ability to recruit volunteers, raise charitable support, and attract board leadership from constituent groups.

Donors are particularly significant. From their perspective, transparency involves honesty in interpreting the organization's needs and open accounting of the sources and uses of donations. Stated needs for financial support must address a number of questions: Why is the contribution needed to further the mission of the organization? Are there other sources of support that the organization is seeking to accomplish the same objectives? How will these funding sources work together to avoid overlap?

Assurance that contributions are applied for the donor's intended purpose is the second area where transparency is essential. A clear trail from the contribution to the expenditure must be maintained and be open for examination by the donor.

Finally, donors must be aware of the organization's fund-raising expenses. This is a basic stewardship question. A historical record of the ratio between fund-raising expenses and dollars raised is vital to assure donors that their contributions actually accomplish the organization's goals.

Business Partners

Relationships with business partners are critical to consistently providing superior service. Suppliers of goods and services are selected based on articulated criteria that represent the best value for money. The quality of products, services, and prices takes precedence over personal relationships. Whether or not the business partner is from the local community or a part of your constituent base is at best a secondary concern. At PHI, the consistency of long-term relationships is valued, but it is clear that the presence of these ties raises, not lowers, expectations of performance. Transparency here means that the organization's decision-making process is known by every potential supplier, and that the information they provide will not be shared with competing organizations. In addition, vendors know that they are held to the same high ethical business standards that PHI follows.

Regulatory Agencies

Full disclosure to governmental and accrediting organizations is part of fulfilling the organization's legal, moral, and ethical responsibilities. The spirit and the letter of the law must be observed in this process as it is, in all aspects, of the organization's operation. State and federal regulations are clear about the need to reveal any problems related to compliance, resident injury, and a host of other issues. Although such information may create short-term difficulties for the organization by triggering a more invasive review, a culture of transparency requires that even the appearance of impropriety be avoided. Many regulators develop a sense about whether or not an organization is open and willing to share information needed to protect the public interest. A transparent environment is the only way to overcome any suspicion that the organization has something to hide.

The Financial Community

There is probably no more important area where transparency is appreciated and rewarded than in accurate reporting to the financial community. Financial integrity is the foundation of the relationships with lending institutions, rating agencies, bondholders, and other interested parties. In earlier years, PHI provided a stream of written reports and briefings to these groups, but the information was often sporadic or sorely inadequate. It seemed that everyone wanted additional insight into PHI's financial condition. In response to the need for more timely and accurate data, PHI developed a system of financial disclosure. In consultation with our lenders, bondholders, and Standard & Poor's, a package of information was developed and made consistently available on PHI's Web site. It is updated as the financial statements are closed every month. Now everyone has access to the most recent information, and can inquire about what we are doing to remedy any areas of weakness.

As a result, the confidence level of the financial community has been enhanced to such a degree that the cost of capital for PHI is consistently lower than for many peer organizations with approximately the same financial performance.

Limitations on Transparency

Even when an organization is committed to transparent leadership, honesty does not require that societal restrictions on disclosure of information, legal imperatives, or concern for the well-being of others be ignored. Much information handled by the organization has legal and ethical restrictions on its use. However, these limitations must never be used as an excuse to withhold information that allows for an open climate.

Understanding the Essentials

Long-Term Care Is a Human Resource Business

From an operational standpoint, effective administration requires that the essentials of the organization are clearly understood, and that everyone is focused on them. In long-term care, it means that the management of human resource inputs is the single most important indicator of success. In recent years, many long-term care facilities have closed. The inability to recruit and retain the kind of staff needed to deliver quality care is often cited as the main reason.

The critical nature of effective use of human resources is supported by data. In a typical skilled nursing environment, approximately 65 percent of all costs are related to human resources, including salaries and wages, benefits, and government-mandated employment costs. Of the remaining 35 percent, there are fixed depreciation and interest expenditures that offer a limited opportunity for savings. From a purely mathematical standpoint, the key to success lies in the effective deployment of human resources. Too few dollars remain in other areas to make up for ineffective performance on the human side of the enterprise. Independent living and assisted living facilities have a less labor-intensive profile, although home- and community-based services are even more so.

If workforce management is the primary key to success, understanding the complexities of the long-term care workforce is essential. The group employed by long-term care organizations is predominantly female, representing a variety of disciplines, almost all of which are infused with a strong caring ethic, and in many cases, with a loyalty to a professional discipline that exceeds allegiance to the organization. Many of these professionals are in very high demand. Nurses and therapists are among the employees who do not fear changing jobs to find an employer whose mission is more closely aligned with their personal goals and values. A large percentage of these individuals must be willing to work weekends and holidays, and spend many hours away from their families. It is no wonder that in many long-term care organizations employee turnover is high.

People who gravitate to the caring professions must be engaged intellectually and emotionally with the mission of the organization and the people they serve. The stability of work relationships is extremely important, as is the consistency of leadership. Studies conducted by the Institute for the Future of Aging Services (IFAS) have demonstrated the interplay between supervision and frontline employees and the effects on quality of care, job satisfaction, and retention (Stone et al., 2002; Institute for the Future of Aging Services, Kansas Association of Homes and Services for the Aging, 2003).

Combining Technology and Human Resources

Developments in technology have permitted long-term care providers to access critical information on a real-time basis. This trend is expected to accelerate in the foreseeable future. However, the benefit of new technology is only realized when underlying systems are overhauled correspondingly. In the past five years, PHI has significantly improved its accounting department's performance as measured in accuracy and speed of providing data to employees throughout the organization. In addition, the accounting department staff has been reduced by 25 percent through attrition in the same period. Increased productivity was the result of changing systems, applying new technology, and completely engaging the accounting workforce in the larger aims of the organization.

Sharing of information and an open decision-making process are among the first steps in establishing an intellectual and emotional bond as well as a team identity or culture. As mentioned earlier, PHI has developed a dashboard approach to information sharing at the governance level, and has expanded this approach to the operational level to ensure that the workforce is well informed on the key metrics of PHI's performance. Each area of the organization is analyzed and a limited number of metrics highlighted for use by the entire team. Employees are able to connect their personal and departmental efforts with the achievement of the identified targets. The timing of information is critical in assisting managers in making operational decisions; any significant delay can lead to inertia or decisions based on inaccurate assumptions or imperfect information.

Information related to essential PHI issues is placed on the dashboard. Periodic discussions are held to decide the measures that should be added or dropped. However, some areas are likely to continue receiving very close attention. In addition to the periodic dashboard reports, variables critical to the organization's mission are monitored daily. For example, at PHI, human resource information is considered so vital that systems are in place to provide reports on the previous day's staffing. A graphic display for the entire month is included to provide immediate feedback on how well the staffing plan is being executed daily in each one of the 19 locations in a three-state area.

Fear of technology is common among healthcare professionals, and is a major obstacle to change. People in the caregiving professions frequently complain about the burden of paperwork and other tasks that keep them from the resident and family contact that inspired them to become caregivers in the first place. Therefore, the primary goal of introducing technology into a long-term care environment should be measured by the answer to the following two questions:

- How will the change improve the quality of care from the consumer's point of view?
- How will use of this technology allow more time to maximize human contact between staff and residents?

Creating a Culture of Leadership

Recently, a great deal of emphasis has been placed on group culture as a critical element in achieving objectives. The concept of organizational change is not new, but some of the current language is more engaging. Whether the approach is called a culture of discipline, as suggested by Collins (2001), or the "software" of organizational beliefs and behaviors, as proposed by Bossidy and Charan (2002), the focus is on the role of culture in getting things done. Although culture is important in every organization, one could argue that it is even more important in the long-term care environment.

Many years ago, PHI acquired a skilled nursing facility from a for-profit agency that was a subsidiary of an insurance company. During a meeting at the time of the sale, the facility's director indicated that his experience as a steel company executive served as excellent training for his role as a long-term care administrator. He explained, "Long-term care is not unlike the steel business. There are inputs and outputs in every business. One simply has to manage the inputs in a way to create the desired outputs." It proved otherwise. The facility was losing money and had high employee turnover, low occupancy, poor survey results, and unhappy customers; ultimately it had to be sold. The industrial culture, as practiced by this executive, did not transfer successfully into the long-term care environment.

Mark Thomas, CEO of the Ebenezer Society in Minneapolis, observed that "Culture eats strategy for lunch." This is not to say that an impressive culture will necessarily turn a flawed strategy into a winning situation. However, it does imply that a solid strategy may put an organization in a position to become successful, but even the best one cannot be properly executed within a poor culture. One of the most vivid examples of the power of culture is Southwest Airlines, a company that has always had a clear and effective strategy as a low-cost regional airline. However, many other airlines have failed to replicate Southwest's success because they just could not replicate its culture (Gittell, 2002).

Why is culture even more important in long-term care? First, the number of persons who have direct contact with the customer (resident or family) represents a very high percentage of the total workforce. Second, the length of stay means that staff, residents, and family members have frequent contact over a long period of time, and get to know each other well. Expectations can be raised because, for most people, relationships are a reason to expect more, not less. In this environment, values such as a strong work ethic, compassion, kindness, and attention to detail in providing care must permeate the entire organization.

In long-term care, culture cannot be a veneer but must be solid throughout the organization. Moreover, in long-term care, leadership is the soil in which a culture of care can grow. The most dedicated adherents to a grassroots cultural change initiative will be overpowered by lack of support by management. An unhealthy leadership culture will ultimately result in a weak and impoverished culture of care. Conversely, successful change has roots in healthy leadership. Organizational values such as integrity, humility, transparency, stewardship, and continual striving for excellence must be articulated and modeled daily by those in charge of the organization.

References

American Association of Homes and Services for the Aging (2004). *AAHSA Leadership Development Survey*. Washington, D.C.

Baum, H. (2004). *The Transparent Leader*. New York: HarperCollins.

Block, P. (1993). *Stewardship: Choosing Service Over Self-Interest*. San Francisco, CA: Berrett-Koehler Publishers, Inc.

Bossidy, L. and Charan, R. (2002). *Execution*. New York: Crown Business.

Butler, R. N. (1975). *Why Survive Being Old in America*. New York: Harper & Row.

Chait, R. P., Holland, T. P., and Taylor, B. E. (1996). *The Effective Board of Trustees*. Phoenix, AZ: American Council on Education and the Onyx Press.

Chait, R. P., Ryan, W. P., and Taylor, B. E. (2005). *Governance as Leadership: Reframing the Work of Nonprofit Boards*. Hoboken, NJ: Wiley.

Collins, J. C. (2001). *Good to Great*. New York: HarperCollins.

Friedsam, H. J. (2006). *A Memoir*. Department of Applied Gerontology, University of North Texas. Denton, TX.

Gittell, J. H. (2002). *The Southwest Airlines Way*. New York: McGraw-Hill.

Institute for the Future of Aging Services, Kansas Association of Homes and Services for the Aging. (2003). *Keeping Frontline Workers in Long Term Care: Research Results of an Intervention*. Topeka, KS.

Ivanovich, D. (2006). Everybody knows Enron's name, for better or worse. *Houston Chronicle*. March p. 1.

Johnson, C. L. and Grant, L. (1985). *The Nursing Home in American Society*. Baltimore, MD: Johns Hopkins University Press.

Kim, W. C. and Mauborgne, R. (2005). *Ocean Blue Strategy: How to Create Uncontested Market Space and Make the Competition Irrelevant*. Boston, MA: Harvard Business School Press.

Mendelson, M. A. (1975). *Tender Loving Greed*. New York: Alfred A. Knopf.

Mintzberg, H. (1994). *The Rise and Fall of Strategic Planning: Reconceiving Roles for Planning, Plans, Planers*. New York: Free Press.

Stone, R., Reinhard, S., Bowers, B., Zimmerman, D., Phillips, C. P., and Hawes, C. (2002). *Evaluation of the Wellspring Model for Improving Nursing Home Quality*. New York: Commonwealth Fund.

Swaim, W. T. (1961). *Short Course on the Organization and Administration of a Home for the Aging, Topic Number 20*. Pillsburg, PA: Pennsylvania.

The Pennsylvania Code, Chapter 39, State Board of Examiners of Nursing Home Administration, adopted 1972, amended June 2006. Harrisburg, PA.

United States Bureau of Labor Statistics. (1941). *Bulletin Number 677*. Washington: U.S. Government Printing Office, pp. 5, 50–52, 100–108.

Van Ryzin, J. (2004). Resident leaders take a seat at the table. *Best Practices* (May/June), no volume 28–29.

Vladeck, B. (1980). *Unloving Care: The Nursing Home Tragedy*. New York: Basic Books.

Chapter 14

Improving the Quality of Long-Term Care with Better Information*

Vincent Mor

Contents

* *Milbank Quarterly*, 83(3), 333–364, 2005, © 2005 Milbank Memorial Fund, Blackwell Publishing. Reproduced with permission.

Improving the quality of health care using clinical information is achieved either by identifying targets for quality improvement (QI) efforts or by reporting intra- or interprovider performance differences to consumers, regulators, or purchasers using accepted indicators of quality of care. QI is a means of improving clinical care in specific areas, with comparative reporting, particularly public reporting, acting as a stimulant for improvement. The rationale is that providers will be stimulated to invest in internal quality improvement efforts *if* they believe that consumers will choose providers based on public reports of provider quality or if they will be otherwise rewarded or penalized because of these comparisons. These two strategies can operate synergistically or be implemented independently. QI uses clinical information to gauge changes in a provider's own performance after changing some existing practices or procedures. Reports comparing providers' performance are predicated on the assumption that the underlying comparisons are valid. Both approaches have advocates, and numerous companies, ranging from software vendors to specialized consulting groups, have emerged to support providers' QI efforts.

The long-term care service sector is a diverse group of institutional and community-based providers but only Medicare- or Medicaid-certified nursing homes (NH) and home health agencies (HHA) are subject to uniform data-reporting requirements. In some states, however, assisted living facilities and state and privately funded home care agencies serve many frail elderly individuals. Among nursing home and home health agency providers, both the QI and the comparative performance reporting traditions have strong advocates and are being supported both intellectually and financially by federal and state quality initiatives. Indeed, the existence of universal, mandated clinical data sets has facilitated the implementation of both internally motivated QI efforts and public reporting. In the case of home health agencies, the uniform clinical assessment tool mandated by the government grew out of an impetus to create case-specific internal and external performance measures to facilitate this integrated application of quality measures. In contrast, the uniform assessment mandated for nursing homes in 1991 was designed primarily to plan care (Morris et al. 1990; Shaughnessy et al. 2002).

In 1998 the Institute of Medicine (IOM) began a follow-up study of the progress, or lack thereof, in improving the quality of care in nursing homes (IOM 2001). A central issue in that report dealt with the adequacy of data regarding long-term care quality on which to make policy, specifically how to evaluate the relative merits of a regulatory approach to quality assurance versus an information-based approach designed to stimulate quality improvement. The IOM report recommended promoting the public reporting of information about the quality of long-term care providers but cautioned that there still were many unanswered questions about the adequacy of the data on which to base such comparisons.

This article examines the conceptual and empirical validity of the data underlying the quality measures now in use in long-term care and highlights the principal assumptions underlying the current and proposed uses. Then the article looks at the impact of quality information on the introduction of CQI efforts, including how the information is presented and used. This is followed by a review of how the public reporting of quality information has influenced long-term care consumers, their advocates, and long-term care provider organizations. Finally, the article recommends further methodological and applied research in this area.

The questions relevant to long-term care providers and policymakers that this article addresses are

- How reliable and valid are the data used to construct quality measures on which public reporting is based? Do the current measures reflect the quality of the provider or the impact of case-mix differences?
- If providers improve their care, will the outcomes actually improve?
- Are the current measures of quality consistent with consumers' interests?
- How can we determine the "overall" best providers, and how should we establish benchmarks of quality?

Background

Assessing Nursing Home Residents

In 1984, a committee of the Institute of Medicine (IOM) began studying the quality of care in nursing homes. Led by Sidney Katz, the committee's recommendations (IOM 1986) led to the 1987 Nursing Home Reform Act (OBRA). One of these recommendations was mandating a comprehensive assessment that would provide a uniform basis for establishing a nursing home resident's care plan, or minimum data set (MDS). The rationale was the perceived inability of staff to identify patients' needs because of inadequate training and education. The MDS was a product of the recommendations of hundreds of experts representing the academic disciplines and the professional organizations serving geriatrics, psychiatry, nursing, physical and occupational therapies, nutrition, social work, and resident rights advocates (Morris et al. 1990). The goal was an instrument to capture the basic information needed to develop a care plan that considered individuals' comorbidities, strengths, and residual capacities. An initial version was nationally implemented in 1991, followed by a revised and larger version introduced in 1996 (Morris et al. 1997).

After universally available patient information was assembled in computerized form in 1998, it was used for policy applications and not just to drive clinical care planning (Mor 2004). Nursing home case-mix reimbursement systems, initially developed for certain states' Medicaid programs, were refined using the more detailed data in the MDS. The resulting resource utilization groups (RUGs-III) system became the basis for Medicare's prospective payment system for skilled nursing facilities (Fries et al. 1994). The availability of clinically relevant, universal, uniform, and computerized information about all nursing home residents raised the possibility of using this information to improve the quality of the nursing homes' care. The Centers for Medicare and Medicaid Services' (CMS) Nursing Home Case-Mix and Quality Demonstration, which had refined the RUGs case-mix classification system, thereupon created readily usable quality indicators based on computerized data from the resident assessment instrument (Zimmerman et al. 1995). These indicators were refined, and MDS-based quality measures accounting for shortstay, postacute patients as well as the long-stay residents were created. In November 2002, the CMS mandated and began publicly reporting them, first in a six-state pilot and then nationally (Harris and Clauser 2002). The revamped quality improvement organizations (QIOs) funded by the Centers for Medicare and Medicaid Services then were assigned to work with nursing home providers to improve their quality of care (Baier et al. 2003, 2004).

Home Health Agency Outcomes

Throughout the 1990s, researchers at the University of Colorado worked with home health agencies to establish a system to monitor the quality of care for HHA patients (Shaughnessy et al. 1994). Based on the Outcome and Assessment Information Set (OASIS), both the state of New York and the Robert Wood Johnson Foundation supported a pilot test of a quality assurance system: Outcome-Based Quality Improvement (OBQI). The OASIS data describe patients' diagnoses, medical condition, treatments, and functional and cognitive status. The participating home health agencies reviewed reports of the proportion of patients who improved or deteriorated in selected domains between their admission to the service and subsequent discharge. Data on the change in patients' status were constructed by comparing their condition at the two points in time. In 1999, the Centers for Medicare and Medicaid Services required the OASIS as a means of uniformly recording information about all

Medicare beneficiaries using a home health service. With the adoption of OASIS, the entire Medicare-certified home health care industry began to submit the required data to the CMS for the new Prospective Payment System (PPS) implemented in October 2000, as well as data for monitoring quality and improvement (Sangl et al. 2005; Stoker 1998). In 2004 this system was extended to the entire nation, and now consumers can compare agencies' QIs in local newspapers, at the CMS website (http://www.cms.hhs.gov/quality/hhqi/), or by telephone.

Conceptual Issues in Quality Measurement

Quality is measured using information about individual patients' experience (e.g., pressure ulcers) and aggregating it to determine the "rate" among all patients of a given type served by the provider. The individual data come from clinical assessments of patients that are recorded and then computerized. Measures designed to reflect the "quality" of the provider are constructed after considering a number of technical, sampling, and statistical stability and adjustment issues, as well as the conceptual issues inherent in measuring quality in nursing homes and home health agencies. Next we address several of these issues, using examples from both types of long-term care providers.

Which Aspects of Quality Are Important?

Publicly reported measures of provider quality should reflect the value that society in general, and consumers (and their advocates) in particular, attribute to various aspects of quality. When we could report only hospitals' mortality rates or countries' number of live births, clinicians and policymakers were disappointed that the more refined and desirable aspects of health care were ignored. Although Mukamel (1997) suggested criteria for selecting quality measures according to their utility and meaningfulness to designated audiences, the existing data tend to emphasize clinical rather than psychosocial issues. But the quality of long-term care is fundamentally multidimensional and encompasses clinical care issues, functional independence, quality of life, and patients' and families' satisfaction with care (Mor et al. 2003c). In the case of NHs and HHAs, despite the availability of much information about patients, consumer advocates and many clinicians do not feel that the data on the Nursing Home Compare website, which is maintained by the CMS, capture important aspects of quality. For example, it does not mention quality of life (Kane et al. 2003). In addition, although patients' and families' satisfaction is widely used, particularly in the nursing home industry, it has not been incorporated into a national reporting system (Castle 2004; Kane et al. 2003; Simmons et al. 1997). Finally, some critics of the OASIS data for home health do not believe that the outcome data reported capture the content of nurses' education of families (Fortinsky et al. 2003).

Aggregated Quality Measures

Standardized, mandatory, patient assessment systems are computerized in all U.S. nursing homes (NH) and in all home health agencies (HHA) serving Medicare beneficiaries. These assessments are made by the nursing staff when the patient is admitted into the service and periodically thereafter (for HHAs, upon discharge). Only those patients cared for long enough to have two assessments are included in the calculation of an aggregated measure of provider quality. Patients who cannot change (i.e., who already have a pressure ulcer or whose functioning will not improve) are excluded (Sangl et al. 2005). Furthermore, because these aggregate measures of provider quality are based on clinical assessments made by different kinds of nurses in different facilities and agencies, the resulting quality measures may reflect differences in clinical assessment practices, such as directly asking patients about their pain (Wu et al. 2003).

Comparing Quality

Consumers using publicly reported data to compare providers are essentially asking whether their experience will be better with one versus another. As noted, basing aggregated quality measures on clinical assessments means that patients and their advocates who are comparing the performance of providers may not be able to differentiate between "real" differences between two providers and those that merely reflect differences in how the nurses in the two agencies conducted their assessments. Thus, differences in how the data are collected may undermine the validity of interfacility comparisons, which is at the heart of efforts to report providers' performance publicly (Sangl et al. 2005).

Care versus Outcomes

Quality measures reflect providers' performance in their administration of treatments as well as the outcomes of those treatments (Mor et al. 2003c; Sangl et al. 2005). The proportion of restrained NH residents indicates the kind of care given in the home, whereas the proportion of HHA beneficiaries who become better able to move by themselves from bed to chair is also an outcome, presumably of the patients' natural recovery rate and the HHAs' treatment, support, and family education. Establishing benchmarks to compare providers assumes agreement on appropriate and inappropriate care and could reveal poor quality of care. Conversely, the quality of the outcome is a measure of the clinically desirable result of the nursing home or home health care.

The kinds of treatments that may be provided vary substantially. For example, treatments of postsurgical patients pertain to wound care and recovery and differ from those for patients admitted with terminal prognoses. In any case, the universal applicability of indicators of care may be limited to evidence of effectiveness (e.g., flu shots) or consensus about inappropriateness (e.g., physical restraints).

Currently, the CMS's publicly reported NH quality measures are a mixture of process and outcomes, whereas the HHA data are almost exclusively based on outcomes. Some critics have argued that both the NH's and the HHAs' approaches overemphasize outcomes, since they fail to address important processes of care (Fahey et al. 2003; Fortinsky et al. 2003; Sangl et al. 2005). A comparison of providers according to the rate at which their patients' function changes is intended to show the impact of rehabilitative, nursing, and medical treatments, whereas the rates of pressure ulcer incidence are presumed to reflect inadequate skin care. Whether in nursing homes or HHAs, nurses are particularly interested in indicators of performance that can be specifically associated with the interventions they provide (Rantz et al. 1996).

Validity of Quality Measures

Establishing measures of performance and interpreting their meaning to various constituencies require a shared understanding of quality. This is why so many quality standard–setting organizations have broadly representative groups reviewing performance measures of quality and why the CMS asked the National Quality Forum to recommend the final indicators of quality that would be posted on the CMS's websites for both nursing homes and home health agencies (Kizer 2001; Kurtzman and Kizer 2005; Sangl et al. 2005). Assessing provider performance, particularly that based on patients' outcomes, implies that providers are accountable for the observed score and that the quality measure resonates with our understanding of what true quality is. The Donabedian model of good structure facilitating excellent care processes, which, in turn, produce the desired outcomes, explicitly or implicitly, informs much of the literature on quality measurement (Donabedian 1980). Many studies have examined the relationship between staffing levels (structure) and various indicators of quality (process and outcome). Harrington and colleagues reported that the performance of nursing homes with more staff is superior, but others have not found such consistent results (Harrington et al. 2000; Rantz et al. 2004a; Schnelle et al. 2004c). Most recently, Rantz and her colleagues identified those nursing homes that performed best on the CMS's publicly reported quality measures, but the medical records reviewed by her researcher were found to be unrelated (Rantz et al. 2004b). However, detailed care processes are difficult to document based only on records. Just as important, Schnelle and his colleagues repeatedly found in the facilities they studied that information in the records did not necessarily match the actual care observed by the research staff (Schnelle et al. 2004a; Simmons et al. 2002).

It is important to differentiate the validity of the aggregated providers' measures from that of the patients' data in the MDS or OASIS assessments. Much research points to the construct and predictive validity of the MDS data, ranging from cognition, diagnoses, ADLs, and the like (Mor 2004; Sangl et al. 2005). Similarly, several studies of the OASIS refer to the validity of the data, both in the correlation of pertinent items and the prediction of events such as hospitalization (Fortinsky et al. 2003;

Fortinsky and Madigan 2004). There is far less information about the validity of the provider measures now being used, both in their relationship to other structural, process, and regulatory indicators of quality (e.g., deficiency citations from inspectors) and whether they capture the impact of real changes in patient care thought to be associated with good quality (Bates-Jensen et al. 2003; Madigan 2002; Mor et al. 2003a; Zimmerman 2003). Research on the CMS's nursing home quality measures now being publicly reported found that they were not significantly correlated and were poorly correlated to the number, or severity, of regulatory deficiencies, even when controlling for the interstate variation in regulatory "severity" (Mor et al. 2003c; Sangl et al. 2005). Furthermore, Schnelle and his colleagues observed little relationship between the indicator of MDS-based restraint quality and care processes in nursing homes, even though the high-restraint facilities revealed other kinds of poor care (Schnelle et al. 2004b).

Establishing Benchmarks or Comparison Groups

Almost all providers are compared as a group or, in some cases, against a specific standard of care. Among the issues in establishing benchmarks are whether to use different benchmarks for different types of providers (peer based), whether benchmarks should be "targets" for improvement that may change as providers improve, or whether benchmarks should be based on the observed quality distribution across providers. There is not necessarily a "right" answer to these questions. For example, establishing minimums as measured by particular quality measures may not be appropriate in all cases, since many areas of performance have no evidence-based standards that could determine a minimum (Mor et al. 2003a; Shaughnessy and Richard 2002). Conversely, relying on only empirically based benchmarks (e.g., below the median) may "institutionalize" the poor performance of providers operating at the median.

Furthermore, while national benchmarks might make sense in the long run, large geographic differences in medical practice may mean that patients entering long-term care from acute care may have had different treatments in different regions of the country. For example, the large interstate variation in the use of feeding tubes among cognitively impaired residents of nursing homes is likely to affect the homes' performance on quality indicators, ranging from weight loss to drug use (Mitchell et al. 2005).

A related issue is whether to consider regional variations in care patterns at all. For example, in markets offering alternative long-term care options, such as home health, inpatient rehabilitation, and even assisted living, a different mix of patients are admitted to and reside in nursing homes. Recent research on the prevalence of long-stay nursing home residents assessed as requiring little functional or medical support services, as well as the mix of cases, revealed substantial interstate variation between 1999 and 2002 (Grabowski and Angelelli 2004; Grabowski et al. 2004). This research confirms that observed differences in hospitalization rates are strongly related to Medicaid payment rates (Intrator et al. 2005; Intrator and Mor 2004).

Thus, states and facilities with higher hospitalization rates of long-stay residents may, paradoxically, appear to be better because their patients are discharged when they become sick, whereas in other states they may remain in the nursing home (Grabowski and Angelelli 2004).

Technical Issues in Quality Measurement

Just because it is possible to construct aggregated measures that reflect providers' performance does not mean the measures are technically sound or valid. Constructing valid measures of provider quality requires addressing issues such as small sample sizes, low prevalence, and therefore instability, as well as knowing how much difference between providers is reflected in differences in the actual care provided.

Variation in Reliability of Measurement

The reliability of the MDS and the OASIS was extensively tested in their development and implementation in the 1990s and more recently (Hittle et al. 2003; Mor 2004; Mor et al. 2003b; Morris et al. 1997). The two instruments' items achieve reasonable to excellent levels of interrater reliability as measured by the Kappa statistic (Sangl et al. 2005).* However, most interrater reliability tests are made under optimal conditions and may not reflect "real-world" conditions, since providers participating in such intrusive field studies tend to differ from the average provider (Mor et al. 2003b). The largest multifacility reliability study undertaken to date asked research nurses with established high levels of interrater reliability to independently assess more than 5,000 nursing home residents in 209 facilities (approximately 28 per facility). Despite the high average rates of interrater reliability recorded, substantial interfacility variation in observed reliability levels was found (Mor et al. 2003b).

Just as important, the direction of disagreement was examined and found to vary both between and among the facilities in the six states that the study examined. Thus, the facilities' Kappas were systematically lower in some states; disagreements between the raters were nonrandom; and in some facilities the raters were less likely to detect a problem like pressure ulcers or pain, whereas in others they were more likely than the research nurses to rate residents as having the clinical problem. Recent statistical analyses of these data reveal that directional bias in the data can result in significant differences in the relative quality ranking of facilities (Roy and Mor 2005).

---

* Volume 3 of the University of Colorado report summarizing the history of the development and testing of OASIS and the OBQI process summarizes the results of several reliability studies. The investigators chose not to present the Kappa statistics for low variance OASIS items or dichotomous items with few discrepancies. Since these invariably result in lower Kappa levels, slightly lower average Kappas would have resulted.

This literature suggests that in both NHs and HHAs, more attention must be directed to training the staff in making the MDS and OASIS assessments, since the interfacility variation in reliability can undermine the validity of the aggregated quality measures. Similarly, the variation among the staff of a HHA or NH can undermine efforts to measure the results of quality improvement initiatives. Consequently, some in the home health and nursing home industry have called for more consistent training practices and commitment to high-quality data (Fortinsky and Madigan 2004; Pentz and Wilson 2001).

Risk Adjustment

Comparing providers on the basis of quality measures assumes comparable patients and similarly reliable data. Risk adjustment seeks to equilibrate the patients that the providers are serving. In addition to specifying which types of patients are included in a given quality measure, statistical regression–based approaches, or stratification, can be used to adjust risk. Stratification promotes transparency, since providers can readily identify which patients are in which stratum (Arling et al. 1997; Berg et al. 2002; Zimmerman 2003). The regression-based approach, used in all OBQI measures for HHAs, essentially compares the observed and the expected rate of the clinical event (e.g., an incident pressure ulcer), where the expected rate is predicated on what would occur were the mix of patients served by one provider like that served by the average provider (Hittle et al. 2003; Mukamel and Spector 2000). Both approaches have advocates and detractors. Stratification may result in small numbers of patients per stratum, making the resulting estimate unstable. But regression-based approaches can be very sensitive to the statistical model used and its stability (Mukamel et al. 2003).

Even when using regression-based risk adjustment techniques, the CMS's publicly reported nursing home quality measures include fewer adjusters than do home health agencies' regression-adjusted models (Sangl et al. 2005). HHA quality measures tend to examine change from the start of service to discharge, whereas many NH measures are based on prevalence, because their residents are served for extended periods. Therefore, it is hard to identify a "baseline" status for nursing home patients, which has not already been influenced by the quality of the nursing home. For example, being bedridden is predictive of acquiring a pressure ulcer (Berlowitz et al. 2001; Mukamel and Spector 2000). However, patients may have become bedridden because of inadequate mobility care earlier. Statistically controlling for this "effect" could adjust away earlier poor care (Zimmerman 2003).

Home health agencies face a different type of risk adjustment issue, since it is well known that social support and family members' help influence patients' outcome or improvement. However, although current HHA outcome measures include many adjusters, they do not adjust for the adequacy of patients' informal support. This could be relevant, as it is reasonable to assume that not all HHA patients have similar family and social support.

The inadequacy of current risk adjustment models is exemplified in research examining correlates of the CMS's NH quality measures. Using annual survey data and the quarterly quality measures, Baier and colleagues found that aggregated measures of case mix (e.g., ADL, high acuity levels) were *lower* among the facilities with high quality measures (Baier, Gifford, and Mor 2005). Furthermore, the study found that facilities serving predominantly Medicaid patients also were ranked high, even though numerous studies found that poor quality, lower staffing levels, more regulatory deficiencies, and a greater risk of termination from the Medicare/Medicaid programs were associated with high concentrations of Medicaid patients (Castle 2002; Grabowski and Castle 2004; Mor 2004).

Composite Quality Measures

Consumers, regulators and even payers would prefer having a single metric to measure the quality of providers (Fortinsky et al. 2000; Mukamel and Spector 2003). Nonetheless, several studies have found very little correlation among the various provider quality measures used in nursing homes (Baier, Gifford, and Mor 2005; Mor et al. 2003c; Sangl et al. 2005; Stevenson and Studdert 2005). A recent report commissioned by the Medicare Payment Commission to study the consequences of offering prospective payments for HHAs acknowledged similarly low correlations among HHA measures but nonetheless created a single quality summary score for the existing HHA measures (Outcome Concepts Systems 2004). When analyzing the data, the authors observed offsetting effects on the composite measure; that is, providers performed very well on one measure but poorly on another, resulting in a finding of no effect, which is one of the dangers of combining uncorrelated measures.

Selection and Provider Specialization

One difficulty of comparing providers is that some types of providers offer a different mix of specialty services and therefore attract different patients. Much of the literature documents how hospital-based HHA or NH providers differ from those without a hospital affiliation (Fortinsky et al. 2003; Mor 2004; Zinn, Aaronson, and Rosko 1994), and the influence of specialty care units in nursing homes also has been well documented (Banaszak-Holl et al. 1997; Zinn and Mor 1994). Analyses of the characteristics of nursing home patients at the time of their admission reveal substantial interfacility variation in the proportion of patients with a preexisting pressure ulcer, lending credence to the notion that facilities may have a reputation for special competence in this area (Mor et al. 2003a). Obviously, geographic proximity has an enormous influence on the facility chosen, but the provider's specialization is important as well.

Experience with Long-Term Care Quality
Improvement Efforts

Almost from the beginning of the design and testing of the OASIS and the MDS, investigators and providers tried to use the information to influence practice for both individual patients and organizations. The MDS was designed to facilitate care planning with "resident assessment protocols" (RAPs) to identify clinical areas of care possibly requiring extra attention (Hawes et al. 1997; Morris et al. 1990). The aggregation of some RAPs to the level of the NH could be used to identify the most common clinical problems. In the case of home health agencies, the outcome-based quality improvement approach was built into the patient documentation process (Kramer et al. 1990; Shaughnessy et al. 1994; Shaughnessy, Crisler, and Bennett 2000). Nurses record patients' functioning and clinical condition at their admission and then again at their discharge. Any changes in condition could be attributed to the care provided, up to and above the natural rate of improvement expected for HHA patients.

Since OASIS was designed explicitly with outcome measurement and agency feedback in mind, early evaluations of the introduction of OASIS focused on responses to the reports summarizing each agency's outcome performance relative to the group averages. Shaughnessy and colleagues undertook a series of interrelated demonstration and evaluation projects as they continued to refine the conceptualization and measurement of home health care outcome–based quality (Shaughnessy et al. 1995, 2002). Their evaluation revealed a significant reduction in the rate of hospitalization and in the risk-adjusted rates of improvement in the OBQI target outcome measures of health status in both demonstration trials ($p < 0.05$) when compared with similar HHAs (Shaughnessy et al. 2002).

Beginning in 1990, the first set of quality indicators derived from the MDS began to be developed and tested under the six-state Nursing Home Case-Mix and Quality Demonstration (Zimmerman et al. 1995). Building on the MDS's universal implementation and computerization, government regulators anticipated that creating indicators of nursing homes' performance would guide and enable more systematic regulatory oversight. The more enlightened administrators felt that such information could improve their own facility's quality, and advocates thought that making this information available would create greater "transparency" to guide consumers' choices of a long-term care facility (Mor et al. 2003c). In the late 1990s, the Center for Medicare and Medicaid Services expanded its commitment to using quality indicators to improve the quality of nursing homes. First, the CMS tried to improve and expand the existing quality indicators (Berg et al. 2002). The CMS also devised measures to respond to the quality-of-life concerns of long-term care facility residents regarding the quality of food and their preferences, autonomy, and perception of treatment with respect, but the CMS soon recognized that these measures were still in the early stages of development.

In November 2002 the CMS applied a set of indicators to the entire country. A new set of chronic, long-stay, as well as postacute, short-stay, quality measures were promulgated in January 2004. Some of the existing measures were dropped while new measures were added based on a review by the National Quality Forum (NQF) (Kizer 2001). As part of this rollout, CMS reinforced its efforts to involve the quality improvement organizations (QIOs) in stimulating providers to improve their performance. Almost all the states' QIOs have now created or adapted quality improvement training materials for the nursing home industry (Kissam et al. 2003).

Unfortunately, despite the many studies describing the scope of quality improvement activities in nursing homes, there have been few systematic evaluations of their impact (Bates-Jensen et al. 2003; Berlowitz et al. 2003; Lee and Wendling 2004). Several surveys of facilities' QI programs revealed them to be limited to nonexistent (Lee and Wendling 2004). Saliba found relatively low adherence to pressure ulcer prevention guidelines in a sample of Veterans Administration facilities (Saliba et al. 2003), and Berlowitz and his colleagues documented considerable variation in the extent of QI implementation in the prevention of pressure ulcers, with greater efforts noted in those nursing homes emphasizing innovation and teamwork (Berlowitz et al. 2003).

In a series of applied studies to train nursing homes to use quality indicators as the stimulus for improvement, Rantz and her colleagues observed similar results in facilities in Missouri (Rantz et al. 2001, 2003; Wipke-Tevis et al. 2004). Their efforts began with a randomized trial of more than 100 facilities exposed to either training or quality measure feedback and consultation. They found no significant improvement, which resulted in their efforts to strengthen the intervention and to identify predictors of successful implementation (Rantz et al. 2001). While several studies have documented improvement following the introduction of specific QI interventions, these studies have generally used highly selective facilities (Baier et al. 2003, 2004). Given the difficulty of implementing and sustaining improvement, some have concluded that the success of the quality improvement movement in nursing homes is predicated on leadership that is ill prepared to implement these innovations (Schnelle, Ouslander, and Cruise 1997). Indeed, one of the main recommendations of the Institute of Medicine's report on long-term care quality was to enhance managerial capacity in nursing homes in order to improve quality (IOM 2001).

The Impact of Public Reporting

As noted, in 2002 CMS released Nursing Home Compare as a national resource for consumers, their advocates, and providers to compare, with state and national averages, facilities' most recent survey and certification inspection reports as well as their MDS-derived quality measures.

In 2004 the CMS released a national version of Home Health Compare, which performed a similar function. Both Nursing Home and Home Health Compare report only a subset of all the measures developed and tested over the years (Berg et al. 2002; Shaughnessy et al. 2002; Zimmerman 2003). In addition, numerous states have assembled their own Web-based "report cards" summarizing the quality of nursing homes using different ways of presenting the information (Castle and Lowe 2005; Harrington et al. 2003; Mattke et al. 2004).

Although there is evidence that interest in this kind of quality information is substantial, according to the number of Internet site "hits" and the attention of several states, we do not know who uses this information and whether, or how, it informs or influences consumer decision-making. Indeed, it is not even clear who is looking at the websites. Several reports suggest that in regard to acute care, the public reporting has attracted the attention of more providers than consumers, although large employers have been somewhat more sensitive to using the health plans' reports of quality (Chernew et al. 2004; Hibbard and Pawlson 2004; Hibbard, Stockard, and Tusler 2003). In addition, there is evidence that reports of the quality of hospital and health plans have only slightly altered practice patterns, choice, and perhaps even the quality of care provided (Mukamel and Mushlin 2001; Mukamel et al. 2000; Romano and Zhou 2004).

The audiences for public reports of long-term care providers' performance include elderly consumers and their family members, but hospital discharge planners might be the most important audience (Potthoff, Kane, and Franco 1997; Sangl et al. 2005). Most patients are admitted to HHAs or NHs directly from a hospital (Intrator and Berg 2002). Hospital stays are short, focused almost exclusively on medical or surgical treatments; discharge planning is often just an afterthought. Decisions about the postacute setting or provider are characteristically made hastily with insufficient knowledge about the patients' prognosis and the anticipated duration of care needed, and virtually no knowledge about the quality of available alternative providers. Bowles and colleagues recently reported that shorter hospital stays have affected nursing activities associated with discharge planning and postacute care for older adults (Bowles, Naylor, and Foust 2002). Indeed, one review found that predischarge assessment, education, and appropriate follow-up reduced readmission by 12 to 75 percent (Benbassat and Taragin 2000). Furthermore, a systematic meta-analysis found that organized discharge planning that included specific mechanisms to effect the transfer of the treatment plan was associated with a variety of positive patient outcomes (Richards, Coast, and Peters 2003). However, a recent survey of discharge planners in California hospitals revealed that they rarely considered data on the quality of nursing homes (Collier and Harrington 2005). Since part of discharge planning is finding an appropriate postacute discharge venue, having information about the relative quality of long-term care organizations could reduce rehospitalizations.

The efforts made by QIOs around the country to direct hospital discharge planners to the Compare websites have apparently been only somewhat successful. A project in Rhode Island designed to examine hospital discharge planners' interaction with patients and families when considering postcancer surgery placement options discovered that discharge planners did not know about, and did not feel that they had time to explain, the various options to patients and their families (Bourbonniere, Mor, and Allen 2003). Furthermore, anecdotal evidence from the results of QIO efforts in various areas around the country reveals that discharge planners and their hospital employers have little incentive to make selecting the discharge setting easier, since their primary goal is to discharge patients quickly.

Although there is little information about the response to public reports of nursing home quality, there is even less information about home health care agencies' response to the public reports of their performance. Many of the same issues are pertinent to both nursing homes and home health agencies, particularly discharge planning, since most markets include multiple HHAs from which discharge planners and patients must choose.

Information about the quality of nursing homes and home health agencies has been reported publicly for only a few years. Since the public continues to trust the opinions of friends and family about the choice of their physician and hospital more than most other sources, perhaps as families begin to accumulate experience with long-term care decisionmaking, they will become increasingly aware of the availability of public reports (Kaiser Family Foundation and the Agency for Health Research and Quality 2000). This relatively inefficient approach parallels how consumers choose their health insurance plans, their hospitals, and their physicians, so why should it be different for long-term care providers? Because most Americans try not to think about requiring long-term care, it is unlikely that they would browse websites linked to the CMS Compare sites. Rather, most Americans will encounter long-term care services following a hospitalization or similar medical encounter, either for themselves or their parents. This means that consumers must rely on professionals to find out about the alternatives and to help them choose.

Even in a planned "elective" admission for a hip or knee replacement, patients and families are likely to assume that the admitting physician directs the hospital admission and the postacute recovery program. Consequently, since only a third of new admissions to NHs or HHAs are directly from home, publicly reported quality information may have only a limited impact on consumers' choice of provider unless hospitals become more proactive (Decker 2005).

Gaps in Research Knowledge

Although long-term care has, in many ways, leaped over the public reports of hospital and physician quality by having adopted uniform clinical measurements, substantial gaps remain in our knowledge about the quality of existing measures, how they are reported, how to get the designated audiences to use the information, and whether and how providers can institute quality improvement programs. Improving the quality of information about providers is one area of research with both technical and conceptual gaps. Conceptually, we need to know what consumers value and what kinds of information about providers they want.

Technically, we need workable models for systematically handling measurement errors that may be confounded with true quality differences and better ways of handling small samples, rare events, and instability. Operationally, we need to know who uses and would use quality performance data and whether the mode of presenting the information and the context in which it is placed would enhance its utility to consumers and their advocates. Finally, we need to understand better the implications of establishing clinically relevant performance benchmarks—not relative to statistical averages or rankings of providers—for consumers' and providers' understanding of the information.

Valuing Quality of Life versus Areas of Quality of Care

Monitoring the quality of long-term care using OASIS- or MDS-derived performance measures necessarily limits the areas of quality reported to the public. Information about quality of life, autonomy, and residents' satisfaction is not currently available from either universally available instrument (Mor 2004; Sangl et al. 2005). However, some argue that it is precisely these dimensions that are of greatest concern to consumers and their advocates (Kane et al. 2003; Kane et al. 2004). Measures of quality derived from a clinical tool are necessarily based on values different from those of the consumer. An updated version of the MDS is now being designed for nursing homes that is supposed to reflect recent research on residents' quality of life (Kane et al. 2003). Future testing of a revised MDS that includes the residents' "voice" should address the fundamental issue of how to obtain unbiased information about residents' views about staff, food, and autonomy, particularly if staff members are asking the questions. These issues are equally important to home care, and the complications of obtaining the information are at least as great, because home care workers cannot ask recipients of HHA services about their "satisfaction" with the care they receive or whether they have unmet needs. While much research has been on nursing home populations, almost none has focused on these issues in home health agencies. In sum, we may end up having to obtain the family members' perspective, as is done for hospice care (Teno et al. 2001a, 2001b).

Another area of quality that is often mentioned but little studied as an indicator of quality is consumers' satisfaction with their experience as a recipient of care (Kane et al. 1997, 2003). Numerous resident satisfaction instruments have been developed and are being routinely fielded by chains as well as states to assess the preferences of their "customers" (Lowe et al. 2003). The CMS has been pushing for the development of a modified consumer assessment measure that can be applied to nursing homes that is based on the one used for health plans (Carman et al. 1999). The quality-of-life research by Kane and colleagues also addressed consumer satisfaction, and other investigators have developed and tested their own consumer satisfaction surveys (Castle 2004; Kane et al. 2003). In addition to the possible mismatch between clinical performance measures and those that might interest consumers, consumers (and purchasers) would like to know which the "best" overall provider is. The recent emphasis on "pay for performance" requires that several metrics of quality be reduced to a single dimension on which to base the financial incentive (Goldfield et al. 2005). However, existing performance measures are clearly multidimensional (Mor et al. 2003c). We know that NHs performing best on one measure might be performing poorly on another and suspect that this is likely the case among HHAs (Rantz et al. 2004b). Indeed, in a recent study comparing the quality performance of Veterans Administration and community nursing homes, Berlowitz and his colleagues concluded that since nursing homes' performance was not correlated across multiple quality measures, purchasers would not be able to use the data to make decisions (Berlowitz et al. 2005). Whether consumers and their advocates are able to understand this and to identify those measures of greatest interest to them in choosing a provider is a very important research question that must be addressed. Similar problems face those people educating consumers to properly interpret information about the quality of health plans and hospitals (Shaller et al. 2003; Sofaer et al. 2000).

Coping with Measurement and Statistical Complexity

While both the MDS and the OASIS have been subjected to a great deal of reliability testing, and both instruments, under volunteer "test" conditions, perform reasonably well in the items' interrater reliability, recent research reveals that even acceptable levels of reliability still allow for systematic bias in the direction of the errors (Roy and Mor 2005).

This is consistent with evidence from analyses suggesting a consistent underassessment of pain and depression (Miller et al. 2002; Wu et al. 2003, 2005). Because this is likely a universal issue associated with clinical administrative data on which measures of provider quality are based, generalized strategies are needed to audit the reliability and directionality of "disagreements." Statistical models also are needed to use the results of these audits to adjust quality measures for biased measurement error, since it would be highly counterproductive to penalize providers who conduct more thorough assessments. Using statistical analyses of large-scale reliability data, Roy and Mor (2005) proposed a statistical model that could address this problem in conjunction with an audit, but more work is required to generalize this approach.

The Impact of the Public Reporting Format

The format in which information about provider quality is presented has become a lively area of research over the last several years (Hibbard and Peters 2003; Shaller et al. 2003). Hibbard and Peters tested formats for information about quality and found that they dramatically changed consumers' perceptions of the importance of the information (Hibbard and Peters 2003). In both Nursing Home and Home Health Compare, the CMS presents the actual rates of the performance measures. Consumers can compare the rates of a particular provider with all others in the state and with the national averages. However, there is limited guidance regarding the meaning of the differences in rates between a provider and either state or national averages. Acceptable performance measure rates are not defined, and how much departure from the average, or the top, is meaningful is not explained. Furthermore, the stability of a measure is not indicated, particularly for small facilities with relatively few patients contributing to the performance measure. Even though both NH and HHA Compare have minimal sample sizes, the stability of a measure based on only 20 observations is questionable (Mor et al. 2003a). Several states that have invested in nursing home reporting systems of their own have adopted a different perspective, which was summarized by Mattke and his colleagues (Mattke et al. 2003). They identified numerous deficits in these sites related to the ease of understanding the content and the ease of navigating the website and accordingly tried to avoid these pitfalls in designing and testing a site for the state of Maryland. Rather than using the actual rates for each quality measure, they divided facilities into the top 20th percentile, the bottom 10th percentile, and the remainder. They also chose to use more quality measures but then grouped them into clinical care domains, with a count of the number of measures in each domain that fell into each of the three classes. While giving consumers and purchasers the actual rate may be desirable, we do not know whether this approach is the best for this target audience or whether a simpler format that identifies facilities that perform better or worse than expected would be better (Marshall, Romano, and Davies 2004). But this approach would require that experts and advocates agree on the approach to determining "better" or "worse," since the Maryland model uses an empirical distribution to identify good and poor facilities, an identification that can be problematic if most providers do not do well in some areas.

Summary

The adoption of uniform, clinically relevant patient information systems for both nursing homes and home health agencies has already begun to transform these industries. Not only do they provide the basis for a common clinical language, they also form the groundwork for two interrelated initiatives designed to improve the care of long-term patients. By feeding back quality performance data to provider organizations, leaders at all levels can begin examining and changing their current practices to reduce the occurrence of undesirable clinical events and to increase the rate of functional improvement. This impetus, which may be willingly adopted by only a minority of providers in each industry, is reinforced by reporting the same information to the public and the providers' local competition (Castle 2001; Crisler and Richard 2002; Lucas et al. 2005; Zinn, Weech, and Brannon 1998). Spurred by either competition or fear of what consumers might find out about them on public websites, providers have signed up for their state's quality improvement initiatives (Lee and Wendling 2004). Nursing home chains also are using some of these quality improvement approaches internally and are using competition among their different subunits or facilities to stimulate action (Mukamel and Spector 2003). This is not to say that all this will necessarily improve the care offered by the average NH or HHA, nor will it necessarily affect the bottom tier of facilities, since they are unlikely to be able to make the needed organizational changes (Mor 2004). But the providers, though worried, appear to be more energized and are beginning to feel that they have the tools to make the changes needed to improve the quality of their care.

The research community and the government have a responsibility to make sure that the technical aspects of the quality measures being used to compare NH and HHA providers are up to the challenge of being used both to stimulate the organizational changes needed to redesign care processes and to allow for legitimate and valid comparisons across providers. The current crop of measures, albeit a great improvement over the limited validity of the admittedly idiosyncratic survey and certification process, continue to leave much to be desired (Sangl et al. 2005). While they appear to be reliably measuring quality in certain areas, the measures cannot capture a global notion of quality. Furthermore, problems with the consistency of measurement across providers may undermine the legitimacy of the comparisons for which these measures were created. There is evidence that this is the case in nursing homes, but the research on home health care has not even begun. Nonetheless, we should not stop the public reporting or other uses of these quality measures simply because they continue to have significant deficits; rather, we should treat them as merely one other product that should be continuously improved.

Acknowledgments

This article was supported in part by NIA grant AG11624, the Robert Wood Johnson Foundation Health Policy Investigator grant, and the Commonwealth Fund grant 20040412. The opinions expressed are those of the author and do not necessarily reflect those of the funding agencies.

References

Arling, G., S.L. Karon, F. Sainfort, D.R. Zimmerman, and R. Ross. 1997. Risk Adjustment of Nursing Home Quality Indicators. *The Gerontologist* 37(6):757–66.

Baier, R.R., D.R. Gifford, C.H. Lyder, M.W. Schall, D.L. Funston-Dillon, J.M. Lewis, and D.L. Ordin. 2003. Quality Improvement for Pressure Ulcer Care in the Nursing Home Setting: The Northeast Pressure Ulcer Project. *Journal of the American Medical Directors Association* 4(6):291–301.

Baier, R.R., D.R. Gifford, and V. Mor. 2005. Reporting Nursing Home Quality in Rhode Island. *Medicine and Health/Rhode Island* 88(6):186–91.

Baier, R.R., D.R. Gifford, G. Patry, S.M. Banks, T. Rochon, D. DeSilva, and J.M. Teno. 2004. Ameliorating Pain in Nursing Homes: A Collaborative Quality-Improvement Project. *Journal of the American Geriatrics Society* 52(12):1988–95.

Banaszak-Holl, J., J.S. Zinn, D. Brannon, N.G. Castle, and V. Mor. 1997. Specialization and Diversification in the Nursing Home Industry. *Health Care Management* 3(1):91–9.

Bates-Jensen, B.M., C.A. Alessi, N.R. Al-Samarrai, and J.F. Schnelle. 2003. The Effects of an Exercise and Incontinence Intervention on Skin Health Outcomes in Nursing Home Residents. *Journal of the American Geriatrics Society* 51(3):348–55.

Benbassat, J., and M. Taragin. 2000. Hospital Readmissions as a Measure of Quality of Health Care: Advantages and Limitations. *Archives of Internal Medicine* 160(8): 1074–81.

Berg, K., K.M. Murphy, V. Mor, T. Moore, J.N. Morris, and Y. Harris. 2002. Identification and Evaluation of Existing Nursing Homes Quality Indicators. *Health Care Finance Review* 23(4):19–36.

Berlowitz, D.R., G.H. Brandeis, J.J. Anderson, A.S. Ash, B. Kader, J.N. Morris, and M.A. Moskowitz. 2001. Evaluation of a Risk-Adjustment Model for Pressure Ulcer Development Using the Minimum Data Set. *Journal of the American Geriatrics Society* 49(7):872–6.

Berlowitz, D.R., A.K. Rosen, F. Wang, D. Tsilimingras, P.N. Tariot, J. Englehardt, B. Kader, and D.B. Mukamel. 2005. Purchasing or Providing Nursing Home Care: Can Quality of Care Data Provide Guidance. *Journal of the American Geriatrics Society* 53(4):603–8.

Berlowitz, D.R., G.J. Young, E.C. Hickey, D. Saliba, B.S. Mittman, E. Czarnowski, B. Simon, et al. 2003. Quality Improvement Implementation in the Nursing Home. *Health Services Research* 38(1, part 1):65–83.

Bourbonniere, M., V. Mor, and S.M. Allen. 2003. Symptom Management and Rehospitalization for Older Persons Following Surgical Treatment for Colorectal Cancer. Paper accepted for presentation at the 7th National Conference on Cancer Nursing Research, San Diego.

Bowles, K.H., M.D. Naylor, and J.B. Foust. 2002. Patient Characteristics at Hospital Discharge and a Comparison of Home Care Referral Decisions. *Journal of the American Geriatrics Society* 50(2):336–42.

Carman, K.L., P.F. Short, D.O. Farley, J.A. Schnaier, D.B. Elliott, and P.M. Gallagher. 1999. Epilogue: Early Lessons from CAHPS Demonstrations and Evaluations. Consumer Assessment of Health Plans Study. *Medical Care* 37(3, suppl.):MS97–105.

Castle, N.G. 2001. Innovation in Nursing Homes: Which Facilities Are the Early Adopters? *The Gerontologist* 41(2):161–72.

Castle, N.G. 2002. Nursing Homes with Persistent Deficiency Citations for Physical Restraint Use. *Medical Care* 40(10):868–78.

Castle, N.G. 2004. Family Satisfaction with Nursing Facility Care. *International Journal for Quality in Health Care* 16(6):483–9.

Castle, N.G., and T.J. Lowe. 2005. Report Cards and Nursing Homes. *The Gerontologist* 45(1):48–67.

Chernew, M., G. Gowrisankaran, C. McLaughlin, and T. Gibson. 2004. Quality and Employers' Choice of Health Plans. *Journal of Health Economics* 23(3):471–92.

Collier, E.J., and C. Harrington. 2005. Discharge Planning, Nursing Home Placement, and the Internet. *Nursing Outlook* 53(2):95–103.

Crisler, K.S., and A.A. Richard. 2002. A Basic and Practical Overview of the Six Steps of Outcome-Based Quality Improvement. Interpreting Outcome Reports: The Basics. *Home Healthcare Nurse* 20(8):517–22.

Decker, F.H. 2005. *Nursing Homes, 1977–99: What Has Changed, What Has Not?* Hyattsville, Md.: National Center for Health Statistics.

Donabedian, A. 1980. Methods for Deriving Criteria for Assessing the Quality of Medical Care. *Medical Care Review* 37(7):653–98.

Fahey, T., A.A. Montgomery, J. Barnes, and J. Protheroe. 2003. Quality of Care for Elderly Residents in Nursing Homes and Elderly People Living at Home: Controlled Observational Study. *British Medical Journal* 326(7389):580.

Fortinsky, R.H., R.I. Garcia, T. Joseph Sheehan, E.A. Madigan, and S. Tullai-McGuinness. 2003. Measuring Disability in Medicare HomeCare Patients: Application of Rasch Modeling to the Outcome and Assessment Information Set. *Medical Care* 41(5):601–15.

Fortinsky, R.H., and E.A. Madigan. 2004. Data, Information, and Quality Indicators for Home Healthcare: Rapid Implementation, What's Next? *Journal for Healthcare Quality* 26(3):44–51.

Fortinsky, R.H., E.A. Madigan, and S. Tullai-McGuinness. 2000. Resource Use & Patient Outcomes in Medicare Home Care. *Caring* 19(11):20–22.

Fries, B.E., D.P. Schneider, W.J. Foley, M. Gavazzi, R. Burke, and E. Cornelius. 1994. Refining a Case-Mix Measure for Nursing Homes: Resource Utilization Groups (RUG-III). *Medical Care* 32(7):668–85.

Goldfield, N., R. Burford, R. Averill, B. Boissonnault, W. Kelly, T. Kravis, and N. Smithline. 2005. Pay for Performance: An Excellent Idea That Simply Needs Implementation. *Quality Management in Health Care* 14(1):31–44.

Grabowski, D.C., and J.J. Angelelli. 2004. The Relationship of Medicaid Payment Rates, Bed Constraint Policies, and Risk-Adjusted Pressure Ulcers. *Health Services Research* 39(4, part 1):793–812.

Grabowski, D.C., and N.G. Castle. 2004. Nursing Homes with Persistent High and Low Quality. *Medical Care Research & Review* 61(1):89–115.

Grabowski, D.C., Z. Feng, O. Intrator, and V. Mor. 2004. Recent Trends in State Nursing Home Payment Policies. *Health Affairs* Supplement Web Exclusives: W4-363–73.

Harrington, C., J. O'Meara, M. Kitchener, L.P. Simon, and J.F. Schnelle. 2003. Designing a Report Card for Nursing Facilities: What Information Is Needed and Why. *The Gerontologist* 43(2):47–57.

Harrington, C., D. Zimmerman, S.L. Karon, J. Robinson, and P. Beutel. 2000. Nursing Home Staffing and Its Relationship to Deficiencies. *Journals of Gerontology Series B–Psychological Sciences and Social Sciences* 55(5):S278–87.

Harris, Y., and S.B. Clauser. 2002. Achieving Improvement through Nursing Home Quality Measurement. *Health Care Finance Review* 23(4):5–18.

Hawes, C., V. Mor, C.D. Phillips, B.E. Fries, J.N. Morris, E. Steele-Friedlob, A.M. Greene, and M. Nennstiel. 1997. The OBRA-87 Nursing Home Regulations and Implementation of the Resident Assessment Instrument: Effects on Process Quality. *Journal of the American Geriatrics Society* 45(8):977–85.

Hibbard, J.H., and L.G. Pawlson. 2004. Why Not Give Consumers a Framework for Understanding Quality? *Joint Commission Journal on Quality & Safety* 30(6):347–51.

Hibbard, J.H., and E. Peters. 2003. Supporting Informed Consumer Health Care Decisions: Data Presentation Approaches That Facilitate the Use of Information in Choice. *Annual Review of Public Health* 24:413–33.

Hibbard, J.H., J. Stockard, and M. Tusler. 2003. Does Publicizing Hospital Performance Stimulate Quality Improvement Efforts? *Health Affairs* 22(2):84–94.

Hittle, D.F., P.W. Shaughnessy, K.S. Crisler, M.C. Powell, A.A. Richard, K.S. Conway, P.M. Stearns, and K. Engle. 2003. A Study of Reliability and Burden of Home Health Assessment Using OASIS. *Home Health Care Services Quarterly* 22(4):43–63.

Intrator, O., and K. Berg. 2002. Comparing Outcomes of Post Acute Care Following Hip Fracture. *The Gerontologist* 42:75.

Intrator, O., Z. Feng, V. Mor, D. Gifford, M. Bourbonniere, and J. Zinn. 2005. The Effect of State Medicaid Policies on the Employment of Nurse Practitioners and Physician Assistants in U.S. Nursing Homes. *The Gerontologist* 45(4):486–95.

Intrator, O., and V. Mor. 2004. Effect of State Medicaid Reimbursement Rates on Hospitalizations from Nursing Homes. *Journal of the American Geriatrics Society* 52(3):393–8.

Institute of Medicine (IOM). 1986. *Improving the Quality of Care in Nursing Homes.* Washington, D.C.

Institute of Medicine (IOM). 2001. *Improving the Quality of Long-Term Care.* Washington, D.C.: National Academy Press.

Kaiser Family Foundation and the Agency for Health Research and Quality. 2000. National Survey on Americans as Health Care Consumers: An Update on the Role of Quality Information.

Kane, R.A., A.L. Caplan, E.K. Urv-Wong, I.C. Freeman, M.A. Aroskar, and M. Finch. 1997. Everyday Matters in the Lives of Nursing Home Residents: Wish for and Perception of Choice and Control. *Journal of the American Geriatrics Society* 45(9):1086–93.

Kane, R.A., K.C. Kling, B. Bershadsky, R.L. Kane, K. Giles, H. Degenholtz, J. Liu, and L.J. Cutler. 2003. Quality of Life Measures for Nursing Home Residents. *Journals of Gerontology Series A—Biological Sciences and Medical Sciences* 58(3):240–48.

Kane, R.L., B. Bershadsky, R.A. Kane, H. Degenholtz, J. Liu, K. Giles, and K.C. Kling. 2004. Using Resident Reports of Quality of Life to Distinguish among Nursing Homes. *The Gerontologist* 44(5):624–32.

Kissam, S., D.R. Gifford, P. Parks, G. Patry, L. Palmer, M. Fitzgerald, L. Wilkes, A. Stollenwerk Petrulis, and L. Barnette. 2003. Approaches to Quality Improvement in Nursing Homes: Lessons Learned from the Six-State Pilot of CMS's Nursing Home Quality Initiative. *BMC Geriatrics* 3(1):2.

Kizer, K.W. 2001. Establishing Health Care Performance Standards in an Era of Consumerism. *Journal of the American Medical Association* 286(10):1213–7.

Kramer, A.M., P.W. Shaughnessy, M.K. Bauman, and K.S. Crisler. 1990. Assessing and Assuring the Quality of Home Health Care: A Conceptual Framework. *Milbank Quarterly* 68(3):413–43.

Kurtzman, E.T., and K.W. Kizer. 2005. Evaluating the Performance and Contribution of Nurses to Achieve an Environment of Safety. *Nursing Administration Quarterly* 29(1):14–23.

Lee, R.H., and L. Wendling. 2004. The Extent of Quality Improvement Activities in Nursing Homes. *American Journal of Medical Quality* 19(6):255–65.

Lowe, T.J., J.A. Lucas, N.G. Castle, J.P. Robinson, and S. Crystal. 2003. Consumer Satisfaction in Long-Term Care: State Initiatives in Nursing Homes and Assisted Living Facilities. *The Gerontologist* 43(6):883–96.

Lucas, J.A., T. Avi-Itzhak, J.P. Robinson, C.G. Morris, M.J. Koren, and S.C. Reinhard. 2005. Continuous Quality Improvement as an Innovation: Which Nursing Facilities Adopt It? *The Gerontologist* 45(1):68–77.

Madigan, E.A. 2002. The Scientific Dimensions of OASIS for Home Care Outcome Measurement. *Home Healthcare Nurse* 20(9):579–83.

Marshall, M.N., P.S. Romano, and H.T. Davies. 2004. How Do We Maximize the Impact of the Public Reporting of Quality of Care? *International Journal for Quality in Health Care* 16:57–63.

Mattke, S., J. Needleman, P. Buerhaus, M. Stewart, and K. Zelevinksky. 2004. Evaluating the Role of Patient Sample Definitions for Quality Indicators Sensitive to Nurse Staffing Patterns. *Medical Care* 42(2, suppl.):II21–II33.

Mattke, S., K. Reilly, E. Martinez-Vidal, B. McLean, and D. Gifford. 2003. Reporting Quality of Nursing Home Care to Consumers: The Maryland Experience. *International Journal for Quality in Health Care* 15(2):169–77.

Miller, S.C., V. Mor, N.Wu, P. Gozalo, and K. Lapane. 2002. Does Receipt of Hospice Care in Nursing Homes Improve the Management of Pain at the End of Life? *Journal of the American Geriatrics Society* 50(3):507–15.

Mitchell, S.L., J.M. Teno, S.C. Miller, and V. Mor. 2005. A National Study of the Location of Death for Older Persons with Dementia. *Journal of the American Geriatrics Society* 53(2):299–305.

Mor, V. 2004. A Comprehensive Clinical Assessment Tool to Inform Policy and Practice: Applications of the Minimum Data Set. *Medical Care* 42(4, suppl.):III50–III59.

Mor, V., J. Angelelli, D. Gifford, J. Morris, and T. Moore. 2003a. Benchmarking and Quality in Residential and Nursing Homes: Lessons from the U.S. *International Journal of Geriatric Psychiatry* 18(3):258–66.

Mor, V., J. Angelelli, R. Jones, J. Roy, T. Moore, and J. Morris. 2003b. Inter-Rater Reliability of Nursing Home Quality Indicators in the U.S. *BMC Health Services Research* 3(1):20.

Mor, V., K. Berg, J. Angelelli, D. Gifford, J. Morris, and T. Moore. 2003c. The Quality of Quality Measurement in U.S. Nursing Homes. *The Gerontologist* 43(spec. no. 2):37–46.

Morris, J.N., C. Hawes, B.E. Fries, C.D. Phillips, V. Mor, S. Katz, K. Murphy, M.L. Drugovich, and A.S. Friedlob. 1990. Designing the National Resident Assessment Instrument for Nursing Homes. *The Gerontologist* 30(3):293–307.

Morris, J.N., S. Nonemaker, K. Murphy, C. Hawes, B.E. Fries, V. Mor, and C. Phillips. 1997. A Commitment to Change: Revision of HCFA's RAI. *Journal of the American Geriatric Society* 45(8):1011–6.

Mukamel, D.B. 1997. Risk-Adjusted Outcome Measures and Quality of Care in Nursing Homes. *Medical Care* 35(4):367–85.

Mukamel, D.B., and A.I. Mushlin. 2001. The Impact of Quality Report Cards on Choice of Physicians, Hospitals, and HMOs: A Midcourse Evaluation. *Joint Commission Journal on Quality Improvement* 27(1):20–27.

Mukamel, D.B., A.I. Mushlin, D.Weimer, J. Zwanziger, T. Parker, and I. Indridason. 2000. Do Quality Report Cards Play a Role in HMOs' Contracting Practices? Evidence from New York State. *Health Services Research* 35(1, part 2):319–32.

Mukamel, D.B., and W.D. Spector. 2000. Nursing Home Costs and Risk-Adjusted Outcome Measures of Quality. *Medical Care* 38(1):78–89.

Mukamel, D.B., and W.D. Spector. 2003. Quality Report Cards and Nursing Home Quality. *The Gerontologist* 43(spec. no. 2):58–66.

Mukamel, D.B., N.M. Watson, H. Meng, and W.D. Spector. 2003. Development of a Risk-Adjusted Urinary Incontinence Outcome Measure of Quality for Nursing Homes. *Medical Care* 41(4):467–78.

Outcome Concepts Systems. 2004. The Effect of the Prospective Payment System on Home Health Quality of Care. Report submitted to the Medicare Payment Advisory Commission, Seattle Washington.

Pentz, C., and A. Wilson. 2001. Ensuring the Quality of OASIS Data: One Agency's Plan. *Home Healthcare Nurse* 19(1):38–42.

Potthoff, S., R.L. Kane, and S.J. Franco. 1997. Improving Hospital Discharge Planning for Elderly Patients. *Health Care Finance Review* 19(2):47–72.

Rantz, M.J., L. Hicks, V. Grando, G.F. Petroski, R.W. Madsen, D.R. Mehr, V. Conn, et al. 2004a. Nursing Home Quality, Cost, Staffing, and Staff Mix. *The Gerontologist* 44(1):24–38.

Rantz, M.J., L. Hicks, G.F. Petroski, R.W. Madsen, D.R. Mehr, V. Conn, M. Zwygart-Staffacher, and M. Maas. 2004b. Stability and Sensitivity of Nursing Home Quality Indicators. *Journals of Gerontology Series A—Biological Sciences and Medical Sciences* 59(1):79–82.

Rantz, M.J., D.R. Mehr, V.S. Conn, L.L. Hicks, R. Porter, R.W. Madsen, G.F. Petroski, and M. Maas. 1996. Assessing Quality of Nursing Home Care: The Foundation for Improving Resident Outcomes. *Journal of Nursing Care Quality* 10(4):1–9.

Rantz, M.J., L. Popejoy, G.F. Petroski, R.W. Madsen, D.R. Mehr, M. Zwygart-Staffacher, L.L. Hicks, et al. 2001. Randomized Clinical Trial of a Quality Improvement Intervention in Nursing Homes. *The Gerontologist* 41(4):525–38.

Rantz, M.J., A. Vogelsmeier, P. Manion, D. Minner, B. Markway, V. Conn, M.A. Aud, and D.R. Mehr. 2003. Statewide Strategy to Improve Quality of Care in Nursing Facilities. *The Gerontologist* 43(2):248–58.

Richards, S.H., J. Coast, and T.J. Peters. 2003. Patient-Reported Use of Health Service Resources Compared with Information from Health Providers. *Health Social Care Community* 11(6):510–18.

Romano, P.S., and H. Zhou. 2004. Do Well-Publicized Risk-Adjusted Outcomes Reports Affect Hospital Volume? *Medical Care* 42(4):367–77.

Roy, J., and V. Mor. 2005. The Effect of Provider-Level Ascertainment Bias on Profiling Nursing Homes. *Statistics in Medicine*. In press.

Saliba, D., L.V. Rubenstein, B. Simon, E. Hickey, B. Ferrell, E. Czarnowski, and D. Berlowitz. 2003. Adherence to Pressure Ulcer Prevention Guidelines: Implications for Nursing Home Quality. *Journal of the American Geriatrics Society* 51(1):56–62.

Sangl, J., D. Saliba, D.R. Gifford, and D.F. Hittle. 2005. Challenges in Measuring Nursing Home and Home Health Quality: Lessons from the First National Healthcare Quality Report. *Medical Care* 43(3, suppl.):124–132.

Schnelle, J.F., B.M. Bates-Jensen, L. Chu, and S.F. Simmons. 2004a. Accuracy of Nursing Home Medical Record Information about Care-Process Delivery: Implications for Staff Management and Improvement. *Journal of the American Geriatrics Society* 52(8):1378–83.

Schnelle, J.F., B.M. Bates-Jensen, L. Levy-Storms, V. Grbic, J. Yoshii, M. Cadogan, and S.F. Simmons. 2004b. The Minimum Data Set Prevalence of Restraint Quality Indicator: Does It Reflect Differences in Care? *The Gerontologist* 44(2):245–55.

Schnelle, J.F., J.G. Ouslander, and P.A. Cruise. 1997. Policy without Technology: A Barrier to Improving Nursing Home Care. *The Gerontologist* 37(4):527–32.

Schnelle, J.F., S.F. Simmons, C. Harrington, M. Cadogan, E. Garcia, and B.M. Bates-Jensen. 2004c. Relationship of Nursing Home Staffing to Quality of Care. *Health Services Research* 39(2):225–50.

Shaller, D., S. Sofaer, S.D. Findlay, J.H. Hibbard, D. Lansky, and S. Delbanco. 2003. Consumers and Quality-Driven Health Care: A Call to Action. *Health Affairs* 22(2):95–101.

Shaughnessy, P.W., K.S. Crisler, and R.E. Bennett. 2000. We've Collected the OASIS Data, Now What? *Home Healthcare Nurse* 18(4):258–65, quiz 266.

Shaughnessy, P.W., K.S. Crisler, R.E. Schlenker, and A.G. Arnold. 1995. Outcome-Based Quality Improvement in Home Care. *Caring* 14(2):44–9.

Shaughnessy, P.W., K.S. Crisler, R.E. Schlenker, A.G. Arnold, A.M. Kramer, M.C. Powell, and D.F. Hittle. 1994. Measuring and Assuring the Quality of Home Health Care. *Health Care Finance Review* 16(1):35–67.

Shaughnessy, P.W., D.F. Hittle, K.S. Crisler, M.C. Powell, A.A. Richard, A.M. Kramer, R.E. Schlenker, et al. 2002. Improving Patient Outcomes of Home Health Care: Findings from Two Demonstration Trials of Outcome-Based Quality Improvement. *Journal of the American Geriatrics Society* 50(8):1354–64.

Shaughnessy, P.W., and A.A. Richard. 2002. Performance Benchmarking. Part 1: What It Is & How to Use It. *Caring* 21(11):18.

Simmons, S.F., S. Babineau, E. Garcia, and J.F. Schnelle. 2002. Quality Assessment in Nursing Homes by Systematic Direct Observation: Feeding Assistance. *Journals of Gerontology Series A—Biological Sciences and Medical Sciences* 57(10): M665–71.

Simmons, S.F., J.F. Schnelle, G.C. Uman, A.D. Kulvicki, K.O. Lee, and J.G. Ouslander. 1997. Selecting Nursing Home Residents for Satisfaction Surveys. *The Gerontologist* 37(4):543–50.

Sofaer, S., J. Gruman, S. Connaughton, R. Grier, and C. Maule. 2000. Developing Performance Indicators That Reflect an Expanded View of Health: Findings from the Use of an Innovative Methodology. *The Joint Commission Journal on Quality Improvement* 26(4):189–202.

Stevenson, D.G., and D.M. Studdert. 2005. Nursing Home Consumer Complaints and Their Potential Role in Assessing Quality of Care. *Medical Care* 43(2):102–11.

Stoker, J. 1998. OASIS as a Mandatory Medicare Requirement. *Home Healthcare Nurse* 16(9):595.

Teno, J.M., V.A. Casey, L.C. Welch, and S. Edgman-Levitan. 2001a. Patient-Focused, Family-Centered End-of-Life Medical Care: Views of the Guidelines and Bereaved Family Members. *Journal of Pain & Symptom Management* 22(3):738–51.

Teno, J.M., B. Clarridge, V. Casey, S. Edgman-Levitan, and J. Fowler. 2001b. Validation of Toolkit After-Death Bereaved Family Member Interview. *Journal of Pain & Symptom Management* 22(3):752–8.

Wipke-Tevis, D.D., D.A. Williams, M.J. Rantz, L.L. Popejoy, R.W. Madsen, G.F. Petroski, and A.A. Vogelsmeier. 2004. Nursing Home Quality and Pressure Ulcer Prevention and Management Practices. *Journal of the American Geriatrics Society* 52(4):583–8.

Wu, N., S.C. Miller, K. Lapane, and P. Gozalo. 2003. The Problem of Assessment Bias When Measuring the Hospice Effect on Nursing Home Residents' Pain. *Journal of Pain and Symptom Management* 26(5):998–1009.

Wu, N., S.C. Miller, K. Lapane, J. Roy, and V. Mor. 2005. The Quality of the Quality Indicator of Pain Derived from the Minimum Data Set. *Health Services Research* 40(4):1197–1216.

Zimmerman, D.R. 2003. Improving Nursing Home Quality of Care through Outcomes Data: The MDS Quality Indicators. *International Journal of Geriatric Psychiatry* 18(3):250–57.

Zimmerman, D.R., S.L. Karon, G. Arling, B.R. Clark, T. Collins, R. Ross, and F. Sainfort. 1995. Development and Testing of Nursing Home Quality Indicators. *Health Care Finance Review* 16(4):107–27.

Zinn, J.S., W.E. Aaronson, and M.D. Rosko. 1994. Strategic Groups, Performance, and Strategic Response in the Nursing Home Industry. *Health Services Research* 29(2):187–205.

Zinn, J.S., and V. Mor. 1994. Nursing Home Special Care Units: Distribution by Type, State, and Facility Characteristics. *The Gerontologist* 34(3):371–7.

Zinn, J.S., R.J. Weech, and D. Brannon. 1998. Resource Dependence and Institutional Elements in Nursing Home TQM Adoption. *Health Services Research* 33 (2, part 1):261–73.

Chapter 15

Long-Term Care Housing Types and Design

Shannon M. Chance

Contents

Today, a myriad of housing types support long-term care—a myriad that results from an array of complex issues that surrounds the planning and design of these care facilities. This chapter describes major distinctions between various kinds of housing facilities available today. It also provides an overview of services and amenities typically offered in each category of housing. It then outlines the basic process used to create long-term care facilities, explaining the general sequence of events that occurs from the initial conception of a facility through its design and construction. The chapter concludes by discussing three critical points in the design sequence where health professionals can have the greatest impact on design quality: choosing the architect, selecting the site, and programming the facility. These aspects deserve special attention to overcome deficiencies that negatively impact the quality of life in many existing facilities. Healthcare planners and administrators can help remedy or avoid standard problems by understanding these issues and the processes used in building facilities for long-term care.

The overall objectives of this chapter are to prepare the reader to (1) identify various housing types; (2) understand what groups of amenities are generally offered together; (3) distinguish the roles and responsibilities of the various members of the development team as well as the sequence in which they work; and (4) recognize design issues traditionally neglected in long-term care facility development.

Types of Housing for Long-Term Care

Long-term care facilities provide support to the frail elderly as well as people who have mental retardation, head trauma, Alzheimer's disease, or who need physical rehabilitation or psychiatric care (Scaggs and Hawkins, 1994). At present, facilities provide various combinations of housing, healthcare, medical care, assistance with the "activities of daily living," and support services (such as housekeeping and transportation). The contemporary proliferation of offerings results not only from various combinations of these services, but also from how they are combined with various types of physical facilities, delivery systems, and payment mechanisms (Gordon, 1998).

The size and shape of facilities for long-term care run the gamut. Facility forms range from standard single- and multifamily housing units to sprawling campuses, from single-story to mid- and high-rise structures, and from stand-alone buildings to large complexes. Housing for long-term care contains various types of dwelling units: efficiency units, one- or two-bedroom apartments, and houses that stand alone or are attached to other houses (Scaggs and Hawkins, 1994). Almost all long-term care facilities include shared service space to support administration, housekeeping, dining, indoor and outdoor gatherings, and at least some medical services.

Naming and defining clear categories of facility types presents a definite challenge. Housing options are often grouped according to the level of dependence (or the service needs) of their users. However, no single organization regulates the terms used to describe the categories. Some definitions are determined by national policies such as Medicare and Medicaid rules, but most of these decisions are left to state regulation. They vary widely across the nation and remain in constant flux. Even within the long-term care literature, the thresholds differentiating categories remain unclear; terms such as "congregate housing" carry many different meanings.

It is, however, possible to distinguish two basic categories that have typified long-term care housing in America, although the lines defining them have blurred in recent years as new hybrid forms have appeared. Laws have generally differentiated facilities operating on a medical-type model from the lesser-regulated residential-model places that are less concerned with their occupants' healthcare needs. In recent years, hybrid permutations of these two forms have gained popularity as developers tailor facilities to users' requirements through various combinations of building types, services, and financing and in accord with state regulations and federal policies.

Twentieth-Century Paradigms

Two distinct paradigms for long-term care—a medical model and a residential model—emerged in the United States as a result of the regulation of hospitals but more lax rules for nursing homes. As medical technology improved and people lived longer, a growing number of individuals required higher levels of medical services over longer periods of time. This fostered the demand for long-term care outside of medical institutions. Indeed, the traditional divide between regulated and unregulated facilities emerged when the national government required the states to license healthcare facilities within their boarders by 1970 (Shore, 1994). This requirement formally separated long-term care along the two historic paradigms: a fairly technical and standardized medical model and a distinctly different residential one that was allowed to provide housing with very few health-related services. Both aesthetically and medically, long-term housing facilities within the residential model resemble many of the early almshouses that had a domestic appearance but which provided no organized medical care.

Medical-model facilities do provide medical and other health-related care. This paradigm of long-term care grew out of the medical hospital tradition that emphasized organization, efficiency, and sanitation. Housing within the medical model has a much more institutional appearance and bureaucratic structure than housing that grew from the residential model. Medical-model facilities have faced considerable state regulation in addition to being shaped by federal policies.

Many people who found themselves in a medically focused environment for lengthy periods missed the comforts of a homelike residential setting. Turner (2002, p. 20), a bioethicist, explains:

> I am used to experiencing hospitals and geriatric facilities as bright, white, sanitized, utilitarian institutions where little attention is given to the moral, aesthetic, and spiritual dimensions of place. Trudging through most hospitals, it is easy to understand why patients and visitors regard them as such impersonal, dehumanizing institutions. There are ways, however, of making hospitals and geriatric facilities more humane and hospitable.

Efforts to bridge the divide between "residential" and "medical" facilities have fostered new hybrid accommodations. Many of the features distinguishing residential from medical places are now packaged together in various combinations, but this shift has not been easily accomplished. Gordon (1998, p. 24) contends that

> it is the tension among the housing, care, and services components of seniors' communities that makes their operation and regulation unique and sometimes presents a tightrope walk for developers and operators seeking to combine these disparate elements in a single setting.

In light of the current plethora of hybrid offerings, it is important to understand traditional types of residential and medical-model housing to distinguish what specific attributes are provided by a given hybrid facility.

The Residential Model

Residential-model housing has historically accommodated people who are healthy and independent as well as many semi-independent or moderately impaired persons. A number of younger individuals who have mental illness or developmental disabilities also reside in long-term residential-model housing. Owing to the high cost of such service, only the frailest, most dependent people reside in medical-model facilities.

Building types within the residential model include standard single- and multifamily dwellings found in typical neighborhoods or in age-restricted complexes. The latter often are referred to as congregate housing, senior living, independent living, or planned retirement communities. These options avoid the cost and complexity involved with state licensure of medical care. They focus on providing housing alone—and sometimes meals. Thus, residents must obtain medical and most other services from outside sources. States generally allow these housing providers to either supply or arrange a few additional services (such as meal delivery and transportation) for their residents. However, because they are not licensed, residentially focused facilities are seldom permitted to coordinate residents' medical care or even assistance with activities of daily living (such as bathing or taking medication).

Regardless, many people who reside in unlicensed residential-model housing still need occasional support. A range of programs has been developed to provide home care to them. Such assistance includes home modification, day facilities, chore services, meals, shopping, transportation, and housecleaning, as well as healthcare assistance (ranging from help with the activities of daily living to more medical forms of care). For the elderly, these services may be obtained directly from individuals, for-profit companies, or nonprofit organizations; services may also be secured and coordinated with the help of Area Agencies on Aging.

Common services involve in-home therapies. These include physical and rehabilitation therapy, mental health therapy, speech therapy, and occupational therapy, among others. Many states require licensure for agencies that provide these types of services. However, licensure is often not required of providers who only offer assistance with activities of daily living such as dressing, bathing, and climbing stairs.

Home modifications can help people live independently longer and more comfortably. Alterations are especially advantageous when they increase the usability of kitchens, bathrooms, and stairways. They can make a place safer and more user friendly by enhancing mobility, facilitating the work of caregivers, and thereby delaying the need to move elsewhere. However, Pynoos and Matsuoka (1996) note that a number of barriers deter people from modifying their dwellings. Consumers (and even the healthcare professionals who advise them) are often unaware of the risks posed within their existing housing, or of the changes that could be made to enhance their daily experience. According to Pynoos and Matsuoka, surprisingly few people are able to identify potential modifications that could offer physical support. Even fewer understand the process of constructing or installing such features, or even how to contract for construction services. These researchers cite numerous obstacles in financing the work, noting that individuals must often pay for housing modifications out of pocket or apply to several different assistance programs to obtain adequate funding.

Adult day facilities, senior centers, and the geriatric day hospitals common in the United Kingdom can also help delay institutionalization and can provide relief for caregivers (Cox and Groves, 1990; Vierck and Hodges, 2003). Seniors living independently can use such facilities, along with semi-independent and chronically ill people who reside with their family members or with other informal caregivers. These facilities provide meals, community interaction, and organized activities, in addition to supervision and personal care assistance during the day (Pratt, 1999; Vierck and Hodges, 2003). They may also provide counseling, therapy, rehabilitation, and outdoor recreation (Cox and Groves, 1990; Scaggs and Hawkins, 1994). Some of these facilities are freestanding, whereas others are housed within schools, churches, recreational centers, nursing homes, or continuing care retirement community (CCRC) complexes (Scaggs and Hawkins, 1994). As in other areas of long-term care, states' licensure requirements may affect the range of services provided by these facilities.

In addition to Title III funding under the 1965 Older Americans Act, federally subsidized services are available through Social Service Block Grants and Community Service Block Grants (Vierck and Hodges, 2003). However, there are limited government resources for such community-based assistance, especially in comparison to those allocated for institutional care, which captures about 72 percent of total national spending on long-term care (Vierck and Hodges, 2003).

Although home care services are greatly needed by seniors who reside in all kinds of residential-model housing, their utilization drastically declined between 1996 and 2000. In fact, the Balanced Budget Act of 1997 decreased Medicare expenditures by half between 1997 and 1999, which forced the closure of many agencies (Vierck and Hodges, 2003). Currently, slightly less than 3 percent of seniors use home care service; in 2000, this represented 1.5 million Americans, or 49 percent fewer people than in 1996 (Goldsmith, 2005; Vierck and Hodges, 2003).

Although residential-model housing accommodates the lion's share of the older population, it is clear that these arrangements often provide inadequate services and physical supports. When asked if they receive enough assistance, 37 percent of older persons who live in regular communities describe that they receive either no help or less than they need (Jackson and Doty, 1997, as cited by Vierck and Hodges, 2003).

Inadequacies are common in the places that house most seniors, including standard single- or multifamily dwellings, and even in many age-restricted, senior-oriented communities.

Moreover, a comprehensive and coordinated system for delivering in-home care has yet to be developed. Some multiunit housing facilities do assist residents in securing home care services, but the amount of help they can legally offer varies from state to state.

Standard Family Housing

Standard "family housing" is available through private ownership or rental-type fee arrangement. Most of the senior population lives in housing that is privately owned, either by themselves or by another individual. This owner is typically a relative who provides care as well as housing, or an unrelated person who provides "adult foster care." Private ownership often involves detached housing (such as single-family dwellings and mobile homes) or attached housing (including multifamily structures organized as condominiums or cooperatives) with privately owned townhouses or flats. Alternatively, rental methods can also be employed to secure many of these same housing types. Rental arrangements proliferate among residential hotels and publicly subsidized housing (complexes or dispersed units).

Single-family housing remains the top preference among seniors, who often stay in the homes they obtained earlier in life (Gordon, 1998). About 77 percent of elders own their homes and, although homeownership rates do tend to decrease at higher ages, "67 percent of older adults over age 85 residing in the community still own their own homes" (Pynoos and Matsuoka, 1996, p. 118). However, a significant number of these homes do not include physically supportive features that promote independence. Seniors who find their abilities declining are often forced to move in with their children or relocate to more medically oriented facilities.

Most of the non-homeowners who live independently reside in apartments, and 21 percent of them live in structures that include more than 50 dwelling units (Naifeh, 1993, as cited in Pynoos and Matsuoka, 1996). Urban residence hotels are inhabited by about 76,000 older people who rent rooms on a monthly or long-term basis (Gordon, 1998). In addition, over one million seniors reside in government-assisted housing, funded through programs such as Section 202, Section 8, or Farmers Home Administration (Pynoos and Matsuoka, 1996).

Although multifamily housing options (including apartment complexes, urban residence hotels, and public housing projects) are distinctly less popular than single-family housing, they present a major advantage due to their greater density (Gordon, 1998). Concentrated populations of seniors provide ready markets for products and services that can be offered economically. They can also boost competition among private-sector providers. Although dense multifamily housing often provides a ready market for senior services, this potentially lucrative market is just beginning to gain recognition. In some places like New York City, where large groups of older people living in close proximity have formed Naturally Occurring Retirement Communities (NORCs), providers sometimes do offer services known as "cluster care."

Urban planners coined the acronym NORC to designate areas with disproportionately high numbers of senior residents (Dover, 2006). NORCs also represent pockets where increased levels of service will be needed as the health of their residents continues to decline. NORCs are emerging in many older existing neighborhoods, because these places already offer ready access to many diverse services, activities, and neighbors. Although older houses may have features that impede mobility, their location in "walkable" inner-city neighborhoods allows easy access to a range of products and services, and often to rich and vibrant community life.

Age-Restricted Housing

Most of the same forms of dwellings available on the standard housing market can also be found in age-restricted housing communities. The use of age restrictions simply allows housing providers to collect more homogeneous, and generally quieter, resident populations. U.S. "fair housing" legislation established in 1968 does make it illegal to discriminate based on personal characteristics that include age, and so only officially certified communities are legally permitted to control the demographics of their residents.

Age-restricted housing complexes are often called "active adult" or "planned residential" communities. They can be utilized through a variety of payment mechanisms including private ownership, rental, or other periodic fee systems. Age-restricted complexes provide various levels of amenities—such as grounds maintenance and shared recreational space—typical in regular housing complexes (Gordon, 1998).

Because these age-restricted residential communities provide concentrated markets of people who need frequent healthcare, medical-type facilities are often constructed near them. In many cases, adjoining medical- and residential-model facilities are built by a single owner or provider. These include the increasingly popular CCRCs that are described in the section on hybrid models.

Congregate Housing

Various public and private organizations offer congregate housing facilities, which generally hold anywhere from four to forty residents each (Pynoos, 1987; Pynoos and Matsuoka, 1996). They are often referred to as "independent living" facilities and are used most often by healthy and independent seniors who desire a number of convenience services (Gordon, 1998; Pynoos and Matsuoka, 1996). Congregate housing is generally rental-based, and differs from other forms of age-restricted housing in that it includes prepared meals as well as facility maintenance. Although the individual units typically include private kitchens and baths, these facilities also provide shared dining rooms and other gathering spaces (Pynoos and Matsuoka, 1996). Residents may be assisted in taking medications, but other medical and personal care services are usually contracted separately by the individual, as needed.

Congregate housing is a popular form of housing among semi-independent people as well as completely independent seniors. Many moderately impaired individuals also reside in these settings, where they sometimes live with family members or share their units with other seniors (Gordon, 1998). One advantage that congregate and multiunit housing complexes often offer over traditional single-family homes is some level of supportive physical and architectural features, including bathroom grab bars and wide doorways (Zook, 2005).

The Medical Model

Although hospitals evolved out of the almshouses that had provided little in the way of medical care and which had served primarily residential functions, the character of hospitals changed drastically following the Industrial Revolution. Round-the-clock availability of trained nursing personnel became, and remains, common to all medical-model facilities (Gordon, 1998). A medical model of care emerged in the twentieth century that left domestic and residential-life issues on the periphery of concern. Instead, it stressed scientific technology, sanitation, and efficiency.

National policies were developed throughout the past century which served to regulate and standardize the service delivered by hospitals, and after 1970, state licensure extended some degree of standardization to nursing homes as well. Although licensure has been implemented at the state level, national mandates have resulted in definitions and requirements regarding medical-model facilities that are quite consistent from coast to coast. As a result, medical-model facilities provide a highly regulated and comparatively consistent system of care. States almost always group nursing facilities together with hospitals. Generally, such medically oriented facilities are distinguished legally from residential-type facilities. Overall, state regulation of residentially based facilities is drastically less than that of medical-model facilities. In fact, Gordon (1998) asserts that some states do not regulate residential housing for seniors any differently than regular housing.

Nursing Facilities

In 2000, more than 1.5 million people lived in over 17,000 nursing homes certified by Medicare and Medicaid (Goldsmith, 2005; Nursing Homes, 2005). Vierck and Hodges (2003) have found that these facilities average 105 beds, with an 87 percent occupancy rate. They note that about 27 percent of nursing homes are run by non-profits, less than 7 percent by governmental entities, and the remaining two-thirds by private, profit-making companies. About 60 percent of all nursing homes are affiliated with large franchise operations (Vierck and Hodges, 2003).

Medicare and Medicaid policies have fostered consistency among medical-model facilities with regard to delivery of acute, semiacute, and long-term care. These federal programs categorize nursing facilities as intermediate care facilities

(ICFs), skilled nursing facilities (SNFs), or special care facilities (SCFs). The admission policies and levels of care offered by these facilities are often tailored to Medicaid and Medicare payment allowances.

Nursing facilities provide room and board in addition to nursing services and therapies, with the major distinction between ICF and SNF involving intensity of care (Pratt, 1999). It is common for nursing facilities to offer both ICF and SNF in separate areas.

ICFs provide minimal nursing assistance. ICF residents are usually able to move around by themselves, but they often require physical, occupational, and recreational therapies. They also tend to need continuous supervision with their medications and with various activities of daily living (Scaggs and Hawkins, 1994).

The residents of SNFs generally require ongoing supervision by nursing staff, mostly aides. A high percentage of residents are bedridden; some are incontinent or severely debilitated and many have multiple health problems. These facilities usually do not provide acute care services in-house. However, they may provide long-term maintenance programs and short-term rehabilitation for individuals who need physical, substance abuse, or physiological rehabilitation (Goodman and Smith, 1992).

SNFs usually contain 40–60 beds (Scaggs and Hawkins, 1994), although large facilities may include 250 beds or more. Single- or double-occupancy rooms, with attached toilet and shower rooms, typically surround shared spaces. These "shared spaces" shelter various services or accommodate collective activities such as dining, recreation, and therapy; they sometimes include collective bath facilities (Goodman and Smith, 1992). Regulations mandate that SNF residents may choose to take meals at bedside or in the collective dining room, although nursing personnel may encourage them to leave their rooms in an effort to promote mobility, socialization, and an overall sense of independence (Goodman and Smith, 1992).

SCFs offer services that are similar to SNFs. However, the former have special design features that accommodate the needs and conditions of specific user groups; they may provide focused care for people who are dependent on ventilators, who suffer head trauma or comas, or who have Alzheimer's disease. States often require SNFs to include specialized facilities for the acute care procedures that are typically needed by the facility's special user group (Scaggs and Hawkins, 1994).

Ambulatory Care

Ambulatory care facilities, which tend to be regulated by the states, provide medical-type services that prolong a person's ability to live in residential-model facilities.

They include "physicians' offices, hospital outpatient departments, hospital emergency rooms, and a range of other facilities such as surgical day centers, optometrists' offices, day-care centers, neighborhood health centers, substance abuse clinics, mental health centers, and pharmacies" (Goldsmith, 2005, p. 13).

Acute and Subacute Care Facilities

Hospitals provide acute care and are geared toward treating patients quickly so that they may be discharged to private homes or to lower-cost facilities that provide "stepdown" levels of care. Subacute care facilities provide intermediate or "post-acute care" at levels between that offered by hospitals and the nursing homes. Like hospitals, subacute care facilities are intended for short stays, with multidisciplinary teams of care providers focused on moving patients elsewhere. They provide more intensive supervision, skilled nursing, and therapies than do nursing homes (Pratt, 1999).

Hybrid Models

Although this chapter uses the term "hybrid" to describe new types of long-term care housing that blend aspects of more traditional models, hybrid forms are more commonly referred to by the umbrella term "residential care" (RC). The range of housing available within the hybrid model is often difficult to describe; however, these facilities can generally be classified as adult foster homes, "assisted living" (AL) or board-and-care facilities, or CCRCs.

Hybrid facilities are designed to create a feeling that is more residential and less institutional than the traditional medical model. They use various strategies to extend regulated medical and other health services to residents. Such facilities include the domestic, homelike attributes associated with residential-model housing, while bolstering residents' access to the type of healthcare services available at more medically oriented facilities. As such, they often support the resident's ability to "age in place." However, AL facilities are often prohibited from offering medical care beyond assistance in taking medication; instead, they may help residents obtain such care from outside the facility.

Hybrid facilities are visually similar to standard American residential housing. However, they also include components that support the various medical and personal care services crucial to more comprehensive, long-term care. The form and nature of shared service spaces in hybrid facilities vary greatly, due to different combinations of regulatory, financial, and design constraints. Services may be provided in separate facilities near the housing site, in the same building as the dwellings, or within individual housing units.

Eckert et al. (2001) applaud the hybrid model's lack of standardization. They emphasize the "remarkable diversity" of the hybrid model which they label as RC/AL: "Settings vary in size; ownership; profit or not-for-profit status; religious or nonreligious affiliation; and urban, suburban, or rural location, to mention but a few." They maintain that this diversity offers important possibilities for "linking person (in terms of prior life circumstances, history, and preferences) with place. In this regard, until there are data to the contrary, every effort should be made to resist rules and regulations that homogenize RC/AL through a 'one size fits all' formula" (p. 310).

By 2004, there were 36,450 facilities for RC across the United States that provided 937,601 units or beds. These figures from Mollica and Johnson-Lamarche (2005) do not include some types of hybrid facilities, such as those specifically licensed to provide adult foster or family care, or SCFs for people with developmental disabilities, mental retardation, or psychiatric needs.

Adult Foster Homes

Adult foster care may be provided to one or more individuals in a single setting. Because most states do not regulate facilities that serve just a few individuals, very small-scale operations often fit within the residential model described previously. However, as their resident population grows, adult foster care homes face increasing levels of regulation typical of facilities within the hybrid category. Regulation ultimately affects the physical facility's design and layout. Contemporary facilities for adult foster care and AL have roots in the board-and-care facilities that were available in many places during the 1960s and 1970s.

Mollica and Johnson-Lamarche (2005) found that 13 states regulate facilities with one or more residents; three states, with two or more residents; and eight states, with three or more residents. North Carolina classifies homes with two to six residents as "adult family homes," and those with seven or more residents as "adult care homes." North Carolina, like some other states, licenses both of these types as AL. Although population size is no longer the main factor used to distinguish adult foster care from AL, these researchers note that many states "still designate the number of people who may be served to distinguish between types of settings for other regulatory purposes, e.g., staffing requirements" (p. 1).

Assisted Living Facilities

AL facilities have steadily gained popularity since the 1990s. Residents generally live in private apartments and utilize a variety of common areas (Goodman and Smith, 1992). AL facilities offer essentially the same services and emulate the residential character of traditional board-and-care facilities (Regnier, 1994). However, they are subject to increasing levels of regulation and enjoy a better reputation than previous forms of board and care. The negative stigma associated with the latter resulted when some operators abused their unregulated status; they became notorious for fraud, abuse, and deadly fires (Gordon, 1998). The term "assisted living" is becoming standard today; the application of a new term, as well as increasing levels of regulation, has helped counteract the stigma.

Twenty-nine states had policies regarding AL or other forms of board-and-care homes in 2000 (Mollica, 2000, as cited in Bernard et al., 2001). However, there is constant modification of these rules, with 28 states revising them in 2003 and 2004 alone (Mollica and Johnson-Lamarche, 2005). There is still no uniform model or definition for AL, and this has allowed levels of financial assistance among hybrid facilities to vary widely (Bernard et al., 2001). Recently, a number of states have been granted Medicaid waivers to fund a small portion of AL facilities.

In essence, AL facilities offer a less intensive level of care than nursing homes; they can provide some healthcare but only with limited nursing services available on-site (Goodman and Smith, 1992; Scaggs and Hawkins, 1994). As with congregate housing, in some AL facilities medical services are provided by home health agencies that are licensed but are not affiliated with the housing operator (Goodman and Smith, 1992).

Because AL facilities tend to provide care at about 30 percent less cost than nursing homes (Gordon, 1998), they have become very popular and competitive alternatives to SNFs (Goodman and Smith, 1992). However, the component of personal care that they do provide carries a cost. As such, they are used by people who need some daily personal assistance but who are mostly ambulatory and independent (Gordon, 1998; Scaggs and Hawkins, 1994). Most personal assistance services are provided only as needed, both to keep costs down and to promote independence.

AL facilities aim to retain each resident for as long as possible and to delay the resident's need to move into a more care-intensive nursing facility (Regnier, 1994). Achieving this goal requires a high level of flexibility. Both the physical facility and the AL operator must be able to accommodate the resident's changing levels of function, mobility, and cognition (Bernard et al., 2001; Sloane et al., 2001). AL facilities are often designed to provide a sense of freedom and encourage the resident's continued independence (Goodman and Smith, 1992). This can be enhanced by using the various home modification techniques described earlier.

Gordon (1998) notes that the population of seniors able to support themselves financially is growing. At the same time, government continues to search for ways to care for an aging population, cut costs, and create less demand on medical-model facilities. Thus, "we are seeing a significant rise in the development of high-quality assisted-living facilities as an alternative to nursing care" (p. 35). The design of the physical facilities that support AL is constantly changing as the industry grows and evolves.

Continuing Care Retirement Communities

CCRCs are also referred to as "life care" communities (Gordon, 1998). They are considered the most accommodating form of care because they provide the full extent of services throughout a resident's life. CCRCs often offer congregate or independent housing, AL, and nursing facilities within one site. These may include intermediate and SNFs, and they sometimes include SCFs such as a hospice (Goodman and

Smith, 1992; Scaggs and Hawkins, 1994). On-site acute care hospitals are rarely found within these communities; CCRCs generally negotiate with nearby facilities to provide residents with coordinated care (Gordon, 1998).

CCRCs generally involve large-scale complexes, in the form of campuses or high-rise buildings. They offer an assortment of residential and healthcare facilities necessary to accommodate residents across changing levels of dependency. Although residents must sometimes relocate from one facility within the CCRC to another, they continue to live within a single community despite their changing needs.

Vierick and Hodges (2003) indicate that only about 2 percent of seniors use CCRCs; nearly 625,000 people reside in 2,100 facilities across the United States. They are generally run by private, nonprofit agencies, many of which have a religious affiliation (Gordon, 1998).

According to the American Association of Retired Persons (AARP), "costs of living in a CCRC can be quite high and unaffordable to those with low or moderate incomes and assets." Most CCRCs require monthly payments in addition to the entry fee (which may or may not have provisions for refund if unused). AARP further indicates that entry fees "can range from lows of $20,000 to highs of $400,000. Monthly payments can range from $200 to $2,500. In some places, residents own their living space, and in others the space is rented." Monthly fees average $1,500 and some newly developed CCRC programs are utilizing cooperative and condominium approaches (Gordon, 1998).

The Building Process

Long-term care presents a very specialized set of design constraints. Creating effective long-term care facilities requires input from many sources. The current flurry of construction strives to meet the growing demand for housing tailored to the needs and desires of America's aging baby boomers. Long-term care providers are utilizing both renovation and new construction to create housing that will meet the aspirations of these customers. The following overview of the building process is intended to provide long-term care administrators and policy makers with an understanding of the professional expertise and the sequence of events involved in developing long-term care facilities.

Housing for long-term care must provide function, versatility, and beauty. These attributes enhance the quality of life for the many diverse users who will rely on a single facility to sustain most of their needs. Many of the specific design qualities and features that have come to be considered most desirable in new housing—and most lacking in traditional forms of long-term care housing—are described in Chapter 12, on housing trends. Creating welcoming, efficient structures for aging long-term residents requires careful management, a solid understanding of the user group, and strong architectural design skills. The same basic process applies to new construction, adaptive reuse (which retrofits buildings originally constructed for some nonhousing purpose), and renovation (which modifies or upgrades facilities initially constructed for residential use).

Roles and Responsibilities

When an organization proposes to develop a long-term care facility, the first steps involve determining the type of facility to build. The terms "developer" or "owner" refer to this organization, which may be for-profit, nonprofit, public, or even a conglomeration of entities structured as a "joint venture." This developmental organization generally appoints an individual or group of people to serve as the "project coordinator." Project coordinators can be most effective when they have a clear understanding of the developer's goals and awareness of retirement facility operations, as well as experience with developing real estate and supervising the many different types of consultants who will help produce the housing product (Gordon, 1998).

The project coordinator establishes a preliminary project schedule and assembles a team of experts in various fields. Securing a range of expertise is mandatory because this team is expected to identify and define the consumer market, determine the types of facilities and services that will be offered, navigate legal and financial issues, and design and construct the housing product.

To provide a well-rounded understanding of the task and to create a realizable work plan, this team should include healthcare facility consultants, as well as financial, legal, and architectural consultants. The development process works most effectively with input from all these fields from the outset of the project. Developers may contract with one single source in each of these categories. In other cases, they may choose to contract directly with a number of specialized consultants within each of the mentioned areas. Once the project team has been established, it begins by structuring the basic concept for the housing product that will be developed.

The healthcare consultant, who often eventually serves as the facility's administrator, provides advice regarding the daily operations of a long-term care facility (Gordon, 1998). This person develops service packages, provides insight regarding local market conditions, projects staffing needs and operational expenses, develops policies and procedures, and helps define the architectural building program (Gordon, 1998; Scaggs and Hawkins, 1994).

Financial consultants include a range of specialists such as experts in marketing and economic feasibility; they base their assessments on market conditions, need projections, and financial capacity (Scaggs and Hawkins, 1994). Their goal is to develop a product that is competitive with regard to services, housing amenities, and payment mechanisms (Gordon, 1998). Marketing—of both sale and rental housing—often begins before any construction takes place (Gordon, 1998).

Legal consultants typically assist the owner or developer by interpreting aspects of zoning and land use, as well as preparing and reviewing various financing agreements and contracts. Developing a long-term care facility involves a high level of legal intricacy. Gordon (1998) maintains that clearly defining the regulatory constraints at the start of the process is critical to shaping an appropriate product, business plan, and residence agreement. All these aspects influence spatial requirements, overall layout of the physical facility, and construction standards and schedules.

The architectural consultant oversees the design and construction aspects of the project. The architect will determine the building form and spatial layout—coordinating these with the site plan and the structural, electrical, plumbing, heating, and air conditioning systems. In this endeavor, the architect usually employs individuals or outside firms that are specialized in structural, civil, mechanical, and electrical engineering.

Design Sequence

The American Institute of Architects (1997) B141 contract known as the Standard Form of Agreement between Owner and Architect defines the five "basic services" typical to most building design projects. These are schematic design, design development, construction documents, bidding and negotiation, and construction administration. Projects as complex as long-term care facilities usually require contracting for "additional services" besides the five basic ones. The AIA-B141 contract provides a framework for delineating extra services that are needed on a specific project, including the scope of the architect's involvement and methods of payment. Additional services commonly required in long-term housing include "predesign," landscape design, interior design, and graphic or signage design (Scaggs and Hawkins, 1994; Spreiregen, 2004).

Predesign Phase

Although listed as additional services, many "predesign" activities are absolutely critical to the success of a project. These include site selection and analysis, master planning, building programming, and feasibility studies. Predesign services have been held outside the five basic ones because they may be conducted before the project's architect has been selected. Although the practice of having these activities done by someone outside the design process became commonplace in the United States over the past century, it has weakened the continuity of the design process. Getting the project architect involved at the earliest stages of conceptualizing a long-term facility will ensure a higher overall quality of design (Scaggs and Hawkins, 1994).

The architect selected for this job should have experience with the intricacies of designing long-term care facilities, and should be contracted to provide detailed site analysis. This consultant should also provide leadership in defining the building program, a critical aspect that traditionally receives inadequate attention—largely a result of being classified as "pre-design" by the AIA. The AIA and healthcare experts are now stressing the importance of site design and building programming in creating high-quality physical environments.

A design that emphasizes function and technology at the expense of life quality often results when the initial building program identifies only tangible, quantifiable goals such as cost, size, use, and schedule. To ensure that ephemeral qualities are not overlooked in the maze of technical issues, it is important to identify desirable, intangible qualities at the outset and to specify these in the formal building program.

Schematic Design Phase

During schematic design, the architect proposes various schemes and then develops one or more of these into a tentative design proposal. It shows the basic arrangement of rooms, as well as the building's form, appearance, and orientation on the site. On the technical side, the architect balances the functional and adjacency requirements outlined in the building program with various structural and legal considerations.

Legal issues always include attention to municipal zoning as well as health and safety codes and the Americans with Disabilities Act (ADA). The architect should look for opportunities to tie the new building to its natural, built, and social context and provide artistic expression. In many cases, the architect will propose an overarching concept that helps tie the design together and give it meaning beyond the obligatory function. This overarching concept is used to guide future design decisions and to foster a cohesive, evocative design.

The architect's job involves tasks such as sizing the building(s), establishing building layouts, choosing structural and mechanical systems, and arranging the components on the site (Scaggs and Hawkins, 1994). Because each of these tasks influences the others, the architect must synthesize a great deal of information. Every design project requires the architect to make thousands of decisions, cross-referencing these various aspects and resolving conflicts (Regnier, 2002). The architectural language—massing, form, and appearance—is developed in relation to the owner's spatial, operational, and functional needs. Technology, cost, and schedule constitute one set of concerns for the architect creating a meaningful design that will support and foster life represents another.

The owner, the owner's consultants, and the architect's consultants usually provide input throughout the schematic design phase. The architect meets with the owner's representatives periodically during this phase to discuss options, confirm preferences, and determine which scheme or schemes should be developed in further detail. When the schematic design has been completed, it is presented to the owner with a preliminary estimate of construction costs (Heuer, 2004).

Design Development Phase

The project moves into design development following formal review and approval of the schematic design. This phase entails refining the schematic design, which requires a high level of coordination and a great deal of input from the architect's consultants. The end result is a polished final draft that is again provided to the owner—along with a more refined cost estimate—for formal review and approval (Heuer, 2004).

Construction Document Preparation

During the subsequent construction documents phase, detailed "working drawings" and written specifications are created that will instruct the contractor in assembling the building. The working drawings graphically present information regarding layout, adjacencies, and dimensions. The specifications describe quality expectations, performance ratings, assembly methods, and so on. The contractor uses these documents to determine construction fees.

Bidding, Negotiation, and Construction Administration

The bidding and negotiation phase is used in the traditional design-bid-build approach, wherein the architect helps the owner select a contractor and negotiate the construction fee (Heuer, 2004). The process traditionally involves obtaining and comparing bids from a number of qualified companies. The architect's role throughout construction is described as "construction contract administration," and entails providing experienced oversight to ensure that the owner's interests are represented (Kornblut, 2004). During this administration phase, the architect typically observes progress to confirm that the quality of construction meets the design intent as described in the construction documents.

Quality Considerations

A facility's design will have tremendous influence over the long-term quality of life for residents, staff, and visitors. Healthcare consultants, long-term care administrators, housing developers, and even policy makers need to understand several key aspects of the design process. There are three main points in the process of developing a new facility where input by these individuals is critical to producing a quality design: selecting the architect, choosing and designing the site, and programming the facility.

Selecting the Architect

Public financing almost always dictates a formal selection process—including prequalification and competitive bidding—to choose both the architectural and construction firms that will be hired (Heuer, 2004). In the private market, however, it is common for a developer to select the architect and the contractor based on personal familiarity, without regard to the firm's specialization. Selection by convenience poses risk. The complexities of developing a long-term care facility—which may integrate housing, dining, recreation, AL, with health and medical services—necessitate that the architect as well as the builder possess special skills (Gordon, 1998). These facilities must meet a myriad of very specialized codes and regulations, and provide higher-than-typical levels of strength, fire resistance, exiting capacity, and air exchange (Gordon, 1998; Regnier, 1994). Long-term care facilities must also support the specific physical and emotional needs of the residents, and they must facilitate care giving.

Although some formal methods of selecting the architect and builder do improve chances of achieving quality, the competitive bidding process that is commonly used has its own potential drawbacks. Public financing generally requires that the lowest qualified bidder be offered the job. This system inadvertently encourages architects and contractors to underbid to win the contract. Low-bid selection prioritizes cost above other concerns. As such, the low bidder may discover that the winning fee is inadequate to produce a refined product.

Creating a design that will enhance the quality of life for users of long-term care facilities requires dedicated commitment from the architect and from the owner or developer. Allotting sufficient resources to the design process is crucial to shaping a quality, cost-effective product that will enhance the lives of users (Kobus, 2000; Purves, 2002). The demand to control the costs associated with design and construction must be weighed against the ultimate goal of life quality—efficiency should not overshadow concerns for the users' experience (Kobus, 2000).

Dedicating sufficient time and effort to proper coordination during programming and design leads to a more efficient and functional facility, and often results in lower life-cycle costs. It renders "hospitals, geriatric facilities and other health care institutions more human, decent, aesthetically and spiritually moral habitats" (Turner, 2002, p. 19). All of these aspects raise the quality of life in these facilities for residents, workers, and even visitors.

Selecting and Connecting the Site

One of the most overlooked but critical features influencing quality of life at a long-term care facility involves its location (Regnier, 2002). Although acreage requirements for a site will vary depending on the size and complexity of the facility, there are other site attributes that are desirable regardless of the specific type of long-term care facility. The site must accommodate the necessary buildings, roadways, and parking. It must also provide ample outdoor spaces for communal gathering, recreation, and introspection. Long-term care facilities require larger sites than one might anticipate. For instance, ICFs and SNFs with 100–120 beds usually need about 5 acres of land that can be developed (Scaggs and Hawkins, 1994). Facilities for residents who are more ambulatory require additional space for outdoor activities.

Transportation represents a critical aspect of site selection (Heuer, 2004; Purves, 2002; Spreiregen, 2004). The site must be large enough to provide clear circulation for automobiles as well as delivery and emergency vehicles. It should be located on public transportation routes to enhance access by residents, staff, and visitors alike. The facility should also be placed near hospitals (Payette, 2000), specialized health-care and other "ambulatory" facilities, shopping, entertainment, churches, and so on (Scaggs and Hawkins, 1994).

The unique features of a site—its existing views, topography, vegetation, rock outcroppings, or water features—can enhance the user's experience as well (Wood, 2004). Sites with security issues, high traffic or noise, or problematic odors should be avoided (Goodman and Smith, 1992; Scaggs and Hawkins, 1994).

Municipal zoning plays a major role in the use of land, and often regulates every-thing from the size and use of buildings placed on a site, to the public utilities and services that the municipality will provide. "Zoning ordinances" dictate setbacks and easements, building heights, and densities, while "building codes" regulate other health, safety, and welfare issues (Scaggs and Hawkins, 1994; Spreiregen, 2004; Wood, 2004). Code issues include fire rating, egress requirements, and construction classifications (Heuer, 2004).

Zoning represents one method for controlling the way a new construction project will fit into the larger community; it is a means to protect the rights of surrounding property owners and taxpayers (Spreiregen, 2004; Wood, 2004). As such, zoning may dictate certain design types, especially where the site is adjacent to (or within) a recognized historic building or district. Zoning regulations also tend to distinguish single-family areas from denser multiunit dwelling areas, and to subdivide residential districts based on house size (Wood, 2004). This system has segregated the American population by income level, and often by age and ethnicity as well. It has fostered urban sprawl because our low-density residential districts are not located near the areas where we shop and work.

Our zoning models are shifting as more and more people recognize the value of fostering diverse experiences, services, and resident groups in American communities. Although long-term care facilities often provide housing to those with very specific needs, these buildings should be carefully woven into vibrant communities to gain from and contribute to social diversity. Long-term care facilities should welcome and accommodate visitors. They should be located and designed to provide residents with easy access to the outside world (including stores and services). To promote social interaction, many long-term facilities today offer classes, activities, and services that will appeal to residents of both the facility and the surrounding community. Some long-term care facilities even include child care facilities on-site.

Zoning is inherently tied to community perceptions, attitudes, and political clout because it primarily serves to protect the rights of surrounding property owners (Spreiregen, 2004; Wood, 2004). Gaining approvals will be easier in areas where the local community supports developing multiunit residences and health facilities (Gordon, 1998). By law, variance hearings, which are usually required for large-scale development such as a long-term care facility, must involve area citizens. As such, it is critically important to gauge community support for the project before investing large sums of time and effort.

Programming the Facility

The "building program" is a written description of expectations and requirements for the projected facility; it is best shaped by the owner's project coordinator under the direction of the architect with ample guidance from the owner's other consultants (Spreiregen, 2004). This program almost always includes functional descriptions, but it should also describe the character of the place to be built. Thus, it is good practice to open with a statement of intent, or general overview that conveys the desired psychological and social qualities of the place (Ballast, 1995; Purves, 2002). Overall, a good building program describes the pertinent needs and limitations of the project, conveys a comprehensive vision, and lists specific attributes that are necessary to achieve the owner's goals and the users' needs (Ballast, 1995).

The programming process provides an invaluable opportunity to investigate and describe various tangible and intangible qualities of the future design. Purves (2002) writes "There are many . . . guides to the management of design briefing which are logical, analytical and scientific in their approach to the problem." But he notes that these guides often omit the most critical aspect, failing to "build in the 'delight' factor. Time must be allocated to thinking about emotions, and discussing ideas, which must be encapsulated in a written document" (p. 120). Finding ways to address those aspects that will create the "spirit of the place" can help ensure that these qualities will not be overlooked during the technical periods of design. The program must do more than list functions, costs, and time schedules. It must promote meaning and protect the human and moral aspects of living in the facility.

Conclusion

Over the past century, American society has emphasized functional aspects in healthcare and in architectural design, but has recently begun to develop a more holistic way of thinking. In healthcare, the boundaries separating residential and medical offerings are blurring at an ever-increasing rate. The resultant hybridization allows individuals to select the grouping of provisions that best suits their personal needs. Their increasing ability to choose—coupled with their rising purchasing power—encourages competition, research, and development of new combinations, products, and services.

There is a growing insistence for attention to "quality of life" and "aging in place" by experts and citizens alike. The ethos of building is changing as we come to understand that the therapeutic benefits of good design are as important as flexibility and efficiency (Purves, 2002). As the bioethicist Turner (2002, p. 21) posits, "the way in which places are designed, built, and sustained over time has an important effect upon the moral, aesthetic, and spiritual lives of the inhabitants of these settings . . . [and] upon the kinds of moral experiences that occur in these settings." It is critically important that those who create and maintain healthcare environments understand these human aspects as well as the technical and scientific components of long-term care.

References

American Institute of Architects. (1997). AIA-B141 Standard Form of Agreement Between Owner and Architect. Contract Document.

Ballast, D. K. (1995). *Architectural Exam Review, Volume II: Nonstructural Topics* (3rd ed.). Belmont, CA: Professional Publications, Inc.

Bernard, S. L., Zimmerman, S., and Eckert, J. K. (2001). Aging in place. In S. Zimmerman, P. D. Sloane, and J. K. Eckert (Eds.), *Assisted Living: Needs, Practices, and Policies in Residential Care for the Elderly*. Baltimore, MD: Johns Hopkins University, pp. 224–241.

Cox, A. and Groves, P. (1990). *Hospitals and Health Care Facilities: A Design and Development Guide* (2nd ed.). Boston, MA: Butterworth Architecture.

Dover, V. (2006, July 21). *Draft Fort Monroe Reuse Concepts*. Dover, Kohl and Partners public presentation to the Hampton Federal Area Development Authority, Hampton, Virginia.

Eckert, K., Zimmerman, S., and Morgan, L. A. (2001). Connectedness in residential care: A qualitative perspective in the changing health care environment. In S. Zimmerman, P. D. Sloane, and J. K. Eckert (Eds.), *Assisted Living: Needs, Practices, and Policies in Residential Care for the Elderly*. Baltimore, MD: Johns Hopkins University, pp. 292–313.

Goldsmith, S. (2005). *Principle of Health Management Care: Compliance, Consumerism, and Accountability in the 21st Century*. Boston, MA: Jones and Bartlett.

Goodman, R. J. and Smith, D. G. (1992). *Retirement Facilities: Planning, Design, and Marketing*. New York: Whitney Library of Design.

Gordon, P. A. (1998). *Seniors' Housing and Care Facilities: Development, Business, and Operations* (3rd ed.). Washington: Urban Land Institute.

Heuer, C. R. (2004). *Construction Documents and Services 1*. Chicago, IL: Kaplan AEC Architecture.

Kobus, R. L. (2000). Perspective. In S. A. Kilment (Ed.), *Building Type Basics for Healthcare Facilities*. New York: Wiley, pp. 1–7.

Kornblut, A. (2004). *Construction Documents and Services 2*. Chicago, IL: Kaplan AEC Architecture.

Mollica, R. and Johnson-Lamarche, H. (2005, March 31). *State Residential Care and Assisted Living Policy: 2004*. National Academy for State Health Policy of the United States Department of Health and Human Services. Retrieved August 10, 2006, from http://aspe.hhs.gov/daltcp/reports/04alcom1.pdf.

Nursing Homes. (2005, July 25). Medicare: The Official U.S. Government Site for People with Medicare. Retrieved August 9, 2006, from http://www.medicare.gov/Nursing/Overview.asp.

Payette, T. M. (2000). Ambulatory care facilities. In S. A. Kilment (Ed.), *Building Type Basics for Healthcare Facilities*. New York: Wiley, pp. 193–240.

Pratt, J. R. (1999). *Long-Term Care: Management across the Continuum*. Gaithersburg, MD: Aspen Publishers.

Purves, G. (2002). *Healthy Living Centers: A Guide to Primary Health Care Design*. New York: Architectural Press.

Pynoos, J. (1987). Housing the aged: Public policy at the crossroads. In V. Regnier and J. Pynoos (Eds.), *Housing the Aged: Design Directives and Policy Considerations*. New York: Elsevier Science, pp. 25–40.

Pynoos, J. and Matsuoka, C. E. (1996). Housing. In C. J. Evashwick (Ed.), *The Continuum of Long-Term Care: An Integrated Systems Approach*. New York: Delmar Publishers.

Regnier, V. (2002). *Designing for Assisted Living: Guidelines for Housing the Physically and Mentally Frail*. New York: Wiley.

Regnier, V. A. (1994). *Assisted Living Housing for the Elderly*. New York: Wiley.

Scaggs, R. L. and Hawkins, H. R. (1994). Architecture for long-term care facilities. In S. B. Goldsmith (Ed.), *Essentials of Long-Term Care Administration*. Gaithersburg, MD: Aspen Publishers, pp. 254–280.

Shore, H. H. (1994). History of long-term care. In S. B. Goldsmith (Ed.), *Essentials of Long-Term Care Administration*. Gaithersburg, MD: Aspen Publishers, pp. 1–10.

Sloane, P. D., Zimmerman, S., and Walsh, J. F. (2001). The physical environment. In S. Zimmerman, P. D. Sloane, and J. K. Eckert (Eds.), *Assisted Living: Needs, Practices, and Policies in Residential Care for the Elderly*. Baltimore, MD: Johns Hopkins University, pp. 173–197.

Spreiregen, P. D. (2004). *Pre-Design. Volumes 1 and 2*. Chicago, IL: Kaplan AEC Architecture.

Turner, L. (2002). Medical facilities as moral worlds. *Journal of Medical Ethics: Medical Humanities, 28*, 19–22.

Vierck, E. and Hodges, K. (2003). *Aging: Demographics, Health, and Health Services*. Westport, CT: Greenwood.

Wood, P. H. (2004). *Site Design*. Chicago, IL: Kaplan AEC Architecture.

Zook, P. (2005). *Accessibility in Multi-Family Housing for Design Professionals*. Richmond, CA: Virginia Fair Housing Office.

POLICY MAKING AND FINANCING

Chapter 16

Long-Term Care Politics and Policy

William Weissert

Contents

Long-term care is not a subject Congress knows much about, and it tends to care about it even less. Nor have most presidents been cheerleaders for long-term care. Mostly, the making of policy within broad federal program guidelines is left to the states, the federal bureaucracy, and when they cannot agree, to the courts. Even when the Gulf of Mexico floodwaters pushed by Hurricane Katrina rose inexorably to drown some nursing home patients because evacuation plans were not implemented by various nursing home owners and public officials, there was little outrage and less policy change in response other than indictments of two hapless owners (www.cnn.com, 2005).

Long-term care policy is the policy of neglect. Somehow this does not seem to fit with our representative system of government, in which members of Congress hotly debate issues of great concern to their constituents and about which they feel a passionate thirst for good policy. Americans are dying in nursing homes of negligence, abuse, and policy indifference. Books have been written about the problem, exposing scandalous conditions approaching the level of outrage of the original muckrakers (Mendelson, 1974; Butler, 1975; Vladeck, 1980). Nursing homes rank near the bottom in surveys measuring perceptions of healthcare providers. Nearly three-quarters of the public think nursing homes do not have adequate staff. And nearly two-thirds say that the government inadequately regulates nursing home quality (Kaiser Public Opinion Spotlight, 2006). Yet elderly people are active voters. So why have policymakers not risen in anger over this abuse of a potentially important constituency?

This chapter argues that several factors contribute to this policymaking disconnect in a situation for which public policy is largely responsible as the primary payer for long-term care through the federal-state Medicaid program. Explanations lie at the heart of the way America makes policy. In this country, it is made through a pluralistic system of power shared by levels of government, impelled and constrained by the legacies of past policy choices, altered only when a mobilized committed constituency demands change, and very much shaped by organized private interests even in the face of constituent interests. Few policies succeed in the uphill struggle against powerful interest group opposition, and fewer still succeed when no interest group is pushing them. Exceptions prove the rule: only when a "policy entrepreneur"—a political leader with sufficient clout and skill—brings to bear concentrated and persistent pressure for change in a venue where policy is made, do neglected policies garner sufficient support to move from dormancy to deliberation and sometimes passage.

This chapter argues that long-term care has few of the necessary elements to motivate policy change and is compounded by the intractability of the underlying problems and lack of the solutions necessary to place problems on the public policy agenda. The key elements of policymaking addressed here are the very difficult nature of the problem, lack of solutions available, absence of mobilized constituents, dearth of reform-minded interest groups, the inexorability of path-dependent policy, and a lack of policy entrepreneurs available to lead the charge for change.

Barriers to Agenda Setting: Tough Problem, No Ready Solutions

Models of how the policy process works—what it takes to pass legislation—make it clear that political change occurs only when issues move to the public policy agenda. But for long-term care, the problem itself and a lack of ready solutions make that unlikely to happen very often. There is nothing easy about long-term care. The patients have used up most of their resources (physical, mental, social, and financial), and are frail and vulnerable. For many, their health status trajectory is downward, meaning that good quality care, if it were to be designed and delivered, could hope at best to improve only pain management, comfort, dignity, and privacy. It would do little more than slow the rate of decline. Many of the long-term care population's underlying health and disease problems are chronic or incurable with present technologies. Because so much of medical training is focused on curative interventions, too little attention is paid to finding better ways to manage chronic problems. The challenges are made more difficult by the multiplicity of diseases suffered by many long-term care patients and the large number of drugs, with multiple side effects, which many long-term care patients consume daily. Worse, the small numbers of patients in any given subgroup suffering a particular combination of diseases and conditions make research or even assessment of health status change difficult. Nor is the situation helped by the very limited state of our knowledge of the marginal benefits for marginal treatment investments in this population. Improvement of healthcare quality in general—even simple procedures to fix routine problems—has proven all but impossible in the years since the Institute of Medicine highlighted the often unsatisfactory nature of American healthcare delivery (Kohn et al., 1999). For the long-term care population, an equivalent systematic assessment has not even been written, let alone major solution options proffered.

Long-term care is also fragmented, moving from physicians' offices to hospitals, to care at home, to nursing homes, and around the loop again, with few consequences for failure and few rewards at any point along the way. There is also no good way to attribute success or failure to any set of providers because of the frequently long lapses between care and outcome. Staffs are poorly paid, often inadequately trained, often overburdened, and likely to change jobs frequently. Perhaps worst of all, states know that the surest way to cap their expenditures is to limit the construction of nursing home beds. Some states directly limit Medicaid payment amounts to discourage building of new beds. The result is that although nursing homes compete for private pay patients, they have no need to compete for those whose charges are paid by Medicaid. Facilities do not need to offer a better product to publicly supported patients.

In short, no one really knows how to fix long-term care, and no one seems ready to pay for a fix if one were found. From a political perspective, this problem's complexity and lack of ready solutions are deadly. When a window of opportunity opens in the policy process, something that occurs only rarely, three streams must intersect: a problem, a solution, and a receptive moment in the political venues where legislation is made—the White House and Congress (Kingdon, 1995). With no ready solution available—ideally one that has been around for a while and shaped by debate and compromise—even if events were to push long-term care onto the public policy agenda, an opportunity for legislation is not likely to lead to enactment.

Constituents

Constituents can be a force for policy change. For other causes, those with the most to gain from reform have organized themselves to demand it. Workers have traditionally organized to demand higher wages and better working conditions. Blacks mobilized for equal access to public transportation and housing, school integration, voting rights, and job opportunities. Gays and lesbians are insisting on equal protection and equal treatment in the institution of marriage and workplace benefits. People with disabilities have at least partially succeeded in pressing their case for job opportunities and public accommodations. Animal rights advocates have raised awareness to the special needs and high vulnerability of pets, animals used in medical testing, and even the plight of geese force-fed to fatten their livers for *pâté de foie gras*.

It is not just because old people are not politically active. Some are. And when they are, their grassroots lobbying has often worked. For example, elderly Chicago constituents of Dan Rostenkowski (powerful Ways and Means Committee chair in the late 1980s) left a senior center meeting to chase him down the block and across parking lots in their rage over his support of means-tested Medicare premium increases. This event made the evening news on all the three network channels and played a major role in causing Congress to reverse itself and repeal the Catastrophic Health Insurance Act, passed only a year earlier by a wide margin (Kollman, 1998). Two Florida congressmen received 75,000 pieces of mail opposing the new law (Kollman, 1998). Arizona Senator John McCain said, "Every Member of Congress was getting accosted at town meetings" (Kollman, 1998).

Baby boomers have money, political savvy, and a long history as a generation that gets what it wants. Why have long-term care users and their families not mobilized to get policy action? Two reasons explain the lack of an organized long-term care constituency. The first one is obvious: nursing home residents, even home care patients, are simply too disabled, often disoriented and functionally impaired, frequently too poor, and certainly too immobile to offer much hope of organized action. Among nursing home patients in particular, perhaps two-thirds suffer from dementia. Moreover, there are not very many institutionalized people at any given moment. Despite their impressive costs to Medicaid budgets, the fact that nearly half of all Americans spend some time in a nursing home (Murtaugh et al., 1997), and nearly 85 percent say that they have some experience with nursing homes directly or through a friend (Kaiser Public Opinion Spotlight, 2006), at any given time, nursing home patients still represent only about 5 percent of elderly Americans.

Numerous problems may also plague their families. Although daughters—the primary caregivers of frail elderly people (and to a lesser extent, sons)—could in theory mobilize to demand better treatment of their elders, the reality is that most caregivers are themselves beyond the age at which people are willing to take to the streets, sleep in parks, and participate in demonstrations. Moreover, no group is more overburdened than family caregivers of long-term care patients; they have enough to do already without expecting them to mobilize and march in the streets. Respite care was invented to give caregivers a rare break in an often unrelenting and isolated routine of caregiving that leaves little free time for even the most pressing problems.

It also appears that once their loved ones have passed away (most nursing home patients die within two or three years of admission), few family caregivers are much interested in involving themselves in long-term care reform issues. Thus, the potential for constituent mobilization seems to be hamstrung by small numbers, physical and mental limitations, caregiving burdens, and finally, the transient nature of the long-term care caregiver role.

Of course, political scientists have argued that it is not the broad geographically defined population of a congressman's district that defines his or her constituency on a given issue. Instead it is the "attentives" (Arnold, 1990), people within the district who are concerned about a particular issue. Unfortunately, the attentives for long-term care are likely to be the nursing home lobby and other narrow economic interests, discussed in the section titled Interest Groups. But first, the inertia of past policies must be considered.

Federalism and Path Dependency

Some political science theory suggests that policies tend to remain in their steady state unless some major upheaval occurs to change them (Pierson 2000). This description of policy is called "path dependency," the tendency of a policy once launched on a path to continue along that path unless a major force comes along to change it. The path for nursing home policy, and for that matter, home care policy as well, has long been state dominance, and since the mid-1960s, all but exclusively a state responsibility. Medicaid, the primary payer for nursing home residents, is regulated primarily by the states. Federal policy sets broad guidelines, but states make the important choices, especially the important budget-driven ones. Even when national policy is adopted, surveillance and enforcement is typically delegated to the states.

But state responsibility tends to mean tight budgets, very strong competition for resources from primary and secondary education, prisons, highways, and other state spending priorities, and very little willingness to raise taxes for social welfare improvements. Moreover, Medicaid is a poverty program. Why it should be that acute care (provided under Medicare) is a universal entitlement for elderly people, while public funding of long-term care is conditioned on abject poverty, is nothing short of an accident of history. The conditions set in place for Medicaid's treatment of the poor were never intended to be applied to institutionalized elderly people who had outlived their resources. It just happened that way when life expectancy stretched out the years of postemployment living from months or a few years to many years and often decades. Long-term care policy is now a derivative of poverty policy, funded by a program designed to pay for the healthcare needs of poor people, but twisted and adapted to support the end-of-life care of huge swaths of the population. As long as long-term care remains a state-federal responsibility, with leadership vested principally in the states, it will suffer only the most limited financing: Medicaid is always among the fastest growing components of state budgets despite cost-containment efforts. These funding constraints invariably breed the curse of very low quality expectations and little vision for improvement.

Interest Groups

Interest groups are an essential element of America's pluralistic form of government in which power is widely shared among formal representative bodies such as Congress and state legislatures, the courts, and private businesses interests, citizens' groups, and foundations. Without interest group pressure, few issues make it to the top of the policy agenda. Those that do rise to saliency as a result of disaster or crisis often do not get turned into legislation without a major interest group framing the issue, brokering deals to line up supporters, and dogging members and leaders in both the houses of Congress. When there is no active interest group supporting an issue, it tends to get caught at one of the many veto points that are purposely designed into the political system to limit the number of congressional enactments. Committees and subcommittees tend to work on one problem at a time. When an issue is pushed by a group, others must wait their turn, wait until the next Congress, or just keep waiting.

The New York Times (Rudoren and Pilhofer, 2006) recently reported an excellent example of the dramatic difference it can make when lobbyists become involved in a cause. Unable for years to win federal support of $15 million for a bridge-rebuilding project, the small town of Treasure Island, Florida, hired a lobbyist to achieve its goal. A few weeks later, he came back with $50 million for the project, more than triple of what had been asked for. Since that time, he has continued to win new federally funded projects for the town.

To be sure, there are a number of organizations interested in long-term care. But they come in two major types: economic interests and externality groups. The American Health Care Association (previously called the National Nursing Home Association), American Association of Homes and Services for Aging, the National Organization of Home Care, Alliance for Quality Nursing Home Care, National Hospice and Palliative Care Organization, and the Alabama Nursing Home Association represent the economic interests. Their efforts are focused on their own industry's well-being: improving reimbursement rates, stifling competition, relaxing regulatory burdens, and shielding themselves from tort liability. When they help themselves, only sometimes are nursing homes and home care patients assisted as well. For example, higher payments to nursing homes or home care agencies do not necessarily translate into more attentive care, better food, or cleaner and safer facilities. Indeed, considerable research shows that higher across-the-board Medicaid payment rates may actually reduce access for Medicaid patients because facilities may use the extra reimbursement to improve their appeal to private clients who pay more (Nyman, 1985).

One example is the Alliance for Quality Nursing Home Care, a coalition group organized in 2000 by 15 for-profit members of the nursing home industry's trade group, the American Health Care Association. Its members include HCR Manor Care, Sun Healthcare Group, Tandem Health Care, Kindred Healthcare, and Advocate Inc. According to the group's Web site, "Its founding members include the nation's 11 largest nursing home companies," whose operators support "reduced federal regulation—and the Republicans who promise it" (www.sourcewatch.com). Major system reform is not mentioned as a goal of the group.

However, externality groups seek benefits that do not accrue only to their members but to the larger society (e.g., the Sierra Club, the American Public Health Association, and AARP). Not many groups such as these exist on behalf of long-term care patients, far fewer, for example, than serve the interests of environmental concerns or even poor people generally. But how many groups does it take to achieve a particular end? If AARP is on the job, why is long-term care not a larger policy concern in Congress? The answer lies in the absolute necessity of successful lobbyists to set priorities, concentrate their efforts on "winnable" issues, and leverage support from other groups that can gain something for themselves.

Unfortunately for long-term care patients, AARP works on a broad range of issues as the champion of elderly people. Long-term care is only one of the group's many priorities (AARP, 2006), including Social Security, pensions, prescription drug coverage, health insurance, workplace age discrimination, and a host of other issues. It is also worth noting that for AARP, aging begins at 50. The group puts much of its effort into the concerns of those who have been called the "young-old" (not frail, not dependent), especially those who are middle class and are still important consumers. On long-term care at the federal level, AARP is often the dog that does not bark much. Although its staff pays more attention to long-term care than most groups do, and an entire chapter of its 2006 policy book is devoted entirely to long-term care reform proposals, for AARP the frail elderly population in nursing homes is seldom its primary focus (AARP, 2006). Indeed, AARP changed its name in 1998 as part of a major effort to recruit baby boomers into its ranks and rid itself of "retirement" in its name (AARP Woos Reluctant Boomers with a High-Priced Makeover, 2000).

The long-term care reforms it pushes often tend to be lobbied through its local chapters, on a state-by-state basis, and generally in the context of Medicaid. The latter is limited by spending constraints, low expectations, minimal popular awareness, and provider resistance to any reforms that would increase their costs or regulatory burdens. These initiatives are unlikely to succeed, including such AARP-endorsed proposals as social insurance for long-term care. Rarely does AARP make the all-out effort for long-term care that it did for Medicare drug coverage, although two-thirds of elders already had drug coverage before the Medicare Modernization Act was passed. However, most Americans have no good idea how they will pay for long-term care (Kaiser Public Opinion Spotlight, 2006). Moreover, AARP does list long-term care reform as fourth on its list of five items shown on its Web site (under "AARP on the Issues" the two reforms AARP advocates are long-term care insurance and consumer-directed at-home services—www.aarp.org/issues). That these two limited proposals could be supported by many Republicans may reflect the need for lobbying efforts to be directed at achievable goals during a Republican administration unlikely to support major regulatory reforms in nursing homes or home care.

In the final analysis, however, the reality is that a major effort on behalf of long-term care would be a bad investment of its resources for AARP. Leaving aside the concerns of some that the organization may be too focused on selling insurance and other products, AARP, like every other interest group, confronts a major flaw in the nature of organized interests: the free rider problem. Free riders are those people who benefit from a group's efforts, but do not join or buy its products. Focusing on the issues of importance to the young-old, and to some extent the well-heeled among them, makes sense because these individuals will pay membership dues, consume products, vote, and remain with the group for many years.

Interest groups rely on what are called solidarity and material benefits to control the free rider problem. Solidarity benefits relate to policy goals and improvements for the interest group and its members. Material benefits are items such as newsletters, magazines, and travel discounts. But neither of these is likely to be an effective membership incentive to a frail, very old population, many of whom are demented. Resources spent pursuing the interests of the very old group of Americans who make up the long-term care population would be unlikely to increase AARP's membership, dues receipts, or political clout. In the final analysis, AARP lacks many of the powerful tools used by economic interest groups. It has no political action committee (PAC) that can funnel campaign contributions from its membership to members of Congress on key committees and subcommittees. AARP can be very good at grassroots lobbying, and it has an excellent track record in its direct lobbying efforts with legislators and their staffs, the bureaucracy, state legislatures, and even local Medicaid agencies. But not having campaign contributions to offer deprives it of an important strategy that other groups competing for members' attention have available to them. AARP has little to offer, for example, in the biennial battles for legislative and congressional committee chairmanships, when much of the focus is on how much campaign money a member has been able to raise on behalf of other committee members. In the limited time and space available for agenda setting, deftly placed campaign contributions may just tip the scales. This may partly explain why every year physicians and hospitals, drug companies, the insurance industry, medical equipment suppliers, and a host of other health interests see their issues rise to the top of the congressional agenda while long-term care reform remains in the queue.

Another way to think about the important role of interest groups in dominating the political environment was offered by Wilson (1989). He categorized issues into a four-cell matrix representing the different kinds of politics associated with issues of different types. He labeled each one based on whom they benefited and who paid the costs. "Interest group" issues were those with competing interests, such as employers and labor unions fighting over minimum wage requirements and worker safety. Benefits to one group are costs to the other. Policies must be negotiated between the positions of the two groups, with every aspect of the issue not only raising the ire of one or the other group but also inducing politicians to pick sides.

"Client" issues are those like farm subsidies that concentrate benefits on farmers and food processors, causing them to closely follow policy changes and make sure that Congress keeps the issue at the top of its agenda. Although the costs are paid by taxpayers, the amounts are so small (only a few cents per person in tax increases) that most Americans pay little attention.

"Entrepreneurial" issues include nursing home regulations—they concentrate costs on an industry, giving its members incentives to mobilize, while bestowing benefits on a disorganized group of often vulnerable citizens. The industry will support legislators who oppose stronger rules (as the mission statement of the Alliance quoted earlier suggests), but there is a conspicuous lack of groups which will mobilize on the patients' side of the issue.

Finally, issues such as broad long-term care system reform are called "majoritarian" ones because they diffuse both costs and benefits to the large swath of society that will eventually need such care. But most people will not benefit from them sufficiently to mobilize broad support. President George Bush learned in 2005 just how difficult it is to mobilize citizens in favor of another majoritarian reform when he sought to enlist public and congressional support of the Social Security reform. These kinds of issues just do not appeal strongly enough to the average American to win many supporters.

Congressional Structure and the Critical Role of Policy Entrepreneurs

Congress is a large organization, and as such, suffers from all the problems of collective action typical of large groups. With 435 House members and 100 senators, all trying to get benefits for their districts, pursue their own notions of good public policy, and make their tries at moving up to leadership positions, the potential for chaos and disorder is profound. Without positive institutional controls, the classic dilemmas of collective action would lead to self-interested behavior: individualistic opportunism, broken promises, free riding, outright dishonesty, and little attention paid to the needs for expert information, conflict resolution, routine scheduling, staff sharing, and even regular order.

Like all successful large groups, Congress relies on its institutional powers to bring order from chaos. Members must be assured that if they promise their vote in exchange for another's vote on their different priorities, the commitment will be honored. They must know that if one member agrees to become an expert on complex issues such as Medicaid, others will learn about energy policy, defense weaponry, pharmaceutical regulation, etc. Moreover, each Congress adopts certain rules of behavior. Among the most important of these are election of a speaker, majority and minority leaders, and their assistants. They set the agenda for the group, assuring that if members will wait for their turn, their personal priorities will be taken up, that those who work to become experts will be rewarded with deference by others on their respective topics, and that members selected to handle the complex and powerful tasks of appropriations will channel money fairly and appropriately, not simply to their own districts. Congress does all this through rules, leaders, party control, and committee jurisdiction.

Those who care about healthcare policy volunteer to join the health committees and subcommittees and work hard to learn the complex details of the topic. The committees are endowed with power within their jurisdiction: any healthcare-related bill introduced will be directed to the health committee and will die or survive depending almost exclusively on its committee chair and members' preferences. Members not on the health committees cannot hold hearings on health bills. Only health committee members can participate in the closed-door markup sessions during which the legislators rewrite their bills. The health committee will likely be given deference when requesting a rule from the Rules Committee. The health committee chair will manage the bill on the House floor. Amendments offered by non-committee members will probably be rejected by the House majority in deference to the committee (Hall, 1992).

Throughout the process, subcommittees will wield more influence over issues in their jurisdiction than that of the full committee (Hall, 1992). Indeed, in subcommittees, for most issues, no more than a mere handful of members will hold much influence over any given issue. Charles Clapp reports that "less than half of committee's members regularly participated in its deliberations" (Hall, 1996, p. 23).

For example, John Manley found that for the Ways and Means Committee, "on many important issues a 'subgroup . . . sometimes as small as three individuals dominated the executive session deliberations'" (Hall, 1996, p. 23). Similarly, Lynette Perkins reported that "two-thirds of the House Judiciary Committee's membership were described by committee staff as not interested . . ." (Hall, 1996, p. 23).

In short, jurisdictional rules and party control are used by the House to make it function, resulting in dominance of its agenda on most issues by a small handful of members, sometimes one or two people. If no members are committed to an issue, it has no chance of getting on a subcommittee agenda, surviving markup, and making it through the rest of the congressional process in both chambers (the full committee, the Rules Committee, onto the speaker's agenda, House floor vote, the Senate, and the conference committee). After that, if it survives, it must go through the process again to be funded through an appropriations bill, or get tucked into a reconciliation act.

For all these reasons, if difficult, complex, neglected issues such as long-term care policy are to be reformed, the effort must be led by a policy entrepreneur (Kingdon, 1995). These are individuals who by passion, hard work, deft bartering, and most importantly, persistence, move an issue onto the agenda and push it through its many hurdles to become law. Typically, they hold some position that permits them to speak with authority. Examples include the president, speaker, majority leader, committee or subcommittee chair, and department secretary. They know how to negotiate and use their institution's rules and norms to make things happen; and they do the hard work that makes them an expert on a given topic.

Policy Entrepreneurs

Policy entrepreneurs for long-term care have been few and far between over many decades.

Senator Frank Moss (D-UT 1959–1977)

Nursing home quality assurance problems had begun to emerge long before Frank Moss moved the issue to the top of his legislative agenda in the mid-1960s to late 1970s. The Old Age Assistance provisions of the Social Security Act (Title I), which provided limited matching funds to states that offered assistance to their elderly citizens, predated his efforts by decades. That legislation permitted payments to individuals in private homes but not public poorhouses, the latter disdained for their abysmal conditions, and led to the expansion of what would become the nursing home industry (Congressional Research Service, 1972). This prohibition was removed in 1950 after advocacy by the Advisory Commission on Social Security (Congressional Research Service, 1972). Standard setting and enforcement were left to the states. Rampant problems were particularly well documented by the 1956 Commission on Chronic Illness, and a year later by the Council of State Governments, which synthesized a number of state reports (U.S. Senate, 1957). U.S. Public Health Service surveys validated these concerns, showing that states had few standards, limited enforcement, and little or no training or qualifications requirements for staff; nearly half of all skilled nursing beds did not even meet fire safety standards as late as 1960 (U.S. Department of Health, Education and Welfare, 1963). Congress responded by establishing the Senate Subcommittee on Problems of the Aged and Aging in 1959, which found that states feared that enforcement of standards would close most nursing homes. Six years later, the U.S. Public Health Service produced a manual of guidelines for nursing home licensure by the states (Congressional Research Service, 1972). The Senate next created the Special Committee on Aging in 1961, chaired by Utah Senator Frank Moss, who became famous for dressing himself in old clothes and checking into facilities to get firsthand exposure to conditions. His committee again confirmed weak enforcement and concern that it would lead to closure with nowhere to send residents. Moss pushed for the Medicare Extended Care Facility (ECF) as a substitute for skilled nursing homes. Of 6,000 applicants for ECF certification, only 740 could meet the standards; another 3,000 were given a provisional status called "substantial compliance" (Institute of Medicine, 1986). Nonetheless, Senator Moss pushed for yet higher quality requirements, and in 1967 led the fight for passage of Skilled Nursing Facility (SNF) standards for Medicare-certified facilities that did not meet them (Institute of Medicine, 1986). Implementing regulations, delayed by the Johnson administration, were later issued by the Nixon administration in 1969, but *sans* Intermediate Care Facility (ICF) standards. The Department of Health, Education and Welfare (DHEW) wrote and then declined to issue them for a number of reasons, including fear that they would weaken industry compliance with SNF requirements. Moss wanted enforcement: he mounted a series of hearings that stretched from 1969 to 1973 and produced reports that demonized and scandalized the nursing home industry for its poor quality of care (U.S. Senate, 1974). Over the course of these hearings—and with Moss's help—some of the scandals became front-page news, including the deaths of 32 Ohio nursing home residents and 36 Maryland residents caused by fire and food poisoning, respectively.

Moss also used the investigative powers of the congressional staff agency, the U.S. General Accounting Office (GAO). After auditing state facilities, it found that Medicaid was not enforcing its own ICF standards that required the states to certify facilities as a condition for the receipt of Medicaid funds. In addition, the Senate Finance Committee found that states were certifying facilities as ICFs without their inspecting them (U.S. Senate, 1974). Because of the Moss hearings, "substantial compliance" was dropped as a certification standard.

The Nixon administration responded to the furor that Moss, the fires, and the salmonella contamination had created in 1971 with two major speeches. The president condemned nursing home conditions and asked Congress to approve an eight-point initiative aimed at increased DHEW enforcement staff, state surveyor training, establishment of a nursing home ombudsman program, creation of an Office of Nursing Home Affairs in DHEW, and a "comprehensive study of federal long-term care policies" (U.S. Senate, 1974, p. 244). A year later, Congress included many of these initiatives as part of its Social Security Act Amendments (redefining ECFs as SNFs, unifying Medicare and Medicaid SNF standards, and raising some standards, but lowering others).

In 1974, new ICF standards were adopted for the Medicaid program. Efforts in the DHEW office of Nursing Home Affairs shifted to developing standards for patient evaluation to include as a part of the certification survey process that previously had been overly facility focused. Competing evaluation instruments, industry opposition to compliance costs, and a new focus added late in the Carter administration on "residents' rights" slowed publication of the survey instrument and procedures until 1980. When the Reagan administration came into office, it immediately rescinded the new rules.

As Baumgartner and Jones (1993) predicted, although the issue cycle that Moss helped start was over and long-term care had fallen off the agenda, institutional changes spawned by his efforts persisted and added to the momentum when the issue was put back on the agenda years later. As will be shown, the Institute of Medicine took up the long-term care issue at the behest of another policy entrepreneur, Henry Waxman, D-CA.

Congressman Claude Pepper (D-FL 1948–1989)

An advocate for vulnerable populations, the working person, and the little guy throughout his very long public career, and for elderly people during at least the last two decades of it, Claude Pepper predicted what would happen if Congress failed to spend money on elderly and other needy groups. He told *Time* magazine in 1986, "I would rather live with $200 billion deficits and have more people living, than the reverse. And if we don't spend the money fighting cancer and arthritis and poverty and poor housing and all the rest, they'll just spend it on the military or something else" (Fessler, 1989).

From his chairmanship of the House Aging Committee, Pepper could do little more than hold hearings, toss bills into the hopper, and challenge his colleagues to do more for elderly people. His committee had no legislative authority and at times may have undercut its credibility with press releases, including one which claimed that large increases in pet food sales were perhaps because some elderly people were forced to eat it.

When he chaired the powerful Rules Committee, the broad range of concerns of that committee and the practical needs of his party to pass legislation forced him into compromises. Yet he would have forced a Medicare long-term care coverage amendment onto the ill-fated Catastrophic Health Insurance Act of 1988, had the Democratic Speaker of the House, Jim Wright (Texas), not promised him a direct floor vote on a separate bill, bypassing the recalcitrant House Commerce

Committee. When it was eventually brought to the floor and voted on, he lost; John Dingell (D-MI) vehemently opposed the measure on grounds that his committee's jurisdictional rights had been violated.

Pepper next seized on the renewal of the Older Americans Act to attach an amendment that would broadly cover home care services for people requiring assistance with activities of daily living. (Critics complained that it was so broadly written that it would cover all children who needed help dressing and using the toilet—Rovner, 1987.) The program would have been financed by removal of the cap on earnings to which Medicare taxes are applied. This would have raised an estimated $30 billion, possibly enough to cover the $20–40 billion cost of the Pepper home care bill. Again, Pepper tried to end-run the jurisdiction of the Ways and Means and Commerce committees, incurring their wrath. He did get the bill out of his Rules Committee with a favorable rule. "When you own the umpire, chances are you're going to win the ball game," growled Ways and Means Committee Chair Dan Rostenkowski (D-IL) (Rovner, 1987). Ultimately, however, Pepper was again defeated on the House floor amid concerns about both the procedural violations and the looming budget deficit, which the Democrats were committed to reducing (Rovner, 1987).

Pepper was also a critical factor in the formation of the 1989 congressional "Pepper Commission," charged with solving both long-term care issues and problems related to people lacking healthcare coverage. But alas, commissions are a favorite way Congress has of pushing real problems with no easy solutions off the agenda while taking credit for having done something. The Pepper Commission offered a proposal that outlined a detailed coverage plan with no budget attached (later estimated to cost $66 billion). Everyone (rightly as it later turned out) assumed that the cost would be too high to get a serious hearing in Congress. The commission disbanded, the report was ignored, and when Congressman Pepper died in 1989, the House abolished its Aging Committee altogether. The House Rules Committee was eventually taken over by a conservative Republican whose primary concern was agriculture policy. Nonetheless, at Pepper's death, colleagues acknowledged his earnest and important appeal on behalf of the nation's neglected populations: "He was a giant," one colleague observed (Fessler, 1989).

Congressman Henry Waxman (D-CA 1975–)

President Ronald Reagan's policy choices were not intentionally friendly to long-term care. His top priority for Medicaid was to cap spending, but his efforts were eventually turned inside out by Congressman Henry Waxman. After rescinding the Carter administration's nursing home reform regulations, the Reagan administration's attempts to modify and weaken the rules ran into fierce congressional opposition. To quell the anger, Department of Health and Human Services (DHHS) Secretary Richard Schweiker withdrew the effort as well. He suggested changes in survey procedures that would have permitted some nursing homes to have less frequent evaluations. In response, Congressman Waxman proposed a moratorium on any modifications to nursing home regulation until the Institute of Medicine did a study of nursing home quality. Not only did he achieve the study but its 1986 report also led to the important 1987 and 1989 nursing home reforms that he authored (Institute of Medicine, 1986).

Although the 1980 Omnibus Reconciliation Act was the centerpiece of the Reagan administration's efforts to shrink the size and regulatory prowess of the federal government, Congressman Waxman, chair of the Health and Environment Subcommittee of the House Commerce Committee—a position he held for nearly 24 years—used the same legislation for his own purposes: he wrote the Social Security Amendments that added Section 1915(c), authorizing home- and community-based care demonstration projects under Medicaid. These have been used over the subsequent decades to substantially expand Medicaid services for home and community care. Waxman also authored long-term care coverage improvements in the short-lived Medicare Catastrophic Healthcare Act of 1988 that was repealed the following year.

Since the Republicans took control of the House in 1994, and he lost his chairmanship, he has been seriously constrained by his minority status in the House and on the Commerce Committee and its Health and Environment Subcommittee. No Republican subcommittee chair has stepped up to take on his limited role as a policy entrepreneur on behalf of long-term care. Indeed, under Republican leadership, the issue did not even get listed in the Health and Environment Subcommittee's priority list. Nonetheless, even from his minority assignment on the Government Operations Committee, where he also serves, Waxman has been able to initiate investigations by the Government Accountability Office (formerly General Accounting Office) and House minority staff that have exposed long-term care abuses.

Other Advocates

In the Senate, both Senator Edward Kennedy (D-MA) and later, Senator Jay Rockefeller (D-WV) have at times pressed for long-term care issues. But both men have a broad range of interests, and in their minority party status have had few opportunities to push for new initiatives. For instance, although Senator Rockefeller previously chaired the Senate Long-Term Care Subcommittee for several years, he lost interest in the topic by 2003.

The Senate Aging Committee, chaired by Gordon Smith (R-OR), did not even list long-term care on its Web site's "issues" page this year, although the committee did hold a hearing on financing long-term care. The committee chair also sent a letter to Centers for Medicare and Medicaid Services (CMS) protesting regulatory changes that would prohibit states from continuing their long-time practice of maximizing their federal cost-sharing contributions for Medicaid. Senator Smith's interests in long-term care reform have been rather limited, as indicated in his statement to the committee when it opened hearings in March 2006. To solve the pending long-term care financing problem facing the baby boomers, he advocated incentives to induce greater purchase of long-term care insurance (Smith, 2006). Yet most experts regard long-term care insurance as a solution available only to the few who can afford to pay the costly premiums. Senator Smith also introduced the Long-Term Care Trust Account Act of 2006.

Republicans have not typically championed reforms that would increase Medicaid spending and they are even less likely to suggest that Medicare takes over responsibility for funding long-term care. That they enacted prescription drug coverage was surprising; some observers suggest that they had to do so only to take the issue away from the Democrats. Because long-term care has little or no prominence in the Democratic Party's agenda either, it is unlikely to be a major political concern in the foreseeable future. Nonetheless, very important and ultimately expansionary changes in long-term care policy have taken place during Republican administrations. Whatever his motives, President Reagan did not veto the 1980 Omnibus Reconciliation Act despite its inclusion of the expansionary home- and community-based waiver program. More recently, two Republican Department of Health and Human Services (DHHS) secretaries have greatly enlarged that program.

Former Republican Wisconsin Governor Tommy Thompson used waivers to gain national attention for his welfare reform program, and as DHHS secretary he led the charge for greater use of them under Medicaid. He endorsed broad changes in their scope, permitting states to revise service delivery systems and payment methods as well as introduce patient copays. As a result, home- and community-based waivers eventually increased from 227 (in 2000) to 252 (in 2002 and 2005) (Kitchener et al., 2005).

Thompson was followed into DHHS by an equally fervent fan of individualized care choices, former Bush White House staffer and the then Food and Drug Administration (FDA) Commissioner Mark McClellan, who believed in vouchers to permit disabled individuals to make their own choices as long-term care consumers. Secretary McClellan had also supported the legislative changes in waiver authority included in the Deficit Reduction Act (DRA) of 2005, signed by President George W. Bush on February 8, 2006. The law contains six chapters and 39 sections devoted to Medicaid. Among them, the new law allows states to offer home- and community-based care and self-directed personal care services without a waiver, allowing states to include these as optional services in their state plans. Importantly, for the states, home- and community-based services can be provided to a predetermined number of recipients, essentially capping the program and assuring states more fiscal control than if the services were guaranteed to all those eligible. States can now also tighten the medical standards for admission to institutions and refine eligibility for home- and community-based waiver services (HCBS) on their own.

Many ideas that found their way partially or completely into the DRA came from the other broad set of entrepreneurs for long-term care reform, the nation's states (Weissert and Weissert, 2002). The National Governors Association (NGA), the

National Conference of State Legislatures (NCSL), individual governors, Medicaid directors, and others who are responsible for Medicaid, push ideas that can become state programs; many of them are eventually adopted by Medicaid as broad national policy. The DHHS office of the Assistant Secretary for Planning and Evaluation—the major policy design office within DHHS—compiled a summary of recent proposals that had been considered for inclusion in the DRA, noting their source and the extent to which they wound up in the law (Medicaid Commission Staff, 2006). A number of the proposals came from the states' associations, NGA, NCSL, and other groups, ranging from the Heritage Foundation to a Michigan consulting firm that works with Medicaid programs around the country (Health Management Associates). The proposals were new to the 2005 DRA, but they represent a long history of healthcare innovations by the states related to long-term care, Medicaid quality and information technology, and program administration (Medicaid Commission Staff, 2006). Ideas generated locally have proven useful over the years for reforms in long-term care payment policy, eligibility expansions and implementation, alternative service settings, the development of home care options, case management, and ombudsman programs. Although the changes are incremental, they are often innovative.

Some of the most important developments at the state level have been in HCBS, implemented by the states under Section 1915(c), authored in 1981 by Congressman Waxman. Nominally intended to save costs and make long-term care more efficient (which they do not), these programs have grown from their original demonstration project status to broad, nearly permanent expansions of the Medicaid program (Weissert, 1981; Weissert, 1985; Weissert et al., 1988; Weissert and Hedrick, 1994; Weissert et al., 2001; Weissert et al., 2003). Clients range from people who are elderly and disabled or developmentally disabled to those with mental illness or chronic brain disorders. Many services are included: acute and posthospital home care visits, personal care, aid and attendant care, foster care, chore services, friendly visits, and more. After a slow start in 1981, with half a dozen programs in as many states, by 2002 there were 252 programs, at least some functioning in every state, at a total cost of over $17 billion annually (State Health Facts, 2006). These programs have expanded steadily, with little or no congressional involvement, and once approved by DHHS, they receive only the most minimal (or nonexistent) oversight (U.S. Government Accounting Office, 2003). The DRA expanded waiver authority even further, converting most of the waivers to optional services under Medicaid. Thus, states can now adopt them without filing a special application. Again, they were adopted as a cost-saving strategy, intended to improve program efficiency by giving the states more control, the opportunity to place more responsibility on individual patients to pay their own bills, and generally relaxing further the already limited role of DHHS in protecting patients from restrictive state fiscal policies.

A related development is expansion of the so-called consumer-directed care. These programs permit would-be home care clients to hire and supervise their own home care workers, using a voucher. Some programs offer case management supervision to support the client-purchaser. Given their inherent expectation for consumer sovereignty, however, they tend to be an option only for disabled clients—or their families—capable of rendering such decisions. An additional concern should be the quality of services in home care settings. Enforcement of standards has long been a challenge in congregate housing and nursing homes. Inspecting the quality of services in each and every house is an even greater problem.

Nonetheless, there is no denying that states are the engines of innovation in long-term care as in other aspects of public policy, an important legacy of our federal system. As DRA 2005 further frees them to try out their own plans, new ideas may emerge (Kane et al., 2004).

Conclusion

Long-term care is a technically difficult problem with no ready solutions. Constituents tend to be frail, often immobile, and most importantly, transient. There are few effective interest groups for the clients of long-term care, and those that do exist are preoccupied with their own limited concerns. The legacy of past long-term care policy has condemned it to treatment as poverty policy, dependent on constrained state budget. At the national level, long-term care tends to be at the bottom of congressional committee agendas. The dearth of policy entrepreneurs interested in the topic contributes to its neglect as well.

Yet some reforms have occurred, and in every case a policy entrepreneur led the charge. What motivated them was not obvious, although the usual suspects—sense of good policy, desire to get ahead in the House or Senate, take credit back home for good policy, and reelection payoff potential—all contributed. What has to happen for the nation to see the next modest round of long-term care improvements is for policy entrepreneurs (chair of a committee, secretary of DHHS, vice president, or first lady) to take on the issue and make it their *cause célèbre*. The history briefly recapped here, the complex nature of the problem, and the organizational structure of Congress suggest that success is likely to come from a legislative policy entrepreneur, and most probably a Democrat. Items on the agenda could include improved training of nursing home aides, strengthening state inspections of nursing homes, and federal oversight of regulatory compliance. Other possibilities include expansion of nursing home ombudsman programs, increased home care and design of innovative ways to monitor quality of care delivered there, and payment systems that encourage efforts to achieve maximum outcome potential for all clients (Kane et al., 2004). Or perhaps reform will come on cat's feet, as home care has experienced, quietly expanding as state-by-state policy makers try to respond to the needs of their most vulnerable populations within budgets constrained by economic cycles and competing demands. Indeed, state innovations may be most likely because, for the most part, long-term care remains both the poor stepchild of state policy making and a product of congressional neglect.

References

AARP Woos Reluctant Boomers With A High-Priced Makeover. 2000. *American Demographics* (September). InfoTrac OneFile. Thomson Gale.

AARP. 2006. The Policy Book: AARP Public Policies 2006. Available at http://www.aarp.org/issues/policies/policy_book. Downloaded October 3, 2006.

Arnold, D. R. 1990. *The Logic of Congressional Action.* New Haven, CT: Yale University Press.

Baumgartner, F. and B. Jones. 1993. *Agendas and Instability in American Politics.* Chicago, IL: University of Chicago Press.

Butler, R. N. 1975. *Why Survive: Being Old in America.* San Francisco, CA: Harper & Row.

Congressional Research Service. 1972. *Nursing Homes and the Congress: A Brief History of Developments and Issues.* Washington: Library of Congress.

Fessler, P. 1989. Florida's unabashed Liberal Left 41-year mark on hill. *CQ Weekly* (June 3). p. 1298.

Hall, R. L. 1992. Measuring legislative influence. *Legislative Studies Quarterly.* 17(2): 205–231.

Hall, R. 1996. *Participation in Congress.* Ann Arbor, MI: University of Michigan Press. http://find.galegroup.com.proxy.lib.umich.edu. Downloaded October 9, 2006.

Institute of Medicine. 1986. *Improving the Quality of Care in Nursing Homes.* Washington: National Academy Press, p. 241.

Kaiser Public Opinion Spotlight. 2006. The Public's Views on Long-Term Care. Updated June 2005. www.kff.org. Downloaded October 3, 2006.

Kane, R. L., B. Bershadsky, R. A. Kane, H. H. Degenholtz, J. (Jason) Liu K. Giles, and K. C. Kling. 2004. Using resident reports of quality of life to distinguish among nursing homes. *The Gerontologist.* 44: 624–632.

Kingdon, J. 1995. *Agendas, Alternatives, and Public Policy.* 2nd ed. New York: Harper Collins.

Kitchener, M., T. Ng, N. Miller, and C. Harrington. 2005. Medicaid home and community-based services: national program trends. *Health Affairs.* 24(1): 206–212.

Kohn, L. T., J. M. Corrigan, and M. S. Donaldson (Eds.). 1999. *Committee on Quality of Health Care in America, Institute of Medicine.* Washington: National Academy Press.

Kollman, K. 1998. *Outside Lobbying.* Public Opinion and Interest Group. Strategies, Princeton, NJ: Princeton University Press.

Medicaid Commission Staff. 2006. *Medicaid Reform Proposals Summaries.* Washington. http://www.hhs.gov/medicaid/. Downloaded October 10, 2006.

Mendelson, M. A. 1974. *Tender Loving Greed: How the Incredibly Lucrative Nursing Home "Industry" Is Exploiting America's Old People and Defrauding Us All.* Vancouver, WA: Vintage Books.

Murtaugh, C., P. Kemper, B. Spillman, and B. Carlson. 1997. The amount, distribution, and timing of lifetime nursing home use. *Medical Care.* 35(3): 204–218.

Nyman, J. A. 1985. Prospective and "cost-plus" Medicaid reimbursement, excess demand, and the quality of nursing home care. *Journal of Health Economics.* 4(3): 237.

Pierson, P. 2000. Increasing returns, path dependence, and the study of politics. *American Political Science Review.* 94(2): 251–267.

Rovner, J. 1987. Pepper wins a round on long-term care bill. *CQ Weekly* (November 21). p. 2874.

Rudoren, J. and A. Pilhofer. 2006. Hiring federal lobbyists, towns learn money talks. *The New York Times.* July 2. www.nytimes.com.

Smith, G. H. 2006. Long-Term Care Financing: Are Americans Prepared? Statement of Chairman Gordon H. Smith. U.S. Senate Special Committee on Aging. March 9.

State Health Facts. 2006. Kaiser Family Foundation. www.statehealthfacts.org. Downloaded October 3.

U.S. Department of Health, Education and Welfare. 1963. Nursing Home Standards Guide: Recommendations Relating to Standards for Establishing, Maintaining, and Operating Nursing Homes. Public Health Service, Division of Chronic Diseases, Nursing Homes and Related Facilities Program.

U.S. Government Accounting Office. 2003. Federal Oversight of Growing Medicaid Home and Community-Based Waivers Should Be Strengthened. GAO-03-576.

U.S. Senate. 1957. Recommendations of the commission on chronic illness on the care of the long-term patient. In *Studies of the Aged and Aging.* Vol. 1, November. Committee on Labor and Public Welfare. Washington: Government Printing Office, pp. 275–309.

U.S. Senate. 1974. Nursing Home Care in the United States: Failure in Public Policy. An Introductory Report. Senate Report No. 93-1420, 93rd Congress, 2nd Session, December 19. Subcommittee on Long-Term Care, Special Committee on Aging.

Vladeck, B. C. 1980. *Unloving Care: The Nursing Home Tragedy.* New York: Basic Books.

Weissert, W. 1981. Toward a continuum of care for the elderly: a note of caution. *Public Policy.* 29(33): 331–340.

Weissert, W. 1985. Seven reasons why it is so difficult to make home and community based long-term care cost-effective. *Health Services Research.* 20(4): 423–433.

Weissert, W., M. Chernew, and R. Hirth. 2001. Beyond managed long-term care: paying for home care based upon risks of adverse outcomes. *Health Affairs.* 20(3): 172–180.

Weissert, W., M. Chernew, and R. Hirth. 2003. Titrating versus targeting home care services to frail elderly clients: an application of agency theory and cost-benefit analysis to home care policy. *Journal of Aging and Health.* 15(1): 99–123.

Weissert, W., C. M. Cready, and J. E. Pawelak. 1988. The past and future of home and community based long-term care. *The Milbank Quarterly.* 66(2): 309–388.

Weissert, W. and S. C. Hedrick. 1994. Lessons learned from research on effects of community-based long-term care. *Journal of the American Geriatrics Society.* 42(345): 348–353.

Weissert, C. and W. Weissert. 2002. Table 5.6, Some state innovations in health policy, 1965–2000. *Governing Health: The Politics of Health Policy.* Baltimore, MD: Johns Hopkins University Press, p. 277.

Wilson, J. Q. 1989. *Bureaucracy: What Government Agencies Do and Why They Do It.* New York: Basic Books.

www.cnn.com. 2005. Nursing Home Owners Face Charges. September 13. Downloaded October 8, 2006.

www.sourcewatch.org. Accessed December 24, 2006.

Chapter 17

Geriatric Mental Health Policy: Impact on Service Delivery and Directions for Effecting Change*

Bradley E. Karlin and Michael Duffy

Contents

* *Professional Psychology: Research and Practice.* Copyright 2008 by the American Psychological Association, 35(5), 509–519, 2004. Reproduced with permission.

The mental health needs of the nation's geriatric population (defined here as individuals age 65 years and older) have been significantly neglected. This longstanding neglect has contributed to the enduring underuse of mental health services by older adults and has resulted in a service delivery system unable to adequately respond to mentally ill elderly persons. Over the next couple of decades, the need for mental health treatment by older adults will become even greater in light of evidence of increased prevalence of mental disorders in future elderly cohorts (Gfroerer, Penne, Pemberton, & Folsom, 2002) and anticipated demographic changes in this country and in nations abroad. Because of increases in life expectancy and the aging of the baby boom generation, the number of Americans age 65 or older is expected to double by the year 2030 (U.S. Department of Health and Human Services, 1999).

Unfortunately, little has been done to address enduring barriers and new challenges to service access and availability. Psychologists and others have lacked critical knowledge and advocacy acumen necessary to promote substantive change. This article provides a more complete knowledge base of the barriers to the use and provision of mental health services for older adults, identifying the significant but previously neglected role of regulatory policies and administrative practices in inhibiting service use and provision. These factors, although the least understood and recognized by psychologists, researchers, and laypersons, are also the very factors on which psychologists and the public can have the most potential influence. This article then examines several recent legislative proposals and regulatory developments that offer potential for advancing the field of clinical geropsychology, while addressing the importance of advocacy on legislative agenda setting and policy enactment. Last, the article provides several proposals and directions at various levels for improving geriatric mental health care delivery.

Enduring Underuse

For years, the rates at which older adults have received mental health services in this nation have been strikingly low, particularly in the outpatient sector. Data from the Epidemiological Catchment Area (ECA) Program conducted in the early 1980s revealed that 4.2% of young–old (65–74 years) and 1.4% of old–old (75 years) individuals received any mental health treatment compared with 8.7% of younger (18–64 years) adults (German, Shapiro, & Skinner, 1985). Older adults were even less likely than their younger counterparts to use specialty mental health services. Only 0.3% of young–old and no old–old respondents visited a mental health specialist, whereas 4.1% of younger adults saw a specialty mental health provider. Moreover, elderly individuals have been found to receive only 2.7% to 4.0% of clinical services rendered by private-sector psychologists and psychiatrists (Swan & McCall, 1987; VandenBos, Stapp, & Kilburg, 1981). Underuse is even more profound in rural regions (Durenberger, 1989; Stefl & Prosperi, 1985).

In the public sector, underuse of mental health services by elderly individuals is just as dire, even though the public mental health care system has been specifically charged by the U.S. Congress with targeting the mental health needs of older adults. Several studies conducted in the 1970s and 1980s consistently found older adults to constitute between 4% and 6% of community mental health center (CMHC) consumers (Flemming, Buchanan, Santos, & Rickards, 1984; General Accounting Office, 1982; Goldstrom et al., 1987; Redick, Kramer, & Taube, 1973).

Unfortunately, contrary to social, political, and professional developments that portend a recent increase in mental health care use by older adults, including greater understanding of mental health and aging, increased Medicare coverage of mental health services, the recognition of psychologists as independent providers pursuant to the Omnibus Budget Reconciliation Act of 1989 (Sherman, 1996), and the development of empirically validated geropsychological treatments (Gatz et al., 1998), substantial underuse remains. A recent study examining service use and delivery throughout the Texas public mental health care system found that only 5% of adults beginning mental health treatment at CMHCs in Texas in 1999 were 60 years old or older, though that age cohort represents one quarter of the state adult population (Karlin & Norris, 2001). Demmler (1998) similarly found that older adults continue to use outpatient specialty mental health services at disproportionately low rates.

Previously Identified Barriers to Mental Health Services for Older Adults

The limited use of mental health services by older adults is not due to lack of mental health need. Conservative estimates are that 12% of community-dwelling individuals age 65 or older suffer from one or more clinically diagnosable mental disorders (Gatz, Kasl-Godley, & Karel, 1996; Regier et al., 1988). Recent reports on mental illness released by the U.S. Surgeon General (U.S. Department of Health & Human Services, 1999) and the U.S. Administration on Aging (2001) have estimated that approximately 20% of younger and older Americans suffer from mental disorders. Rates of subclinical emotional disturbances (particularly depression and anxiety) have been found to be considerably higher and often greater than the corresponding rates in younger adults (Blazer & Williams, 1980; Himmelfarb & Murrell, 1984; Mc-Kegney, Aronson, & Ooi, 1988). Furthermore, the prevalence of psychopathology in nursing home residents, who are among the least likely to receive mental health care (Burns et al., 1993; Lombardo, 1994), is between 65% and 90% (Lair & Lefkowitz, 1990; German, Rovner, Bertner, & Brant, 1992).

Over the last couple decades, various dynamics implicating individual, system, and policy domains have been cited as contributing to the disproportionately low use of mental health services by the nation's geriatric population. These barriers include stigma toward geriatric mental health held by professionals and the public

(Gaitz, 1974; Lasoski, 1986), physicians' underdetection of psychopathology in older adults (Gatz & Smyer, 1992), the medical community's overreliance on pharmacotherapy with older patients (Kisely, Linden, Bellantuono, Simon, & Jones, 2000), physicians' low referral rates of older patients for psychotherapy (Alvidrez & Areán, 2002) and limited confidence in the efficacy of geropsychological treatments (Mackenzie, Gekoski, & Knox, 1999), a shortage of geropsychology professionals (Halpain, Harris, McClure, & Jeste, 1999), older adults' limited knowledge of mental health and mental health services (Yang & Jackson, 1998), and restrictive legislative policies, namely limited Medicare mental health reimbursement (Sherman, 1996).

Although these obstacles are significant, they only paint part of the picture. In addition to the foregoing barriers, discriminatory regulatory policies and administrative practices have considerably restricted Medicare beneficiaries from receiving, and practitioners from providing, mental health treatment. In fact, it is in the regulatory arena where some of the most considerable constraints to the practice and provision of geriatric mental health care lie. At the same time, the nature and scope of regulatory and administrative policies and practices, and the processes underlying their development and revision, have been neglected in the extant literature. These factors are examined below.

The Role of Regulatory and Administrative Barriers

Restrictive Local Medical Review Policies

The Health Care Financing Administration (HCFA), recently renamed the Centers for Medicare and Medicaid Services (CMS) as part of an effort to improve the agency's image (Centers for Medicare and Medicaid Services, 2001b), is the regulatory body responsible for managing the Medicare program. In implementing the Medicare mental health benefit, HCFA and its contractors have restricted psychological services for older adults through inconsistent and limited reimbursement of claims and, in many cases, through outright preclusion of appropriate services. CMS administers the Medicare program by contracting with private insurance companies, known as Medicare carriers and intermediaries. (A list of Medicare carriers and intermediaries by state is available at www.cms.hhs.gov/contacts.) Part A (hospital insurance) claims for mental health services are processed by intermediaries. Part B (physician and outpatient medical insurance) claims for mental health services are processed by carriers. There are 10 CMS regional offices that oversee carriers and intermediaries. (A list of CMS regional offices and their respective jurisdictions is available at www.cms.hhs.gov/about/regions/professionals.asp.) Medicare carriers administer outpatient mental health care claims. Through their medical directors, carriers develop policies for what is "medically necessary," which is required for a service to be covered by Medicare. These policies are known as "local medical review policies" (LMRPs). Coverage decisions are based on a specific carrier's LMRP, which must be consistent with clinical science and standard practice (Centers for Medicare and Medicaid Services, 2003).

Many psychologists, because of overly restrictive LMRPs or narrow interpretations thereof, have been denied coverage for services. Moreover, because of the decentralized nature of the regulatory system, it is not uncommon for a psychologist in one state to be denied reimbursement for a claim whereas a psychologist elsewhere receives reimbursement for the identical service provided in the same context.

Furthermore, a review of carrier LMRPs by the first author revealed that several carriers do not have guidelines addressing the provision of psychological services in nursing homes, leaving psychologists in the dark. The silence of many LMRPs on this issue renders psychologists vulnerable to claims denials and with limited recourse to appeal. Moreover, a recent report by the Office of the Inspector General (OIG) of the Department of Health and Human Services found that several carriers had no LMRPs for mental health services (U.S. Department of Health and Human Services, 2002). Furthermore, some LMRPs that included provisions for mental health services lacked sufficient detail and specificity, and documentation requirements for psychotherapy and medication management were often limited and inconsistent.

Medicare–Medicaid Crossover Restrictions

Indigent older adults are eligible for both Medicare (government health insurance for the elderly) and Medicaid (government health insurance for indigent persons). These individuals, also known as "dually eligibles" or "crossover" patients, have typically been able to receive psychological services under Medicare and would not be responsible for Medicare deductibles and copayments (usually 50% for outpatient psychological treatment), which would be covered by Medicaid. However, in an effort to curtail spending during the sluggish economy, many states have recently restricted or limited Medicaid crossover payments for psychological services (Nelson, 2002). Consequently, copayments have been left unpaid, and many indigent older adults are not able to receive mental health treatment.

Nursing Home Quality-Indicator Exclusion of Psychotherapy

The provision of psychological services in nursing homes is further limited by the process used by the federal government to assess the level of quality of care in skilled nursing facilities. The quality of care provided by nursing homes is assessed using 24 quality indicators (QIs) that are based on the Minimum Data Set (MDS), which contain data from mandatory quarterly resident assessments. The QI related to the treatment of depression (QI 5) provides an incentive for nursing homes to treat depressive symptomatology with pharmacological means and discourages the use of psychotherapy. QI 5 considers only medication as antidepressant therapy. Thus, a nursing home resident receiving psychotherapy but not medication would be considered "without antidepressant therapy," according to the indicator. Nursing homes, wishing not to be marked as deficient in its care of depressed residents, therefore have a clear motivation to favor pharmacotherapy over psychotherapy.

Carrier Restriction of Psychological Services for Patients with Dementia

Perhaps the most egregious example of discrimination and restraint on mental health treatment of older adults concerns the past policy of many Medicare carriers to preclude the provision of psychological services to individuals with dementia, on the basis of the erroneous belief that dementia patients cannot benefit from psychological interventions. This mentality is unsupported by clinical science, with which, as noted above, LMRPs and carrier decisions must be consistent. There is growing research demonstrating the efficacy of various psychological interventions for a multitude of psychological and behavioral conditions, including agitation, aggression, depression, verbal disruption, wandering, sleep disturbance, and certain cognitive functions in dementia patients, contrary to the policies of many Medicare carriers. Reviews of studies evaluating psychosocial interventions for behavioral and psychological symptoms associated with dementia are available (Burgio & Fisher, 2000; Opie, Rosewarne, & O'Connor, 1999).

The likely effects of the foregoing regulatory policies and practices are significant and pervasive. First, they impede older adults' access to needed treatment, even those with Medigap (Medicare supplement) policies because these policies only take effect and cover the 50% copay requirement for Medicare-approved claims. Second, payment restrictions and denials, administrative time requirements, auditing procedures, and bureaucratic complexity are significant disincentives for practitioners to serve older adults. Finally, because Medicare sets the tone and establishes standards that private insurers, employers, and the rest of the private sector follow (Ourand, 2003), restricting mental health services and limiting reimbursement send the message that mental illness has little significance in late life and that geropsychological treatment is not a priority.

Why the Schism?

For several years, CMS and providers have not been amiable bedfellows. There is current consensus among health care professionals and government officials that CMS has neglected providers' concerns (Centers for Medicare and Medicaid Services, 2001b; Miller, 2001). The agency's disposition toward mental health care has been particularly unfavorable. The recent schism between CMS and the general health care community may be attributed in significant part to the antifraud and abuse zeitgeist within the government agency during the 1990s when the Clinton administration spearheaded a drive to curtail the exponential rise in Medicare spending. Efforts to crack down on the wasteful provision of services and the submission of fraudulent and inflated claims by providers attempting to bilk the Medicare Trust Fund came at the expense of then HCFA's relationship with the health care community. As detailed below, the mental health sector was no stranger to Medicare fraud and abuse, which likely accounts for much of HCFA's heightened scrutiny of, and vigilance toward, mental health care services.

With the enactment of the Omnibus Budget Reconciliation Act of 1990, Congress expanded Medicare coverage of partial hospitalization (PH) services to include services provided by CMHCs. Although this was expected to have limited effect and result in an increase of only $15–$20 million per year, the change led to an exponential rise in costs. Between 1993 and 1997, Medicare reimbursement for PH claims increased nearly 500%, from $60 million to $349 million. Average payments per patient increased 530% during this period (U.S. Department of Health and Human Services, 1998). Rather than the benefit extending merely to state sponsored CMHCs established by the CMHC Act of 1963, a spate of private centers calling themselves CMHCs were created to benefit from the new PH benefit that previously applied only to hospitals. HCFA failed to realize that many states do not have CMHC licensure requirements, making it relatively easy for these entities to set up shop and bill Medicare for PH services in those states. Furthermore, many unallowable services were billed as PH to Medicare by unscrupulous providers. Medicare contractors poorly monitored PH claims and had little direction from HCFA in doing so. When HCFA eventually caught on, it responded in stern fashion. In addition to heightening its scrutiny and denial of claims, it shut down many facilities across the nation. Thus, directly and indirectly, the PH calamity restricted older adults' access to care. Perhaps most significant, it changed the way in which HCFA would come to administer Medicare mental health benefits (Karlin & Norris, 2000).

To add insult to injury, a misleading and unjustifiably scathing report regarding the delivery of psychiatric services in nursing homes was released by the OIG in January 2001. The report, entitled *Medicare Payments for Psychiatric Services in Nursing Homes—A Follow Up*, concluded that 27% of psychiatric services provided in nursing homes are medically unnecessary (U.S. Department of Health and Human Services, 2001). Among the shortcomings of the report was the exclusive determination of what is and is not medically necessary. For example, the report implied that psychological treatments are inappropriate for cognitively impaired nursing home residents. This false notion is the same scientifically inconsistent belief that, as noted above, has led many Medicare carriers to preclude the provision of psychological services to individuals with dementia. In addition, the report criticized the use of several psychological measures, including the Geriatric Depression Scale (Sheikh & Yesavage, 1986), with nursing homes residents, though it did not elaborate on its basis for this conclusion. Furthermore, carrier guidelines on this issue and on mental health care reimbursement in nursing homes, in general, were lacking or nonexistent (U.S. Department of Health and Human Services, 2002). Unfortunately, the OIG's report falsely implied that mental health services in nursing homes are excessive when, in fact, they are in great need but short supply (Lombardo, 1994). The report also failed to acknowledge the substantial degree of unmet mental health need in nursing homes. Also unmentioned in the report were important recent steps by the psychological community to limit unethical practice in long-term care. For example, standards have been developed by Psychologists in Long Term Care (Lichtenberg et al., 1998) for the responsible provision of psychological services in nursing homes, and guidelines have been approved by the American Psychological Association (APA; 2003b) for psychological practice with older adults. Indeed, the OIG's efforts to reduce fraud and abuse are important, although, contrary to its goal of ensuring medically necessary services in nursing homes, the consequential effects of the report are likely to increase unmet mental health need following in part from increased coverage surveillance and stringency.

Recent Legislative and Regulatory Developments

In the past few years, there have been a handful of legislative efforts to eliminate the disparity in Medicare's coverage of outpatient mental health services, eliminate the lifetime limit on inpatient mental health care, and extend other mental health benefits, including the Medicare Mental Health Modernization Act of 2000 (S. 3233) and 2001 (S. 690, H.R. 1522) and the Medicare Mental Illness Nondiscrimination Act of 2000 (H.R. 5434) and 2001 (H.R. 599, S. 841). Unfortunately, these proposals failed to emerge from committee. The Medicare Mental Health Modernization Act was reintroduced in the Senate (S. 646) by Senator Jon Corzine (D-NJ) and in the House (H.R. 1340) by Representative Pete Stark (D-CA) on March 18, 2003. The bills were last referred to the Senate Committee on Finance and the House Subcommittee on Health. Senators Olympia Snowe (R-ME) and John Kerry (D-MA) and Representative Ted Strickland (D-OH) introduced similar legislation, entitled the Medicare Mental Health Copayment Equity Act of 2003 in the Senate (S. 853) and House (H.R. 2787) on April 10, 2003, and July 17, 2003, respectively. Similar to the Medicare Mental Health Modernization Act, this proposal provides for parity in Medicare's coverage of outpatient mental health services, but through a gradual phasing down of the copay from 50% to 20% over 6 years. The Senate bill was referred to the Committee on Finance, and the House bill was last referred to the Subcommittee on Health.

In July 2002, Representative Patrick Kennedy (D-RI) introduced in the House legislation designed to improve mental health care access, service integration, outreach, and quality. Entitled the Positive Aging Act of 2002 (H.R. 5077), the bill was the most expansive piece of legislation of its kind. It called for the development of implementation projects to integrate psychological screening and treatment services at primary care facilities, the establishment of a new federal grant program to support mental health outreach teams in social service settings serving older adults, the creation of a new deputy director for geriatric mental health services within the Center for Mental Health Services and advisory council positions for geriatric mental health providers, as well as other provisions. The bill, which was referred to the Subcommittee on Health, was not acted on before the close of the legislative session. The Positive Aging Act of 2003 was introduced in the House (H.R. 2241) by Representative Kennedy on May 22, 2003, and an identical bill (S. 1456) was introduced in the Senate on July 25, 2003, by Senator John Breaux (D-LA). The bills were referred to the House Subcommittee on Health and the Senate Committee on Health, Education, Labor, and Pensions, respectively. Another bill designed to provide for Medicare coverage of prevention services, including screening for depression, entitled the Medicare Wellness Act of 2003 (H.R. 1860), was introduced by Representative Carl Levin (D-MI) on April 29, 2003. The bill was referred to the House Subcommittee on Health.

The failure of significant policy change, including recent legislative proposals, is undoubtedly largely a consequence of limited mobilization and advocacy. In fact, in his study on legislative agenda setting, political scientist John W. Kingdon (1995) found that mental health was the subject least likely to be discussed by health policymakers and specialists, even though it undeniably deserved much greater attention. Unfortunately, many psychologists are unaware of public policy issues affecting older adults and are detached from the legislative process. This passivity is perplexing and disconcerting in a profession of individuals that epitomize the very skills of a successful advocate, including analytical proficiency, communication skills, persuasive abilities, and interpersonal skills. In fact, psychologists have been conspicuously absent whereas other professions have consistently contributed to past policy debates, including social work, nursing, medicine, and psychiatry (see, e.g., Heaney, 2003; Sosi & Caulum, 1983). Furthermore, psychologists often underestimate their potential political influence. As constituents, experts, and members of interest groups, psychologists can have significant influence on legislative agenda setting and on policymakers' voting decisions (Kingdon, 1995). In fact, constituents are one of the two most important factors influencing how legislators vote (Kingdon, 1989).

The limited involvement of professional psychology in recognizing and influencing geriatric mental health care policy exists not only at the individual or grassroots level, but also at the organizational and leadership hierarchy. The APA has historically exerted little effort on legislative and regulatory policy issues relating to older adults and mental health care delivery. On the other hand, geriatric psychiatry, represented by the American Association for Geriatric Psychiatry (AAGP), has been successful in providing coordinated advocacy responses. For example, the Positive Aging Act of 2002 (H.R. 5077), noted above, was originally initiated by the AAGP, and its influence was clearly evident in the legislative language of the initial bill, which excluded psychologists. In addition, the APA has been missing in the past among organizations mentioned by members of Congress in hearings or introductions of Medicare mental health parity (or similar) bills and in letters of support printed in the *Congressional Record*, whereas the AAGP, the American Psychiatric Association, and other medical associations are often prominent (see, e.g., Kerry, 2003). In fact, the medical profession as a whole has historically done a better job than the psychology profession in responding to managed care and other health care changes and in initiating and providing coordinated legislative and regulatory responses. In a recent study examining organizations' reputations for influence in health policy, the American Medical Association ranked 2nd among 171 organizations because of significant grassroots presence (Heaney, 2003). The APA ranked 94th (78th when a more liberal ranking method was applied). Significantly, many high rankings were more a function of successful grassroots organization than of financial resources (Heaney, 2003).

More recently, the APA has exhibited greater attention to important policy issues affecting mental health care for older adults, efforts that have begun to yield significant dividends. This renewed commitment is reflected in the APA's hiring of its first full-time aging issues officer, who was at the center of the advocacy efforts behind the reintroduction of the Positive Aging Act of 2003 (H.R. 2241; S. 1456) and the inclusion of new legislative language more inclusive of psychologists. The experience with the Positive Aging Act is an interesting example of psychology's past and present involvement in advocacy for clinical aging issues and the success that such advocacy (and the pitfalls silence) can bring. A recent legislative development to improve geropsychology training is another mark of victory and advocacy success for the geropsychology community. In December 2001, Congress approved the creation of the Graduate Psychology Education (GPE) program. The GPE program is designed to support programs that train health service psychologists working with underserved populations, including older adults. Beyond additional funding, the GPE program, and its location in the Bureau of Health Professions, increases positive recognition of, and legitimacy for, the profession for psychology. Congress approved $3 million for the GPE program as part of its Fiscal Year 2003 appropriations bill. This represents a two-fold increase over the previous appropriation. Of even greater significance to geropsychology is the fact that $1.5 million of the appropriation was allocated for geropsychology education and training, as part of the new Graduate Geropsychology Education Program (GGEP). The passing of this appropriation is especially noteworthy in that it is the first time Congress has allocated funding specifically for geropsychology education and training. Contributing to this development was an advocacy campaign spearheaded by the APA Public Policy Office. This success is an example of the importance of what political scientists call "problem definition" in legislative agenda setting, which involves linking private problems to public causes and a possible governmental solution (see Stone, 1989). The APA and others helped bring legislative attention to the seriousness of mental illness in late life and the impending growth of mental health need, as well as a controllable public cause, namely the shortage of geropsychology professionals.

A recent development in Medicare reimbursement for health care services has the potential of transforming the delivery of psychological services to older adults. In 2002, six "Health and Behavior Assessment and Intervention" (H&B) codes were established, extending the nature and scope of services psychologists may provide and the circumstances in which they may do so. Psychologists and other health care professionals bill Medicare for services provided to a Medicare beneficiary using codes from the Current Procedure Terminology (CPT) system developed by the American Medical Association and approved by CMS. The six new CPT codes provide for reimbursement for behavioral, social, and psychophysiological services to prevent, treat, or manage physical health problems or illnesses, rather than for the treatment of mental illness or symptoms related thereto. Prior to the H&B codes, which became effective January 1, 2002, Medicare reimbursement for psychological services required that such services be provided only to individuals with a mental health diagnosis. The new CPT codes have the potential of greatly increasing older adults' access to psychological services. They provide particular opportunities for providing services in residential and institutional facilities, including nursing homes and hospitals. The new codes cover services for assessment, reassessment, individual intervention, group intervention, family intervention with the patient present, and family intervention without the patient presence. Significantly, Medicare reimbursement for services billed under the H&B codes is provided from funding for medical services and will not reduce funding earmarked for mental health services. Furthermore, the 50% copay requirement for outpatient mental health services does not apply to the health and behavior assessment and intervention codes.

In addition to the obvious benefits to the delivery of psychological services the new codes provide, the creation of them affirms the benefit of biopsychosocial services and further certifies that psychologists and other qualified health professionals should provide such services. The new codes may also reduce the stigma older adults attach to seeing a psychologist or other mental health professional. Last, the H&B codes have the potential of reducing fragmentation of services and increasing interdisciplinary collaboration that can provide psychologists another point of entry into the care for older adults and, most important, lead to better health outcomes. The new codes were first published in *CPT 2003* (American Medical Association, 2002).

In a highly significant regulatory development, CMS issued a memorandum (Transmittal AB-01-135) to its contractors on September 25, 2001, instructing them to no longer preclude reimbursement for psychological services provided to dementia patients (Centers for Medicare and Medicaid Services, 2001a). However, implementation of this instruction must be monitored by the mental health community because the memorandum specifically stated that contractors may not install computer edits that result in the automatic denial of services provided to patients with dementia. Contractors still have considerable discretion in processing the claims, including the ability to deny such claims.

Forthcoming regulations will establish important changes to the Medicare claims appeals process and have the potential to improve the reimbursement process for mental health (and medical) services by increasing fairness and accuracy and decreasing economic and time constraints on providers (67 Fed. Reg. 69312, 2002). Perhaps most significant, the proposed rule establishes "qualified independent contractors" (QICs) to conduct reconsiderations of claim determinations made by contractors in an effort to introduce greater impartiality to the Medicare appeals process. In an acknowledgement of the reimbursement system's past imperfections, CMS has stated that it believes that the establishment of QICs "can result in significant improvements in the Medicare fee-for-service appeals system" (67 Fed. Reg., 69312, 2002). The reduced bureaucracy and increased efficiency and equity intended by the new regulations can potentially reduce disincentives facing current and prospective practitioners serving older adults. The changes also offer psychologists the potential opportunity for greater involvement in the appeals system.

A final development offering potential for improving geriatric mental health care concerns the findings of the New Freedom Commission on Mental Health, which was established by President George W. Bush to conduct a comprehensive study of the U.S. mental health service delivery system, including public and private sector providers (New Freedom Commission, 2003). The study is the first extensive federal study of the nation's public and private mental health care systems in nearly 25 years. The interim final report highlighted the significant access difficulties that limit mental health treatment in the United States, specifically for older adults. Unfortunately, the final report made little reference to older adults and lacked specific recommendations for this population. Nevertheless, by identifying the inadequacies of the mental health care delivery system at the federal level, the report offers opportunities for action and change that will hopefully be acted on with input from the geropsychological community. In the words of policy experts, the report provides a "policy window" (Kindgon, 1995, p. 165).

Future Directions

Despite these developments, there is considerable work that needs to be done at various levels to reduce barriers to geriatric mental health care. The remainder of this article provides proposals and strategies to aid psychologists, other advocates of elderly persons who are mentally ill, and policymakers to improve the state of geriatric mental health care delivery.

To enhance access and reimbursement for psychological services for older adults, it is important that psychologists who serve elderly individuals be active advocates for their clients and their profession at legislative and regulatory levels. Admittedly, this will require a shift in professional identity that recognizes the important role psychologists, as agents of change, can have at the macro level (Levant et al., 2001). Broader level change may seem formidable to psychologists more familiar with exerting influence within the confines of the therapy room; however, psychologists can have significant political influence as individual advocates, constituents, and members of organized interest groups. Specific legislative advocacy efforts include promotion of legislation that would eliminate the disparity in Medicare reimbursement for psychological services (e.g., the Medicare Mental Health Modernization Act, the Medicare Mental Health Copayment Equity Act) as well as reforms that would enhance funding for geriatric mental health outreach, prevention, research, and training (e.g., the Positive Aging Act).

Mechanisms for legislative advocacy include individual and organizational letter-writing campaigns, attendance at town hall meetings, and individual conferences with legislators. The latter two processes are particularly effective for reducing the "signal-to-noise" ratio. The signal-to-noise ratio represents the likelihood a constituent's message or concern will be perceived by his or her elected official. The degree to which a concern or request (signal) is recognized by an elected official depends on the ability of that message to get through the thousands of messages (noise) from other constituents and interest groups competing for attention (personal communication, Representative Brian Baird, October 6, 2000). For example, in a town hall meeting, often convened by elected officials (although sometimes attended by only a handful of constituents), noise is greatly reduced and signal detection enhanced. This forum also allows the importance of messages to be better recognized (problem definition). Furthermore, it puts elected officials on the record, thus promoting accountability. Town hall meetings, which are held by elected officials in many localities throughout the country, are largely unknown to many and, for this reason, provide ideal opportunities for psychologists and other mental health advocates to relay their signal. A central database of town hall meetings is maintained by the U.S. Chamber of Commerce. The database is accessible at www.uschamber.com/government/townhall.htm. In addition, advocates can join the Grassroots Action Information Network (GAIN) at the same Web site to receive regular e-mail or fax notifications of upcoming town hall meetings and legislative events in their local community. Communication of important issues through the popular press can be another effective method of legislative agenda setting (Levant et al., 2001). The media's focus on issues affects legislators' attention through both direct and indirect channels. Legislators often follow the mass media (direct influence), and they are influenced through the media's effect on constituents (indirect influence; Kingdon, 1989).

Urging local representatives to cosponsor existing or impending legislation is also an important step to enactment. Moreover, in addition to soliciting support and cosponsorship, thanking elected officials for introducing favorable legislation is important, because it lets them know that their actions are recognized and valued. Involvement in the drafting and revision of legislation and advocacy for legislative language that is favorable toward, and inclusive of, psychologists, are important and effective ways for professional psychology to influence and effect change.

In addition to advocacy at the individual policymaker level, direct advocacy at the Congressional committee level is essential. Committees (and subcommittees) are typically the first main hurdle in the legislative process and, as such, act as gatekeepers. If a committee fails to consider a piece of legislation, which is common, the bill is effectively defeated. Committees may also reshape the bill through markups, hold hearings, and debate legislation. Advocacy efforts include requesting legislators to vote for or against a bill and supporting or objecting to legislative language included in the bill in committee markups. Constituents of committee or subcommittee members can have particular influence. Methods of contact include letters, e-mail messages, telephone calls, and in-person meetings. Discussions with Congressional staffers, particularly legislative directors, are also important because staffers typically have significant influence in setting and shaping a legislator's policy agenda and positions. Advocates can identify their House representatives and Senators and even send direct correspondence at www.house.gov and www.senate.gov. It is also important that psychologists, as well as other mental health professionals, urge professional organizations (e.g., APA, state associations) to advocate for aging-related issues and hold these organizations accountable for doing so. APA has pledged continued support in advocating on behalf of aging issues (DiGilio & Levitt, 2002). State psychological associations are also good vehicles for advocacy, though, unfortunately, they have not historically been highly involved in advocacy on aging-related issues.

It is important to note that interest groups in and of themselves often have limited influence on policymaking. The most effective way for interest groups, such as the APA, to exert influence on a policymaker is to engage in advocacy through the legislator's home constituency. In addition to connecting with local constituents, another effective strategy of influence is to use members of Congress sympathetic to or supportive of mental health issues to persuade others. Legislators often look to their congressional colleagues in deciding if and how to act on an issue (Kingdon, 1989). There are several psychologists and friends of psychology in Congress today who could serve as effective advocacy agents.

Practitioners can also have influence by becoming familiar with and involved in regulatory policymaking and administrative procedures. The time appears ripe for improving regulatory practices relating to geriatric mental health service delivery. Since taking its new name, CMS has been working to revamp its image and "bring a culture of responsiveness to the Agency" (*Medicare Regulatory and Contracting Reform*, 2001). As part of this effort, CMS has pledged to be more provider friendly. One method by which it is trying to accomplish this mission and increase providers' role in shaping regulatory polices and administrative procedures is through open-door telephone meetings. Among other benefits, the open-door forum is a good way for providers to put concerns on the radar screens of influential government officials and promote accountability. A meeting schedule and list of topics, as well as information on how to participate, can be found at www.cms.gov/opendoor/schedule.asp.

To promote service access and reimbursement for mental health services to older adults, it is important that practitioners be knowledgeable of Medicare reimbursement and relevant decision making policies and respond quickly and assertively to unfavorable or unjust decisions. Because of improper denials and restriction of appropriate services by Medicare carriers, as well as ambiguous and often medically inconsistent LMRP provisions, carriers should be held accountable by CMS, practitioners, and provider organizations for ensuring that their mental health medical review policies are comprehensive, clear, and consistent with clinical science. CMS has instructed carriers to reduce ambiguities in their medical review policies, although there is little evidence that this guidance has had any effect. Policies governing outpatient psychological services are typically found in the LMRP section entitled "Psychiatry and Psychology Services." Centralized access to all LMRPs is now available through the Medicare Coverage Database, a user-friendly Internet resource recently developed by CMS, greatly simplifying the process for obtaining LMRPs. The database (available at www.cms.hhs.gov/mcd/) allows one to search by state and coverage topic (e.g., outpatient mental health). Practitioners can also obtain LMRPs by contacting their local Medicare carrier or visiting their carrier's Web site. Moreover, it is imperative that carriers consider the views and experiences of psychologists, who have been absent from the LMRP development process. Carriers have been required for several years to develop LMRPs in an open forum and to periodically review these policies; psychologists, however, have been largely left out of this development phase. Therefore, psychologists are encouraged to initiate efforts, not only to become knowledgeable of their carrier's LMRP but also to be actively involved in LMRP development and revision phases, involvement that can and does have important impact. Proposed draft LMRPs can also be obtained through the Medicare Coverage Database.

Practitioners and others are encouraged to request elaboration of vague local medical review policies and appeal provisions that are inconsistent with clinical standards and quality care. Psychologists can appeal inappropriate, inconsistent, or unclear LMRP provisions by writing to the carrier medical director (CMD), with copies sent to the administrator of the CMS regional office, the executive director of the state psychological association, and the APA Practice Directorate. A letter written by the first author appealing a highly restrictive LMRP for psychiatry and psychological services provided in nursing homes in Wisconsin, Illinois, Michigan, and Minnesota was included as a model in a LMRP toolkit recently developed by the APA and is also available on request of the first author. The toolkit can be accessed at: www.apa.org/pi/aging/lmrp. Furthermore, it is important that state associations establish relationships with local carriers and provide comments on new and revised LMRPs. Practitioners are also advised to respond to claims denials for services they deem appropriate by writing an appeal to the Medicare carrier, first examining the carrier's LMRP for provisions that may relate to the denied service.

As part of its commitment to be more responsive to providers' concerns, CMS has required that carriers establish a standard *reconsideration process* in which practitioners and beneficiaries may request a revision to an LMRP (Centers for Medicare and Medicaid Services, 2002, Ch. 13, §11). As part of this process, carriers are required to place on their Web site information describing the reconsideration process and instructions for submitting reconsideration requests.

The monitoring and involvement of psychologists (and state and national associations) in the development and implementation of regulatory policies will be particularly important as the new Health and Behavior CPT codes are implemented and to ensure that the new CMS policy disallowing the automatic preclusion of psychological services provided to patients with dementia is appropriately implemented by carriers. In light of HCFA's past experience with the implementation of new benefits (e.g., the PH benefit), vigilance and communication are essential. In fact, there have already been problems with the implementation of the new H&B codes. Some carriers have denied reimbursement to psychologists for services billed under the new codes because of the erroneous assertion that psychologists are not eligible to use them. The APA Practice Directorate has been working with CMS and local Medicare carriers to resolve inappropriate denials under the codes (American Psychological Association, 2003a).

It is also important that the psychology community monitor and respond to proposed changes to Medicare regulations. Before final implementation, federal regulations are published as a proposed rule in the *Federal Register*. In the proposed rule, the issuing agency solicits comments from providers and other interested parties, with instructions and a timeframe for submitting feedback. Professional psychology therefore has an opportunity to help shape final regulations during the comment period to ensure that they are inclusive of and favorable toward the profession. The *Federal Register* can be accessed at www.gpoaccess.gov/nara/index.html. If advocacy and oversight are to be successful, they must have collaboration and coordination. According to Kingdon (1995), "Part of a group's stock in trade in affecting all phases of policymaking—agendas, decisions, or implementation—is the ability to convince government officials that it speaks with one voice and truly represents the preferences of its members" (p. 52). Unfortunately, collaboration and coordination have been lacking in the psychology profession. Professional psychology is a highly disjointed community. Fragmentation has been especially prevalent among practitioners serving older adults, a problem identified by Niederehe, Gatz, Taylor, and Teri (1995): Clinical geropsychology will not advance substantially as a field until other organizational structures are developed with greater potential for transforming the current professional context, in which geropsychologists are isolated from each other, strapped for resources, and struggling just to maintain a toehold. (p. 144)

As noted above, the limited coordination in clinical geropsychology is not seen in many related professions. Improving coordination, communication, and cohesion among psychologists serving older adults (and between professions, including geriatric psychiatry) would yield significant effects on reducing social, policy, and system barriers to care and benefit the professional image of psychology.

Collaboration among young and seasoned professionals in mental health and aging is also important for developing and implementing a coordinated research agenda and procuring necessary funding. In a significant step along these lines, the National Institute of Mental Health (NIMH) recently released a program announcement (PA) entitled *Research on Mental Illnesses in Older Adults* (National Institute of Mental Health, 2002). The PA is the most expansive of its kind. It delineates specific research questions in the areas of risk factors and basic research, diagnosis, treatment, prevention and services, mood disturbance, and bioethics. In addition, the NIMH recently established an aging research consortium to increase research on mental health in late life, enhance coordination and collaboration of aging research within and outside of NIMH, and improve training in research on mental illness and late life.

Furthermore, the fact that older adults lack knowledge of mental health and mental health treatment should not be surprising in light of the disconnected service delivery infrastructures in this nation and the limited degree of mental health outreach provided to the elderly. In its investigation of the Texas and New York public mental health systems, the GAO found that no CMHC officials indicated that they engaged in any outreach efforts to attract elderly clients (General Accounting Office, 1982). The fragmented mental health care delivery system was identified as a key obstacle to quality mental health care by President Bush (Bush, 2002). The Positive Aging Act of 2003 (H.R. 2241; S. 1456), discussed above, would help close the service gap, if enacted. In addition to limited outreach and service coordination, even less effort is devoted to mental health prevention in late life, even though psychological risk factors for mental and physical illness in late life are significant (Smyer, 1995). Mental health prevention strategies in late life could have profound social, economic, emotional, and health benefits. There is a growing body of research demonstrating the impact of psychological factors and early intervention on physical health and independence in younger and older adults (e.g., Lebowitz & Pearson, 2000; Ritchie, Touchon, & Lendesert, 1998; Smyer, 1995; Smyth, 1998). This research suggests that, among other consequences, psychological interventions could delay or perhaps prevent the onset of physical and psychological illness, extend the period of independent living, and delay or render unnecessary nursing home placement. One randomized study of counseling and support versus usual care for family caregivers of patients with Alzheimer's disease found that the intervention delayed patients' nursing home admission by over 300 days (Mittelman, Ferris, Shulman, Steinberg, & Levin, 1996). Accordingly, greater efforts to increase late-life mental health outreach (including nontraditional case finding), service coordination, and prevention should be taken by federal agencies (e.g., CMS, Substance Abuse and Mental Health Services Administration, NIMH), professional organizations (e.g., APA, AAGP, American Medical Association, American Psychiatric Association), and health care professionals, including incorporating mental health prevention into Medicare. A campaign to increase medical prevention benefits under Medicare is currently being spearheaded by the Partnership for Prevention, a national nonprofit organization dedicated to preventing disease and promoting health.

Local area agencies on aging (AAAs) could play an important role in mental health care outreach, education, and referral. Established by the Older Americans Comprehensive Services Amendments promulgated in 1973, AAAs provide information and access services, in-home and community-based services, and housing and elder rights services to elderly individuals throughout the country. AAAs have had limited involvement in mental health outreach and referral, though they are well suited to serve in this capacity. In fact, Lebowitz, Light, and Bailey (1987) found that coordination between CMHCs and AAAs was associated with higher mental health care use by older adults. Accordingly, linkages between AAAs and community mental health resources should be further developed.

To reduce the unmet mental health need in nursing homes, it is essential that the favoring of pharmacotherapy over psychotherapy following from the narrow method of QI 5, discussed earlier in this article, be eliminated. Specifically, the QI should be revised to capture both treatments. There is a simple method for making this change. The MDS includes an item that assesses whether residents receive psychotherapy (Item P1be). Including this item in the calculation of QI 5 would count both psychotropic medication and psychotherapy as antidepressant therapy.

Finally, greater education of professionals, paraprofessionals (e.g., nursing assistants), and the public, including older adults, family members, and other potential referral sources, regarding the nature and treatment of mental illness is essential. One method for increasing physicians' knowledge, detection, and referral of mental illness in older adults that offers considerable potential concerns a recent effort within the profession of child clinical psychology to do the same with children. In 1996, the American Academy of Pediatrics developed a mental health classification system for children and adolescents, compatible with the *Diagnostic and Statistical Manual of Mental Disorders, fourth edition* (*DSM–IV*; American Psychiatric Association, 1994), for use by primary care physicians, known as the *Diagnostic and Statistical Manual for Primary Care (DSM–PC) Child and Adolescent Version* (American Academy of Pediatrics, 1996). In addition to diagnostic information, the *DSM–PC* includes additional information such as diagnostic vignettes to help physicians make more informed diagnoses and provide referrals when necessary. Furthermore, the project advisory committee identified training faculty to teach pediatric residents how to use the manual. Using this initiative as a model, geropsychologists and the medical community should consider developing similar resources to facilitate non–mental health specialists' detection and diagnosis of mental illness in older adults and provide appropriate referrals. In a general sense, the foregoing initiative suggests that geropsychologists could learn from the experiences of child psychologists, as the two professions confront many similar issues in service delivery. Accordingly, greater collaboration between the two professions should be explored.

Widespread public education campaigns should be implemented to improve the public's knowledge of mental illness in elderly persons and the availability of effective treatments for them. A recent major public education campaign initiative to educate older adults and family members about Alzheimer's disease (AD) is a model for this proposal. The initiative, known as the IDentify Alzheimer's Disease (ID.A.D.) Resource Kit (National Family Caregivers Association, 2002), is designed to educate older adults and families on recognizing and managing early symptoms of AD and how to seek treatment. The toolkit is sponsored by the National Family Caregivers Association and the Novartis Pharmaceuticals Corporation, and it is free of charge to the public. The initiative, which has been publicized through national radio, print media, and the Internet (www.AlzheimersDisease.com), is the most aggressive and widespread of its kind. It offers promise for increasing the diagnosis and treatment of AD and related disorders. Similar public education campaigns should be developed to increase awareness and treatment of depression, anxiety, and other mental disorders in late life.

In conclusion, this article provides for a more complete understanding of the restrictions to geriatric mental health care use and provision and offers several micro- and macro-level processes and proposals for effecting change. It is hoped that this article will stimulate individual advocacy and collective action to improve mental health service access and availability. With greater knowledge and a broader conceptualization of and commitment to change can come substantial dividends to both the profession of psychology and the clients (and potential clients) we serve.

References

Alvidrez, J., & Areán, P. A. (2002). Physician willingness to refer older depressed patients for psychotherapy. *International Journal of Psychiatry in Medicine, 32,* 21–35.

American Academy of Pediatrics. (1996). *The classification of child and adolescent mental disorders in primary care: Diagnostic and statistical manual for primary care (DSM-PC) child and adolescent version.* Washington, DC: American Psychiatric Press.

American Medical Association. (2002). *CPT 2003.* Chicago: Author.

American Psychiatric Association. (1994). *Diagnostic and statistical manual of mental disorders* (4th ed.). Washington: Author.

American Psychological Association. (2003a). 2002 annual report of the American Psychological Association. *American Psychologist, 58,* 510–539.

American Psychological Association. (2003b). *Guidelines for psychological practice with older adults.* Retrieved September 30, 2003, from http://www.apa.org/practice/Guidelines_for_Psychological_Practice_with_Older_Adults.pdf

Blazer, D., & Williams, C. D. (1980). Epidemiology of dysphoria and depression in an elderly population. *American Journal of Psychiatry, 137,* 439–444.

Burgio, L. D., & Fisher, S. E. (2000). Application of psychosocial interventions for treating behavioral and psychological symptoms of dementia. *International Psychogeriatrics, 12,* 351–358.

Burns, B., Wagner, R., Taube, J., Magaziner, J., Purmutt, T., & Landerman, L. (1993). Mental health service use by the elderly in nursing homes. *American Journal of Public Health, 83,* 331–337.

Bush, G. W. (2002). *President says U.S. must make a commitment to mental health care.* Retrieved December 28, 2002, from http://www.whitehouse.gov/news/releases/2002/04/20020429-1.html

Centers for Medicare and Medicaid Services. (2001a). *Medical review of services for patients with dementia* (Transmittal AB-01-135). Baltimore, MD: Author.

Centers for Medicare and Medicaid Services. (2001b). *The new Centers for Medicare & Medicaid Services.* Retrieved November 23, 2002, from http://www.hhs.gov/news/press/2001pres/20010614a.html.

Centers for Medicare and Medicaid Services. (2002). *Medicare program integrity manual.* Baltimore, MD: Author.

Centers for Medicare and Medicaid Services. (2003). *Medicare program integrity manual* (Pub. 100-8). Baltimore, MD: Author.

Changes to the Medicare Claims Appeal Procedures, 67 Fed. Reg. 69,312 (Nov. 15, 2002).

Community Mental Health Centers Act of 1963, 42 U.S.C. § 2689 *et seq.* (1963).

Demmler, J. (1998). Utilization of specialty mental health organizations by older adults: U.S. national profile. *Psychiatric Services, 49,* 1079–1081.

DiGilio, D. A., & Levitt, N. G. (2002). APA bridging the gap on aging related issues. *Professional Psychology: Research and Practice, 33,* 443–445.

Durenberger, D. (1989). Providing mental health care services to Americans. *American Psychologist, 44,* 1293–1297.

Flemming, A. S., Buchanan, J. G., Santos, J. F., & Rickards, L. D. (1984). *Mental health services for the elderly: Report on a survey of community mental health centers* (Vol. I). Washington, DC: Action Committee to Implement the Mental Health Recommendations of the 1981 White House Conference on Aging.

Gaitz, C. M. (1974). Barriers to the delivery of psychiatric services to the elderly. *Gerontologist, 12,* 210–214.

Gatz, M., Fiske, A., Fox, L. S., Kaskie, B., Kasl-Godley, J. E., McCallum, T. J., & Wetherell, J. L. (1998). Empirically validated psychological treatments for older adults. *Journal of Mental Health and Aging, 4,* 9–46.

Gatz, M., Kasl-Godley, K. E., & Karel, M. J. (1996). Aging and mental disorders. In J. Birren & K. Schaie (Eds.), *Handbook of the psychology of aging* (4th ed., pp. 365–382). San Diego, CA: Academic Press.

Gatz, M., & Smyer, M. A. (1992). The mental health system and older adults in the 1990s. *American Psychologist, 47,* 741–751.

General Accounting Office. (1982). *The elderly remain in need of mental health services* (GAO-82-112). Washington, DC: Author.

German, P. S., Rovner, B., Bertner, L., & Brant, L. J. (1992). The role of mental morbidity in the nursing home experience. *Gerontologist, 32,* 152–158.

German, P. S., Shapiro, S., & Skinner, E. A. (1985). Mental health of the elderly: Use of health and mental health services. *Journal of the American Geriatrics Society, 33,* 246–252.

Gfroerer, J. C., Penne, M. A., Pemberton, M. R., & Folsom, R. E. (2002). The aging baby boom cohort and future prevalence of substance abuse. In S. P. Korper & C. L. Council (Eds.), *Substance use by older adults: Estimates of future impact on the treatment system* (DHHS Publ. No. SMA 03-3763). Rockville, MD: Substance Abuse and Mental Health Services Administration.

Goldstrom, I. D., Burns, B. J., Kessler, L. G., Feuerberg, M. A., Larson, D. B., Miller, N. E., & Cromer, W. J. (1987). Mental health services use by elderly adults in a primary care setting. *Journal of Gerontology, 42,* 147–153.

Halpain, M. C., Harris, M. J., McClure, F. S., & Jeste, D. V. (1999). Training in geriatric mental health: Needs and strategies. *Psychiatric Services, 50,* 1205–1208.

Heaney, M. T. (2003, August). *Coalitions and interest group influence over health policy.* Paper presented at the 99th annual meeting of the American Political Science Association, Philadelphia, PA.

Himmelfarb, S., & Murrell, S. A. (1984). The prevalence and correlates of anxiety symptoms in older adults. *Journal of Psychology, 116,* 159–167.

Karlin, B. E., & Norris, M. P. (2000, November). *Mismanagement, fraud and abuse in the implementation of Medicare partial hospitalization mental health policy.* Paper presented at the 53rd annual scientific meeting of the Gerontological Society of America, Washington, DC.

Karlin, B. E., & Norris, M. P. (2001, August). *Underutilization of community mental health services by older adults.* Poster presented at the 109th Annual Convention of the American Psychological Association, San Francisco, CA.

Kerry, J. (2003, April 10). Introduction of the Medicare Mental Health Copayment Equity Act of 2003. *Congressional Record, 149,* S5179–S5180. Washington, DC: Government Printing Office.

Kingdon, J. (1989). *Congressmen's voting decisions* (3rd ed.). Ann Arbor: University of Michigan Press.

Kingdon, J. (1995). *Agendas, alternatives, and public policies* (2nd ed.). New York: Harper Collins.

Kisely, S., Linden, M., Bellantuono, C., Simon, G., & Jones, J. (2000). Why are patients prescribed psychotropic drugs by general practitioners? Results of an international study. *Psychological Medicine, 30,* 1217–1225.

Lair, T., & Lefkowitz, D. (1990). Mental health and functional status of residents of nursing and personal care homes. In *National medical expenditure survey research findings* (DHHS Publication No. PHS90-3470). Rockville, MD: Public Health Service, Agency for Health Care Policy and Research.

Lasoski, M. C. (1986). Reasons for low utilization of mental health services by the elderly. *Clinical Gerontologist, 5,* 1–18.

Lebowitz, B. D., Light, E., & Bailey, F. (1987). Mental health center services for the elderly: The impact of coordination with area agencies on aging. *Gerontologist, 27,* 699–702.

Lebowitz, B. D., & Pearson, J. L. (2000). Intervention research in psychosis: Prevention trials. *Schizophrenia Bulletin, 26,* 543–549.

Levant, R. F., Reed, G. M., Raguesa, S. A., DiCowden, M., Murphy, M. J., Sullivan, F., Craig, P. L., & Stout, C. E. (2001). Envisioning and accessing new roles for professional psychology. *Professional Psychology: Research and Practice, 32,* 79–87.

Lichtenberg, P. A., Smith, M., Frazer, D., Molinari, V., Rosowsky, E., Crose, R., et al. (1998). Standards for psychological services in longterm care facilities. *Gerontologist, 38,* 122–127.

Lombardo, N. E. (1994). *Barriers to mental health services for nursing home residents.* Washington, DC: American Association of Retired Persons.

Mackenzie, C. S., Gekoski, W. L., & Knox, V. J. (1999). Do family physicians treat older patients with mental disorders differently than younger patients? *Canadian Family Physician, 45,* 1219–1224.

McKegney, F. P., Aronson, M. K., & Ooi, W. L. (1988). Identifying depression in the old old. *Psychosomatics: Journal of Consultation Liaison Psychiatry, 29,* 175–181.

Medicare Mental Health Copayment Equity Act of 2003, H.R. 2787, 108th Cong., 1st Sess. (2003).

Medicare Mental Health Copayment Equity Act of 2003, S. 853, 108th Cong., 1st Sess. (2003).

Medicare Mental Health Modernization Act of 2000, S. 3233, 106th Cong., 2d Sess. (2000).

Medicare Mental Health Modernization Act of 2001, H.R. 1522, 107th Cong., 1st Sess. (2001).

Medicare Mental Health Modernization Act of 2001, S. 690, 107th Cong., 1st Sess. (2001).

Medicare Mental Health Modernization Act of 2003, H.R. 1340, 108th Cong., 1st Sess. (2003).

Medicare Mental Health Modernization Act of 2003, S. 646, 108th Cong., 1st Sess. (2003).

Medicare Mental Illness Nondiscrimination Act of 2000, H.R. 5434, 106th Cong., 2d Sess. (2000).

Medicare Mental Illness Nondiscrimination Act of 2001, H.R. 599, 107th Cong., 1st Sess. (2001).

Medicare Mental Illness Nondiscrimination Act of 2001, S. 841, 107th Cong., 1st Sess. (2001).

Medicare Regulatory and Contracting Reform Act of 2001: Hearings Before the House Ways and Means Subcommittee, 107th Cong., 1st Sess. (2001) (testimony of Thomas Scully).

Medicare Wellness Act of 2003, H.R. 1860, 108th Cong., 1st Sess. (2003).

Miller, M. (2001). *Testimony on HCFA's relationship with providers and contractors.* Testimony before the House Energy and Commerce Subcommittee on Health. Retrieved September 29, 2003, from http://cms.hhs.gov/media/press/testimony. asp?Counter_623

Mittelman, M. S., Ferris, S. H., Shulman, E., Steinberg, G., & Levin, B. (1996). A family intervention to delay nursing home placement of patients with Alzheimer disease: A randomized controlled trial. *Journal of the American Medical Association, 276*, 1725–1731.

National Family Caregivers Association. (2002). *IDentify Alzheimer's disease: A resource kit.* Kensington, MD: Author.

National Institute of Mental Health. (2002). *Research on mental illnesses in older adults* (Publ. No. PA-03-014). Bethesda, MD: Author.

Nelson, E. (2002). Change in pricing made for Medicare part B crossover claims. *Massachusetts Psychologist, 10*, 2.

New Freedom Commission. (2003). *Interim report to the President.* Retrieved December 28, 2002, from http://www.mentalhealthcommission.gov/reports/FinalReport/toc.html

Niederehe, G., Gatz, M., Taylor, G. P., & Teri, L. (1995). The case for certification in clinical geropsychology and a framework for implementation. In B. Knight, L. Teri, P. Wohlford, & J. Santos (Eds.), *Mental health services for older adults: Implications for training and practice in geropsychology* (pp. 143–151). Washington, DC: American Psychological Association.

Older Americans Comprehensive Services Amendments of 1973 (Publication L. No. 93-29).

Omnibus Budget Reconciliation Act of 1989 (Publication L. No. 101-239).

Omnibus Budget Reconciliation Act of 1990 (Publication L. No. 101-508).

Opie, J., Rosewarne, R., & O'Connor, D. W. (1999). The efficacy of psychosocial approaches to behaviour disorders in dementia: A systematic literature review. *Australian & New Zealand Journal of Psychiatry, 33*, 789–799.

Ourand, P. (2003). The impact of Medicare on private health plans. *The ASHA Leader, 8*, pp. 8–9, 12–13.

Positive Aging Act of 2002, H.R. 5077, 107th Cong., 2d Sess. (2002).

Positive Aging Act of 2003, H.R. 2241, 108th Cong., 1st Sess. (2003).

Positive Aging Act of 2003, S. 1456, 108th Cong., 1st Sess. (2003).

Redick, R. W., Kramer, M., & Taube, C. A. (1973). Epidemiology of mental illness and utilization of psychiatric facilities among older persons. In W. W. Busse & E. Pfeiffer (Eds.), *Mental illness in later life*. Washington, DC: American Psychiatric Association.

Regier, D. A., Boyd, J. H., Burke, J. D., Rae, D. S., Myers, J. K., Kramer, M., et al. (1988). One-month prevalence of mental disorders in the United States: Based on five epidemiologic catchment area sites. *Archives of General Psychiatry, 45*, 977–986.

Ritchie, K., Touchon, J., & Lendesert, B. (1998). Progressive disability in senile dementia is accelerated in the presence of depression. *International Journal of Geriatric Psychiatry, 13*, 459–461.

Sheikh, J. I., & Yesavage, J. A. (1986). Geriatric Depression Scale: Recent evidence and development of a shorter version. *Clinical Gerontology, 5*, 165–172.

Sherman, J. J. (1996). Medicare's mental health benefits: Coverage, utilization, and expenditures. *Journal of Aging & Health, 8*, 54–71.

Smyer, M. (1995). Prevention and early intervention for mental disorders of the elderly. In M. Gatz (Ed.), *Emerging issues in mental health and aging* (pp. 163–182). Washington, DC: American Psychological Association.

Smyth, J. (1998). Written emotional expression: effect size, outcome types, and moderating variables. *Journal of Consulting and Clinical Psychology, 66*, 174–184.

Sosi, M., & Caulum, S. (1983). Advocacy: A conceptualization for social work practice. *Social Work, 28*, 12–17.

Stefl, M. E., & Prosperi, D. C. (1985). Barriers to mental health service utilization. *Community Mental Health Journal, 21*, 167–177.

Stone, D. A. (1989). Causal stories and the formation of policy agendas. *Political Science Quarterly, 104*, 281–300.

Swan, J., & McCall, N. (1987). Mental health components and the aged. In E. Lurie & J. Swan (Eds.), *Serving the mentally ill elderly: Problems and perspectives* (p. 111). Lexington, MA: Lexington-Heath.

U.S. Administration on Aging. (2001). *Older adults and mental health: Issues and opportunities*. Washington, DC: U.S. Department of Health & Human Services.

U.S. Department of Health and Human Services. (1998). *Five-state review of partial hospitalization programs at community mental health centers* (Publ. No. A-04-98-02145). Washington, DC: Author.

U.S. Department of Health and Human Services. (1999). *Health, United States, 1999*. Washington, DC: Author.

U.S. Department of Health and Human Services. (2001). *Medicare payments for psychiatric services in nursing homes—A follow up* (Publ. No. 02-99-00140). Washington, DC: Author.

U.S. Department of Health and Human Services. (2002). *Medicare carriers' policies for mental health services* (Publ. No. OEI-03-99-00132). Washington, DC: Author.

VandenBos, G. R., Stapp, J., & Kilburg, R. R. (1981). Health services providers in psychology: Results of the 1978 APA human resources survey. *American Psychologist, 36*, 1395–1418.

Yang, J. A., & Jackson, C. L. (1998). Overcoming obstacles in providing mental health treatment to older adults: Getting in the door. *Psychotherapy, 35*, 498–505.

Chapter 18

Private Financing for Long-Term Care

Galen H. Smith and William P. Brandon

Contents

Introduction

In 2005, an estimated $206.6 billion was spent on long-term care services in the United States (Georgetown University, Health Policy Institute, 2007). Medicaid represents the greatest proportion of total long-term care expenditures

363

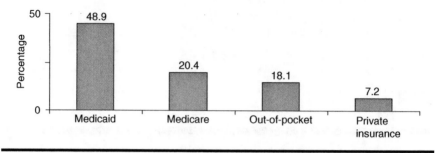

Figure 18.1 **Long-term care financing sources in the United States (2005).**
(Adapted from Georgetown University, Health Policy Institute. 2007. *National*
***Spending for Long-Term Care.* Fact Sheet. Washington. Retrieved April 4, 2007,**
from http://ltc.georgetown.edu/pdfs/natspendfeb07.pdf.)

(48.9 percent), paying for about one-third of long-term care spending on the elderly in 2004 and about 60 percent of long-term care spending for nonelderly persons with disabilities in 1998 (Congressional Budget Office, 2004).* The Medicare program, with its limited coverage of nursing home care and home healthcare, finances about 20 percent of total long-term care spending. Medicare is followed closely by out-of-pocket spending, which constitutes 18.1 percent of total long-term care expenditures. Private health and long-term care insurance accounts for only 7.2 percent of expenditures (see Figure 18.1). Despite the relatively low current market share of private insurance in paying for all forms of long-term care, recent evidence indicates that the private market is growing (America's Health Insurance Plans, 2004).

These descriptive statistics reflect the disparate nature of long-term care financing in the United States, where the combination of private and public mechanisms has historically been inadequate in terms of pooling risks or spreading costs over time (Rivlin et al., 1988). The important role that private options can play in financing long-term care is underscored by the fact that most individuals who enter nursing homes do not, at least initially, qualify for financing by public programs such as Medicaid. Financing of long-term care through the Medicaid program is means-tested; individuals with income or asset levels in excess of a critical threshold level fail to qualify. In contrast, Medicare-related financing of long-term care was originally designed for convalescence posthospitalization, and therefore requires individuals to enter a skilled nursing facility (SNF) directly from a hospital. The emphasis

---

* Because a large proportion of long-term care for the nonelderly disabled is financed by the Medicaid program, the remainder of the chapter will focus largely on the private financing of long-term care for individuals aged 65 or above.

on home and community-based services as an alternative to nursing home care and its public financing developed after the enactment of Medicare in 1965.

In the future, likely constraints on public budgets may further compromise the provision of public long-term care financing for those individuals who do qualify for public assistance. These considerations suggest that when it comes to long-term care, the United States will need to continue for the foreseeable future to rely on private risk-sharing mechanisms to provide financial security and well-being. Most experts concede that private insurance of long-term care has so far been underutilized as a strategy to protect an individual's wealth against the pernicious effects of costly episodes of long-term care. However, inherent structural problems, which may be unavoidable, constitute significant barriers.*

This chapter examines several facets of private long-term care insurance in the United States and the reasons for its relative insignificance. Initially, the focus is on economic principles such as market failure, incomplete markets, externalities, moral hazard, and adverse selection that characterize insurance markets. A brief discussion of risk pooling is included because a number of the existing and potential private funding mechanisms are based on this important concept. Next, the various structural components of private long-term care risk sharing are identified and described, with attention to their strengths and weaknesses and how each might improve the portfolio of private long-term care funding alternatives. Subsequent portions of the chapter describe emerging trends within this market and examine ways in which access and affordability of private long-term care financing might be improved to create incentives for expanded consumer participation.

Economic Principles Related to Private Long-Term Care Insurance

Friedman (2002, p. 593) defines market failures as "situations in which ordinary market coordination does not lead to an efficient (perfectly competitive) equilibrium." Weimer and Vining (2005) and Friedman describe at least four common types of market failure: public goods, externalities, natural monopolies, and information asymmetries (also referred to as imperfect information). Rosen (2002) explains the remarkable efficiency and productivity that markets provide in his discussion of the first fundamental theorem of economics, arguing that a market

---

* The proportion of long-term care services paid by private insurance specifically for long-term care compared to other forms of private insurance (i.e., private health insurance and automobile insurance) is quite low. Only $1.4 billion in claims was paid by private long-term care insurance policies in 2002 (Desonia, 2004). In contrast, approximately $16 billion in long-term care services was covered by all private insurance policies in 2003 (Kaiser Commission on Medicaid and the Uninsured, 2005).

economy best promotes social welfare because individuals will only make Pareto-optimal exchanges.* Market failures arise when the two underlying assumptions associated with the theorem are compromised. The first assumption states that all producers and consumers act as perfect competitors. However, the presence of "market power," where some individuals or firms engage in "price-making" behavior (monopsony or monopoly) instead of the "price-taking" behavior that characterizes competitive markets, undermines this assumption. The second assumption necessary to realize the first fundamental theorem of welfare economics maintains that a market exists for each and every commodity. "Nonexistence of markets" violates this assumption and leads to market failure.

Few would dispute that a market for privately funded long-term care insurance exists, however anemic. But, as suggested earlier, it has so far failed to provide a meaningful alternative to the public sources of long-term care financing. Why? According to Weimer and Vining (2005), "incomplete insurance markets" arise from voluntary (noncompulsory) participation in insurance markets and from several other factors including

- *Moral hazard*, or "the reduced incentive that insurees have to prevent compensable losses" (p. 121)
- *Adverse selection*, where high-risk enrollees are attracted to insurance and low-risk enrollees decline insurance coverage, resulting in only those with the highest risk choosing to remain covered
- *Limited actuarial experience* and therefore uncertainty regarding the cost of claims, which will cause insurers to charge very high premiums to cover the unknown probability of high loss ratios

The market for long-term care insurance suffers from each of these handicaps. Brandon (1989) describes distorted incentives in the Medicaid program that promote the use of its nursing home coverage features as a form of public catastrophic nursing home insurance for the middle-class elderly. The existence of Medicaid long-term care financing as a "free" substitute to private insurance after individuals "spend down" to Medicaid eligibility thresholds supports the role of moral hazard in establishing an incomplete insurance market. Adverse selection also occurs in the private long-term care insurance market, largely due to low take-up rates by younger people; individuals tend to postpone the decision to purchase insurance until later in life when they are at greater risk of requiring long-term care services. Additionally, Weimer and Vining (2005, p. 254) point to suboptimal purchasing decisions by consumers as a result of "biases inherent in the heuristics commonly used to estimate and interpret probabilities." This point becomes apparent in terms

---

* A Pareto-optimal exchange is one in which no party is made worse off than before the exchange and one or more are better off. Side payments by winners to losers that bring the latter back to their initial position are a common way of achieving Pareto-optimality.

of an individual's inability to assess or predict accurately his or her risk for needing long-term care services, thereby supporting the imperfect information argument. All of these factors support the argument for categorizing the private long-term care insurance market as incomplete, if not a failure.

The outcomes associated with incomplete insurance markets often entail negative externalities* imposed on society because of losses suffered by uncovered individuals. These negative externalities may serve as the basis for public intervention expressed either directly by government provision of insurance or indirectly in the form of industry regulation. Feder (2001) argues that public sector interventions are necessary because reliance on personal saving is inefficient (people will save either too much, too little, or not at all) and the ability of private insurance to spread risk is limited (if few purchase it). However, Pauly (1990, p. 167) argues that the nonpurchase of private long-term care insurance is rational behavior and that "the mere absence of coverage does not necessarily imply the existence of a problem of market failure requiring government intervention."

An Illustration of Risk Pooling

From an individual's perspective, there is great uncertainty as to whether or not he or she will require long-term care in his or her lifetime and the extent of the costs associated with those services. The aggregate risk and concomitant costs can be more accurately predicted, however, when various populations or subgroups become the unit of analysis. Several techniques described in this section explain the measurement and evaluation of risk. This brief discussion establishes a baseline understanding of the principles that are employed by several of the private long-term care financing strategies and outlines the economic barriers that may limit the provision of and accessibility to these goods and services.

By definition, uncertainty is associated with more than one possible outcome. One way of measuring the effects of a number of possible outcomes is to calculate the "expected value" of all possible outcomes. Pindyck and Rubinfeld (2001) analyze expected value in terms of weighted probabilities of values associated with possible outcomes and illustrate it using the following convention:

$$E(X) = \Pr_1 X_1 + \Pr_2 X_2 + \cdots + \Pr_n X_n$$

where

$E(X)$ = sum of the expected value of all possible outcomes
$\Pr_1 X_1$ = probability of outcome 1 multiplied by the value of outcome 1
$\Pr_2 X_2$ = probability of outcome 2 multiplied by the value of outcome 2
$\Pr_n X_n$ = probability of outcome n multiplied by the value of outcome n

---

* A negative externality occurs when the action of one party imposes costs on another party that are not accounted for by the market price (Pindyck and Rubinfeld, 2001).

One of the cornerstones of private long-term care financing is the concept of "risk pooling." The mechanics of risk pooling are illustrated by the following hypothetical example. Suppose that each of two households has wealth totaling $100,000 and that each household has a 10 percent probability of total loss of wealth (wealth = $0) due to an extended stay in a long-term care facility. If the households bear the risks independently, the expected value of wealth for each household is $90,000 because there are only two possible outcomes: $100,000 with a probability of 0.9 and $0 with a probability of 0.1.

$$E(X) = [(\$100,000)0.9 + (\$0)0.1] = \$90,000$$

If the individual households decide to pool their risks, then any losses from an extended stay in a long-term care facility will be evenly divided between them. Under this arrangement, there are three possible outcomes:

■ Neither of the households experiences a loss from the extended long-term care facility stay (average wealth for the two households = $100,000 each)
■ Both the households experience total loss of wealth from the extended long-term care facility stay (average wealth for the two households = $0 each)
■ One household has a total loss of wealth and the other does not (average wealth for the two households = $50,000 each)

The probability that neither of the households experiences a loss of wealth from the extended stay in a long-term care facility is 0.81(0.9 × 0.9); the probability that both the households experience a total loss of wealth from the extended long-term care facility stay is 0.01(0.1 × 0.1); and the probability that one household experiences no loss of wealth and the other experiences a total loss is 0.18(1 − 0.81 − 0.01). The probability of extreme outcomes declines as a result of the risk-pooling arrangement, yet the expected value of wealth remains the same at $90,000:

$$E(X) = [(\$100,000)0.81 + (\$0)0.01 + (\$50,000)0.18] = \$90,000$$

$$E(X) = [\$81,000 + \$0 + \$9,000] = \$90,000$$

The risk costs are reduced even further as more households join the pool. In practical terms, this example means that families can reduce their chances of major losses by pledging to pay some of the costs of a risk pool that guarantees large numbers of individuals against large-scale losses.*

---

* See Friedman (2002, pp. 220–243) for a comprehensive analysis of risk control and risk-shifting mechanisms under uncertainty.

Private Long-Term Care Financing Strategies

A handful of strategies have been either implemented or proposed to provide long-term care financing within the private sector. These strategies are broadly classified into two major categories (Rivlin et al., 1988; Alecxih and Kennell, 1994). The first one consists of financing mechanisms that involve risk pooling and include private long-term care insurance, continuing care retirement communities (CCRCs), and social/health maintenance organizations (S/HMOs) and the Program of All-Inclusive Care for the Elderly (PACE). Risk-pooling strategies involve "mechanisms by which individuals spread the costs of incurring a risk among all persons who contribute to the pool" (Alecxih and Kennell, 1994, p. 2).

The second broad category involves an individual's accumulation of assets and includes individual medical accounts (IMAs), home equity conversions (HECs), and accelerated life insurance benefits. Individual asset accumulation strategies encourage people to save or use each household's own existing assets to finance current or future long-term care needs. Each of these specific risk-pooling and individual asset accumulation mechanisms is discussed in detail in the following sections on Risk-Pooling Strategies and Individual Asset Accumulation Strategies, and is summarized in Table 18.1.

Risk-Pooling Strategies

Friedman (2002, p. 235) tells us "Risk-pooling occurs when . . . individuals, each facing a risk that is independent of the risks faced by others, agree to share any losses (or gains) among themselves." Risk-pooling strategies are based on the "law of large numbers," a theoretical premise, which states that risk is minimized when the average outcome of many similar events can be predicted, despite the random and unpredictable nature of a single occurrence (Pindyck and Rubinfeld, 2001). As noted earlier, the specific risk-pooling strategies for financing long-term care include private long-term care insurance, CCRCs, and S/HMOs, including their recent iteration as PACE.

Long-term care insurance represents the predominant form of private financing of long-term care. It is a mechanism by which individuals pay premiums to create financial reserves that are used to pay the costs of those individuals in the pool who actually end up needing long-term care (Alecxih and Kennell, 1994). In addition to its primary effect of providing financial support for individuals in need of long-term care services, long-term care insurance may also be beneficial for those who do not yet require services by relieving anxiety and the need to plan further for future catastrophic needs. The broad benefits conveyed by long-term care insurance are the primary source of its social value.

Long-term care insurance is distinguished from health insurance in two distinct ways. The former provides coverage for extended care services (at least 12 months) and covers services not provided in acute care settings. Nursing home stays and

Table 18.1 Summary of Private Long-Term Care Financing Mechanisms

	Risk-Pooling Strategies
Private long-term care insurance	Individuals pay premiums to create financial reserves that are used to pay the costs (up to the specified limits) of those individuals in the pool who actually end up needing long-term care
CCRCs (analogue: NORCs)	"Residential campuses consisting of independent apartments and cottages and a variety of social and health services in one setting" (Rivlin et al., p. 83)
S/HMOs and PACE	Use case-managed utilization controls and other restrictions in acute and long-term care to generate cost savings designed to reduce premiums and improve affordability of long-term care services for the low-income elderly; keep residents in the home and community and out of SNFs or intermediate care facilities (ICFs)
	Individual Asset Accumulation Strategies
IMAs	Create a form of savings account, with deposits earmarked for long-term care services or the purchase of private long-term care insurance
HECs	Elderly homeowners transfer the equity in their homes into an income stream that enables them to purchase long-term care insurance or long-term care services
Accelerated life insurance benefits and riders to life insurance	Convert existing universal or whole-life insurance policies into long-term care coverage

Sources: Adapted from Rivlin et al., *Caring for the Disabled Elderly: Who Will Pay?* The Brookings Institution, Washington, 1988; Alecxih, L. and Kennell, D., *The Emerging Private Financing System*, U.S. Department of Health and Human Services and Lewin/ICF, Washington, 1994.

home care visits, especially for supportive services, comprise the services not covered in acute care settings.

Most of the long-term care insurance products sold in today's marketplace are indemnity products that vary greatly in terms of cost, covered benefits, and eligibility criteria. Long-term care insurance policies typically pay for at least two years of nursing home coverage and involve a deductible period with no coverage for the first 20–100 days. The premiums for most long-term care insurance policies are based on the age of the individual purchaser and can be either "issue age" or "attained age" premiums (Alecxih and Kennell, 1994). Issue age premiums are charged based on the age at which an individual initially purchases the insurance, whereas attained age premiums represent premiums that alter with the insured individual's age. Both types of premiums are susceptible to modifications based on the experience of others in the risk pool. Premiums may increase if more claims than expected are incurred.

The private long-term care insurance market of the twenty-first century is subdivided into two broad categories. These include the "individual market," where the insurance policies are sold by insurance companies directly to individuals or through group associations that are individually underwritten, and the "group market" (Johnson and Uccello, 2005; Alecxih and Kennell, 1994; America's Health Insurance Plans, 2004). Most private long-term care insurance policies are sold through the individual market (America's Health Insurance Plans, 2004).

Employer-sponsored plans are examples of group insurance. Few employers actually subsidize plan premiums; therefore, most employees who choose long-term care coverage bear the full cost of the policy. However, premiums paid by participants in employer-sponsored plans are usually smaller, due to their lower administrative costs and the younger age of the typical purchaser. Another attractive feature is that employer-sponsored group plans offer long-term care insurance to the employee's spouse and parents as well. Policies sold in the individual market continue to represent the vast majority of total long-term care insurance coverage (Singh, 2005), but the growth of employer-sponsored plans in the group market has been impressive in recent years.

Companies that provide private long-term care insurance products offer policies that cover a wide range of services. Thirteen insurance providers accounted for approximately 80 percent of the private long-term care insurance policies sold in 2002, and all 13 companies offered plans that covered nursing home, assisted living facility, home healthcare, hospice care, and alternate care services. Case management services, homemaker or chore services, restoration of benefits, reimbursement of bed reservations in long-term care facilities, coverage of some medical equipment, survivorship benefits, and caregiver training were other common benefits (America's Health Insurance Plans, 2004). All plans covered Alzheimer's disease and were "guaranteed renewable," meaning that the insurer is required to renew the policy for a specified amount of time, regardless of changes to the health of the insured. All companies offered plans that have inflation protection at an annual 5 percent compounded rate as well as a "nonforfeiture" benefit, which promises return of the value of the premiums paid, even if the insured ceases to pay on the coverage.*

The administrative and overhead costs of private long-term care insurance products are generally higher on a per unit basis compared to those of health insurance policies. Health insurance plans benefit from economies of scale that are unlikely

---

* Because long-term care insurance coverage with affordable premiums generally requires the insured to take out the coverage at a relatively young age, it is quite common for individuals to cease paying premiums if their economic circumstances change.

to be matched by the small number of private long-term care insurance policies currently in force. The higher administrative costs of long-term care insurance lead to higher premiums, which adversely affect affordability and the uptake rates of private long-term care insurance.

Another problem with long-term care insurance is inherent in the fundamental structure of this kind of insurance. Long-term care insurance creates the potential for insurance companies to seek immediate financial success and sacrifice long-term financial stability or even solvency. Unlike health insurance, which typically functions as prepayment for ongoing consumption of acute healthcare that is covered by that year's premium, affordable long-term care insurance depends on healthy insureds who pay premiums for years before claims are likely. Especially if intense competition leads insurers to shave long-term care profit margins to gain market share, insurers may prosper over the years when healthy insureds are paying premiums without receiving any benefits. However, this strategy leads to losses in later decades when high cost claims begin to accumulate.

One way to avoid such losses is to deny or delay paying benefits when insureds require long-term care. Achieving cost savings by avoiding payment on valid policies is easier in the relatively new long-term care insurance market than in more established insurance sectors: first, the typical claimant is impaired and likely to die in a short period of time; and second, state insurance commissioners (the relevant government regulators) are not greatly concerned with this relatively small portion of the insurance industry. A recent investigation in *The New York Times* reveals that this has been a real problem for policyholders of at least three of the ten largest long-term care insurance companies in the United States (Duhigg, 2007).

Long-term care insurance represents the major form of private financing. A second type of private sector long-term care financing strategy that has historically been classified as risk pooling is the CCRC. Rivlin et al. (1988, p. 83) define CCRCs as "residential campuses consisting of independent apartments and cottages and a variety of social and health services in one setting." Access to CCRCs usually requires a relatively large lump sum entry fee plus a monthly fee that covers facility operating and maintenance costs. These fees vary considerably from institution to institution, but are typically based on the size of the dwelling and the number of occupants (Rivlin et al., 1988). In exchange for the entry and monthly fees, CCRCs offer

- Residential housing
- Basic long-term care services, including nursing home care, which is often financed by additional cost-sharing mechanisms
- Access to other health services

Access to nursing services is the feature that attracts most elderly individuals to CCRCs. Utilization of this form of long-term care financing occurs more frequently among the upper-income elderly because of the high costs, especially the entry fees.

In addition to their residential and care-providing capabilities, some CCRCs are insurance vehicles where portions of the entry fee finance the provision of long-term care or the purchase of long-term care insurance (Rivlin et al., 1988). Prepaid financing through entry payments may create an incentive to provide fewer services; CCRCs may capitalize on the fact that they are often the lone access mechanism to long-term care services for CCRC residents and that management can move the location of care delivery from more expensive settings (i.e., nursing homes) to less expensive settings (i.e., home care).

In theory, CCRCs have the potential to finance a significant portion of long-term care for the elderly, due to their risk-pooling features. However, many of them no longer provide long-term care insurance, opting instead to provide long-term care services on a fee-for-service basis, with users at full risk for the cost (Rivlin et al., 1988; Alecxih and Kennell, 1994). This change has limited the role that CCRCs might play in expanding private financing of long-term care initiatives.

There are CCRC analogues that serve low- and moderate-income elders, but they also do not function as insurance. Because disproportionate numbers of older persons often reside in specific apartment buildings or neighborhoods, especially in urban areas, gerontologists have long recognized the existence of "naturally occurring retirement communities" (NORCs) (Masotti et al., 2006). Often such "affordable clustered housing care" provides an important sense of community for low-income elderly persons who cannot afford to live in CCRCs (Golant, 2005). Such housing patterns afford an economical opportunity to locate needed social and health services near the homes of elderly recipients, and sometimes within the same apartment building, thereby functionally replicating many of the advantages enjoyed by more affluent elders who live in CCRCs. The federal government in the United States has done little to mobilize social and health services around these naturally occurring housing patterns (Golant, 2005). Canadian scholars emphasize that local governments in Canada and the United States have the primary responsibility for fostering "healthy NORCs" by improving the physical and social environment of the elderly population. However, they indicate that the strategic focus of policymakers has been directed more toward improving traditional health services, resulting in a haphazard approach toward achieving healthy NORCs (Masotti et al., 2006).

A third type of private long-term care financing strategy is the S/HMO, which functions much like an HMO in the acute care setting, and a similar managed care arrangement largely financed by the public sector, known as PACE. Experience with S/HMOs has been limited to demonstration projects, initiated in the mid-1980s, within the Medicare program. S/HMOs are financed with prepayments similar to acute care HMOs. Generally, the HMO links payers (insurers) with acute care providers by capitated reimbursement mechanisms that shift financial risk from the insurer to the provider. S/HMOs do much the same thing, except that both acute and long-term care services are consolidated into a single, risk-pooled financing mechanism, thereby leading to the integration of acute and long-term care. The goal of S/HMOs is to achieve cost savings in both acute care and the more expensive long-term care arena by instituting case-managed utilization and other controls (such as restrictions on service eligibility and benefit packages), increasing cost sharing, rationing the supply of services, and restricting access to specialty care providers (Rivlin et al., 1988). The savings achieved by these means are subsequently used to reduce premiums and improve affordability for the low-income elderly (Rivlin et al., 1988; Weiner et al., 1994).

Like CCRCs, S/HMOs represent the single point of access to long-term care for participants. S/HMOs cover a variety of long-term care services for the qualified disabled elderly, including "homemaker services, personal care services, respite care, adult day care, transportation, case management . . . and nursing home care" (Rivlin et al., 1988, p. 97). Considerable control over utilization and price accrues to the payer (insurer) when access to a wide range of services is combined with financial incentives. This consolidation could foster enhanced services and lower overall costs but, alternatively, could lead to diminished quality of and restricted access to care.

The long-term viability of S/HMOs as a private funding source of long-term care depends on how well organizational management "can control the use of services and on the market demand for managed care services" (Rivlin et al., 1988). To date, S/HMOs have depended on the demonstration project funding from the federal government. The acute care experience with HMOs indicates that long-term cost reductions may be difficult to sustain. Additionally, the market demand for HMO-specific managed care services has waned in recent years, due in large part to the consumer backlash against stringent gatekeeping activities. These circumstances, coupled with a major adverse selection problem (Rivlin et al., 1988), cast doubt on the long-term viability of this strategy as a long-term care financing mechanism.

PACE, which combines Medicare and Medicaid funding in a capitated arrangement, was built on the promising experiences with S/HMOs demonstration projects in 11 cities in the 1990s. Integrated, comprehensive medical and social services, which allowed impaired and frail Medicare beneficiaries to remain at home rather than become institutionalized, saved Medicare dollars and resulted in longer life than a comparison group.* This striking finding led Congress to incorporate PACE as a permanent Medicare option in the Balanced Budget Act of 1997 (P.L. 105-33). Despite this legislative endorsement, widespread availability of PACE programs has not ensued: only 10,500 individuals were covered in 73 programs, according to a 2002 report by the National PACE Association (Leatherman and McCarthy, 2005).

Gross et al. (2004) discuss a number of possible barriers to participation in the PACE program, including the high out-of-pocket outlays for the elderly who fail to

---

* An Abt Associates evaluation reported that PACE enrollees required 38 percent fewer Medicare dollars in the first six months and 16 percent fewer in the second six months than if they had remained in fee-for-service Medicare. Moreover, clinical outcomes were superior, with PACE enrollees having a median life expectancy of 5.2 years compared to 3.9 years for a comparison group (Leatherman and McCarthy, 2005).

qualify as dual eligibles under both Medicare and Medicaid. These costs are based on Medicaid capitation rates for PACE, which varied from $1,624 to $4,706 per patient per month in January 2003 (National PACE Association, 2003). As such, they represent a substantial out-of-pocket burden for middle-income senior citizens who must pay the Medicaid share if they want to buy into PACE.

Individual Asset Accumulation Strategies

IMAs represent a fourth strategy for funding private long-term care, but, as of this writing, they have not been implemented. Nonetheless, IMA continues to draw considerable attention, particularly because of the claims of its supporters.

IMAs resemble individual retirement accounts (IRAs) in terms of their functionality and administration. Unlike CCRCs or S/HMOs, IMAs are an individual asset accumulation strategy and do not involve the pooling of risk. IMAs would create a form of savings account, with deposits "earmarked for long-term care services or (the purchase of) private long-term care insurance" (Rivlin et al., 1988, p. 109). They would convey tax advantages to those who save for long-term care services by allowing deductions for IMA contributions and exempting interest earnings on deposited funds. Withdrawals without penalty would be made at the applicable tax rate on reaching a certain predetermined age, as long as the funds are used exclusively for long-term care services.

The major advantage of IMAs is their ability to provide discretionary income to the disabled elderly that can be directed to those long-term care services deemed most appropriate for the specific individual's needs. There are, however, several problems that undermine the effectiveness of IMAs. One is the tendency of people to postpone "aging preparation" (retirement, long-term care, etc.) until middle age or older, thereby losing the benefit of compounded interest. The result would be less-than-adequate funding to cover worst-case scenarios. A second problem with IMAs is that participants are likely to save more than necessary for catastrophic expenses that probably will never occur. Depending on the plan's provisions, failure to use the savings in the fund for the earmarked purpose of long-term care could result in forfeiture. This relates to the fact that IMAs are not structured as risk-pooling instruments. Another drawback of IMAs, similar to the experience with IRAs, is that participants are likely to be individuals at upper-income levels, with very low participation rates among those with low or moderate incomes (Rivlin et al., 1988).

HECs represent a fifth type of long-term care financing instrument, where elderly homeowners transfer the equity in their homes into an income stream that enables them to purchase long-term care insurance or long-term care services. Risk pooling is not an integral component of this type of financing arrangement. HECs do provide an opportunity for low-income individuals who are homeowners, especially those with significant amounts of equity in their houses (Rivlin et al., 1988).

There are two types of HEC options. The first is a "reverse mortgage," in which a bank or other lending institution gives the homeowner a loan, usually in the form of monthly installments, with repayment of the loan occurring when the home is sold by the homeowner or his or her heirs. Reverse mortgages are structured as either a "fixed-term loan," where it is repaid after a set period of time (usually five to fifteen years) regardless of the borrower's long-term care status, or an "open-term loan," where it is repaid after the borrower dies, moves, or sells the home (Rivlin et al., 1988; Alecxih and Kennell, 1994). Under the second HEC option, the familiar "home equity line of credit," the homeowner can borrow funds up to a credit limit secured by the equity in the house.

The major advantage of HECs is their ability to permit discretionary spending by borrowers for those long-term care services deemed most necessary or useful by the individual. They are also quite promising in terms of increasing the participation of the low-income elderly in the private long-term care financing market. One major drawback is the reluctance of elderly individuals to part with their homes. Another is the uncertainty that results to lenders if borrowers desire to remain in their homes at the end of a fixed-loan reverse mortgage or if they live much longer than expected, thereby postponing repayment of the loan. Fluctuations in property values also contribute to uncertainty for the lender, particularly in the context of a 20- to 30-year time horizon that may accompany a reverse mortgage. This form of uncertainty may result in higher interest rates or lending only small portions of the established equity (Rivlin et al., 1988). These perceptions have resulted in a low volume of HECs.

However, the U.S. Department of Housing and Urban Development (HUD) and Fannie Mae provide reverse mortgages for borrowers and coborrowers aged 62 and above that greatly reduce the risk borne by commercial lenders and older homeowners who wish to convert an illiquid asset into cash. The HUD program, Home Equity Conversion Mortgage (HECM), involves Federal Housing Administration (FHA) mortgage insurance that costs a mere 2 percent (two points) of the maximum being claimed at closing and 0.5 percent per year on the actual-outstanding HECM loan balance. Both costs can be paid by the income generated. This mortgage insurance guarantees that the lender will receive complete repayment, even if the value of the mortgaged home at sale fails to equal the amount loaned or if a homeowner receiving a promised income stream lives longer than expected. The Fannie Mae offering, Home Keeper Mortgage, requires no insurance other than normal property coverage on the home; presumably, allowances for default (i.e., declining value of the home when the elder vacates it) are built into its fees.

Neither of these HEC plans is restricted to low-income homeowners. The only limitations are the amounts that can be loaned. HUD will provide the full appraised value of a home up to the limits of FHA mortgages in a given geographical area. Fannie Mae's Home Keeper limits its loans by the life expectancy of the borrower (to ensure that it receives actuarially fair fees), the appraised value of the specific property to be mortgaged, and the average U.S. home price (which functions as a maximum that can be loaned).

In both programs, older homeowners can live in their homes as long as they wish; the house is sold only after it ceases to be an owner's principal residence. Fannie Mae and HUD also give the homeowner flexibility in how they wish to receive payment, ranging from lump sums and revenue streams (time limited or for as long as the home is a principal residence) to standby lines of credit to be used only when needed. Moreover, because the loan is only converting an illiquid real estate asset owned by the homeowner into cash, the lump sum or income stream is tax-free (Fannie Mae, 2002).

Both programs involve commercial mortgagers, but the private sector does not appear to have marketed these opportunities vigorously. Moreover, despite the attractive features of such federal guarantee programs, these opportunities appear to be underutilized. Government-guaranteed reverse mortgages should be particularly useful in allowing sophisticated homeowners in a real estate bubble to monetize the inflated value of a principal residence while they continue to reside in it, thereby protecting themselves against future declines in home values. Any appreciation in the value of the home beyond the amount that is borrowed under HECM or Home Keeper programs goes to the homeowner or the homeowner's heirs. FHA or Fannie Mae will also reimburse commercial lenders for any losses (Fannie Mae, 2002).

Technically different, but conceptually very similar to HECs, accelerated life insurance benefits and riders to life insurance are examples of individual asset accumulation strategies that convert existing universal or whole-life insurance policies into long-term care coverage. Accelerated life insurance arrangements pay lump sum accelerated death benefits to the insured in the event of terminal illness, a specific disease, or nursing home confinement (Alecxih and Kennell, 1994). Riders to life insurance arrangements, which also pay benefits to the insured from universal or whole life, must meet the following criteria:

- Conform to National Association of Insurance Commissioners (NAIC) guidelines
- Payments must be used for long-term care services
- Payments must not be made in a lump sum fashion

Riders to life insurance plans were a fashionable means of providing long-term care insurance coverage in the early 1990s, but their popularity has declined in recent years. Indeed, many insurance providers no longer extend this option (America's Health Insurance Plans, 2004). Riders to life insurance pay a percentage of the policyholder's death benefit each month that the policyholder needs long-term care in exchange for a small extra premium. The policyholder's death benefit is reduced accordingly.

Accelerated life insurance benefits as a means of financing long-term care would display promise only if significant numbers of the elderly had high-value whole-life or universal life policies, which is not the case. America's Health Insurance Plans

(2004, p. 11) reports that sales of life insurance rider products have peaked in recent years and they surmise that "consumers view their life insurance and long-term care insurance needs differently and therefore do not want to combine these risks and needs in one product."

Barriers to Private Long-Term Care Insurance Coverage

A number of long-term care financing experts have identified factors that prevent or dissuade individuals from pursuing or maintaining private long-term care insurance coverage (Weiner et al., 2000; Alecxih and Kennell, 1994; Duhigg, 2007; Johnson and Uccello, 2005; Brandon, 1989). Most point to "affordability" as the primary barrier, with the magnitude of the problem exacerbated for those who delay purchasing long-term care insurance coverage until older ages. Social Security Administration data in Johnson and Uccello (2005) show that 12 percent of married couples and nearly half (44 percent) of single adults aged 55 to 61 received less than $25,000 as income in 2000. For ages 70 to 74, the proportion of adults receiving incomes less than $25,000 in 2000 increased to 29 percent of married couples and 62 percent of single adults. Yet the annual premium in 2002 for a policy that provided up to four years of long-term care benefits with a $150 daily benefit, a 90-day waiting period, and 5 percent per year inflation protection was $1,134 if issued at 50 years of age; $2,346 if issued at 65 years of age; and $7,572 if issued at 79 years of age (America's Health Insurance Plans, 2004). In fact, Cohen (2003, p. 82) notes that "many regulators and policymakers suggest that individuals with annual incomes below $20,000 and low levels of assets should not purchase the insurance" and should instead look to Medicaid as their institutional long-term care financing vehicle. According to Weiner et al. (2000), the daunting premiums are mainly due to the large proportion of individually sold policies, which involve significant administrative and marketing costs and the disproportionate number of policies bought by higher-risk, older people.

Imperfect information, particularly among potential consumers, is another major barrier to the development of the private long-term care insurance market. Many individuals lack knowledge about their risks of needing long-term care (Weiner et al., 2000) and many believe that their long-term care needs can be financed unconditionally through the Medicare program (Alecxih and Kennell, 1994; Weiner et al., 2000). Additionally, the vast array of coverage features, options, conditions, and related terminology may be confusing to many potential buyers (Alecxih and Kennell, 1994). They are also less likely to purchase long-term care insurance if reports about insurance companies not paying claims, similar to *The New York Times* investigative account, become common (Duhigg, 2007).

Another important barrier to the purchase of private long-term care insurance is the presence of health problems (Johnson and Uccello, 2005). Many private insurers either deny coverage to those individuals with medical infirmities or charge considerably higher premiums that are often not affordable.

Johnson and Uccello (2005) argue that the most significant obstacle to private insurance coverage for affluent, impoverished, and near-impoverished individuals may be the presence of Medicaid coverage for long-term care needs. Low-income individuals will look to the Medicaid safety net more or less by default. Moreover, the authors argue that at least some of the affluent conclude that they will not derive much utility from their wealth if institutionalized (presumably in a nursing home) and, therefore, lack an incentive to protect their assets with coverage for long-term care. In other words, if bad luck causes them to have expensive long-term care costs, they do not mind exhausting their resources at the end of an active life. Meanwhile, this group prefers to enjoy their income in more rewarding endeavors than paying long-term care premiums.

Cultural characteristics, including religious beliefs and ethnic customs, may deter some individuals from seeking institutional forms of long-term care. Clemetson (2006) describes the struggle of many American Muslims who face conflicts between religious injunctions about a child's responsibility to care for his or her parents and the realities of providing the degree of care that a loved one's condition may require. The conflict may be particularly intense when the major long-term care option involves institutionalization and may escalate if family members are divided about which option(s) to pursue. The demand for long-term care insurance will decrease in response to cultural characteristics that dampen the more general market for paid long-term care. It may be possible, however, for other financing mechanisms such as CCRCs to bridge the cultural divide and become a more acceptable form of long-term care under these circumstances. Religious sponsorship of culturally grounded programs and facilities may also ease the dilemma faced by religious and ethnic minorities. A brief summary of the barriers to purchasing long-term care insurance is presented in Table 18.2.

Table 18.2 Barriers to Purchasing Long-Term Care Insurance

Inadequate affordability
Imperfect information
Presence of health problems
Presence of Medicaid coverage of long-term care services
Cultural barriers

Sources: Adapted from Johnson, R. and Uccello, C., *Is Private Long-Term Care Insurance the Answer?* Issue in Brief No. 29, Trustees of Boston College, Center for Retirement Research, Boston, MA, 2005; Clemetson, L., *The New York Times,* June 13, A1, 2006.

Trends and Recent Developments in the Private Financing of Long-Term Care

Despite the relatively small proportion of total long-term care expenditures currently financed by the private sector, recent evidence indicates that there has been considerable growth in the number of long-term care insurance policies purchased. In time, these policies can be expected to pay claims that amount to a larger proportion of the cost of long-term care services (unless policyholders cease paying premiums). Although sales in the life insurance rider market sector have stalled in the past decade, more than 900,000 policies in the total private insurance market were sold in 2002, the largest surge in single-year sales since 1987 (America's Health Insurance Plans, 2004).

The individual private long-term care insurance market is fairly concentrated in terms of the number of providers selling policies and the geographic regions where policies are sold. Thirteen insurance companies accounted for approximately 80 percent of all individual policies sold in 2002. Additionally, half of all the individual policies sold since the inception of private long-term care insurance in 1987 through 2002 occurred in ten states: California, Florida, Illinois, Iowa, Minnesota, New York, Ohio, Pennsylvania, Texas, and Washington. Market penetration rates in 2002 were highest in the Midwest, with the top ten states consisting of Iowa, Kansas, Indiana, Minnesota, Missouri, Montana, Nebraska, North Dakota, South Dakota, and Washington (America's Health Insurance Plans, 2004).

There has also been substantial recent growth in the number of policies sold in other markets, particularly in the employer-sponsored market. In 2002, 28 percent of long-term care insurance carriers sold policies in either the employer-sponsored or life insurance markets, compared to only 14 percent in 1988. The growth in the employer-sponsored market has been particularly impressive. In 2002, more than 280,000 new long-term care insurance policyholders purchased coverage through their employer; these policies constituted nearly one-third of all long-term care policies sold that year. Approximately 1,700 employer-based plans were introduced in 2001 and 2002 alone. The increasing popularity of these policies is striking, especially in light of the fact that most are not subsidized by employers (America's Health Insurance Plans, 2004).

Government Interventions in the Private Long-Term Care Insurance Market

Weiner et al. (2000, p. 61) discuss three general strategies of governmental intervention intended to increase the market share of private long-term care insurance. These include (1) "providing individuals with tax incentives that encourage purchase of long-term care policies by reducing the net price of such policies"; (2) "encourag[ing] employer-based private long-term care insurance through tax incentives and through the federal and state governments serving as role models for private employers by providing governmental employees, retirees, and their dependents the opportunity to purchase insurance"; and (3) "waiv[ing] some or all of the Medicaid asset depletion requirements for purchasers of qualified long-term care insurance policies, allowing them to retain more of their assets and still qualify for Medicaid."

The Health Insurance Portability and Accountability Act (HIPAA) of 1996 (P.L. 104-191) currently provides some federal tax incentives for purchasing long-term care insurance by allowing individuals to add the value of their long-term care insurance premiums to their medical expenses on their income tax returns and granting tax deductions for total expenses above the 7.5 percent adjusted gross income (AGI) threshold. Weiner et al. (2000) analyze several new federal tax-related proposals that may enhance the incentive to purchase long-term care insurance. One of them would expand the deduction for long-term care insurance premiums by removing the AGI threshold requirement, thereby permitting deductibility of the entire premium. Another proposal is to allow employers to include long-term care insurance as part of their cafeteria plans and flexible spending accounts and permit individuals to withdraw tax-free funds from their retirement accounts to pay long-term care insurance premiums. Of course, the attractiveness of these measures should be considered in the larger context of their impact on "tax revenue loss, the distributional effect of the tax incentive, and the efficiency of the subsidy in encouraging additional [long-term care insurance] purchases" (Weiner et al., 2000, pp. 65–66).

State governments also have attempted to stimulate growth in the private long-term care insurance market by extending both individual and employer-based tax credits and deductions. "In general, these tax incentives are likely to have only a minimal impact on long-term care insurance premiums because of the relatively low state tax rates, which make a deduction or credit less attractive" (Weiner et al., 2000, p. 68).

Weiner et al. (2000, p. 72) also assess the government's role in providing incentives to secure private long-term care insurance in the employer-sponsored market. The centerpiece of this strategy was codified in HIPAA, which allowed "employer contributions to the cost of qualified private long-term care insurance to be tax-deductible as a business expense in the same way that employer contributions to health insurance are deductible." However, the researchers argue that despite this important tax incentive for health benefits, many employers find the costs of long-term care coverage increasingly prohibitive and are even curtailing benefits currently provided to retirees by dropping them altogether or imposing considerably greater cost sharing. Certainly, few companies will be willing to pay for their retired workers' long-term care coverage now or in the future.

The government also has a role as an employer at both the state and federal levels in terms of providing long-term care insurance to public employees. Such a "lead-by-example" strategy to heighten awareness of the relative dearth of private long-term care insurance has not been particularly effective in spurring the market.

One major factor is the low take-up rates by employees, most of whom are discouraged by the pay-all nature of the premiums and the use of medical underwriting by state governments to prevent adverse selection and moderate premium costs (Weiner et al., 2000).

The third major government initiative to expand the market for private long-term care insurance involves public–private partnerships, where "partnership" policyholders can protect a portion of their assets and still qualify for Medicaid. Under this arrangement, "consumers are able to purchase insurance equivalent to the amount of assets they wish to preserve [before becoming eligible for Medicaid], potentially reducing the amount of insurance individuals need to buy" (Weiner et al., 2000, p. 85). Despite the apparent attractiveness of this strategy, consumer interest in it has been low. One reason is that potential beneficiaries regard the "partnership" policies as relatively expensive and view the Medicaid program unfavorably (Weiner et al., 2000). Participation has also been stymied because until recently the program had been limited to only four states. The Deficit Reduction Act of 2005 (P.L. 109-171) expanded this option to all the states and, consequently, the situation may change.

Policy Considerations to Improve Private Long-Term Care Financing

Stone (2001, p. 99) argues for a "disability approach" to long-term care financing, where the focus is support "to enhance a person's quality of life, to help ensure as much independence as possible, and to provide flexibility and choice to individuals and their families." According to the author, it trumps the "care/indemnity approach" prevailing in most private long-term care insurance plans that are characterized by purchase of a discrete amount of service *per diem*. Financing long-term care using the disability model would entail cash payments to beneficiaries or implementation of a voucher system. There appears to be a strong support for the disability approach method of financing long-term care among disabled people below 65 years of age (Simon-Rusinwitz and Mahoney, 1997; Barents Group of KMG Consulting, 2001) and higher satisfaction among those purchasing such policies compared to indemnity coverage (Cohen and Miller, 1999).

According to Stone (2001), the major advantages of the disability approach to financing long-term care are

- Providing consumers with the flexibility to address their individual needs
- Circumventing the tendency for benefits under the indemnity approach to become obsolescent as the scope of needed services changes over time
- Providing resources that family caregivers may use to purchase complementary services
- Expanding the pool of long-term caregivers

She notes that the primary disadvantages include the following:

- Difficulty in monitoring how benefit dollars are spent (particularly in the context of the potential for fraud or abuse)
- Costs associated with determining eligibility for benefits (i.e., costs associated with determining disability status)
- Quality assurance
- Limited application to consumers with substantive cognitive impairments

Although the market share of employer-sponsored long-term care insurance plans has increased in recent years, private long-term care insurance on the whole lags far behind publicly financed programs. To date, the risk-pooling strategies described earlier in this chapter (long-term care insurance, CCRCs, and S/HMOs and the PACE program) have been the mainstay for the private financing of long-term care. If the overarching policy goal is to expand the private market for long-term care financing, it seems logical that the government should promote the disability approach, particularly through various funding mechanisms that increase its viability. Perhaps the time has come for bolder action to expand and develop the individual asset accumulation strategies (IMAs, HECs, and accelerated life insurance benefits). These tactics are especially adept at generating discretionary funds that characterize the disability approach and are most capable, at least in theory, of expanding participation among the middle- and lower-income strata of the population.

References

Alecxih, L. and D. Kennell. 1994. *The Emerging Private Financing System.* Washington: U.S. Department of Health and Human Services and Lewin/ICF. Retrieved July 22, 2006, from http://aspe.hhs.gov/daltcp/reports/emerges.htm.

America's Health Insurance Plans. 2004. *Long-Term Care Insurance in 2002.* Washington: America's Health Insurance Plans. Retrieved July 22, 2006, from http://www.ahipresearch.org/pdfs/18_LTC2002.pdf.

Barents Group of KMG Consulting. 2001. *Summary Findings from Long-Term Care Focus Groups,* April 26–June 6, 2001. McLean, VA: KPMG.

Brandon, W. 1989. Cut off at the impasse without real catastrophic health insurance: three approaches to financing long-term care. *Policy Studies Review,* 8(2): 441–454.

Clemetson, L. 2006. For U.S. Muslims, an aversion to nursing homes. *The New York Times,* June 13, 2006, A1.

Cohen, M. 2003. Private long-term care insurance: a look ahead. *Journal of Aging and Health,* 15(1): 74–98.

Cohen, M. and J. Miller. 1999. *A Descriptive Analysis of Patterns of Informal and Formal Caregiving among Privately Insured and Non-Privately Insured Disabled Elders Living in the Community.* Washington: U.S. Department of Health and Human Services.

Congressional Budget Office. 2004. *Financing Long-Term Care for the Elderly.* Washington: Congressional Budget Office.

Desonia, R. 2004. *The Promise and the Reality of Long-Term Care Insurance.* Washington: National Health Policy Forum.

Duhigg, C. 2007. Aging, frail and fighting insurers to pay up. *The New York Times*, March 26, 2007, A1, A16.

Fannie Mae. 2002. *Money from Home: A Consumer's Guide to Reverse Mortgage Options.* Washington: Fannie Mae.

Feder, J. 2001. Long-term care: a public responsibility. *Health Affairs*, 20(6): 112–113.

Friedman, L. 2002. *The Microeconomics of Public Policy Analysis.* Princeton, NJ: Princeton University Press.

Georgetown University, Health Policy Institute. 2007. *National Spending for Long-Term Care.* Fact Sheet. Washington. Retrieved April 4, 2007, from http://ltc.georgetown.edu/pdfs/natspendfeb07.pdf.

Golant, S.M. 2005. Affordable clustered housing-care for poor and frail older Americans: a promising but still immature long-term care strategy. Revised manuscript originally presented at the 2005 Colloquium "Building Bridges: Making a Difference in Long Term Care" conducted by AcademyHealth, Boston, MA, 25 June 2005.

Gross, D., H. Temkin-Greener, S. Kunitz, and D. Mukamel. 2004. The growing pains of integrated health care for the elderly: lessons from the expansion of PACE. *The Milbank Quarterly*, 82(2): 257–282.

Johnson, R. and C. Uccello. 2005. *Is Private Long-Term Care Insurance the Answer?* Issue in Brief No. 29. Trustees of Boston College, Center for Retirement Research, Boston, MA: Center for Retirement Research at Boston College. Retrieved July 24, 2006, from http://urbaninstitute.org/UploadedPDF/1000795.pdf.

Kaiser Commission on Medicaid and the Uninsured. 2005. *Long-Term Care: Understanding Medicaid's Role for the Elderly and Disabled.* Washington: Kaiser Commission on Medicaid and the Uninsured. Retrieved April 5, 2007, from http://www.kff.org/medicaid/upload/Long-Term-Care-Understanding-Medicaid-s-Role-for-the-Elderly-and-Disabled-Report.pdf.

Leatherman, S. and D. McCarthy. 2005. *Quality of Health Care for Medicare Beneficiaries: A Chartbook—Focusing on the Elderly Living in the Community.* New York: The Commonwealth Fund.

Masotti, P.J., R. Fick, A. Johnson-Masotti, and S. MacLeod. 2006. Healthy naturally occurring retirement communities: a low-cost approach to facilitating healthy aging. *American Journal of Public Health*, 96(7): 1164–1170.

National PACE Association. 2003. *PACE Census and Capitation Rate Information, 2002/03.* Unpublished manuscript.

Pauly, M. 1990. The rational nonpurchase of long-term care insurance. *The Journal of Political Economy*, 98(1): 153–168.

Pindyck, R. and D. Rubinfeld. 2001. *Microeconomics* (5th ed.). Upper Saddle River, NJ: Prentice-Hall.

Rivlin, A., J. Wiener, R. Hanley, and D. Spence. 1988. *Caring for the Disabled Elderly: Who Will Pay?* Washington: The Brookings Institution.

Rosen, H. 2002. *Public Finance* (6th ed.). New York: McGraw-Hill Irwin Publishing.

Simon-Rusinwitz, L. and K. Mahoney. 1997. Determining consumer preferences for a cash option: Arkansas survey results. *Health Care Financing Review*, 19(2): 73–96.

Singh, D.A. 2005. *Effective Management of Long-Term Care Facilities*. Sudbury, MA: Jones and Bartlett Publishers.

Stone, R. 2001. Providing long-term care benefits in cash: moving to a disability model. *Health Affairs*, 20(6): 96–108.

Weimer, D.L. and A. Vining. 2005. *Policy Analysis: Concepts and Practice* (4th ed.). Upper Saddle River, NJ: Pearson Prentice-Hall.

Weiner, J., L. Illston, and R. Hanley. 1994. *Sharing the Burden: Strategies for Public and Private Long-Term Care Insurance*. Washington: The Brookings Institution.

Weiner, J., J. Tilly, and S. Goldenson. 2000. Federal and state initiatives to jump start the market for private long-term care insurance. *Elder Law Journal*, 8(1): 57–102.

Chapter 19

Public Financing of Long-Term Care

Stephen A. Stemkowski and William P. Brandon

Contents

Introduction

Generally, like the financing of U.S. healthcare, current financing arrangements for long-term care (LTC) in the United States are confusing and fragmented, and promote a delivery system that is increasingly unable to serve the needs of American elderly and disabled individuals. Over the next several decades, LTC issues will become increasingly important to individuals and policymakers alike. Increases in longevity and decreases in birthrate have increased the proportion of the U.S. population aged 65 or above by more than 34 percent from 1960 to 2000. Over the coming decades, the increase in the percentage of the population above 65 years will be even more profound. By 2040, the proportion of the total population aged 75 or above will be greater than those aged 65–74, doubling from 6 to 12 percent of the total population by 2050 (National Center for Health Statistics, 2005). The transition from serving the needs of 31 million persons aged 65 and above in 1990 to an estimated 40 million Americans in 2020 will require a significant reorganization of the health and social service system in the United States (National Center for Health Statistics, 2005; Ikegami, 1997).

Although the impending problems of providing LTC may seem overwhelming and significant public funds already pay for much LTC, few analysts currently support the development of a tax-funded LTC system. Without active public support, the issue of publicly funded LTC has not been prominent in the public agenda in recent years. Yet a *Handbook of Long-Term Care Administration and Policy* would be incomplete without a chapter on public financing for LTC. The discussion of public LTC funding in this chapter attempts to provide a comprehensive overview of the subject. Thus, it will cover

- Public programs that currently fund LTC, Medicaid, Medicare, the Veterans Administration, and the Indian Health Service (IHS)
- Recent changes to Medicaid and Medicare that affect LTC financing
- Policy options at the state level to alleviate pressure on the financial and delivery systems that range from efforts to promote the purchase of private LTC insurance to delivery system reform
- The general principles of social insurance and examples of universal, tax-financed LTC programs in other countries

■ A concluding discussion that asks why the United States is an exception among advanced industrial nations in its reluctance to enact social insurance programs to promote the welfare of its citizens in need of LTC, healthcare, etc.

Despite a prevailing opinion that LTC is a private affair, the facts reveal that LTC financing has evolved from private, out-of-pocket sources to slowly growing private LTC insurance and finally to the expansion of public expenditures, primarily Medicaid and Medicare. Despite the shift from private to public financing, the United States remains reluctant to implement any form of explicit government program. Instead, we rely on voluntary insurance programs and safety net approaches to help citizens pay the cost of caring for the elderly and persons with disabilities.

Several reasons explain the fragmented approach to financing LTC. The public's attitude reflects a psychological reaction of denial when confronted with the painful realities of aging and debilitating conditions. A second reason is that current fiscal pressures and uncertainties about future costs make governments reluctant to promise to pay for a general entitlement to LTC. A third reason involves the medical profession. Physicians, recognizing limited resources, favor directing them to acute care services and the application of biomedical interventions that are more likely to show measurable improvement in their patients' health status. Physicians may also be concerned that their professional dominance and autonomy would be threatened if the focus of patient care is shifted from curative acute services to LTC, where nurses and social workers constitute the dominant professional workforce.

Spending for LTC is an increasing portion of total U.S. healthcare costs. Yet it continues to be financed by a disorganized and disparate mixture of government, commercial, and private sources. In 1995, nearly $105 billion was spent on nursing home and home healthcare with more than half coming from public sources (Stone, 2000). Since 1995, expenditures have increased by more than 51 percent to nearly $155 billion in 2004 (National Center for Health Statistics, 2006). Since 1960, the percentage of freestanding nursing home care paid for by private, out-of-pocket sources has declined dramatically from nearly 78 percent to less than 28 percent in 2003, whereas the share paid from government sources has risen to nearly 61 percent. Figure 19.1 outlines the proportion of funds by source for 2004 and clearly illustrates that very little of the coverage for LTC services is reimbursed by commercial and employer-provided insurance (Stone, 2000).

Estimates in 1998 put the number of Americans who reported needing nursing home services at 12.8 million people. More than 57 percent were above 65 years; the others were disabled adults below 65 years and children. Yet for the same period, there were only an estimated 1.8 million certified nursing home beds available. By 2003, the number of beds decreased by 3 percent, and the occupancy rate by 1 percent (Gibson et al., 2004). Thus, the vast majority of the elderly with activities of daily living (ADL) impairments live in community- and home-based settings. One-third of people in these settings continue to report that they do not

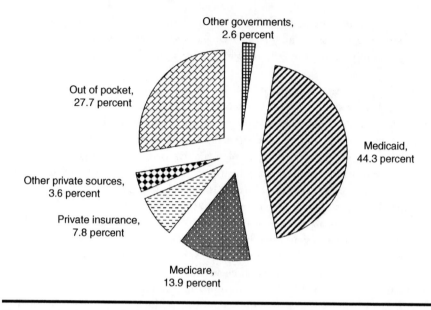

Figure 19.1   Source of nursing home care funds—2004. (From National Center for Health Statistics (2005). *Health, United States 2005* **(DHHS Publication No. 2005-1232). Washington: U.S. Government Printing Office.)**

receive the help that they need. Because the demand for LTC increases significantly with age, special attention is needed for people aged 85 and above (Stone, 2000).

Chapter 18 of this volume by Smith and Brandon discussed the failure of private LTC financing options to provide adequate financial protection for most older and disabled Americans. Insurance is typically considered more attractive as the magnitude of a potential loss or the probability of loss increases. National estimates indicate that a year in a nursing home may cost between $36,000 and $70,000 (ConsumerAffairs.com, Inc., 2006) and that more than 40 percent of all elderly individuals will require nursing home services at least once in their lifetime. Yet LTC insurance is not widely purchased and the recent increase in the number of policies has not significantly increased its share of LTC payments (Norton and Newhouse, 1994; Smith and Brandon, Chapter 18 of this volume).

Two factors help explain the low demand for private LTC insurance. The first is selection. Insurance is more appealing to those who are more likely to use it. Termed "adverse selection," the problem stems from consumers knowing more about their own health risks than do the insurers, which is likely to result in insurance premiums that do not accurately reflect the risk of the insured. Like life insurance, LTC insurance requires an application process that enables insurance carriers to decline applicants or offer coverage for a high premium that reflects the perceived risk. Because of adverse selection, high-risk individuals are more likely to accept the terms of the policy despite higher premiums. In addition, premiums reflect the high administrative costs to insurers that result from individual sales approaches and the expense of underwriting and administering policies. The costly LTC insurance premiums that result typically do not attract healthier individuals (Norton and Newhouse, 1994).

Second, Medicaid is the payer of last resort, functioning as catastrophic LTC insurance (Longest, 2006; Brandon, 1989). Almost all legal residents of a state are covered for LTC under Medicaid once they have spent nearly all of their nonhousing assets to secure the care that they need. States are prohibited from trying to seize the principal residence of beneficiaries or their automobile to recover state Medicaid payments before the recipient's death. Most other assets, however, are subject to liquidation before a beneficiary can qualify. Known as "spending down assets," in effect this practice serves as an individual deductible that must be satisfied to qualify for LTC benefits. For those with few assets to protect, Medicaid is clearly a better deal because the "deductible" is low and there are no premiums. Private LTC insurance for such individuals is hardly worth the monthly premiums that must be paid before the need for LTC arises. For those with significant assets at risk, Medicaid may not be an attractive alternative due to its potentially high "deductible"; for them, LTC insurance is often a more attractive means of protecting individual wealth, particularly for individuals who are risk averse.

Whether these factors or others explain the dearth of private LTC insurance, the fact is that few individuals have purchased private LTC coverage. Consequently, public programs have been enacted to help individuals secure LTC care when the need arises and private resources fail. The U.S. public LTC policy has involved incremental attempts to alleviate a growing social problem by adapting existing programs and instituting new, highly targeted programs that benefit select portions of the population. Such minimally invasive public policy approaches have most often been incorporated in Medicaid and Medicare, the two most prominent public programs that together constitute nearly 57 percent of all LTC financing (National Center for Health Statistics, 2005).

Public Programs Providing Long-Term Care

As a result of the failure of the private sector to provide financial protection to the majority of the population, public programs have been enacted or modified to provide assistance for individuals facing expensive LTC requirements. Despite a 533 percent increase in private insurance as a source of funds for freestanding nursing home services since 1980, all types of private coverage financed only 7 percent of LTC services in 2003 (National Center for Health Statistics, 2005). Other private and out-of-pocket sources have declined considerably, leaving Medicaid and Medicare to finance an increasing proportion of total LTC expenditures.

Medicaid continues to be the single largest source of financial assistance for LTC. Revisions to the Medicare regulations related to home health services and acute LTC have increased the portion of public funds for LTC from this program. The remaining expenditures, about 2.6 percent, are financed through public service agencies such as IHS and the Veterans Administration (National Center for Health Statistics, 2006).

Although the Federal Employees Health Benefit program is sometimes proposed as a model for general healthcare reform, it functions just as any other employer-sponsored insurance in its LTC coverage. In fact, active and retired federal employees must pay the entire premium by a payroll deduction to purchase a private LTC insurance contract if they choose to have LTC coverage. Therefore, this federal employment benefit is not included among the public programs considered in this chapter.

Medicaid

Title XIX of the Social Security Act (P.L. 89-97) created Medicaid, a federal-state entitlement program that pays for medical assistance for certain individuals and families with low incomes and few financial resources. Medicaid is the largest program for LTC benefits for the elderly and the disabled of all ages. It also includes the State Children's Health Insurance Program (SCHIP) for uninsured children in low-income families.

Within broad national guidelines governed by federal statutes, regulations, and policies, each state establishes its own eligibility standards; determines the type, amount, duration, and extent of covered services; sets the rate of payment for services; and administers its own program. Medicaid was initially conceptualized as a program for mothers and children who received income support from Aid to Families with Dependent Children (AFDC), now known as Temporary Assistance for Needy Families (TANF). In addition to covering in- and outpatient acute care services, Medicaid pays for care in skilled or intermediate care nursing homes or in intermediate care facilities for the mentally retarded if medically necessary. The patient's income cannot exceed a threshold established in state Medicaid regulations. If the patient or his or her representative gifts assets or sells them below market value to prevent those assets from being considered in determining the patient's eligibility, he or she may be ineligible for benefits.

Ironically, the Medicaid program's benefit and eligibility structure contributed significantly to the creation and growth of the nursing home industry, an unanticipated effect of the program. Those who previously would have never considered nursing home care due to its cost were now able to access nursing home services because of Medicaid. Not only did this coverage enable Medicaid recipients to afford nursing home care, but it also offered publicly financed LTC options to those with higher income levels who were willing to disperse their nonliquid assets to qualify for Medicaid benefits. A new market that encouraged expansion opened up for nursing home providers.

Medicaid policies for eligibility, services, and payment are complex and vary considerably from state to state (U.S. Department of Health and Human Services, Centers for Medicare and Medicaid Services, 2006). States receive matching federal funds for services provided to the categorically needy, those whose income falls below the eligibility level established by the program. In addition, the federal government finances acute care services and medical care provided in LTC facilities for the elderly and permanently disabled. As a result of the initial focus in Medicaid, there is a strong institutional bias toward more expensive inpatient services for LTC.

However, states are increasingly interested in utilizing home- and community-based services to lower their costs and extend coverage to those with incomes too high to qualify for Medicaid as categorically needy (U.S. Department of Health and Human Services, Centers for Medicare and Medicaid Services, 2005). Known as the "medically needy," these people represent an additional burden on state health expenditures for which states do not receive federal funding. The medically needy option allows states to extend Medicaid eligibility to certain individuals whose income and resources are above the eligibility level for the categorically needy. Individuals may qualify immediately based on income and the extent of their personal assets or they may "spend down" by incurring medical expenses that reduce their income to a level at or below the state-designated eligibility level.

Federal matching funds are available for some medically needy programs if they coincide with funds for categorical groups; however, there are federal requirements that certain groups and certain services must be included for the state to receive them. As of 2003, 35 states and the District of Columbia offered medically needy programs. All the remaining states utilize a "special income level" option to extend Medicaid to the "near poor" in medical institutional settings (U.S. Department of Health and Human Services, Centers for Medicare and Medicaid Services, 2006; Crowley, 2003).

Medicare

The Health Insurance for the Aged and Disabled Act, Title XVIII of the Social Security Act (P.L. 89-97), known as "Medicare," is available to nearly every American 65 years of age and above. It is primarily a health insurance program designed to assist elderly people with meeting hospital, medical, and other health-care costs. Health insurance coverage is also available to people below 65 years who have been disabled for 24 months or longer and those suffering from end-stage renal disease (ESRD) or amyotrophic lateral sclerosis (Lou Gehrig's disease). In addition to acute medical care services, Medicare pays for medically necessary skilled nursing care and home health services. Typically, it does not cover custodial care, although some Medicare advantage plans include limited benefits for skilled nursing and home health. Medicare is composed of three related health insurance programs—hospital insurance (Part A) and supplementary medical insurance consisting of Parts B and D, which provide prescription drugs. LTC-associated coverage is provided by Parts A and B (U.S. Department of Health and Human Services, Centers for Medicare and Medicaid Services, 2004, 2005).

Part A (hospital insurance) is financed by payroll taxes and does not require an individual premium for most beneficiaries. Medicare Part A helps cover inpatient care and prescription medications provided in hospitals, critical access hospitals, long-term care hospitals (LTCHs), and skilled nursing facilities (SNF) but does not cover custodial or LTC services. It also helps pay for hospice care and medically necessary home healthcare services required after a patient is discharged from a hospital. Beneficiaries must meet certain conditions to receive these benefits.

Part B (medical insurance) helps cover doctors' services and outpatient care and is financed in part by individual premium payments and general revenues of the federal government. It also covers other medical services that Part A does not cover, such as the services of physical and occupational therapists and medically necessary home healthcare and medical supplies (U.S. Department of Health and Human Services, Centers for Medicare and Medicaid Services, 2006).

As a result of the Medicare Prescription Drug, Improvement, and Modernization Act of 2003 (MMA, P.L. 108-173), the distinction between medically necessary home health services and assistance services to the homebound is further blurred. The MMA contains provisions that alter existing LTC components of the Medicare program such as home health services, definitions of homebound, and coverage of religious, nonmedical institutional services provided in the home (U.S. Department of Health and Human Services, Centers for Medicare and Medicaid Services, 2004). The MMA redefines homebound to include those who are in adult day care and institutional settings that provide for the ADL-impaired. This change effectively increases the extent to which Medicare finances LTC services. The subtle shift may ultimately be more profound than anticipated, because historically, Medicare focused only on acute care expenses and only reimbursed short-term skilled nursing and home health services for patients in postoperative recovery following an acute hospital discharge.

Beginning with the implementation of prospective payment for acute care hospitals in 1983, an increase in the number of nursing home residents, particularly short stay residents, increased Medicare funding of postacute care in nursing homes (Decker, 2005). The single greatest increase in the proportion of total expenditures for freestanding nursing home services is from the Medicare program. Between 1980 and 2003, Medicare nursing home expenditures had increased by about 600 percent; by 2003, it provided more than 12 percent of total nursing home expenditures (U.S. Department of Health and Human Services, 2005).

Over time, the program began to include a greater number of nonmedical, personal care services. As a result, the growth in Medicare home health spending through the mid-1990s came from greater utilization of nonmedical, low-tech personal services that were previously not covered by Medicare. The program continued to serve an increasing number of ADL-disabled beneficiaries who required more personal services. For these reasons, many policymakers observed that an increasing number of beneficiaries receive long-term care through the Medicare program despite Medicare's stated focus on acute care (Stone, 2000).

In October 2005, there were 8,082 home health agencies certified to care for Medicare patients; at least one home health agency provided services in geographical areas where 99 percent of Medicare beneficiaries resided. The volume of services measured in terms of number of users and episodes of care was higher in 2004 than in 2003. In 2004, 2.8 million beneficiaries received about 4.6 million episodes of care. The volume of services was the same in 2003 and 2004, averaging 18.4 visits per episode (Medicare Payment Advisory Commission, 2006). The number of Medicare-certified home health agencies was 14 percent higher in 2005 than in 2000. However, there was a decline in the more than 10,000 home health agencies that served Medicare beneficiaries in 1997, when prospective payment was mandated for home health.

Many states and home health providers have attempted to take advantage of this liberalization in Medicare by instituting maximization programs that help Medicaid beneficiaries become dual-eligible for both Medicare and Medicaid, thereby allowing states to shift a portion of the Medicaid cost to the federal government. In addition, subacute care experienced more comprehensive coverage under Medicare than under Medicaid. The Medicare program fails to define subacute care specifically and therefore excludes reimbursement for such services, which leaves ample opportunity to reclassify services and expand coverage to include home care.

Veterans Health Administration

In March 1989, the Veterans Administration, as it was then known, became the Department of Veterans Affairs, a cabinet department. More than 5.3 million veterans and eligible dependents of deceased veterans receive medical care and LTC services from the Veterans Health Administration, part of the U.S. Department of Veterans Affairs (VA). The single largest integrated healthcare delivery system in the country, the VA operates 154 hospitals, 136 nursing homes, and 88 comprehensive home care programs as well as hundreds of community-based outpatient clinics, rehabilitation centers, and veteran's centers across the country. Overall, nearly 25 percent of the U.S. population is potentially eligible for VA benefits (U.S. Department of Veterans Affairs, 2006a).

The VA offers a broad range of geriatric and LTC services to enrollees including home-based services, adult day-service programs, and institutional care in VA nursing homes or state nursing homes. The VA focuses on home- and community-based programs both in accordance with its members' preferences and as a more cost-effective care setting. In 2005, nearly 90 percent of VA LTC recipients received care through such programs. In addition, the VA estimated its average daily inpatient LTC census at more than 70,000 for 2005 (U.S. Department of Veterans Affairs, 2006b).

Indian Health Service

The IHS, an agency of the U.S. Department of Health and Human Services, administers the health programs for enrolled members of 557 federally recognized Native American tribes in 35 states. It provides services directly to more than 1.3 million members through 61 health centers, 38 hospitals, and 12 IHS-run nursing homes. Unlike Medicare and Medicaid, which are entitlement programs, IHS funding requires an appropriation in the annual budget process; that is, funding depends on congressional discretion rather than the commitment of an entitlement. Tribes also receive funds from the Older Americans Act, sharing about $25 million among 233 federally recognized tribes.

Federal funding has declined significantly in recent years as a result of an unfavorable political climate that has not supported discretionary increases. Average federal expenditure per patient for Indian patients has decreased from 75 percent of the national average per person healthcare cost in 1977 to only 34 percent in 1999 (Benson, 2002). Limited federal financing has restricted the IHS' ability to expand LTC services for its beneficiaries. Its most widely offered LTC services are transportation, home-delivered meals, housekeeping, and home modification for disabilities, whereas the least offered services include Alzheimer's or dementia care, adult day care, and nursing home services. Indeed, the 12 IHS-run nursing homes have only 627 LTC beds in total.

As a result, tribal members have had to rely more on Medicaid to finance services from an increasing number of non-IHS providers. Yet Native American elders remain underserved, with only 6.5 percent of them receiving any LTC services. Poor economic conditions, transportation issues, and rural isolation make obtaining home and community services even more difficult. Thus, older Native Americans suffer even more than other Americans from fragmented and uncoordinated financing and minimal services (Benson, 2002).

Perhaps the most interesting aspect of the IHS is that structurally and culturally it is more of a government-run, social health system than is the case with health and LTC programs provided to other Americans. The social structure of the tribe encourages the development of services that are provided directly to the members of the tribe from facilities that are owned by the tribe for its collective benefit. Many of the tribal strategies involve generating financial resources to support such social services through gaming and other tribal enterprises. Perhaps similar publicly financed approaches could usefully be developed to meet the needs of other communities for more LTC services.

Recent Changes Affecting Long-Term Care Hospitals

Two significant legislative acts passed in 1999 and 2000 have had a significant impact on Medicaid and Medicare by further blurring differences between the two programs where LTC coverage is involved. The Medicare, Medicaid, and SCHIP Balanced

Budget Refinement Act of 1999 (BBRA, P.L. 106-113) and the Medicare, Medicaid, and SCHIP Benefits Improvement and Protection Act of 2000 (BIPA, P.L. 106-554) established Medicare prospective payment system (PPS) for hospital inpatient stays in LTCHs under Medicare Part A. Section 1886(d)(1)(B)(iv)(II) of the act also provided alternative definitions of LTCHs that were designed to more clearly distinguish LTCHs from acute care hospitals and to restrict the growth of LTCHs.

LTCHs treat "patients with clinically complex problems, such as multiple acute or chronic conditions who may need hospital-level care for relatively extended periods"; they are defined as hospitals with average lengths of stay (ALOS) greater than 25 days. LTCHs can be freestanding or a "hospital within hospital" (HWH). Centers for Medicare and Medicaid Services, citing concern that the latter may function as a step-down unit for acute care patients of the host hospital, established a rule limiting the number of the host hospital's patients that could be admitted to the HWH LTCH.

In October 2002, a PPS for LTCHs replaced the reimbursement program in place since 1982, which was based on average costs per discharge. The PPS for LTCHs is similar to the diagnosis-related group (DRG) classification that is used to reimburse acute care hospitals for Medicare patients. This system reflects the lower intensity of services and costs in LTCHs and maintains budget neutrality. Like the DRG system for acute care hospitals, LTC-DRGs are based on the patient's principal diagnosis, comorbid conditions, procedures, patient demographics, and the discharge status of the patient. LTC-DRG payments provide adequate reimbursement for the efficient delivery of care and are adjusted by LTCH case mix to reflect variations in patient severity. Annual updates to the LTC-DRG payments determined by the Department of Health and Human Services are based on total patient days and total charges (Federal Register, 2006).

Despite the hopes of policy makers, the change in reimbursement does not seem to have discouraged the development of LTCHs. They have become much more common sources of LTC in recent years. Yet many beneficiaries, especially in rural areas, do not have easy geographical access to an LTCH. In 1990, 90 LTCHs served Medicare patients; at the end of 2004, this figure had risen to 357 with 71 new LTCHs beginning their participation between 2001 and 2004. The number of nonprofit and for-profit LTCHs had increased by 12 and 11 percent, respectively, since the end of the cost-based reimbursement in 2002, whereas the number of government-run LTCHs had declined by 5 percent. During the same period, the number of cases discharged from LTCHs had also increased 12 percent per year and Medicare payment per case rose 10 percent per year (Medicare Payment Advisory Commission, 2006).

Recent Changes in Medicaid to Control Costs

Regulatory efforts to limit the growth of public LTC spending occur at both the federal and state levels. In a direct effort to address Medicaid estate planning, the Deficit Reduction Act of 2005 (DRA, S. 1932) includes provisions to reduce the extent of asset transfers by increasing penalties on individuals who transfer personal assets for less than the market value to qualify for Medicaid benefits. The act extends the look-back period, the period of time before an application for Medicaid benefits, from three to five years. Assets that were transferred during the look-back period remain subject to spend-down requirements. The DRA also makes individuals with substantial home equity ineligible for Medicaid nursing home benefits. These measures are expected to save the federal government $6.3 billion from 2006 to 2015.

States are also required to establish Medicaid Estate Recovery programs to recover expenses from patients' estates. Before the year 1993, such programs were voluntary on the part of the state, but the Omnibus Budget Reconciliation Act of 1993 mandated recovery programs. Thus, states must now recover the costs of medical assistance for nursing home services, home- and community-based services, and hospital and prescription drug expenses (U.S. Department of Health and Human Services, Office of Assistant Secretary for Policy and Evaluation, 2005).

The DRA also reduces payment rates for home health services to 2005 levels and establishes a 5 percent add-on payment for home health services provided in rural areas during 2006. The act also requires home health agencies to report quality-related data for 2007 or face a 2 percent reduction in reimbursement. The Congressional Budget Office (2006) estimates that these measures will save the program $5.7 billion from 2006 to 2015.

Long-Term Care Reform: Federal Failure and State Incremental Strategies

The long-running healthcare debate has only occasionally addressed key choices in LTC policy. Early versions of President Clinton's Health Security Act included a large, state-run, non-means-tested home care program. It also included a proposal to increase the level of protected assets under Medicaid to reduce the amount of spend down required for institutional care in a nursing home. As the last major national LTC proposal, it fostered a greater debate over the relative merits of public programs versus private insurance rather than focusing on the plight of the elderly and disabled.

In the same period, the American Health Security Act of 1993 was introduced by U.S. Representative Jim McDermott (D-WA) and Senator Paul Wellstone (D-MN). More liberal than the Clinton administration's proposal, the proposed plan specified extensive coverage for nursing home and home health benefits within a single-payer health insurance system on a non-means-tested basis.

Ultimately, national LTC reform failed, in part because the LTC proposals were part of the larger healthcare reform packages. Proponents of both the Clinton and McDermott–Wellstone proposals failed to gain sufficient support to overcome the objections of numerous special interest groups. None of the comprehensive healthcare and LTC reform bills ever came to a vote; reform efforts thereafter have focused on incremental changes (Wiener et al., 2001). Until the political will in the United States can support a social insurance program for LTC, other means will be required to increase efficiency in the current system.

In the absence of national reform, states are choosing among three strategies to manage public LTC expenditures. States can attempt to offset state expenditures by increasing private insurance enrollment. They can use traditional cost-containment methods such as managing the number of nursing home beds or reducing reimbursement levels. Or they can try to reform the healthcare and LTC delivery systems.

Promoting Private Long-Term Care Coverage

Many states, most notably California and New York, attempt to induce individuals to purchase private LTC insurance. They do so by allowing those who purchase a state-approved LTC policy to retain a higher proportion of personal assets than they normally would be allowed to retain and still qualify for Medicaid. In California, for example, residents may purchase private LTC coverage up to a level that equals the amount of assets they are trying to protect. Similarly, New Yorkers can exempt personal assets of unlimited value from Medicaid spend-down requirements by buying a private insurance policy with at least three years of coverage. Other states have developed public–private partnerships with private insurance carriers that offer lower premiums to promote the individual purchase of private coverage. To date, all have failed to create any appreciable increase in LTC enrollment (Wiener and Stevenson, 1998). These poor results suggest that such programs and market reforms will not be sufficient. In light of that failure, continuing to promote the purchase of LTC insurance, particularly among lower- and middle-income groups, seems futile.

Policymakers have considered another initiative that involves reducing Medicaid estate planning to reduce state expenditures for LTC and promote the purchase of private LTC coverage. Many policymakers consider the practice of asset transferring, sheltering, and otherwise underreporting personal assets by middle- and upper-class elderly to prepare for Medicaid eligibility without surrendering substantial amounts of family wealth to be an extensive problem. Although there is no universal agreement that transferring assets is a major policy problem, most experts believe that reducing the practice is difficult, but essential to increase the purchase of LTC insurance (Wiener and Stevenson, 1998). As long as there are ways to circumvent prohibitions against them, such practices will continue and efforts to increase enrollment in private coverage will go largely unrewarded. States that adopt strategies to curb Medicaid estate planning hope that eliminating opportunities to transfer wealth will further encourage the purchase of private LTC insurance policies.

Regulatory Approaches

Under federal Medicaid and Medicare rules, states have wide discretion in adopting regulatory cost-control mechanisms such as certificates of need that limit the supply of LTC beds. Because most LTC beds are likely to be filled by Medicaid patients, limiting the number of beds enables states to control the rate of growth of Medicaid LTC expenditures. Of course, the cost of home- and community-based LTC may well rise as Medicaid copes with the unmet need for institutional care. Such approaches may produce short- and midterm reductions in cost, but the increasing need for LTC as the country's population ages is likely to render such strategies ineffective in the long term. Moreover, a strategy that creates a shortage of LTC beds is incompatible with efforts to control costs through competition among LTC institutions.

Another public policy mechanism attempts to contain costs by decreasing reimbursement levels to LTC providers. As the largest payer of LTC services, states can apply leverage on providers to agree to lower rates for the same level of service in much the same way that private health insurance carriers use the promise of large patient volume to negotiate lower rates with providers. The potential effectiveness of this cost-reduction strategy was significantly increased by the repeal of the Boren Amendment in the Balanced Budget Act of 1997 (P.L. 105-33). This amendment had required states to reimburse providers of Medicaid at "reasonable" rates. Losses in a number of lawsuits in the 1980s and 1990s had greatly constrained the ability of states to contain Medicaid costs by restricting reimbursements. Since the repeal of the amendment, many states have become more aggressive in "negotiating" lower rates with providers (Wiener and Stevenson, 1998).

However, states cannot restrict the revenues of LTC facilities too much without damaging the quality of care. Painful policy experiences over the years have taught state officials that egregious lapses in quality rouse public ire to a much greater extent than continuous annual increases in cost, even when those costs reach double digits. Reimbursement reductions may be effective only in the short run or in cases where the reimbursements exceed providers' costs. Putting pressure on providers to maintain quality while reducing their revenue creates a squeeze on operators that will probably result in long-term increases in rates and decreases in quality.

Delivery System Reform

Many states have attempted to reform the LTC delivery system to create greater efficiency, hoping thereby to relieve the pressure to increase reimbursements. In general, delivery system reform efforts fall into two categories: expanding home- and community-based services and integrating LTC and acute care services within the same program.

Substituting Home- and Community-Based Services

Most states support the view that they can reduce the cost of LTC by encouraging providers to substitute alternative, home-based and other outpatient, community-based services for lengthier and presumably more expensive inpatient hospital and nursing home care. States also believe that they can shift the cost of such services to Medicare for those individuals who are covered by both Medicaid and Medicare because Medicare will pay for a greater proportion of home healthcare than for care in SNF. By encouraging enrollment in zero premium Medicare Part C Health Maintenance Associations (HMOs), states may also save money on dual enrollees (Wiener, 2003).

Research on the effects of expanding home services on nursing home costs indicates, however, that the popular notion that savings can be realized by shifting utilization from institutional settings to home- and community-based services is not true. Instead of noninstitutional services expanding as a result of a shift from the institutional setting to home-based settings, use of community-based services has increased without any commensurate decrease in institutional care. The growth in utilization of home-based services resulted from the reality that institutional and community-based services are typically not substitute goods or alternatives to each other, but rather that they are complementary in nature. Overall utilization increased because expanded home-based services attracted patients who were not receiving LTC services previously (Rivlin and Wiener, 1988).

Integrating Long-Term Care and Acute Care Delivery Systems

Integrating LTC and acute care delivery systems is intended to allow states to achieve two key objectives by overcoming the difficulties presented by an incoherent delivery and financing system, which too often treats patients in settings that are suboptimal. First, states hope to improve the quality of care. In most current arrangements, providers must balance the requirements of two different programs to serve the needs of patients requiring LTC services (Wiener, 2003). Second, integration creates opportunities to consolidate funding between two government payment sources and introduce capitated payments so that more efficient care may be provided for the three-quarters of LTC residents who rely on Medicaid and Medicare to pay for the services that they receive.

It is often assumed that increasing the reimbursement rates for LTC programs will lead to improvements in quality. Research by Cohen and Spector (1996), Wiener (2003), and others, however, does not support this idea. Examining the effects of reimbursement on accepted standards of nursing home quality including mortality, incidence of bedsores, and patient functional health, Cohen and Spector (1996) concluded that increased reimbursements had no significant effect on quality. In an earlier study, Nyman (1988) reached similar conclusions regarding the relationship between reimbursement levels and quality of care. Nyman's results suggest that higher reimbursement merely leads to more staffing in LTC settings and is not associated with improvement in LTC quality measures. Increased reimbursement for Medicaid and Medicare does, of course, add to the cost of funding these programs without a commensurate increase in offsetting savings or quality. Thus, the results of research on quality and cost make this policy difficult to support on those grounds (Wiener, 2003).

However, integration efforts enable states to reduce the total number of providers and develop contract standards and performance monitoring mechanisms. Each of these initiatives facilitates the use of capitation payments. Capitation payment systems shift the financial risk from the state to the providers and help stabilize state budgets. Building the budget for these services on a fixed per member per month (pmpm) rate enhances the state's ability to budget effectively and puts the short-term risk for the cost of services in the hands of the providers. Congress developed an option for states to capitate acute care and LTC services when it enacted the Program of All-Inclusive Care for the Elderly (PACE).

Program of All-Inclusive Care for the Elderly

PACE became a state option as a result of the Balanced Budget Act of 1997 (BBA, P.L. 105-33). It is now offered as an integrated acute care and LTC model through qualified providers in a limited number of states. The BBA, which established the PACE model as a permanent entity within the Medicare program, allowed states to provide PACE services to Medicaid beneficiaries as a state option. In 2002, the National PACE Association reported that 73 PACE centers served more than 10,500 enrollees (Leatherman and McCarthy, 2005).

The PACE program is a capitated benefit program that offers a comprehensive service delivery system and integrated Medicare and Medicaid financing to address both medical care and LTC needs of clients. No patient cost-sharing mechanisms such as deductibles or copayments are permitted. By combining funding streams into a single global capitation, PACE overcomes the fragmentation in funding between Medicaid and Medicare and the resulting disintegration in the delivery of care. Integrated financing allows providers to deliver all the services that participants need rather than limiting providers to those reimbursable under the Medicare or Medicaid fee-for-service systems.

PACE is an outgrowth of several notable home- and community-based demonstration projects in the 1970s and 1980s that included "social health maintenance organizations," which enabled frail elderly participants to continue living at home while receiving services rather than entering presumably more expensive LTC institutions. They involved interdisciplinary care teams that coordinated services for frail or impaired elderly patients in conjunction with the patient's regular attendance at an adult day service center. The PACE system of care, like the social health maintenance organizations, enables participants to continue living at home while receiving services. Evaluations of several demonstration projects compared patients receiving PACE interventions to those receiving the standard of care at the time. The results suggest that PACE interventions reduced nursing home and hospital days and the number of nurse visits, while increasing ambulatory care visits which provided the required care in less expensive settings (Leatherman and McCarthy, 2005).

Opponents of integrated LTC, however, make two points against such a strategy. They argue that the managed care industry's relative inexperience in LTC services will increase costs. Managed care tends to shift patients to ambulatory care settings when possible to reduce patient volume in high-cost inpatient settings. The practice raises the question of whether integrating acute care and LTC would foster home- and community-based services at the expense of necessary inpatient or institutional care. Opponents are also concerned about the possibility that LTC would become overmedicalized and eventually consume a greater portion of the healthcare budget (Wiener et al., 2001).

Social Insurance

Among the public programs for LTC discussed so far, only Medicare is a social insurance program. To understand why only a few such public programs exist, especially in the United States, it is first necessary to understand what constitutes a social insurance program.

According to the first welfare theorem of economics, private markets provide commodities in efficient quantities. When a market does not provide a commodity in sufficient quantity at a price that the market will bear, either market conditions must change or government must intervene. In the case of LTC insurance, the market has failed to produce a product that satisfies the need for a comprehensive LTC plan at a price most consumers are willing to pay. Consequently, when faced with the need for extensive LTC, most Americans spend down personal assets to qualify for Medicaid, which places a great burden on the state-run program. The role of Medicaid as the universal LTC insurance is costly for state and federal governments and spending down personal assets creates hardships for families who lack LTC insurance.

Social Security, Medicare, and Federal Unemployment Insurance are the U.S. examples of such social insurance programs. Medicaid does not fulfill the criteria for a social insurance program. Although social insurance programs may address a variety of losses, they share the following common attributes:

- Participation is compulsory
- Eligibility and benefits depend to a great extent on prior compulsory contributions made by the worker or employer
- Benefits are paid as the result of a readily identifiable event or occurrence
- There is no means testing (Rosen, 2002)

Social insurance programs are compulsory, a key aspect that differentiates social from private insurance. The latter must maintain sufficient reserves to cover future claims as well as purchase reinsurance. In contrast, compulsory government programs based on taxing power function in the secure knowledge that government obligations do not require actuarially balanced savings from premiums to cover future payments.*

The fundamental concept behind insurance, social or private, is that as the size of the risk pool increases, the cost of protecting against the risk to the individual becomes negligible. This principle is called the law of big numbers.† The cost to individuals of risk decreases as the risk of an insured independent event is pooled. From this perspective, social insurance serves to create larger risk pools than can be generated by competition among multiple insurance firms and is very consistent with the fundamental principles of insurance. The fact that it is compulsory serves to create this large pool (Friedman, 2002).

Compulsory social insurance programs also provide massive advantages of scale, do not need to generate profits, and have inexpensive promotional requirements. In contrast, private insurance carriers must pay for costly marketing efforts to increase market share and generate profits. These cost advantages allow Medicare to pay out nearly 99 percent of revenues in medical benefits, as compared to 85 percent of premium revenue typically paid by private health insurers (Rosen, 2002).

A danger of compulsory insurance is that the excess of revenue over claims produced in some periods in its history will encourage government to fund its other activities in the short term without raising taxes or borrowing from the capital markets. Thus, assets in the Medicare and Social Security Trust Funds have allowed the annual consolidated federal budget to show smaller deficits than without the surpluses that these trust funds have accumulated.

Another common objection to social insurance is that such programs are really income-transfer programs and not insurance. Positive symbolic value comes from labeling such programs "insurance," for the word suggests that benefits are earned and are therefore neither charity nor the result of an unsavory political deal benefiting some special interest group. The reality is that these are "event-conditioned" programs, which means that benefits are paid on the occurrence of a particular insured event such as disability or, in the case of pension funds, achieving a specific age. Health insurance pays when an individual falls ill and files a claim for reimbursement of a covered charge. Indeed, all insurance programs are event-conditioned (Feldstein, 1976).

---

* The government IOUs in the Social Security Trust Fund are real obligations, but the permanence of Social Security and Medicare do not rest on any projected "solvency" of projected claims balanced against reserves. The U.S. obligation to pay future retired baby boomers, like the obligation to pay the People's Republic of China for all the money that it has loaned the U.S. government, ultimately depends on the willingness of future voters to keep promises that have been made in good faith to fellow citizens since 1935 and 1965. In light of the disproportionately high proportion of older Americans who vote, one can be assured that the United States will renege on its debts to China long before the elderly will lose promised benefits.

† For a more detailed explanation of insurance theory, see Chapter 18 by Smith and Brandon in this volume. It provides a quantitative example of risk sharing.

A further objection to social insurance covering LTC is that it will create unacceptable "moral hazard." Moral hazard, the negative consequences for individual and group incentives that are created by insurance, exists when behavior is likely to be affected by the fact that a potential loss will be indemnified. The presence of insurance may provide an incentive to engage in activities that present greater risk of loss than those that might occur without the insurance (Rosen, 2002). For example, the availability of federal flood insurance encourages building in flood-prone areas and subsidizes the mortgages that make such building possible. If LTC is covered, individuals may seek nursing home care sooner or utilize more home care than they may actually need. Such behavior increases the potential loss to the risk pool and is of great concern to policymakers, who must balance the social benefits of a program with higher program costs that may result from riskier behavior. Medicare, for example, struggles continuously with managing the utilization of services by various cost-containment methods such as case management and benefit limitations.

International Perspectives on Social Insurance for Long-Term Care

Unlike the United States, many industrialized countries have instituted social insurance programs to assist families with the financing of LTC. Germany, Denmark, Japan, and the Netherlands, in particular, have created social insurance programs that address the needs of their growing elderly populations. Each of these countries has a highly developed healthcare system, a strong cultural sense of equity and social solidarity, and increasing LTC needs generated by a rapidly aging population. These nations commonly resort to social insurance solutions for their social welfare problems.

Denmark, for example, operates a national health service that integrates LTC and acute care under a single administrative unit. Local authorities operate the majority of nursing homes and are experimenting with a transition from traditional institutional nursing home settings to specialized, self-contained dwellings designed for the elderly, while maintaining the institutional setting for residents with the greatest need. The other countries, Germany, Japan, and the Netherlands, each operate a social insurance system to finance the cost of LTC services, but services including those provided in institutional residential settings are provided by the private sector and reimbursed by the social insurance funds (Meijer et al., 2000).

Germany established its Pflegeversicherung, an LTC insurance program, in 1995, as a separate component of the German social insurance system. It covers nearly 90 percent of the population. Those whose annual gross income is below a specified threshold must participate in the public LTC system and make contributions to it. Individuals with incomes greater than the specified threshold must choose between participating in the public system and purchasing private LTC insurance. Contributions to the public LTC system are proportionate to the individual's income and are capped every year. More than 75 percent of the population is required to participate based on income. An additional 13 percent of the population chose to participate in the public LTC system even though they were not required to do so.

The German program explicitly provides assistance to those who are unable to perform ADLs due to physical, intellectual, or mental impairment for periods anticipated to be longer than six months. Assistance covers the spectrum from home health services to institutionalization (Geraedts et al., 2000). It organizes services and needs into three stages: stage 1 in which daily care is necessary for a minimum number of activities, stage 2 in which more extensive care for multiple ADLs is required throughout the day, and stage 3 for which around-the-clock care is required. The program covers both ambulatory and institutional care. Belgium and the Netherlands operate similar social insurance programs (Wahner-Roedler et al., 1999).

Of course, these countries also experience the pressures of escalating costs and quality challenges that are the results of an aging population. All of these countries have, therefore, begun reviewing their payment structures and changing policies to address current and anticipated increases in their age-dependency ratios, the number of workers relative to the number of elderly. These countries are trying to restrain cost increases by making entry and admission criteria more selective, regulating the number of beds, and requiring greater amounts of private cost sharing. Establishing market-based approaches and industry regulation within a social insurance context gives these governments hope of increasing competition among providers that will improve quality and provide a restraining force on prices paid by social insurance funds (Meijer et al., 2000).

An obvious question arises at this point. In a world of global convergence, why does the United States resist adopting social insurance programs when other advanced industrial nations, such as those discussed in this subsection, embrace social insurance as the best way to provide for many of the needs of their citizens? European nations and Japan, in particular, have many social insurance programs: examples range from childcare to LTC and notably include universal healthcare. The answer to this revealing question involves addressing the cause of what has come to be called "American exceptionalism." The following section of this chapter will turn away from the minutiae of programs and economics involved in public financing of LTC to suggest some reasons for the profound resistance in the United States to providing universal, tax-based coverage for LTC without means testing.

Why Does the United States Have So Few Social Insurance Programs?

A brief review of the major points established so far in this chapter highlights the policy problem of paying for LTC in the United States.

■ Extensive LTC is the kind of relatively rare but catastrophic expense for which insurance to spread risk and reduce individual loss is appropriate.

- Asymmetric information, when the insured knows more than the insurer about the likelihood of incurring losses, increases the chances of adverse selection and the cost of insurance in a voluntary system.
- Most individuals are financially unable or volitionally unwilling to purchase LTC insurance in the current voluntary system.

When the problems of financing LTC are laid out in this straightforward fashion, the obvious public policy solution is for the government to establish a system covering all residents that is financed by compulsory payment. These payments may be called "premiums" if that term is more appealing than "taxes." The social insurance solution for LTC seems so obvious that reference to fundamental characteristics of the American polity is necessary to understand why this solution does not have a place in U.S. policy discussions of LTC issues.

Historically, Americans have valued personal liberties and individual rights more than public welfare. The focus on liberty entails a concomitant emphasis on personal responsibility. American society admires risk takers, rewards entrepreneurialism, and is structured in ways that promote these attributes. It was founded on the principles of Locke (1960) and Smith (1981) that the government has the responsibility to establish property rights, provide for national and personal security, and protect free enterprise. De Tocqueville (1956) captured the implications of this unique American approach to social organization in his remarkable chapters on the "novel [in 1835] expression *individualism.*" De Tocqueville also "celebrated vibrant American communities where people understood that their own best interest—their 'self interest rightly understood'—required the whole community to pitch in and help one another, to work together, to see their fates as deeply interconnected" (Morone and Jacobs, 2005). When Americans look beyond the individual for support or action, the initial response is to search for that succor in "civil society," also called the nonprofit or voluntary sector, rather than government (Lipset, 1996; Salamon, 1987).

As a result, American society is ready to assist those truly in need, but will not reward or encourage idleness and will discourage even "deserved" social assistance that might sap habits of self-reliance.* This attitude formed the basic premise of welfare reform in the 1990s, which introduced return-to-work requirements and benefit limits to recipients.

Two aspects of this culture, in particular, help explain why so little social insurance infrastructure exists in the United States and why Social Security, Medicare,

---

* A broad range of cultural evidence supports this generalization. For example, Bremner's (1988) discussion on the influence of the Charity Organization Society as "scientific philanthropy" in post-Civil War America or the moral tale "True and False Philanthropy" credited to Anonymous (1848) in the *McGuffey Readers* of the 1840s. The *McGuffey Readers* propagated a specific set of white, Protestant moral and cultural values in the process of teaching basic reading, speaking, and other academic skills. Much of the rhetoric used to discuss the safety net and proposed welfare reform in the 1981–1996 period would have been instantly familiar and comfortable to mid-nineteenth-century American elites engaged in debating essentially the same problems.

and limited unemployment insurance are the only forms of social insurance offered. First, the American government is pluralist in nature and lacks the structural elements of a "neocorporatist" environment like that found in European countries, which have established numerous, comprehensive social insurance programs. Pluralism promotes the self-interested actions of special interests and requires coalitions to form around issues to place policy issues on the national agenda and move them through the approval process. Fewer coalitions generally represent the middle and lower classes that benefit more from social insurance. In contrast, the disciplined multiple-party parliamentary systems commonly found in Europe, especially those with class-based voting patterns, are better structured to withstand the blandishments and threats of special interests (Lipset and Marks, 2000).

Second, within this political environment, society is willing to help those in need, but only to a certain extent. It will not tolerate shirkers. Therefore, benefits in state and federal programs targeted at specific populations are limited in both extent and length of time. Applying for benefits from such programs may be rather involved and may require the individual to undergo means testing to receive benefits. In this way, policies are used to protect programs from the risks of asymmetric information. Administrators often cannot know the intent or real condition of individuals. Bureaucratic barriers are constructed to help busy officials discriminate between those who truly need benefits and those who would like to have them, but do not require them. Obviously, a humane bureaucracy must balance these approaches and use common sense to avoid inadvertently excluding those in greatest need.

Although the elderly and disabled constitute a large and growing segment of the U.S. population and have developed greater political presence, they have not yet established LTC as an item on the public agenda. The special interests advocating for private insurance have succeeded so far in maintaining government support of the current fragmented financing and chaotic organization of LTC. They have endorsed a number of efforts by individual states to entice the public to purchase private LTC plans rather than depend on Medicaid as catastrophic LTC insurance.

Thus, in the United States, only Medicare, Social Security, and federal Unemployment Insurance meet the political and economic criteria necessary to count as social insurance. The social, psychological, and economic costs of the failure to provide additional social insurance programs, such as LTC, do not affect everyone equally: The costs are particularly low for the interests that exert the greatest influence on the political process in the United States, whereas those least able to influence policy bear the greater burden.

Conclusion

This chapter has covered a great deal of material. It started by providing some statistics about current funding sources, demand for LTC, and measures of expected future LTC needs in the United States. Then it explained the principal national programs for financing LTC: Medicaid, Medicare, the Veterans Health Administration, and the IHS. More attention was focused on recent policy changes in Medicare and Medicaid, particularly the growth of LTCHs and the extension of prospective payment to them, policy efforts to foster the purchase of private LTC insurance, and regulatory and budgetary efforts to limit the growth of LTC spending. Two broad strategies for controlling cost through system reform were examined next: the belief that providing alternative home- and community-based services can reduce the demand for and cost of nursing homes and efforts to integrate LTC and acute care, principally through the PACE program.

The last section of the chapter moved to a more theoretical level in its explanation of the concept of social insurance. After discussing insurance and social insurance, it provided several specific examples of nations that have social insurance for LTC. The final substantive subsection addressed the "big picture" question of why social insurance is not part of the "policy stream" (Kingdon, 2003) when policy discussions about LTC arise in the United States.

References

Anonymous. (1848). True and false philanthropy. In McGuffey, W.H. (Ed.). *McGuffey's Newly Revised Eclectic Fourth Reader: Containing Elegant Extracts, in Prose and Poetry, with Rules for Readings and Exercises in Articulation, Defining, etc.* Revised edition. New York: Clark, Austin and Smith.

Benson, W.F. (2002). Long term care in Indian country today: A snapshot. In Kaufman, J.A. (Ed.). *American Indian and Alaska Native Roundtable on Long Term Care: Final Report 2002.* Spokane, WA: Kaufman and Associates.

Brandon, W.P. (1989). Cut off at the impasse without real catastrophic health insurance: Three approaches to financing long-term care. *Policy Studies Review, 8*(2), 441–454.

Bremner, R.H. (1988). *American Philanthropy.* 2nd edition. Chicago, IL: University of Chicago Press.

Cohen, J.W. and Spector, W.D. (1996). The effect of Medicaid reimbursement on the quality of care in nursing homes. *Journal of Health Economics, 15,* 23–48.

Congressional Budget Office. (2006). *Cost Estimate: S. 1932 Deficit Reduction Act of 2005.* Washington: U.S. Government Printing Office.

ConsumerAffairs.com, Inc. (2006). Nursing home cost hits $70,000 per year. Retrieved on July 28, 2006, at http://www.consumeraffairs.com/news04/nursing_home_costs.html.

Crowley, J. (2003). *Medically Needy Programs: An Important Source of Medicaid Coverage, Kaiser Commission on Medicaid and the Uninsured.* Oakland, CA: Henry J. Kaiser Family Foundation.

De Tocqueville, A. (1956). *Democracy in America.* In Heffner, R.D. (Ed.). New York: New American Library.

Decker, F.H. (2005). *Nursing Homes, 1977–1999: What Has Changed, What Has Not?* Hyattsville, MD: National Center for Health Statistics.

Federal Register. (2006). *Rules and Regulations. 71*(92), May 12, 2006. Washington: U.S. Government Printing Office, 27798–27845.

Feldstein, M.S. (1976). Seven principles of social insurance. *Challenge* (November/December), 6–11.

Friedman, L.S. (2002). *The Microeconomics of Public Policy Analysis*. Princeton, NJ: Princeton University Press.

Geraedts, M., Heller, G.V., and Harrington, C.A. (2000). Germany's long-term care insurance: Putting a social insurance model into practice. *The Milbank Quarterly*, 78(3), 375–401.

Gibson, M.J., Gregory, S.R., Houser, A.N., and Fox-Grage, W. (2004). *Across the States: Profiles of Long-Term Care*. 6th edition. Washington: AARP Public Policy Institute.

Ikegami, N. (1997). Public long-term care insurance in Japan. *Journal of the American Medical Association*, 278(16), 1310–1314.

Kingdon, J.W. (2003). *Agendas, Alternatives, and Public Policies*. 2nd edition revised. New York: Longman.

Leatherman, S. and McCarthy, D. (2005). *Quality of Health Care for Medicare Beneficiaries: A Chartbook, Focusing on the Elderly Living in The Community*. New York: The Commonwealth Fund.

Lipset, S.M. (1996). *American Exceptionalism: A Double-Edged Sword*. New York: W. W. Norton.

Lipset, S.M. and Marks, G. (2000). *It Didn't Happen Here: Why Socialism Failed in the United States*. New York: W. W. Norton.

Locke, J. (1960). The second treatise of government: An essay concerning the true original extent and end of government. In Laslett, P. (Ed.). *Two Treatises of Government*. Cambridge, England: Cambridge University Press.

Longest, B.B., Jr. (2006). *Health Policymaking in the United States*. 4th edition. Chicago, IL: Health Administration Press.

Medicare Payment Advisory Commission. (2006, March). *Report to the Congress: Medicare Payment Policy*. Washington.

Meijer, A., van Campen, C., and Kerkstra, A. (2000). A comparative study of the financing provision and quality of care in nursing homes. The approach of four European countries: Belgium, Denmark, Germany, and the Netherlands. *Journal of Advanced Nursing*, 32(3), 554–561.

Morone, J.A. and Jacobs, L.R. (2005). Introduction. In Morone, J.A. and Jacobs, L.R. (Eds.). *Healthy, Wealthy, and Fair: Health Care and the Good Society*. New York: Oxford University Press, pp. 3–16.

National Center for Health Statistics, U.S. Department of Health and Human Services, Centers for Disease Control and Prevention. (2005). *Health, United States 2005* (DHHS Publication No. 2005-1232). Washington: U.S. Government Printing Office.

National Center for Health Statistics, U.S. Department of Health and Human Services, Centers for Disease Control and Prevention. (2006). *Health, United States 2006* (DHHS Publication No. 2006-1232). Washington: U.S. Government Printing Office.

Norton, E.C. and Newhouse, J.P. (1994). Policy options for public long-term care insurance. *Journal of the American Medical Association*, 271(19), 1520–1524.

Nyman, J. (1988). Improving the quality of nursing home outcomes: Are adequacy- or incentive-oriented policies more effective? *Medical Care*, 26(12), 1158–1171.

Rivlin, A.M. and Wiener, J.M. (1988). *Caring for the Disabled Elderly, Who Will Pay?* Washington: The Brookings Institute.

Rosen, H.S. (2002). *Public Finance*. 6th edition. Boston, MA: McGraw-Hill/Irwin.

Salamon, L.M. (1987). Of market failure, voluntary failure, and third-party government: Toward a theory of government-nonprofit relations in the modern welfare state. In Ostrander, S.A. and Langton, S. (Eds.). *Shifting the Debate: Public/Private Sector Relations in the Modern Welfare State*. New Brunswick, NJ: Transaction Books, pp. 29–49.

Smith, A. (1981). *An Inquiry into the Nature and Causes of the Wealth of Nations*. In Campbell, R.H., Skinner, A.S., and Todd, W.B. (Eds.), 2 vols. Indianapolis, IN: Liberty Fund.

Stone, R.I. (2000). Long-term care for the elderly with disabilities: Current policy, emerging tends, and implications for the twenty-first century, Milbank Memorial Fund, August 2000. Retrieved on February 27, 2006, at http://www.milbank.org/reports/0008stone/.

U.S. Department of Health and Human Services, Centers for Medicare and Medicaid Services. (2004). *CMS Legislative Summary: Summary of H.R.1 Medicare Prescription Drug Improvement and Modernization Act of 2003, Public Law 108-173*. Washington: U.S. Government Printing Office.

U.S. Department of Health and Human Services, Centers for Medicare and Medicaid Services. (2005). *Medicare General Information, Eligibility, and Entitlement Manual*. Retrieved on February 27, 2006, at http://www.cms.hhs.gov/MedicareGenInfo.

U.S. Department of Health and Human Services, Centers for Medicare and Medicaid Services. (2006). *Medicare Program General Information*. Retrieved on February 27, 2006, at http://www.cms.hhs.gov/MedicareGenInfo.

U.S. Department of Health and Human Services, Office of Assistant Secretary for Policy and Evaluation. (2005). *Medicaid Eligibility for Long-Term Care Benefits: Policy Brief I* (DHHS-100-03-0022). Washington: U.S. Government Printing Office.

U.S. Department of Veterans Affairs. (2006a). *Facts about the Department of Veterans Affairs*. Retrieved on July 30, 2006 at http://www1.va.gov/opa/fact/index.asp.

U.S. Department of Veterans Affairs. (2006b). *Fact Sheet: VA Long Term Care*. Retrieved on July 30, 2006, at http://www1.va.gov/opa/fact/index.asp.

Wahner-Roedler, D.L., Knuth, P., and Juchems, R.H. (1999). The German Pflegeversicherung (long-term care insurance). *Mayo Clinic Proceedings*, 74(2), 196–200.

Wiener, J.M. (2003). An assessment of strategies for improving quality of care in nursing homes. *The Gerontologist, 43* (Special Issue II), 19–27.

Wiener, J.M., Estes, C.L., Goldenson, S.M., and Goldberg, S.C. (2001). What happened to long-term care in the health reform debate of 1993–1994? Lessons for the future. *The Milbank Quarterly, 79*(2), 207–252.

Wiener, J.M. and Stevenson, D.G. (1998). State policy on long-term care for the elderly. *Health Affairs, 17*(3), 81–100.

LOOKING AHEAD

Chapter 20

Focal Points of Change

Cynthia Massie Mara

Contents

The landscape of long-term care (LTC) is sure to change. Demographics alone will force adjustments. Technological advances will increasingly facilitate the distance monitoring of vital signs, cardiac function, and other indicators of health status, enabling more people to remain in their homes and communities. Economic pressures will necessitate change in the financing of services. Societal perceptions of aging will alter as the baby boomers continue to age, and changing attitudes toward disability, already evident, are sure to evolve further. The business community will increasingly take note of the aging of its customers and exploit new financial opportunities to address their declining functional abilities.

Nonetheless, the many contradictions that exist in LTC must be addressed. Choices are expanding in some geographic areas although gaps in services continue to pose problems in other locations. High-quality care is offered to recipients of LTC services delivered by many organizations even as abuse and neglect are inflicted on clients of others. Technological advances are being developed, but the resources allocated to LTC are not keeping pace with demand, even for basic services. The need for more paid and unpaid caregivers is steadily growing at the same time that fewer and fewer people are available to do the work. Integration of components of healthcare within networks is emphasized even as multiple LTC programs with different eligibility requirements, services, and financing mechanisms continue to proliferate; indeed, certain efforts to coordinate the healthcare system may be "more rhetoric than reality" (Feder et al., 2000).

Creative approaches, with goals such as the following, are needed to address inconsistencies:

- Integrate acute care and LTC more effectively, providing a smoother continuum of services for people needing both types of assistance, without falling into the trap of overmedicalizing LTC.
- Design policies and programs that foster continuing development of a capable workforce in numbers sufficient to meet needs.
- Render LTC entities places where people want to work and receive care.*
- Address housing issues in coordination with a person's medical and LTC service needs.
- Support independence and choice for LTC recipients, within the limits of their abilities.
- Restructure financing mechanisms so as to avoid impoverishment as a prerequisite for receiving Medicaid, the primary source of public payment for LTC services.
- Provide adequate support and training for the vast number of people who informally provide assistance to family members, friends, and neighbors; without them, the costs would be significantly greater, even unbearable.
- Break down even further the institutional bias in Medicaid by pressing for alternative care options.
- Implement public education programs to counter misconceptions about LTC.
- Develop incentives for people to prepare financially for their potential LTC needs.

---

* This approach is in line with the principles of culture change in LTC. Culture change focuses on person-directed values and practices. More information on this organizational change model can be found at http://www.pioneernetwork.net/who-we-are/our-history.php.

- Foster the development of medical advances and care systems aimed at preventing, delaying, and effectively treating chronic illnesses.
- Design technologies and assistive devices that enable people to live more independently.
- Focus our collective attention on the challenges of LTC and make the required changes in the current system.
- Consider seriously the development and implementation of a universal LTC insurance system, especially one that incorporates public–private partnerships.

National Long-Term Care Debate

To prompt significant change in LTC, a national debate is needed on the subject. Certain elements must be part of the discussion, including demographics; economics and financing; politics and policy; social and cultural issues; LTC needs, services, and caregivers; and health status and medical technology. These are issues that have the potential to influence LTC significantly.

Demographics

The future impact of shifting demographics on LTC has been detailed in the preceding chapters. Key changes are summarized as follows:

- Between 2000 and 2040, disability rates for people aged 65 and older are expected to decline from 30 to 28 percent.
- Owing to the rapid growth in this age group, however, the number of older individuals with disabilities will more than double.
- There will be fewer working age adults in relation to retired individuals because the numbers of older people will increase at a faster rate than those of their younger cohorts.
- The number of individuals aged 65 and above needing formal or paid care at home will grow by more than 100 percent.
- The number of people in this age group requiring nursing home care will increase from 1.2 to 2.7 million.
- Because of ongoing societal changes, fewer and fewer people, especially adult daughters, will be available to provide informal care (Johnson et al., 2007).

The LTC system is not equipped for these changes. Yet no adequate preparation is underway.

Economics and Financing

The economic environment of LTC has a particularly important impact on policymaking. Ignoring the issue of LTC may appear less problematic when the economy is growing, tax revenues are increasing, and the ratio of workers to non-workers is high. However, when economic indictors fall, political leaders take action to slow the rate of the increase in LTC expenditures, especially with regard to Medicaid. States are particularly vulnerable. Unlike the federal government, most states must balance their operating budgets. During hard times, when states can least afford it, Medicaid budgets tend to rise. At the same time, LTC costs are taking an increasing share of the Medicaid pie. A number of studies show that, in the absence of policy changes, many states will encounter insurmountable fiscal challenges in the foreseeable future (Czerwinski and McCool, 2007; Rossiter and Neice, 2006).

There will be a wide income disparity among future members of the older population. Baby boomers are reportedly anticipating an extended work life. For these individuals, postponed retirement can result in greater personal savings, Social Security payments, and pension benefits. The extra funds can make later retirees better positioned financially and prepared if LTC needs should arise. However, poverty will be the fate of a significant percentage of boomers, particularly single women (widowed, divorced, and never married) and minorities. African Americans, for example, are at a particularly high risk. At age 67, approximately 12 percent of white but 22 percent of African-American boomers are expected to have incomes less than double the poverty level (Murphy et al., 2007).

Misconceptions among the public about LTC financing must be overcome if we are to achieve better personal decisions. A related goal is increased awareness of the financial risks, both public and private, associated with LTC. Past educational efforts, however, have not prompted significant responses; denial about disability and aging serves as a potent barrier. Regardless of the difficulties, we must place a discussion about LTC on our national political agenda.

Politics and Policy

As noted earlier in the text, no real LTC system exists in the United States, but rather a set of uncoordinated policies. As a result, various programs with different eligibility requirements, funding mechanisms, and covered services have emerged, making the nonsystem difficult to navigate. Policy changes must include not only a more coherent LTC system but also a restructuring of its financing.

Many contradictions in policy alternatives exist and need to be addressed. For instance, state governments want to be relieved of at least some of their growing financial commitment; individuals who face catastrophic financial losses and impoverishment due to LTC expenses would like the government to assume a greater share. A public debate is needed and political leadership is essential for that discussion to take place. One means toward this end is "Divided We Fail,"* a national bipartisan organization that is attempting to stimulate presidential leadership in this policy area (Rother, 2007).

Social and Cultural Issues

Social and cultural factors must also be taken into consideration; restructuring our LTC system is hindered, not only by limited resources but also by attitudes of the past† that continue to shape its direction. Enduring shifts in LTC seem possible only if there is a fundamental change in the way aging and disability are regarded in society. The history of LTC reveals a tendency to gather people with certain characteristics, assign a label, and treat everyone in that category alike. Viewing people with LTC requirements as a homogenous cohort has led to cookie-cutter programs in which individuals must fit the program offerings rather than have their actual needs met. Because people with disabilities are becoming even more diverse, it is imperative that we avoid this oversimplification in any ongoing debate about the future of LTC. For instance, one relatively new challenge is the provision of LTC to growing numbers of older prisoners. Corrections systems across the United States, indeed around the globe, are searching for ways to address the needs of their aging inmate population (Mara, 2002, 2003, 2004).

Perceptions of aging and disability are linked to the frameworks or theories adopted by society. As long as the biological deficiency model or dependency theory is given priority, the role of the consumer will be given less weight. From this outmoded perspective, people with a need for assistance are assumed inevitably to follow a downward trajectory (Allert et al., 1994). A newer concept regarding aging provides a different viewpoint. The "successful aging" approach examines factors that enhance life as people age. It is assumed that by applying prevention approaches and behavior modification techniques, a person can postpone the decline often associated with old age.

Martha Holstein and Meredith Minkler caution, however, that such models can lead to "blaming the victims" for their own poor health. According to these authors, the successful aging concept, while contributing heightened awareness of actions to prevent disability, may minimize factors over which the person lacks control. As a result, the individual's struggle to accept and deal with disabilities can be undervalued (Holstein and Minkler, 2003). Balance is needed between perspectives that see individuals as having little or no control over their

---

* This organization consists of AARP (formerly the American Association of Retired Persons), the State Employees International Union (SEIU), and the Business Roundtable. For additional information, see www.aarp.org/issues/dividedwefail/.
† More details about past attitudes toward LTC can be found in Chapter 1.

disabilities and unrealistic ones that imply that people should have more control than is possible.

Changing perceptions of aging and disability, however, are evident and are reflected even in comic strips. In the past, such characters typically did not age or experience disease or death. More recently, "Funky Winkerbean"* (Batiuk, 2007) featured a young couple in which the woman was dying of cancer, allowing straight-forward discussions of illness, chemotherapy, and death. "For Better or For Worse"† (Johnson, 2007), another comic strip, frequently deals with issues of aging, disability, death and dying, and bereavement.

The growing acceptance of hospice care is another example of changing attitudes. Since the opening of the first U.S. hospice in 1974, these organizations have provided care to hundreds of thousands of individuals. Care of the dying, which normally occurred in a person's home in colonial times, has, at least for some people, returned to the home.

There is also a new language used to denote disability, reflecting increased awareness of prior derogatory terms. The Disability Movement‡ has been instrumental in promoting the phrase "people with disabilities" in lieu of terms such as "the handicapped" or "crippled." Increasingly, the public has been encouraged to expand its idea of disability beyond the functional impairments of individuals to focus instead on the restrictions that they encounter in their social and physical environments.

Long-Term Care Needs, Services, and Caregivers

In our national dialogue on the future of LTC, we need to emphasize the specific requirements of the various LTC populations, most of which have been presented in earlier chapters. At the same time, more discussion about alternatives to nursing homes is imperative if we are to respond more effectively to the preferences of individuals with functional limitations. Critical dialogue must be devoted to quality of care, the concerns of paid caregivers, support for individuals who provide assistance informally, and ways to integrate acute care and LTC. We must also seek approaches that will transform the LTC environment to one in which people want to live and work. For instance, since the 1990s, the Pioneer Network (2007) has championed such changes; its underlying philosophy involves:

> person-directed care [that] offers a relationship-based, values-driven
> alternative to the out of sight, out of mind institutional model that

---

* Additional information about this comic strip can be found at funkywinkerbean.com.
† Further information about "For Better or For Worse" can be found at http://www.fborfw.com/strip_fix/.
‡ Additional information on the Disability Movement can be found in Chapter 6.

has plagued the system for decades. The movement is about promoting household living environments—in congregate settings as well as in home and community-based services—where elders and direct care workers are able to express choice in meaningful ways.

Health Status and Medical Technology

The health status of the nation will have a definite impact on the need for LTC. As addressed in previous chapters, the disability rate among the older population has been declining. There are differing predictions, however, as to whether or not that decrease will continue. Even so, the incidence rates of certain chronic illnesses that often underlie the need for LTC are expected to rise. As an example, approximately four million people currently have Alzheimer's disease, with an estimated annual cost of care being over $100 billion. Because of the sheer number of aging baby boomers, without effective methods to prevent or delay onset of the illness, the number of people with Alzheimer's disease could double by 2050 (Hodes, 2003; Hebert et al., 2001). One result will be a substantial increase in the need for LTC services.

However, medical and technological advances could result in significantly decreased need for LTC; they could also change the way care is provided. Research, for instance, is underway to search for ways to prevent Alzheimer's disease and other chronic illnesses. As Pomidor and Pomidor (2006) write in *The Lancet*:

> the pace of scientific progress has been steadily accelerating, and the recent introduction of such transformative tools as genetic engineering, advanced imaging techniques, and the internet may yet breed a "perfect storm" of medical innovation rivalling that spawned by the advent of antibiotics and immunisation [sic].

Genomic medicine uses an individual's genetic information to tailor health care to that person's needs. Such testing can identify gene variants that accompany certain diseases, especially those that underlie the need for LTC services. According to the National Human Genome Research Institute (NHGRI; 2007), the findings can be used "to confirm a suspected diagnosis, to predict the possibility of future illness, to detect the presence of a carrier state in unaffected individuals (whose children may be at risk), and to predict response to therapy" (Topol et al., 2007).

Genetic testing, of course, raises ethical and policy concerns. Without adequate protections, individuals whose tests reveal the likelihood of medical problems in the future could have great difficulty in acquiring health, life, disability, and

LTC insurance. In response, Congress is considering genetic nondiscrimination legislation.*

Health-related efforts that are less complex than genetic testing also have the potential to lessen the demand for LTC and would need to be part of the debate. Programs that promote healthful lifestyles constitute one example. Compression-of-morbidity endeavors that aim at delaying the onset of LTC-related conditions comprise another approach.

The business community, certainly, will be part of any technological development and change. In the article "Electronics giant seeks a cure in health care: Fleeing chips and TVs, Philips makes big bet on aging consumers" in *The Wall Street Journal*, Abboud (2007) reported that Philips and other corporations such as Siemens AG and General Electric Co. are responding to the aging of the population, the increasing incidence of chronic illnesses, and people's strong preference to remain at home even in the face of increasing functional limitations. Lifeline, which enables a person to call for help at the touch of a button that is embedded in a necklace or bracelet, was an early product line. Other equipment enables distance monitoring of a patient's vital signs. The development of technology that detects balance and motion with the aim of reducing the estimated 350,000 falls per year that result in hip fractures is another example.

Corporate America is involved in LTC in other ways, for example, when elder care is found to affect worker productivity. According to a survey conducted by the National Alliance for Caregiving and AARP, almost six out of ten informal caregivers work full- or part time or have been employed at some point while providing care. Of these workers, 62 percent say that caregiving has affected their work in some way, with 54 percent reporting that it has caused them to arrive late at work, leave work for periods of time, or go home early (Barrett, 2005).

Conclusion

The United States must move toward a coherent LTC system, rather than a collection of disparate policies. A national debate is essential in rendering long-needed changes in LTC administration and policy. Although LTC is an often avoided topic of discussion, it is one that must be addressed, especially because forces in the external environment are pushing it toward a crisis situation. A debate would surface issues that seldom receive sufficient attention due, at least in part, to the denial surrounding aging and physical and cognitive decline. Administrators, policymakers,

---

* The Genetic Nondiscrimination in Health Insurance Act would amend the Employee Retirement Income Security Act (ERISA) and the Public Health Service Act (PHSA) and would "prohibit discrimination on the basis of genetic information with respect to health insurance and employment" (The Library of Congress [LOC], 2007).

and the public will increasingly be challenged to enter into a real and full dialogue from which new ways of approaching LTC can emerge.

References

Abboud, L. (2007). New treatment: electronics giant seeks a cure in health care: Fleeing chips and TVs, Philips makes big bet on aging consumers. *The Wall Street Journal.* A.1.

Allert, G., Sponholz, G., and Baitsch, H. (1994). Chronic Disease and the Meaning of Old Age. The Hastings Center Report.

Barrett, L. L. (2005). *Caregiving in the U.S.* Bethesda, MD: National Alliance for Caregiving and Washington: AARP.

Batiuk, T. (2007). Funky Winkerbean. http://www.funkywinkerbean.com (accessed May 27, 2007).

Czerwinski, S. J. and McCool, T. J. (2007). *State and Local Governments: Persistent Fiscal Challenges Will Likely Emerge within the Next Decade.* Washington: Government Accountability Office. GAO-07-1080SP.

Feder, J., Komisar, H. L., and Niefeld, M. (2000). Long-term care in the United States: An overview. *Health Affairs.* 19(3): 40–56.

Hebert, L. E., Beckett, L. A., Scherr, P. A., and Evans, D. A. (2001). Annual incidence of Alzheimer disease in the United States projected to the years 2000 through 2050. *Alzheimer Disease and Associated Disorders.* 15: 169–173.

Hodes, R. J. (2003). Witness (Director, National Institute of Aging) Appearing Before the Senate Committee on Appropriations, Subcommitee on Labor, Health and Human Services, Education, and Related Agencies, Washington. http://www.nia.nih.gov/AboutNIA/BudgetRequests/HearingADResearch.htm.

Holstein, M. and Minkler, M. (2003). Self, society, and the "new gerontology." *The Gerontologist.* 43(6): 787–797.

Johnson, L. (2007). For Better or For Worse. http://www.fborfw.com (accessed May 27, 2007).

Johnson, R. W., Toohey, D., and Wiener, J. M. (2007). *How Changing Families Will Affect Paid Helpers and Institutions.* Washington: Urban Institute. http://www.urban.org/url.cfm?ID=311451 (accessed May 2, 2007).

Mara, C. M. (2002). Expansion of long-term care in the prison system: an aging inmate population poses policy and programmatic questions. *Journal of Aging and Social Policy.* 14(2): 43–61.

Mara, C. M. (2003). A comparison of long-term care in prisons and in the free population. *Long-Term Care Interface.* 4(11): 22–26.

Mara, C. M. (2004). Chronic illness, disability and long-term care in the prison setting. In Katz, P., Mezey, M. D., and Kapp, M. (Eds.), *Advances in Long-Term Care Vol. 5: Vulnerable Populations in the Long-Term-Care Continuum.* New York: Springer.

Murphy, D., Johnson, R. W., and Mermin, G. (2007). *Racial Differences in Baby Boomers' Retirement Expectations.* Washington: Urban Institute.

National Human Genome Research Institute (NHGRI). (2007). *Overview of Genetic Testing.* Washington: Author. http://www.genome.gov/10002335/Overview (last reviewed May 15, 2007).

Pioneer Network. (2007). Pioneer Network: Our Vision. http://www.pioneernetwork.net/who-we-are/ (accessed May 14, 2007).

Pomidor, B. and Pomidor, A. K. (2006). With great power. . . . The relevance of science fiction to the practice and progress of medicine. *The Lancet.* 368: S13–S15.

Rossiter, L. F. and Neice, R. F. (2006). Medicaid, state finances, and the bottom line for businesses. *Business Economics.* 41(3): 49–54.

Rother, J. (2007). Who will pay for boomers' long-term care? Presentation by the AARP Group Executive Officer of Policy and Strategy at the Urban Institute, Washington.

The Library of Congress (LOC). (2007). *THOMAS: CRS Summary of S.358, The Genetic Nondiscrimination in Health Insurance Act.* Washington: Author. http://thomas.loc.gov/cgi-bin/bdquery/z?d110:SN00358:@@@D&summ2=m& (accessed June 28, 2007).

Topol, E. J., Murray, S. S., and Frazer, K. A. (2007). The genomics gold rush. *Journal of the American Medical Association.* 298(2): 218–221.

Index

O